MARRYING JESUS IN MEDIEVAL AND
EARLY MODERN NORTHERN EUROPE

In loving memory of

Mariana Issa Geha
1910–2005
&
Dorothy Pauline Huston
1927–2009

Marrying Jesus in Medieval and Early Modern Northern Europe
Popular Culture and Religious Reform

RABIA GREGORY
University of Missouri-Columbia, USA

ASHGATE

© Rabia Gregory 2016

All rights reserved. No part of this publication may be reproduced, stored in a retrieval system or transmitted in any form or by any means, electronic, mechanical, photocopying, recording or otherwise without the prior permission of the publisher.

Rabia Gregory has asserted her right under the Copyright, Designs and Patents Act, 1988, to be identified as the author of this work.

Published by
Ashgate Publishing Limited
Wey Court East
Union Road
Farnham
Surrey, GU9 7PT
England

Ashgate Publishing Company
110 Cherry Street
Suite 3-1
Burlington, VT 05401-3818
USA

www.ashgate.com

British Library Cataloguing in Publication Data
A catalogue record for this book is available from the British Library

The Library of Congress has cataloged the printed edition as follows:
Gregory, Rabia.
  Marrying Jesus in medieval and early modern northern Europe: popular culture and religious reform / by Rabia Gregory.
    pages cm
  Includes bibliographical references and index.
   ISBN 978-1-4724-2266-8 (hardcover) — ISBN 978-1-4724-2267-5 (ebook) — ISBN 978-1-4724-2268-2 (epub)
  1. Marriage—Religious aspects—Christianity—History of doctrines. 2. Mystical union—History of doctrines. 3. Jesus Christ—Mystical body—History of doctrines. 4. Europe—Church history. 5. Spirituality—Christianity—History of doctrines. I. Title.
  BT706.G74 2016
  274'.05—dc23
                                                                            2015029927
ISBN: 9781472422668 (hbk)
ISBN: 9781472422675 (ebk – PDF)
ISBN: 9781472422682 (ebk – ePUB)

Printed in the United Kingdom by Henry Ling Limited,
at the Dorset Press, Dorchester, DT1 1HD

Contents

List of Figures and Tables		*vii*
Preface and Acknowledgements		*xi*
1	Portraits of the Bride of Christ	1
2	Any Body's Bridegroom	31
3	Transmedia Stories of Jesus and the Loving Soul	67
4	Created to Be a Bride	117
5	Taking Jesus as a Second Husband	145
6	Sisters and Brides of Christ	169
7	Confessions of "True" Brides of Christ	191
8	Brides of Christ, Contemporary Christianity, and American Popular Culture	215
Bibliography		*227*
Index		*255*

List of Figures and Tables

Figures

2.1   *Sponsa et Sponsus, Exposition on the Song of Songs*. Bayerische
Staatsbibliothek München, CLM. 18125, 1v., c. 1200.   38

2.2   *Sponsa et Sponsus, Exposition on the Song of Songs*.
Bayerische Staatsbibliothek München, CLM. 4550, third quarter
of the twelfth century.   39

2.3   *Sponsa et Sponsus, Exposition on the Song of Songs*.
Bayerische Staatsbibliothek München, CLM. 30172, 1403.   40

2.4   *Christ in Majesty, Speculum Virginum*, book 10. The Walters Art
Museum, Baltimore, MS W 72, fol. 98 r.   42

2.5   *Jesus Attracting the Faithful to Heart*, 1480/1490. Courtesy of
National Gallery of Art, Washington, Rosenwald Collection,
1943.3.853.   43

2.6   Dirck Volckertsz Coornhert, *Mensheid wordt door de duivel
geketend*, 1550, after a design by Maarten van Heemskerck.
Rijksmuseum, Amsterdam, RP-P-BI-6540X.   46

2.7   Dirck Volckertsz Coornhert, *Zaligheid wordt bereikt door een te
worden met Christus*, 1550, after a design by Maarten van
Heemskerck. Rijksmuseum, Amsterdam, RP-P-BI-6553x.   47

2.8   Unknown artist, *Eternal Embrace and Closing Prayer, Von der
ynnigen selen wy sy gott casteyet vnnd im beheglich mach*.
Erfurt: Wolfgang Schenck, 1499. Biblioteka Uniwersytecka
we Wrocławiu, XV.Q.329 d iii v–d iv r.   58

3.1   *God sends his messengers, Buch der Kunst, dadurch der
weltlich Mensch mag geistlich werden*. Augsburg: Johann
Bämler, 1477, a 4 r RB 85766. Reproduced by permission of
The Huntington Library, San Marino, California.   80

3.2   *The Soul at the altar with Christ as Man of Sorrows, Buch
der Kunst, dadurch der weltlich Mensch mag geistlich
werden*. Augsburg: Johann Bämler, 1477, c 8 v RB 85766.
Reproduced by permission of The Huntington Library,
San Marino, California.   82

viii   *Marrying Jesus in Medieval and Early Modern Northern Europe*

3.3   Title page, *Den gheesteliken minnenbrief die Jesus Christus
        sendet tot synre bruyt.* Leiden: Govert van Ghemen, c. 1495,
        a i r. Cambridge University Library Inc.6.E.102[3117].   84

3.4   *Christ wakes the Soul, Von der ynnigen selen wy sy gott casteyet
        vnnd im beheglich mach.* Erfurt: Wolfgang Schenck, 1499,
        a iii r. Biblioteka Uniwersytecka we Wrocławiu, XV.Q.329.   86

3.5   *Christ undresses the Soul/Christ hangs the Soul, Christus und
        die minnende Seele.* Albertina, Vienna, DG1930/198/6–7.   88

3.6   *The Soul enthroned with her Attendants and Wounding Jesus,
        Buch der Kunst, dadurch der weltlich Mensch mag geistlich
        werden.* Augsburg: Johann Bämler, 1477, m 8 r, RB 85766.
        Reproduced by permission of The Huntington Library,
        San Marino, California.   90

3.7   Title page, Mauburnus's *Rosetum exercitiorum spiritualium
        et sacrarum meditationum.* Zwolle: Peter Os, 1494, RB
        104186. Reproduced by permission of The Huntington Library,
        San Marino, California.   95

3.8   *Coronation of the Virgin* with profession statements, *Biblia
        Pauperum.* Nuremburg: Hans Sporer, 1471–75, 36. Courtesy of
        Scheide Library, Princeton, NJ.   97

3.9   "er hat mich gezieret mitt der cronen als der gemahel" [He has
        adorned me with a crown as the bride], *Biblia Pauperum.*
        Nuremburg: Hans Sporer, 1471–75, 40. Courtesy of Scheide
        Library, Princeton, NJ.   99

3.10   *The Descent from the Cross* (front), c. 1420. Panel, 62 × 30 cm.
        Inv. Nr. 268.a. Museo Thyssen-Bornemisza, Madrid, Spain.
        Photo credit: Scala / Art Resource, NY.   102

3.11   *Christ bearing the Cross* (reverse), c. 1420. Panel, 62 × 30 cm.
        Inv. Nr. 268.b. Museo Thyssen-Bornemisza, Madrid, Spain.
        Photo credit: Scala / Art Resource, NY.   103

3.12   Iconographic finger ring from Godstow Abbey, early fifteenth
        century. Depth: 11.3 millimeters, diameter: 19.6 millimeters,
        weight: 15.448 grams. British Museum, Inv. Nr. AN287704001.
        Copyright of the Trustees of the British Museum.   105

List of Figures and Tables

3.13   "vanden boome des leuens. Dat is dat ghewarighe heylige cruys" [On the Tree of Life, that is that true Holy Cross], Pierre d'Ailly, *Hofkijn van devotien*. Antwerp: Geerard Leeu, 1487, 12 r. Courtesy of the Library of Congress, Incun. 1487. A393.   108

3.14   "Vanden fonteynen ende vanden loopenden wateren die inden seluen hof springhen: ende vander grooter lusticheyt die de siele ontfanghet vanden vogelkens die doer den hof vlieghen al singende" [On the Fountain and the Running Water which springs forth in that same Garden, and on the great desire which the soul receives from the birds who fly through that garden singing], Pierre d'Ailly, *Hofkijn van devotien*. Antwerp: Geerard Leeu, 1487, 22 r. Courtesy of the Library of Congress, Incun. 1487. A393.   109

3.15   *The School of Charity, Exercitium Super Pater Noster*, 1460. Courtesy of Bibliothèque nationale de France, Xylo 31.   111

4.1   *The Servant before the Cross as a Rosebush of Sorrows*, Henry Suso, *Exemplar*. Courtesy of Wolfenbüttel, Herzog August Bibl., Cod. 78.5 Aug. 2°, f 62 r, c. 1473.   134

4.2   *The Servant's Marriage to Christ*, Henry Suso, *Exemplar*. Courtesy of Wolfenbüttel, Herzog August Bibl., Cod. 78.5 Aug. 2°, f 95 v.   137

5.1   Petrus Christus, *Portrait of a Female Donor*, c. 1455. Courtesy of National Gallery of Art, Washington, Samuel H. Kress Collection, 1961.9.11.   152

5.2   Triumphal arch, Götene Church, last quarter of the fifteenth century. Photo courtesy of Lars-Olof Albertson.   158

5.3   *St. Bridget*, c. 1480. Courtesy of National Gallery of Art, Washington, Rosenwald Collection, 1943.3.593.   159

7.1   *De Ziele rust op de Borst Jesu* [*The Soul rests on Jesus's Chest*], Jan Luyken, *Jesus en de Ziel*. Amsterdam: Pieter Arentsa, 1685, 155, RB 35565. Reproduced by permission of The Huntington Library, San Marino, California.   202

7.2   *De Ziele heeft haer herte met Jesus versegelt* [*The Soul seals her heart with Jesus*], Jan Luyken, *Jesus en de Ziel*. Amsterdam: Pieter Arentsa, 1685, 150, RB 35565. Reproduced by permission of The Huntington Library, San Marino, California.   203

x *Marrying Jesus in Medieval and Early Modern Northern Europe*

7.3   Johann Adam Eyer, "You my soul sing" ["Du meine Seele Singe"], 1782. Courtesy of the Free Library of Philadelphia, FLP 541.   212

8.1   Sister Gertrude Morgan (1900–80), *New Jerusalem*, New Orleans, Louisiana, c. 1957–74. Acrylic and/or tempera on metal lid, 12 in. × 19 in. Collection of the American Folk Art Museum, New York, gift of Bliss Carnochan in honor of Gerard C. Wertkin, American Folk Art Museum director (1991–2004), 2004.7.1. Photo by Gavin Ashworth, New York.   223

Tables

3.1   Uniform Titles and Descriptions of Treatises About Christ and the Loving Soul   71

Preface and Acknowledgements

This book examines how Christians in Germany and the Low Countries learned to marry Jesus between the twelfth and the seventeenth centuries and why this phenomenon continues to influence Christian culture in the modern world. It is not the first book about the bride of Christ, nor will it be the last, and it likely is not the book you are expecting. When you or I or any modern person encounters a medieval image of the bride of Christ, we instinctively will situate it within narratives *we* already know. Those already familiar with marriage to Jesus in medieval and early modern western Christianity may anticipate that this volume will focus on celibate women and saints. Though holy women are part of this study, this book is a history of popular religion told through devotional media and other technologies of salvation. By "popular," I mean that this imagery was widely represented in contemporary media, that its origins were spontaneous and diffuse, and that it elided distinctions between sacred and profane. This definition of popular religion challenges an imagined binary dividing the "popular" from the "elite" in medieval Europe and the "sacred" from the "profane" in the history of religion. As I shall demonstrate, positioning the bride of Christ as a particular medieval expression of Christianity belonging primarily to wealthy women originates in an imagined boundary between Latinate and vernacular sources that stems from an anachronistic and undertheorized understanding of religious culture. Because the bride of Christ has previously been understood as belonging to an elite religious culture comprising primarily wealthy Latinate medieval Christian women, married, male, and postmedieval brides of Christ have been misidentified as peculiar outliers. Using popular religious media depicting the bride of Christ as markers of now-lost communities of devotion and discourse, I shall explain why late medieval Christians insisted that Jesus was the spouse for all created souls. Because these marriages were enacted through sacraments such as baptism and reception of the Eucharist made marriage to Jesus into an important element of popular culture.

The method and argument of this book require a brief explanation. I have written for three intersecting but discrete academic enterprises: religious studies, medieval and early modern studies, and gender studies. Because of this, I have made decisions about presenting my research that adopt the norms of one academic discipline over those of another that may surprise some readers; I address the reasons behind these choices here. Because I hope my research will interest readers from a variety of academic backgrounds, I have included background information on the history of medieval and early modern Christianity as well as my methodological approach to religious studies and gender studies and defined technical terms usually left unglossed in specialist literature. This book is informed by gender studies and reconstructs complex histories from archival sources, but I am, above all, interested in examining religion as a human phenomenon. I draw my approach and some of my vocabulary from Religious Studies and New Media Studies to organize networks of medieval and early modern objects—books, rings, devotional images, cheap prints, songs—that preserve the beliefs, investments, and interactions of individuals who believed themselves to be brides of Christ. As I shall explain in Chapter 1, my examination of marriage to Jesus reconstructs the diverse beliefs, practices, and rituals composing Christianity in northern Europe through devotional media, rather than the texts and institutions granted doctrinal approval by institutional leaders. Few historians of Christianity critically examine religion as a category, while many theorists of religion continue using a historically inaccurate model of medieval Christianity and the secularizing influence of the Protestant Reformation to construct definitions of "religion." This book is neither strictly historical theology, the project of describing the ways Christian thinkers have represented nature of God and the relationship between God and the created universe, nor Church History, the reconstruction of the actions and beliefs of Christians and their institutions. My study evaluates public and private claims about marriage to Jesus as something people have done for centuries and still do today. As a religious studies scholar, I recognize that "religion" cannot be limited by the self-authorized claims of practitioners even though it must accurately represent religious individuals and their beliefs, rituals, experiences, and communities. In a study of eros in Middle High German literature, Hildegard Keller, whose work influences my own, once asked her readers if "anyone involuntarily think[s] of a monk when he or she hears the expression 'bride of Christ,'" proposing that a modern impulse to read the bride as female confirms the normative gendering of medieval brides of Christ as female.[1] I ask my readers in turn to keep in mind what, if anything, they first think of when they hear the expression "bride of Christ" because I know that these modern assumptions strongly influence contemporary scholarship on this topic. Keller's question presumes that her audience has encountered modern brides of Christ in their own lives, and that these brides have been overwhelmingly female. This is not necessarily true. For Catholics, especially those who have witnessed ceremonies of monastic profession, the connection between brides of Christ and nuns may indeed be instinctive. However, as I explain in the final chapter of this book, many contemporary Protestants simultaneously understand the bride of Christ to be every Christian, a harbinger of the apocalypse, and a romantic partner for married women and teenage girls. While writing this book, I have also met American Protestants who privately related stories of relatives who were called to evangelize following a marriage to Jesus or attended churches that presented Jesus as a boyfriend, perfect husband, or ideal role model for Christian husbands. I expect that the cases examined in this book may strike readers as alternately disturbing, profane, devotionally useful, or precociously queer according to personal background, aesthetics, and scholarly training. In my view, medieval and early modern readers would likely not have

---

[1]   Hildegard Elisabeth Keller, *My Secret is Mine: Studies on Religion and Eros in the German Middle Ages* (Leuven: Peeters, 2000), 32.

responded to any of the sources I shall discuss as you or I might. The medieval is not relevant only through its relationship to modernity, nor is that modernity itself fully comprehensible in relation to historical precedents, but I do agree with Keller's claim that considering postmedieval evidence may help determine what was normative in the historical past, so long as these comparisons are not made exclusively to the modern Roman Catholic Church.

Medieval and early modern Christians learned about the bride of Christ in segments of a larger story appearing simultaneously on several media platforms—within a single manuscript codex, but also in printed images, sermons, and songs, adapted to the constraints of a particular medium. To describe these complex adaptations, I have borrowed the phrase "transmedia storytelling," language introduced by Henry Jenkins to describe the collision of genres and loss of authorial identity in new media. Jenkins uses this phrase to explain the narration of a single story across multiple media platforms, each iteration adjusted for that medium and audience.[2] Though this term might strike some as anachronistic, and thus inappropriate for examining the world of manuscript scriptoria and hand presses, as an image embedded in late medieval popular culture, the bride of Christ was susceptible to some of the same popular appropriations and fervent responses as cultural icons in contemporary cultural memory. My use of transmedia storytelling and network theory allows me to incorporate into the history of the bride of Christ, for the first time, fragmentary sources with broken chains of provenance.

Reconstructing how Jesus became enmeshed in late medieval popular religious culture has necessitated that I challenge a longstanding scholarly consensus that the bride of Christ was something constructed *by* male religious elites *for* a small group of wealthy, educated female practitioners. For those familiar with medieval hagiography and mysticism, and to anyone who has read feminist scholarship on either subject, my argument may seem to be a polemical reversal of received wisdom. That is certainly not my intention, but my statement takes into account source material those other scholars have not considered. Two other studies of the bride of Christ appeared after I completed this manuscript but before this book's publication: Dyan Elliott's *Bride of Christ Goes to Hell: Metaphor and Embodiment in the Lives of Pious Women 200–1500* (2011) and Carolyn Diskant Muir's *Saintly Brides and Grooms: The Mystic Marriage in Northern Renaissance Art* (2013). Both accept without question that medieval and early modern Christians believed brides of Christ should be pious celibate women. Elliott's feminist historiography uses primarily Latin sources from central and southern Europe to examine how the metaphor of the bride of Christ was used to modify and control women's spirituality, while Muir's art historical approach compares Latin and vernacular hagiographies to visual depictions of male and female saints. Muir's work draws attention to a disparity between visual and literary sources and Elliott's work to a dissonance between male and female understandings of the

---

[2] Henry Jenkins, *Convergence Culture: Where Old and New Media Collide* (New York: New York University Press, 2006), 93–7.

bride of Christ. In contrast, I examine the bride of Christ as cultural phenomenon through which it may be possible to reconstruct popular religious cultures of the past. This book explains how people learned to be brides of Christ, how such marriages were contracted, and why so many Christians prayed to marry Jesus. More manuscripts, images, songs, and sermons about the bride of Christ have been produced by western Christians than any of these books could discuss, and more exist in languages Anglophone scholars rarely learn to read. These newly published studies and my own share many of the same observations, but focus on different periods, use significantly different sources, and set out to answer different disciplinary questions. Unsurprisingly, we have arrived at different but, I hope, complementary conclusions.

In what follows, I track a transformation of beliefs about the bride of Christ driven by and preserved in media. I focus on objects produced in Germany and the Low Countries between 1200 and 1700, regions in well-documented religious dialogue with one another before and after the Reformation. This period spans the introduction of print culture to continental Europe and the political and religious upheaval of the sixteenth-century reformations, two common periodization boundaries between "medieval" and "early modern." The religious culture of medieval German- and Dutch-speaking Christians influenced both Catholics and Protestants in post-Reformation England as well as the German, Dutch, and English settlers who colonized North America. This interlocking relationship between the material remains of medieval and early modern Christianity and the worlds of belief that scholars reconstruct offers an alternate path to recovering popular religious practices. Because my discussion covers several centuries and presents material even specialists will find unfamiliar, at the end of Chapter 1, I offer a brief historical overview of how marriage to Jesus became part of lay piety. The first half of this book explains that marrying Jesus became part of late medieval popular culture because of a theological understanding of the universe that understood that the gendering of souls was distinct from the biology of bodies.[3] The final chapters of the book examine the interpenetration of medieval, early modern, and contemporary Christian history to explain how the religious revolutions of the sixteenth century distort the late medieval innovation that each Christian should strive to marry Jesus. Each chapter opens with a seemingly dissonant image of the bride of Christ and resolves into a consonant chord as its historical context is recovered from a historical network. As a matter of necessity, evidence is arranged thematically, rather than chronologically. None of the sources I work with existed only in the moment they were written. Even those with a known author, a holograph copy, and clear textual histories were owned and used differently over the centuries. Their afterlives, as preserved in records of use and

---

[3] I shall return to this in Chapter 4. My understanding of the relationship between body, soul, gender, and experience closely follows Amy Hollywood's discussion of the relationship between gender, vision, and authority. Amy Hollywood, *The Soul as Virgin Wife: Mechthild of Magdeburg, Marguerite Porete, and Meister Eckhart* (Notre Dame, IN: University of Notre Dame Press, 1995), 9–12, 27–39, 202–3.

Preface and Acknowledgements xv

adaptation, are central to my argument. Though the medieval church fissured into distinct and embattled denominations during the sixteenth century, each new church retained a medieval understanding that Jesus was a spouse for Christian souls, and not even Catholics limited the role of bride to nuns. The concluding chapter examines marriage to Jesus in contemporary Christianity to demonstrate both how the bride of Christ remains part of popular culture and how contemporary Christianity influences the reception of medieval brides of Christ.

I must issue a few final caveats about my editorial choices, including the critical apparatus, and the translations I provide. All translations are my own unless otherwise specified, and though Jennifer L. Welsh and Johanna Kramer have kindly checked several passages and greatly improved their sense, any remaining errors are my own. I have provided transcriptions of the original source language whenever citing a poem as well as all manuscripts and early books, but otherwise have given only my own English translation with a reference to the best available modern edition of the original. I have taken care to differentiate between Christian denominations where appropriate, but because the medieval Church is not the same entity as either the modern Catholic church or any single Protestant denomination, I use "Protestant" only following the Diet of Speyer in 1529 and "Catholic" after the Council of Trent. Before those events, I speak of individual theologians and their followers, the medieval Church, or the Church in Rome. I use European Reformations, rather than Protestant/Catholic/Counter-Reformation, to encompass the religious changes that dissolved the medieval Church into new denominations. All place names are given as they are most commonly known in American English. Although I am aware of the complex colonial and nationalist issues involved in place names, I have used German rather than Polish for medieval cities (Danzig, Marienwerder, rather than Gdańsk, Kwidzyn) but provided contemporary Polish names when citing items held in Polish libraries (Wrocław rather than Breslau). I refer to "Germany and the Low Countries" as shorthand for the modern nations of Germany, Austria, Switzerland, Poland, Belgium, the Netherlands, and Luxembourg, the regions where dialects of medieval German and Dutch were spoken. Personal names have been left in their original spelling (e.g. Elsbet, Alijt, Adelheid, Gertruid, Katharina) unless the individual is commonly normalized for English audiences (e.g. Gertrud of Helfta, Henry Suso). To allow others to locate my sources, I have provided the exact spelling of an author's name in footnotes and bibliography when I am citing a pre-1750 edition or someone else's book title, even if that spelling differs from the one I have adopted in my own text (e.g. Henricus Suso or Heinrich Seuse rather than Henry Suso). I have provided all possible name variations in the index. Finally, for both male and female figures known by geographic surnames, I have elected to refer to people by their first name, unless they are typically addressed by that geographic name in existing scholarship (e.g. Bridget for Bridget of Sweden, Johannes for Johannes von Marienwerder, but Ruusbroec for Jan van Ruusbroec).

Some of the terms I use to discuss books and objects also need clarification. I refer both to handwritten manuscripts and printed quires as "books," whether or not they have been bound into a codex. I also discuss printed images in "blockbooks," manuscripts into which woodcuts or engravings have been pasted, and illustrated printed books. In illustrated books printed on handpresses, woodcuts were positioned within pages composed of moveable type, while blockbooks consisted of series of images on carved woodblocks. Text was usually carved directly onto the blocks as part of the carved illustration (xylographic text) or written by hand on the printed sheet (chirographic text). Copies were made by pressing the paper down onto the block and required far less technical knowledge to produce or financial investment to create. After production, an image from any of these illustrated books might be cut out of its original context and relocated to a new volume. Where possible, I provide codicological context for these images. I refer to printed and manuscript books, decorative objects, devotional paintings, and other cultural artifacts as "objects," representing my indebtedness to scholarship on object-oriented ontology and the influence of Bruno Latour's actor-network theory on my own approach. As I explain in the next chapter, this approach grants agency to material objects, allowing them to speak and act as representatives of those historical movements for which neither text nor context have survived. Rather than providing lengthy textual histories for my sources, as is often done in medieval studies, I have given brief discussions of textual histories only when details of an object's provenance proves relevant to my argument. Some bibliographic information about books and manuscripts, including provenance information and dimensions, has been derived from published catalogues and additional notation in cataloguing databases. Wherever possible, I have given links to those catalogues and databases, as well as provided links to digitized copies of books, manuscripts, and objects when available. When citing inscriptions in printed books, woodcuts pasted into manuscripts, and miscellanies containing multiple texts under discussion, I have given full references in the footnotes, then listed manuscripts and codices by institution or main title in the bibliography. Anonymous sources, pseudonymous sources, and misattributed sources have been listed in the bibliography according to their title, if known, and otherwise according to the first title under which a volume is listed in an institutional catalogue.

Many of the works discussed in this book circulated in diverse formats, so they lack standardized titles in English and have different titles in Latin, French, Dutch, and German. Consequently, after introducing a nonstandardized source and all known variants in the first citation, I refer to it by a shortened English title. Rather than adopting the standard practice among medieval and early modernists of quoting biblical passages from a normalized text such as the Vulgate, I have offered quotations of isolated passages from the New Revised Standard Version, the most recent scholarly critical edition of the text. I have otherwise provided translated biblical verses as they were presented in original sources. This is standard among religious studies scholars and also reflects the historical reality that most medieval readers would never have encountered a "standard" biblical text, but instead would have heard passages paraphrased in sermons or copied in idiosyncratic manuscripts. Similarly, though sixteenth-century print bibles introduced some standardization, many early modern readers owned multiple biblical editions, often from competing confessional organizations.

Preface and Acknowledgements xvii

My decision to refer to individual brides of Christ as "she" or "he" is determined by pronouns in original texts and gender-specific clothing and hairstyles in art. Finally, I write intentionally of "marrying Jesus," not the "mystical marriage of the soul," or "spiritual marriage," to emphasize that becoming a bride of Christ in medieval Europe was as much a physical as a spiritual process. To marry Jesus required the involvement of a sinful, praying human body that could receive sacraments such as baptism, the Eucharist, or holy orders.

Acknowledgements

During the years when I have worked on this project, a number of good and generous people and institutions have granted their assistance. This book originates in texts I first explored in a dissertation venturing feminist analyses of prose and images designed by or for medieval women. Though a very different project, neither that dissertation nor this book would have been written without the patient guidance of Peter Kaufman, Lance Lazar, and Albert Rabil Jr. I am thankful that my mentors' open-mindedness gave me space to write a dissertation that crossed genres and languages, while their good counsel kept me focused on enclosed women before 1500. Though this book uses very different evidence and directly argues against my dissertation, it still benefits from their wise comments and continued support of this project. Peter Kaufman has offered guidance and good cheer whenever I most needed him. Albert Rabil Jr, though long retired, lent his editor's eye and red pen to reshape every milestone draft, and has introduced me to key texts and generous colleagues every step of the way. Over the years, I have presented portions of this project at a number of conferences. Conversations at Kalamazoo, the American Academy of Religion, the American Historical Association, the Southeastern Medieval Association, Sixteenth Century Studies, and Attending to Early Modern Women have broadened my perspective and brought new ideas to this project. Philip Soergel's generous comments helped me find the book I was trying to write. Kent Brintall has clarified my discussion of gender and sexuality. Emma Lipton, Johanna Kramer, Megan Moore, Anne Stanton, Dennis Kelly, Lois Huneycutt, John Frymire, Chip Callahan, Nate Hofer, Ed Drott, and Bob Flanagan all read and commented on parts of this manuscript in writing groups and hallways. Anne Stanton and Mary Pixley offered kind advice about wording, permissions, copyright, and the many other perils which come with writing about images. My dear friend Michlina Nowicka made several phone calls to help arrange permissions for this book's cover photo. Sue Crowley generously filled my margins with welcome editorial corrections and delightful commentary. A number of students have also assisted with this book along the way. Emily S. Clark scanned microfilm and introduced me to Sister Gertrud Morgan; Guy Niederhauser, Andrew Stelling, and Kyla Richtman assisted with bibliography and scanning. Misty Mullin discussed Augsburg's convent culture and woodcutters with me. Autumn Dolan has admirably handled permissions, untangled a very complicated bibliography, and assisted in editing the manuscript with speed, grace, and attention to detail. Of all the colleagues, friends, and mentors who have advised on this book, I owe two special thanks: Jennifer L. Welsh and Kathleen E. Kennedy were always willing to read a draft or answer a question on short notice. They knew the answers to almost anything I asked them, and I knew I could ask them almost anything. My writing and argumentation has benefited from anonymous readers and press proofreaders who kindly corrected even the most obscure typographical errors in German! My experience working with everyone at Ashgate has been an absolute delight. For her swift support, considerable patience when the unexpected occurred, and much-needed editorial guidance, I thank Erika Gaffney. I am grateful to Stephanie Peake for her quick and detailed replies, attentive reading, patience, and generosity.

Funding for research travel, leave for writing, research assistants, and images came from the University of Missouri Research Council, American Academy of Religion, Missouri Research Board, Center for Arts and Humanities Small Grant Program, and the University of North Carolina's Smith Graduate Research Grant. My ideas have been informed by colleagues and conversations at two summer workshops sponsored by the National Endowment for the Humanities. My dissertation developed during a 2005 Summer Institute on women writers in early modern Europe. In 2009, this project matured significantly under the collegial guidance of those attending the NEH summer seminar on the Reformation of the Book. I also owe an abashed thank-you to the many talented, patient, and unfailingly helpful librarians whose names I did not always know and have other times misplaced or forgotten, including those at the Bodleian Library, the British Library, the Wrocław University Library, the King Albert Royal library in Belgium, the Baden State Library, Karlsruhe, and the Bavarian State Library. The underfunded but enormously resourceful Interlibrary Loan offices at the University of Missouri-Columbia and the University of North Carolina at Chapel Hill have unearthed almost every source I requested.

I owe a special thank-you to Brad K. Earnest and everyone else in Hand Therapy at the Missouri Orthopedic Institute, without whom I would not have been able to complete this manuscript. Most of all, I wish to thank my husband, Devon Gregory, for his endless patience and love, and my parents, Cathy and Mounah Geha, for their continual support even though work on this book kept me from visiting them in Lebanon for too many years. My paternal grandmother, Mariana Issa Geha, died in 2005 as I began my dissertation. In 2009, while completing the research for this book in Europe, I said my last farewell to my maternal grandmother, Dorothy Pauline Huston. With love, tears, and gratitude, I dedicate this book to them both.

Rabia Gregory

Chapter 1
Portraits of the Bride of Christ

Disú wort sprichet got zů der geminten sele:
Ein bilde miner ewige gotheit,
ein spiegel miner heiligen drivaltekeit,
daz bistu liebú sele min,
wenne sich min gotheit neiget darin.
Du bist miner claren gotheit ein spiegel,
wanne ich gewan nie creatur lieber.
Dú bist min ebenmasse,
wanne dú alle ding durch minen willen lessest.
Minne mich alz ich dich,
wanne nieman mag erfullen dich denne ich.
Ich gap minen lip, min blůt fur dich,
daz ich mit mir selber erfulte und gewerte dich.

[God speaks these words to the beloved soul:
An image of my Eternal Godhead,
A mirror of my Holy Trinity,
You are those things, my dear soul,
When my Godhead inclines therein.
You are a mirror to my limpid Godhead,
Because I never won a dearer creature.
You are [reflected as] my equal
When you view all things through my will.
Love me as I love you
Because no one can fulfill you better than I.
I gave my body, my blood for you,
So that I could fulfill and defend you with myself.]

—# 43 Ps. Engelhart of Ebrach's *Book of Perfection*

The Strasbourg Sermon

It was late summer in Strasbourg, in 1334. The pope in Avignon had placed the city under interdict, and visits from famous preachers were uncommon. Townsfolk and travelers crowded into one of the city's churches to hear a sermon about the bride of Christ. In the crush were two unmarried women dedicated to a communal life of prayer, work, and abstinence as beguines. Heilke von Staufenberg and Gertrud von Ortenberg shared a home in the Ortenberg beguinage, a collection of homes for women converted to an apostolic form of Christianity focused on poverty. The two often attended sermons in neighboring towns together. Gertrud, a mother and

2　*Marrying Jesus in Medieval and Early Modern Northern Europe*

widow, identified intensely with the human protagonist of the sermon. She was bound to Christ in a spiritual marriage and feared that her many small betrayals had shattered that union. Overwhelmed with remorse, Gertrud wept during the sermon, lingered in tears until the church doors were drawn closed, and continued crying after returning home. When asked why she cried, Gertrud lamented: "I am the pauper who has broken the spiritual marriage between myself and my spouse."[1] That night Gertrud received a vision of Christ, dressed in rags, begging from door to door through the beguinage; he reassured Gertrud that small spiritual lapses could not shatter the marriage vow uniting her and God.

This scene from the spiritual biography of Gertrude von Ortenberg focuses intently on an inconsolable widow's inner turmoil. Gertrud's story is itself remarkable, though little known, and I shall return to it later in this book. The congregation who witnessed Gertrud's tears and those who later recorded and studied her visions comprise an almost impressionistic backdrop to her solo performance of penitent devotion, but their presence is significant. Possibly delivered at the Strasbourg Cathedral or the Dominican chapter house, this sermon addressed a community of acquaintances and strangers discernible now only through this brief passage in the life of a holy woman. The listening audience, those they told about the sermon, and the copyists who recorded its message shared the same vocabulary of salvation, recited the same prayers, read the same books, and, like Gertrud of Ortenberg, were espoused to Christ. I do not mean that they had each spoken vows or married Christ in heaven, as Gertrud had, or that they were professional religious—the clerics and members of monastic orders who sometimes received rings and wed themselves to Christ in a formal ritual of monastic profession that marked their leaving secular life. Rather, as I shall prove, many late medieval Christians believed that every baptized Christian had wed Christ because late medieval preachers and theologians taught that layfolk and religious professionals benefitted equally from guidance in pleasing their heavenly spouse. Just as Gertrud's tears reveal a network of otherwise unknown Christians

---

[1]　"Ein brůder predigete eines moles wol ein halp jor vor irem [Gertrud's] tode wie der mönſch die geiſtlich E brech die er gemacht het mit got / Do wart ſů ermanet der glůbde vnd der E vnd des bandes dz ſů mit vnſerm herren gemaht hette wie ſů die glůbde nit gehalten hette alſo ſů ſolte / vnd gedoht wie minmeklich er ſich zů ir geneiget het / vnd wie ſů im nit alſo getruwe wer noch irem vermugen alſo er ir / vnd wie su die wer die mit iren geiſtlichen gebreſten die geiſtlichen E gebrochen hette zwiſchen ir vnd irem gemahel / cnd kam in ein weinen vnd weine die gantze predige / vnd noch der predige vntz man die kirche beſloſ / vnd do ſů heim kam do nam jungfrowe heilke war an ir dz ſú weinde vnd sprach liebe gertrut wz weineſtu wz iſt dir / do ſprach ſů owe wz ſolte mir me ſin / jch bin die arme die die geiſtlich E gebrochen het zwiſchent mir vnd minem gemahel...." Hans Derkits, "Die Lebensbeschreibung der Gertrud von Ortenberg" (PhD diss., Universität Wien, 1990), 114–15, lines 3593–610. The full incident is on 114–15, lines 3593–644. Only one manuscript copy survives. It is now held by the King Albert Royal Library, Belgium (hereafter KBR), MS 8507–9. All citations are to Derkits's doctoral dissertation, which is the only available edition.

Portraits of the Bride of Christ

who walked alongside her or marveled at her accomplishments, images conjured by preachers' words, devotional books, and contemporary art, expose networks of individual brides of Christ seeking salvation. Some conversed with the subjects of religious biographies; others appear in ownership marks they left in books.

As the verses which open this chapter explain, each created human's soul reflects the image or figure [*Bild, figura*] of her divine creator. The creator's love for humanity is expressed through Christ's ransom on the cross. By submitting to divine will and returning that love, an individual achieved salvation, represented by the interpenetration of human and divine. Surviving alongside the writing of named "mystical" authors in over 100 manuscripts, this anonymous poem characterizes how the bride of Christ suffused late medieval devotion and survived the Reformations. Like the image of God inclining in(to) the beloved Soul, medieval and early modern understandings of the bride of Christ depended on distinct but interpenetrating understandings of the relationship between the Christian God and created beings. Though many were destroyed or defaced during the wars of religion, medieval objects depicting a marital union between Jesus and Christians such as altarpieces and manuscripts remained in use centuries after Europe ceased to be medieval. New technologies and theologies indisputably disrupted Christianity in the sixteenth century, but the devotional objects circulating between religious communities and pious burghers before the introduction of print and paper survived the censorship and warfare in the sixteenth century and inspired imitations. Medievalists sometimes consider marginal or aberrant the belief that every Christian should strive to become Christ's bride. This understanding was widely represented in medieval media and remained relevant through and after the Reformations—and thus, I argue, part of Christian popular culture.

Marriage to Jesus unfolded in a mixed space where popular and sacred, lay and learned, acted upon each other, responding to, and prompting a sometimes-frenzied desire for, objects enabling self-transformation. In the late twelfth century, monasteries produced Latin theological treatises explaining marriage to Jesus and instructing spiritual beginners to wed Christ. In the thirteenth and fourteenth centuries, new ideas about marriage to Jesus were explained to novices, catechumens, and pious layfolk by beguines, traveling preachers, and reputable nuns. By the late fourteenth century, marrying Jesus had become a crucial component of teaching doctrinally orthodox Christian soteriology. By the end of the fifteenth century, vernacular devotional media across Europe explained sacraments through Christ's marriage to the soul. This narrative also framed some sacramental disputes of the early Reformation. As this book documents, the bride of Christ was a mosaic image comprised of beliefs about God and humanity which migrated from Latin to vernacular, from manuscript to fresco to printed page, and from monastic to lay readers, tearing through the boundary between sacred and profane. Through this ongoing dialogue, new combinations of religious images and beliefs were evaluated for relevance in that moment, but those which endured remained meaningful through the long afterwards of the slowly unfolding modern.

4 *Marrying Jesus in Medieval and Early Modern Northern Europe*

A Professor's Response to the Pope

Almost exactly 200 years after the Strasbourg sermon, Protestant theologian Martin Luther explained his doctrine of salvation through the marriage of Christ and humankind in a letter and short treatise responding to Pope Leo X's bull, *Exsurge Domine*. *On the Freedom of a Christian* was one of three treatises leading to Luther's final split with the institutional church in Rome in 1520. An embattled Luther defending himself against the threat of excommunication with the promise of Christ's love for a sin-stained bride is as iconic as the 1517 delivery of the *95 Theses* or the rapid translation of the New Testament into German while in hiding at Wartburg Castle. In *On the Freedom of a Christian*, Luther expresses his understanding of salvation as a late medieval German Christian, using vocabulary appropriate to that time and place: "[T]he soul joins with Christ like bride and bridegroom" with a bridal ring of faith [*braudtring, das ist der glaub*], the soul's sins are cleansed by her sinless spouse as a wedding gift [*mahlschatz*].[2] Anyone who has taught the history of the Reformation will appreciate how elegantly this brief passage encompasses Luther's new doctrine of salvation, just as anyone who has read late medieval German accounts of the bride of Christ will recognize Luther's use of rings and wedding gifts. An anonymous sermon for the dedication of a church in Basel told the congregation that Christ was waiting at the altar for "sine gemahelun. Ivwer iegelichis sele" [his spouse, your individual soul].[3] In late fourteenth-century Strasbourg, a companion of Rulman Merswin preached, "Dirre brútegoume ist Cristus und menschliche nature ist die brut. Ach lieben kint, nuo heissent wir alle Cristus brute" [The bridegroom is Christ and human nature is the bride, Ah dear child, now we are all called Christ's brides].[4] The fourteenth-century Dominican preacher Johannes Tauler explained that the bride was "die brut daz sin wir: din und min sele" [your soul and mine].[5] For these preachers, as for Luther, the exchange of rings, gifts, and vows between Christ and a human bride was a transaction in salvation that cleansed a sinful individual with redemptive love.

Even after finalizing his break with Rome, the soul's marriage to Christ was one of the few elements popular in late medieval Christianity that Luther retained. Though he would reevaluate the sacraments and reject the cult of the saints following his break with Rome, Luther continued to explain his doctrine of

---

[2] Martin Luther, *Martin Luthers Werke; Kritische Gesamtausgabe* (Weimar: H. Böhlau, 1883–1929), vol. 7, 25–6. Hereafter WA.

[3] Wilhelm Wackernagel, *Altdeutsche Predigten und Gebete aus Handschriften* (Hildesheim: G. Olms, 1964), 27. Wackernagel transcribed this sermon from Basel, Universitätsbibliothek MS Cod. G2 II 58, a late fourteenth-century miscellany of sermons and saints' lives.

[4] Though Schmidt attributes this to Nicolaus von Basel, the text has since been tentatively attributed to Rulman Merswin. Charles Guillaume Adolphe Schmidt, *Nicolaus von Basel: Bericht von der Bekehrung Taulers* (Straßburg: Schmidt, 1875), 29. I discuss this sermon in greater detail in Chapter 2, 64–5.

[5] Johannes Tauler, *Die Predigten Taulers* (Berlin: Weidmann, 1910), 431. I discuss this sermon in greater detail in Chapter 4, 117–18, 139.

Portraits of the Bride of Christ 5

salvation through faith as a marriage between Christ and each believing Christian until close to his death in 1546. A more mature elaboration of this image appears in a compilation of Luther's conversations and off-the-cuff exegesis titled *Table Talk* [*Tischreden*]:

> He is our Bridegroom and we are his bride.... Whatever we have, it is [also] his. But it is truly an imbalanced transaction. He has eternal innocence, righteousness, life, and blessedness, which he gives to us when he makes himself eternally ours. We are ensnared by the devil, subject to sin and death. He has delivered us from the devil's sovereignty [by] smashing his skull, capturing him, casting him [back] into hell.... Even though the dear Lord gives [himself in] a spiritual wedding and marriage [*heirath und Ehe*] with us, betrothing himself to us to be our eternal Bridegroom, blesses and adorns us with his celestial goods [innocence, righteousness, life, blessedness] and also vowing that he wants to be our eternal priest, this is in vain; the teeming mass runs on in the name of the devil, whores against him, prays to foreign idols, like the Jews served Baal, Astaroth, etc., and like we beseeched the saints during the Papacy.[6]

In this reported conversation, Luther now draws clear distinctions between those saved through faith and wed to Christ, and those who have broken the bonds of that union by whoring their souls out to false gods and false religious practices.

Like the fourteenth-century preachers whose books he studied and edited, Luther believed that marriage to Christ was possible for humans, that it could be achieved through study, and that Christ's elect spouses were liberated from the devil. Luther excluded large swathes of humanity from this marriage due to their mistaken religious beliefs, limiting the bride of Christ's identity to a community of right-believers, solid in their theological and sacramental knowledge. This view was typical of polemical writing in the 1530s, as Christians of all denominations distinguished between their elect communities wed to Christ and the theologically misguided who fled or broke their marriages.

An Augsburg Scribe

In 1436, almost exactly 100 years between Martin Luther and Gertrud von Ortenberg, a 13-year-old Augsburg scribe recorded his own desire to be eternally joined to the spousal trinity. "[Q]uis hoc schribebat joranimus muller nomen habebat. Her[re] zů ainem gesponsen hab dir aller menschen sel des bit ich dich huet und ymmer mit got dem vater und dem sun und dem hailigen gaist ainen. Amen" [The one who copied this book is named Joranimus Müller. Lord, you have taken as a spouse all human souls; I pray of you today and forever to be made one with God the Father and the Son and the Holy Ghost. Amen].[7] Copied into the empty

---

[6]   Luther, WA, vol. 6, 362–3.
[7]   *Miscellany of Mystical Treatises* [*Sammelhandschrift, z.T. mystiche Texte*], Munich: Bavarian State Library/Bayerische Staatsbibliothek (hereafter BSB), MS CGM 411

6   *Marrying Jesus in Medieval and Early Modern Northern Europe*

space between two entries in a palm-sized German devotional miscellany, Müller's handwritten plea to be eternally joined with his divine spouse characterizes the brides of Christ this book examines. This inscription appears in a fifteenth-century devotional manuscript now owned by the Bavarian State Library in Munich. From a second manuscript Müller collaborated on in 1457, it seems possible that he worked in a professional scribal workshop in Augsburg.[8] Far less is known about the scribe Jerome Müller than Martin Luther or Gertrud von Ortenberg, but his inscriptions and the abridged texts in this miscellany represent a partial network which explains how media technologies dispersed the belief that every individual could wed Christ.

This inscription conjures the image of a young scribe copying out devotional texts, contemplating the meaning of their words as his hand shaped the forms of the letters, inking the red tails of an allegorical scourge, flourishing initials, and rubricating chapter titles, until he was inspired to ask the celestial spouse whose name he kept recopying for an eternal embrace. As a teenage male bride of Christ, Müller may strike some contemporary readers as an impressionably hormonal boy aroused by a queerly erotic desire for a divine male lover. Like the other male brides of Christ whom I shall discuss in this book, Müller's desire for Jesus should not be read as analogous to contemporary same-sex desire for a biologically male incarnation of God. Müller's colophon does not voice sexual desire, nor do Müller or the devotional treatises he copied seem troubled by the masculinity of mortal and heavenly spouses. The manuscript opens with a dialogue between Christ and the Loving Soul appropriate for "ain ietlich menschen" [each and every person] that uses gender-inclusive and masculine language—when the loving soul [*minnende sele*] thirsts for Christ, he promises to bring a drink to "whomever [*wem*] thirsts for my love."[9] As this wording suggests, neither Jesus nor the bride were fixed into "male" and "female" roles by medieval Christians like Jerome Müller or the book's first owner. Rather, switches between male and female were important markers of spiritual progress, and the consummation of these unions, even when sexualized, erased sins. Consequently, Müller's age, gender, and sexuality were no hindrance to his marrying "the Lord."

Müller's manuscript blended fragmentary sermons, prayers, legends, allegories, and bible paraphrases into a new devotional narrative or mosaic image.

(Augsburg, 1436), 48v. Münchener Digitalisierungszentrum (hereafter MDZ), http://daten. digitale-sammlungen.de/~db/0006/bsb00064431/images. Müller lists his age as 13 in an inscription on 193ra.

   [8] Karin Schneider, *Die deutschen Handschriften der Bayerischen Staatsbibliothek München*, CGM 201–350, Catalogus codicum manu scriptorum Bibliothecae Monacensis V, 2 (Wiesbaden, 1970), 36–8. Karin Schneider, CGM 3:192–9.

   [9] "Es spricht die minnenden sel: O lieber her ihesus Christus wie mich nach deiner minnen durst Do spricht der himel fürst wem nach meinem minnen dürst dem wel ich rilich schenken und wil in selber trenken das glaß das mman here tret das ist genant kewschikait das sol man dick schwencken mit lauteren gedancken mit rüu und mit bicht so wirt terlicht. Dis fur ding sol ain ietlich menschen haben amen." BSB CGM 411 f. 1r.

Portraits of the Bride of Christ 7

As a scribe, Müller marks a node connecting the disparate authors whose texts he copied to the readers who would handle the book he had created. Like the texts from which he copied, and those who used his book, Müller understood marriage to Christ as part of a process of personal spiritual reform related to virtuous living and contemplative practice which comprised the religious routines of the fifteenth century. The manuscript also demonstrates how texts associated with women's religious communities were adapted for broader audiences. The meditative poem *Eine geistliche Geißel* [*A Spiritual Scourge*], for which Müller drew and labeled a mnemonic diagram of an eight-thonged flail, records a longer prose version of a short poem associated with contemporary women's Dominican communities. Where two surviving convent manuscripts addressed cloistered persons [*closter mensch*], Müller wrote "gaistlich mensch" [spiritual people] and copied several additional pages describing the allegorical meaning for each tip of the flail, potentially because his patron needed more instruction to interpret the image than the Dominican sisters.[10]

Marrying Jesus in Christian Popular Culture

Müller's inscription and the contents of his manuscript typify how the bride of Christ became enmeshed in late medieval popular culture. Scholars of medieval popular religion typically consider heterodox practices of the unlettered laity, feast days, confraternities, the cult of the saints, and the use of cheap mass-produced items like printed broadsheets and pilgrims' badges.[11] The bride of Christ appears in these types of sources, but was also discussed in doctrinally orthodox sermons and treatises and appeared in luxury manuscripts and church frescoes. Even those who could not have afforded the sources I discuss would likely have understood their content, and certainly would have heard in songs and sermons that Christ was a spouse for every Christian soul.

Popular religion has become a value-laden phrase representing a perceived difference between the religious beliefs and practices of the people (whoever they may be) and a society's elites.[12] Historians sometimes discard the phrase as

---

[10] I depend here on Jeffrey Hamburger's transcription. Jeffrey F. Hamburger, *The Visual and the Visionary: Art and Female Spirituality in Late Medieval Germany* (New York: Zone Books; MIT Press, 1998), 462–3. Müller's copy spans BSB MS CGM 411 f 1v–11ra.

[11] Elizabeth L. Eisenstein, *The Printing Press as an Agent of Change: Communications and Cultural Transformations in Early Modern Europe* (Cambridge: Cambridge University Press, 1979); Robert W. Scribner, *For the Sake of Simple Folk: Popular Propaganda for the German Reformation* (Cambridge: Cambridge University Press, 1981). Emmanuel Le Roy Ladurie, *Montaillou: Cathars and Catholics in a French village, 1294–1324* (London: Scolar Press, 1978); Carlo Ginzburg, *The Cheese and the Worms: The Cosmos of a Sixteenth-Century Miller* (Baltimore: Johns Hopkins University Press, 1980).

[12] Christopher Marsh's elaboration on "popular religion" addresses most of these pitfalls. Christopher W. Marsh, *Popular Religion in Sixteenth-Century England: Holding*

8 *Marrying Jesus in Medieval and Early Modern Northern Europe*

obsolete or incapable of representing continuities between lay and elite practices. Herbert Grundmann argued almost a century ago that medieval religious culture defied simple categorization as lay or monastic, heretical or orthodox, masculine or feminine.[13] Eamon Duffy preferred "traditional religion," which minimizes divisions between the religious practices of the laity and the professional religious through a shared participation in the liturgical calendar, veneration of images, and participation in the furnishing and funding of churches. Soviet anthropologist Aron Gurevich flagged some religious practices as "folkloric" or "vernacular," developed through a dialectic of bicultural communication between scholarly clergy and the general public.[14] College textbooks, perhaps the best metric for scholarly consensus, classify popular religion as belonging to and coming from the laity, and existing in constant tension with the "orthodoxy" of the hierarchical, Latinate Church.[15] But the religious transformations of the bride of Christ are far more complex than a simple laicization of the clergy, monachization of the laity, or religious revivalism.

Oppositional models for medieval religion that posit significant differences between the practices of theologically trained elites and casual believers adopt native terms proposed by the same doctrinal statements, church councils, and disputes that prioritize the views of affluent and well-educated men typically categorized as learned or professional Christians. These medieval authorities distinguished between "sacred" and "profane" or "heretical" and "holy" in written records that attempted to control the chaotic variety of beliefs and practices through which self-identified Christians constructed their religious identities. Adopting their insistence that there is a doctrinally informed and uniquely correct way to be a Christian imports a sexist and racist model for medieval Christianity that ignores the potential for nuanced and nonbinary relationships between gender, power, and piety.

Their Peace (New York: St. Martin's Press, 1998), 6–12. Charles Long's entry on Popular Religion for the second edition of the *Encyclopedia of Religion* gives a far more comprehensive history of the terminology and its problems. Charles H. Long, "Popular Religion," in *Encyclopedia of Religion*, ed. Lindsay Jones, 2nd ed., vol. 11 (Detroit: Macmillan Reference USA, 2005), 7324–33, *Gale Virtual Reference Library*, Web, October 3, 2012.

[13] Herbert Grundmann, *Religious Movements in the Middle Ages: The Historical Links Between Heresy, the Mendicant Orders, and the Women's Religious Movement in the twelfth and thirteenth century, with the historical foundation of German Mysticism*, trans. Steven Rowan (South Bend, IN: University of Notre Dame Press, 1995).

[14] Eamon Duffy, *The Stripping of the Altars: Traditional Religion in England, c.1400–c.1580* (New Haven, CT: Yale University Press, 1992), 1–8; Aron Gurevich, *Medieval Popular Culture: Problems of Belief and Perception*, trans. János M. Bak and Paul A. Hollingsworth (Cambridge: Cambridge University Press, 1988).

[15] Daniel Ethan Bornstein, *Medieval Christianity* (Minneapolis, MN: Fortress Press, 2009); John Raymond Shinners, *Medieval Popular Religion, 1000–1500: A Reader* (Peterborough: Broadview Press, 1997); Miri Rubin, *Medieval Christianity in Practice* (Princeton, NJ: Princeton University Press, 2009).

Scholars of religion and media in contemporary society advocate interpreting religion through media and as mediation, using material culture—books, prayers, pictures, but also toys, music, food, and clothing—to pick apart the tangle of actors and interactions that compile belief and mark its change and evolution.[16] In this way, media becomes more than a tool conveying information to believers; instead, media, creators, and consumers constitute a dialectic that influences religious culture in ways neither creator nor devotee designed. This multidirectional relationship between creators, consumers, and objects also exists for medieval and early modern media. Medieval depictions of the bride of Christ exist and are reinterpreted in the centuries after its creation, and these postmedieval responses can help unravel how the actions and beliefs of medieval and early modern Christians reformed their own religion. As Bruno Latour points out, "[I]nformation technologies allow us to trace the associations in a way that was impossible before ... mak[ing] *visible* what was before only present virtually."[17] Colophons, incipits, inscriptions, glosses, and rubrications like those left behind by Müller are themselves medieval information technologies. With the assistance of digitized manuscript catalogues and other tools, it is possible to begin reconstructing the networks of readers, patrons, and users who surrounded these individual medieval artifacts. Though I do not apply Latour's actor-network theory to images of medieval brides of Christ, his approach guides my own. Like Latour, I acknowledge that objects also have agency, can move and act, and can disclose information about the now-lost worlds to which they belonged. By repopulating the media network which transformed the bride of Christ from an enclosed female virgin into a gender-inclusive community of created humans, I refocus the modern gaze on material remains of the medieval bride of Christ.

Granting objects agency, as Latour does, makes available for critical examination sources that have no known provenance and thus facilitates a reconstruction of the historical past that depends more on interactions and afterlives of ideas within human communities rather than their creators. For even when depictions of the bride of Christ were created by known individuals—leading theologians, popular saints—those creators retained no control over how their work would be used by devotees. The loss of authorial control, media saturation, generational shift, and passionate emotional response characterizing the transmission of late medieval books about the bride of Christ are analogous to the media empire Henry Jenkins describes developing around George Lucas's 1977 film *Star Wars*.[18]

---

[16] While much scholarship on religion in popular culture focuses on theorizing religion through examining seemingly secular analogues of religious phenomena, the focus on media as a point of intersections applies equally on the other end of the spectrum when the seemingly sacred infiltrates and is infiltrated by the material world. The framework behind this approach is summarized by David Morgan, ed., *Keywords in Religion, Media and Culture* (New York: Routledge, 2008), xiii–xiv.

[17] Bruno Latour, *Reassembling the Social: An Introduction to Actor-Network-Theory* (Oxford: Oxford University Press, 2005), 207–8.

[18] Jenkins discusses *Star Wars* extensively in chapter 4. *Convergence Culture: Where Old and New Media Collide* (New York: New York University Press, 2006), 131–68.

10 *Marrying Jesus in Medieval and Early Modern Northern Europe*

Widespread interest in the original film initiated a trademarked Universe, as well as satirical mimicry, unscripted fan-authored fiction, and participation in the Jedi Church, a demographically quantifiable new religious movement. Creator George Lucas pioneered marketing crossovers but he has actively sought to stop some of these adaptations of his work under copyright law. Today *Star Wars* so saturates contemporary western culture that it is possible to recognize its characters and key lines without seeing the film. Medieval narratives about the bride of Christ also generated unscripted imitations rarely endorsed by the medieval church.

Making sense of medieval brides of Christ required the same level of familiarity with the complex narratives about the marriage between Jesus and the soul we now take for granted in the cultural repurposing of media franchises such as *Star Wars*. As I explain in chapters 2 and 3, in the late twelfth century a "master narrative" of Jesus's courtship and marriage emerged and would be retold in part and whole in a way analogous to Jenkins's description of transmedia storytelling. Most medieval Christians understood the complex theological conversations condensed into depictions of the bride of Christ, though with different degrees of knowledge and emotional response. Jenkins documented how contemporary citations of *Star Wars* create a community encompassing even the most casual fans through emotional responses to licensed paraphernalia and quotations while other citations are only intelligible to those fans intimately familiar with competing narratives within and about the *Star Wars* universe. In the same way, medieval representations of the bride of Christ created communities of strangers, only some of whom knew the full narrative of marriage to Jesus. Marriages to Jesus appear in woodcuts, liturgical music, prayers, sermons, and theological treatises and biographies which communicated spiritual concerns and devotional techniques across centuries. These sources reflect developing beliefs about marrying Jesus as a path to spiritual salvation. Each told a different version of Christ's marriage, adapted not only to the needs of an audience, but to the specific media platform. As marrying Jesus became part of popular culture, the fragments of this narrative appeared in diverse sources and audiences began filling in missing lines and finishing half-told stories from an internalized master narrative. This narrative included details such as the bride and groom's clothing, their kisses, squabbles, and courtship, their wedding ceremony, banquet, and consummation, which were recognizable even in isolation. Medieval Christians encountered related images of the bride of Christ so often that the story permeated their perception of the world and became incorporated into their daily lives.

Influenced in part by Rudolph Otto's *Das Heilige* [*The Idea of the Holy*], a comparative examination of religion infused with the late fifteenth- and early sixteenth-century vocabulary of Martin Luther and other Christian writers, classic studies of religion present "religion" as exceptional and deeply personal manifestations of belief and experience that disrupt daily life.[19] Though Otto's

---

[19] Rudolph Otto, *The Idea of the Holy: An Inquiry into the Non-Rational Factor in the Idea of the Divine and Its Relation to the Rational*, trans. John W. Harvey (London: Oxford University Press, 1958).

approach has long been challenged as theological and incomplete, his construction of religion as something *ganz andere* [wholly other], and the "sacred" or "holy" as something unique to religion continues to influence debates about the importance of distinguishing between the sacred and the profane. Following Otto, sociologist Émile Durkheim proposed that "[T]he division of the world into two domains, one containing all that is sacred and the other all that is profane—such is the distinctive trait of religious thought."[20] Mircea Eliade extended the divide between "sacred" and "profane" to differentiate between medieval and modern religious cultures, writing that religion had "long since lost the cosmic values that it still possessed in the middle age."[21] Though Eliade's work has also been the subject of harsh criticism, his distinction between a "medieval" world infused with religion and a "modern" world fully profane and secular persists in both histories of Christianity and theoretical work in religious studies. Scholars still use this purported division between sacred and profane as a tool for differentiating between religion and religion-like phenomena, such as patriotism and sports. In an influential essay on religion and popular culture, David Chidester proposes that "the cutting edge of religion—the radical rift between the sacred and the profane—appears at the cutting edge of American technology."[22] Chidester argues for the religious quality in seemingly secular phenomena, such as sports, music, and junk food, to emphasize that scholars produce "real" religions when we select particular subjects for study. Chidester's observations directly relate to mass-media adaptations of the bride of Christ. Individual Christians invested in clothing, jewelry, books, and time learning prayers as part of their preparation for marriage to Jesus, though most curators, cataloguers, and scholars have excluded these objects from the historical record. Yet artifacts like Müller's inscription or the depiction of the crowd gathered in Strasbourg to hear a sermon about the bride of Christ help explain how Christian bodies dwell in the world and how the personal elements of religion such as belief and experience relate to more tangible aspects of Christian culture.

Technological innovations such as print, paper, and artistic realism changed the ways that medieval people learned about the bride of Christ. Medievalists' assumptions about what is "real" religion and "valuable" literature have guided which books about the brides of Christ are available in reliable editions and which still languish, mostly unknown, in libraries around the world. For instance, the manuscripts containing the biography of Gertrud von Ortenberg and Jerome Müller's inscription were used to compile scholarly critical editions of the writings of Meister Eckhart and Gertrud of Helfta by scholars who were disinterested in other

---

[20]   Émile Durkheim, *The Elementary Forms of Religious Life*, trans. Karen E. Fields (New York: The Free Press, 1995), 34.

[21]   Mircea Eliade, *The Sacred and the Profane: The Nature of Religion*, trans. Willard R. Trask (Orlando: Harcourt, 1987), 178.

[22]   David Chidester, *Authentic Fakes: Religion and American Popular Culture* (Berkeley: University of California Press, 2005), 49.

12   *Marrying Jesus in Medieval and Early Modern Northern Europe*

brides of Christ in those codices.[23] Centuries of editorial choices have determined which brides of Christ would become part of our historical record, discarding others as deviant or obscure. Chidester and other scholars of religion and media in contemporary society have increasingly advocated interpreting religion through media and as mediation to pick apart the tangle of actors and interactions that compile belief and mark its change and evolution.[24] In this model, media becomes more than a tool conveying information to believers; instead, media, creators, and consumers constitute a dialectic. Recognizing this multidirectional relationship in medieval and early modern media shifts the focus from static texts and objects to moments of influence and transformation. As Jerome Müller's manuscript shows, medieval objects continue existing, influencing, and being reinterpreted centuries after creation. These subsequent modes of meaning can sometimes track back to actions and beliefs through which medieval Christians helped reform their religion.

Art historian Michael Camille once wrote that medieval love "on all levels, from the political down to the psychological, the sacred and profane overlapped, shared languages, subjectivities, ... identical visual codes."[25] An image like the bride of Christ circulated across imprecise social boundaries and remained relevant over centuries. Each individual response to and reflection of the bride of Christ, whether marked on a page with ink, suggested through the kiss-stains on a devotional image, or distilled from prose treatises and panel paintings, preserves a personal response or financial investment that influences the system of symbols which comprised historical Christianity. Considered this way, objects depicting the bride of Christ represent an avenue to reconstruct medieval popular religion through an ever-shifting community of individuals remaking, exchanging, and identifying the bride of Christ and the significance of marrying Jesus.

The figure of the bride of Christ in MS CGM 411, the *Life of Gertrude von Ortenberg*, and Luther's *On the Freedom of a Christian* could have been comprehensible only to those familiar with a larger master narrative about marrying Jesus. For those who knew the narrative, however, such references were powerful devotional cues which triggered emotional responses. When they stood before the altar and gazed at the Crucifix, they saw their spouse; when they swallowed the Eucharistic wafer they embraced their lover; when a medieval Christian heard Christ called "Bridegroom," they recalled the *Song of Songs*' reassurance that

---

[23] For a list of all known publications citing BSB CGM 411, http://www.handschriftencensus.de/6130, accessed on March 18, 2013; and for those citing KBR 8507–9, http://www.handschriftencensus.de/7334, accessed on March 18, 2013.

[24] While much scholarship on religion in popular culture focuses on theorizing religion through examining seemingly secular analogues of religious phenomena, the focus on media as a point of intersections applies equally on the other end of the spectrum when the seemingly sacred infiltrates and is infiltrated by the material world. The framework behind this approach is summarized by David Morgan, ed., *Keywords in Religion*, xiii–xiv.

[25] Michael Camille, *The Medieval Art of Love: Objects and Subjects of Desire* (New York: Abrams, 1998), 22.

"I am my beloved's and he is mine." Some, like Jerome Müller and Gertrud von Ortenberg, would pray for that spouse's eternal embrace.

A new kind of religious enthusiasm infused central European cities in the late Middle Ages, as pious individuals like Gertrud von Ortenberg traveled half a day or more to hear sermons or to join new religious movements. Cities' churches, streets, and markets bustled with preachers of penitence [*Bußprediger*] whose fiery sermons demanded heartfelt contrition and conversion from those who listened; with mendicants, the begging orders, who preached, prayed, and sanctified the city streets; and with the semi-religious laity, the beguines and tertiaries, informal communities dedicated to prayer, work, and daily penance. Though most of the men and women swept into this movement are now lost to the historical record, their world can be recovered through the material objects their devotion required.

History, the Bride of Christ, and "Medieval Women Mystics"

We historians of medieval Christianity typically end our work around 1500, as if Christianity suddenly ceased to be medieval when the Church began fragmenting into new denominations, while historians of the Reformation sometimes regard the fifteenth century as a prefiguration of Protestant theology. This approach to negotiating periodization—a "two-sidedness" in historian Berndt Hamm's words—recognizes that history does not fit neatly into packets of centuries or eras. Instead, the religious culture of the early modern world was influenced by its medieval past, and less obviously, the cultural and theological shifts of the Reformation also shape the ways we can now view the medieval past.[26] Hamm's "two-sidedness" acknowledges that the medieval and the early modern are reflections of each other, in dialogue, in motion, across a frame—a boundary line—that interrupts the transmission of belief and culture, positing that the image on one side is only a partial reflection of the other. This aptly represents the differences in scholarship on the bride of Christ in medieval and early modern Europe: scholars working before 1500 evaluate the bride of Christ against a prototype of chaste female sanctity imposed by male clergy regulating women's behavior and religious opportunities, those working after 1500 by degrees of proximity to Luther. I do neither.

I argue that the best evidence that marrying Jesus had become part of late medieval popular religion lies in the religious disputes of the sixteenth century. It may at first seem counterintuitive to look for information about the medieval world in the early modern period, but as I will show throughout this book, the history of the bride of Christ must also account for the histories of medieval books and objects during and after the Reformations. Simply, when we medievalists wish to know why our sources survived and were even duplicated, we should try to reconstruct why medieval and early modern Christians thought them worth holding

---

[26] Berndt Hamm, *The Reformation of Faith in the Context of Late Medieval Theology and Piety: Essays by Berndt Hamm* (Leiden: Brill, 2004), 178.

14   *Marrying Jesus in Medieval and Early Modern Northern Europe*

on to. The Reformations disrupted networks of communication and brought under suspicion almost every theological claim that could not be firmly attributed to a biblical passage. The bride of Christ could—perhaps should—have disappeared in the sixteenth century, abandoned by Protestants with less complaint than the cult of the saints, forgotten by Catholics during the erasure of late medieval popular piety. Catholics and Protestants shunned and even executed one another over biblically based understandings of nature of the Trinity, clerical celibacy, and even the sacraments of baptism and communion. As shall become clear in the last two chapters of this book, the complex medieval exegesis which introduced the possibility that every Christian could wed Christ had become so integral to explaining Christian theology by the early sixteenth century that *each* Christian denomination viewed themselves as true brides of Christ. My evidence clearly shows that beliefs about the bride of Christ changed significantly between the twelfth and fifteenth centuries, but I have chosen to make tracking that historical shift secondary to explaining how networks of devotional media first created and now preserve medieval popular religion. Documenting the interpenetrating lineages between medieval, early modern, and contemporary brides of Christ is an important piece of my argument that marrying Jesus was part of late medieval popular culture, that a range of medieval definitions for "bride of Christ" survived the European Reformations, and that marrying Jesus remains part of contemporary popular Christianity.

We historians of medieval Christianity often begin our studies with patristic sources, scholastic authorities, and saints' lives; consequently, many consider celibate nuns and sainted visionaries to be normative and married and male brides of Christ to be aberrant. A number of influential feminist readings have proposed that the bride of Christ subordinated women's religious opportunities to a male-dominated Church. This "narrative devised by male authors for a female protagonist," as Barbara Newman views it, unfolds in a gendered pattern of men *prescribing* bridal behavior and women *performing* marriage to Christ.[27] Following this narrative, the bride's figure was invented by men to guide or evaluate Christian women's piety, and when women stepped into the role of bride, they were nonetheless embracing a role first "thrust upon them," in Dyan Elliott's estimation.[28] Hildegard Keller described two possible representations of the bride in medieval literature: the insider view "actually or apparently authenticated by experience," a first-person position typically assumed by women, and the outsider views of the third-person narrator, usually male, who relates the marriage between Christ and a historical person or an Everysoul.[29] Medievalists certainly are aware

---

[27] Barbara Newman, *From Virile Woman to WomanChrist: Studies in Medieval Religion and Literature* (Philadelphia: University of Pennsylvania Press, 1995), 138–9.

[28] Dyan Elliott, *The Bride of Christ Goes to Hell: Metaphor and Embodiment in the Lives of Pious Women, 200–1500* (Philadelphia: University of Pennsylvania Press, 2012), 4.

[29] Hildegard Elisabeth Keller, *My Secret Is Mine: Studies on Religion and Eros in the German Middle Ages* (Leuven: Peeters, 2000), 44–5, 51.

of early modern brides of Christ—Barbara Newman cites the sixteenth-century German Lutheran Jakob Boehme's love for Christ as Sophia as a continuation of the feminized Christ and Hildegard Keller discusses both Luther and the seventeenth-century German Pietist Nikolaus von Zinzendorf. Both are, however, primarily interested in writing by and about women, not postmedieval responses to the bride of Christ. Reformation historians Berndt Hamm and Stephen Ozment trace Luther's theological use of marriage to Christ from Bernard of Clairvaux, through celibate centers of male learning and fourteenth-century German writers like Tauler and Merswin, as if the bride of Christ had nothing whatsoever to do with medieval women. Both assume that the young Luther came to this understanding from his religious education by the Brothers of the Common Life and the Augustinians.[30] These Reformation historians were largely correct—early modern sources show that information about the bride of Christ was a standard part of late medieval Christian education, but this information was not confined to Latinate men.

Both medieval and early modern scholars continue to view as "bizarre," "radical," "alarming," or "problematic" brides of Christ who diverge from their own normative models, even when discussing widely circulated sources. Hildegard Keller identifies as "bizarre" the general endeavor of marrying Christ as well as the specific cases of violent love between Christ and his bride in the Middle High German poem *Christus und die minnende Seele* [*Christ and the Loving Soul*] and the eroticism in the seventeenth-century *Songs of the Sifting* authored by the Moravian leader Count Nikolaus von Zinzendorf.[31] Anne Matter declared Brun von Schönebeck's Middle High German verse commentary on the *Song of Songs* "rather odd" and Honorius Augustodunensis's *Expositio in Cantica Canticorum* "extreme."[32] Dyan Elliott described the composition of treatises on marrying Jesus for women religious as a "bizarre liturgical swindle" and frames her study of the bride of Christ with two "alarming instances of credulity."[33] The male bride of Christ, Henry Suso, has been described as "unmännlich" [unmanly]. Art historian Jeffrey Hamburger described Suso's near-contemporary Friedrich Sunder's marriage to the Christchild as "suggestive[ly] ... manipulating gender," and Hildegard Keller finds that these same marriage scenes represent a "suprasexual, non-sexualized concept of the bride."[34] Barbara Newman suggested that before Suso, to avoid homoeroticism "it was highly unusual for a man to play the male role in a scenario of celestial love."[35] Americanist Aaron Fogelman's study of the

---

[30]   Hamm, *The Reformation of Faith*, 128–45.

[31]   Keller, *My Secret Is Mine*, 7, 20, 37–9, 185.

[32]   For instance, Anne E. Matter, *The Voice of My Beloved: the Song of Songs in Western Medieval Christianity* (Philadelphia: University of Pennsylvania Press, 1990), 58, 190.

[33]   Elliott, *Bride of Christ Goes to Hell*, 7, 237.

[34]   Kurt Berger, *Die Ausdrücke der Unio mystica im Mittelhochdeutschen. Berlin, 1935* (Nendeln: Kraus Reprint, 1967), 29. On Sunder, see Jeffrey F. Hamburger, "Overkill, or History that Hurts," *Common Knowledge* 13, no. 2–3 (2007). Keller, *My Secret Is Mine*, 29.

[35]   Barbara Newman, *God and the Goddesses: Vision, Poetry, and Belief in the Middle Ages* (Philadelphia: University of Pennsylvania Press, 2003), 207.

16 *Marrying Jesus in Medieval and Early Modern Northern Europe*

gendering of Jesus in new and old world Moravian communities takes a similar tone, finding that Christ's feminine or androgynous quality poses a "problem" for the erotic union of believers with Christ because "believers were both male and female." Fogelman acknowledges that "one way to overcome the problem of how male believers could have intense sensual relations with a male Savior was to deny that this was a problem and embrace the concept," which he sees proven by alleged homoerotic relationships between gender-segregated young men and women in Moravian communities.[36]

Each of these citations, admittedly taken out of context, voices a modern author's discomfort with what she or he has identified as sexualized images of Jesus in premodern devotional texts. What modern readers find bizarre, that is, "queer," was nonetheless comprehensible to and valued by medieval and early modern readers, for whom the bride held multiple, equally valid meanings. Theorists and theologians who insist that erotic encounters with Christ are, by default, "queer," and that male authors who love and lust after a male deity are transgressing heterosexual gender norms do so because marriage to Christ demonstrably subverted modern and medieval gender roles.[37] In his discussion of demon possessions in early modern convents, Moshe Sluhovsky summarized the problem with this kind of reading precisely: for pre-Freudian Christians, "even a penis can signify a cigar."[38] To be blunt, studying the bride of Christ as feminist medievalists have thus far done, by accepting concepts of doctrinal orthodoxy and deviance presented by Christian "authorities" rather than the diverse acts, acquisitions, and imaginings of those who profess to be Christians is not just ignoring relevant evidence; it is constructing and studying a "Christianity" derived from ideals that likely never existed on the ground. Male-dominated institutional Christianity certainly silenced some women and controlled both male and female access to the divine, but this binary ignores entirely how pious behavior in general and the practice of learning to become a bride of Christ in particular work outside of this institutional hierarchy. Most queer and feminist readings of the apocryphal bride of Christ as a "medieval woman mystic" require a straight-acting male Christ whose body and sexuality can be read against our own normative sexual practices and gender constructions—not the fluidly gendered bodies and souls of the medieval Jesus and his brides. As I outline in chapters 2 and 4, medieval sexual aesthetics are not our own, and transferring modern concepts of gender onto sex-like scenes risks overtly sexualizing theologically nuanced encounters with God.

---

[36] Aaron Spencer Fogleman, *Jesus is Female: Moravians and the Challenge of Radical Religion in Early America* (Philadelphia: University of Pennsylvania Press, 2007), 79.

[37] See especially Richard Rambuss, *Closet Devotions* (Durham, NC: Duke University Press, 1998); Gerard Loughlin, ed., *Queer Theology: Rethinking the Western Body* (Malden, MA; Oxford: Blackwell, 2007), particularly Amy Hollywood's essay, "Queering the Beguines: Mechthild of Magdeburg, Hadewijch of Anvers, Marguerite Porete," 163–75.

[38] Moshe Sluhovsky, *Believe Not Every Spirit: Possession, Mysticism, & Discernment in Early Modern Catholicism* (Chicago: University of Chicago Press, 2007), 252.

Portraits of the Bride of Christ 17

In drawing attention to these readings, my intention here is not to discredit the very rich feminist and queer scholarship on the gender of Jesus and the role of the bride of Christ. Without these perspectives, my book would not exist—but these are modern reactions. My own project is equally modern, but my study focuses on the nature of religion more closely than gender, and I will not address topics such as female agency, sexual sublimation, and patriarchal control unless that has been the primary focus of existing publications on a text or author. Each of these statements originates in a feminist approach to the study of the historical past that is influenced by modern psychoanalysis and a two-sex system. Brides of Christ are identified as either male-bodied or female-bodied, their relationships to Jesus sexualized through post-Freudian assumptions about desire and repression, and, drawing from contemporary Christian-influenced mores, only male-female bridal pairs are normal. As Fogelman points out, for some Christians, same-sex desire for Jesus was not a problem, however problematic it may be for contemporary western readers. The bride and Christ's unfixed, nondualistic gender and identities are emphatically not heteronormative, but, as shall become clear in subsequent chapters, the modern concept of "queer" is not synonymous with the complex theological meanings medieval and early modern Christians found in the spouses' unstable genders. Instead, medieval Christians wrote about male and female genders as inconstant and fluid, power as dependent on piety, and sexual contact on a spectrum of sin and salvation.

The bride of Christ certainly originated within a society that gendered both religion and virtue, but the dualistic hierarchies of medieval gender and class governing physical bodies were accompanied by a flowing system of gender for souls that metered proximity to the divine. Women and men did not have the same religious opportunities or the same religious obligations in medieval Europe, and there were very few ways for any individual to sidestep socially expected gender roles. As Saba Mahmood has shown for women's piety in contemporary Cairo, theories of gender and performativity should take into account both historical and cultural context and the subject's own understanding of his/her actions. Individuals acting piously will sometimes discount or redefine their culture's existing gender hierarchies, and their social circles may accept that properly performing piety supersedes conforming to gender norms. Following Mahmood, I argue that the gendering of virtue and vocation in medieval Christianity must be read on its own terms, with the rules we can best discern from medieval sources. And on those terms, the medieval body, male or female, sometimes operated as a medium for religious practice in ways which cut through the rigid hierarchies of class and consecration and defied gendered constructions of sanctity.[39] This medieval Christian gendering of souls was not any more inclusive than our contemporary two-body-two-gender model, nor did it bypass the hierarchies of class and gender which strictly segregated medieval geographies. However, rituals and prayers

---

[39] Saba Mahmood, *Politics of Piety: The Islamic Revival and the Feminist Subject* (Princeton: Princeton University Press, 2005), 166.

18 *Marrying Jesus in Medieval and Early Modern Northern Europe*

for brides of Christ were available to *both* male and female Christians, and their devotional acts regulated a coherent and stable gender system that was predicated on personal piety rather than the sexuality or the sex of physical bodies. Through spiritual exercises, medieval Christians put their bodies to work developing their souls. The soul's shifts from male to female granted medieval women alternate routes to spiritual authority, allowing individuals to transcend societal parameters for gender by making bodies secondary to souls—but it was not something only women could or should do.[40] Rather, these shifts from male to female represented a drawing together of human and divine until the one so closely resembled the other that they were indistinguishable. Consequently, depictions of Christ as female, of the lovers as same-sex or intrasex, and of the bride as male, are not "queer" in our modern sense, or even queer for medieval sexual norms, however much they might resemble modern categories of queer sexual identity. Instead, medieval Christians would have understood that these blending bodies reflecting and flowing through one another were acting out the incarnation, crucifixion, and final judgment. They might also have understood the shifts from male to female to act out the gendered inflections in their own languages, as discussion shifted from the form and matter of a male-gendered person to the formlessness and spirit of a female-gendered soul.

Sixteenth-Century Distortions

The assumption that the medieval bride of Christ was primarily a chaste holy woman modeled after the Virgin Mary originates not in the literature of medieval Europe, nor even in treatises on virginity authored by early Christian theologians, but in the religious debates of the sixteenth century. This is not to suggest that medieval nuns did not identify as brides of Christ or that Catholic nuns no longer do. As I shall show in Chapter 6, the young nun's transformation into a bride of Christ through her monastic vocation was integral to both women's communal life and to the transmission of marrying Jesus for more general religious instruction. Medieval convents were an important locus through which texts, objects, songs, and sermons about the bride of Christ engaged the laity, until debates about monastic celibacy in the 1520s and 30s spurred the closing of religious houses and the kidnapping (liberation) of nuns. This was part of a developing confessional

---

[40] For instance, Carolyn Bynum's recent caution that though the Trinity was "both feminine and masculine: the devout of both sexes could imagine themselves as brides to Christ the bridegroom, child to God the mother, troubadour seeking a Jesus who as Lady Wisdom or Lady love ... [this] polyvalence of description should warn us once again against any simplistic assumption that the undoubtedly misogynist stereotypes of women as garrulous, oversexed, morally irresponsible and weak of intellect ... were incorporated directly in the self-understanding of nuns." Caroline Walker Bynum, "Patterns of Female Piety in the Late Middle Ages," in *Crown and Veil: Female Monasticism from the Fifth to the Fifteenth Centuries*, ed. Jeffrey F. Hamburger and Susan Marti (New York: Columbia University Press, 2008), 187.

debate over which part of the Church was the "true" bride of Christ that became a frontline for religious disputation. Following the Diet of Speyer in 1529, the new Protestation distinguished itself as the "true" bride of Christ, favored over the adulterous Roman church. As early as the 1530s, emerging Protestant theologians wrote about marriage to Christ as baptism or a harbinger of the apocalypse. In the wake of the disruptive doomsday prophecies of Melchior Hoffman and the bloody fall of the Münster commune, the end-times wedding was inextricably associated with the radical elements of Anabaptism, antinomianism, and religious violence. Even in the mid-sixteenth century, as religious warfare and public executions marked the fault lines of newly developing churches, Protestants and Catholics kept communal the late medieval belief that it was possible to marry Jesus. All sides claimed the bride of Christ, retaining marriage to Jesus in their liturgies, their identities, and their material culture, yet this intense identification as true brides of Christ often framed religious confrontations and confessional statements. By the seventeenth century, Protestants had distanced themselves from the bride as the Virgin Mary and the bride as a celibate nun, Catholics from the bride as a harbinger of the end-times and the marriage as a transaction in sin and salvation, but *no* denomination abandoned the central medieval belief that every human being had the potential to wed Jesus.

Proving a community's status as the "true" bride of Christ and explaining to converts the obligations of being espoused to Christ were central to the formation of religious, civic, and cultural identities which early modern historians Heinz Schilling, Wolfgang Reinhard, and others have termed confessionalization.[41] Positing that the Catholic and Protestant Reformations were distinct neither materially nor temporally, the confessionalization thesis considers the early modern period as unfolding through symbiosis rather than reaction. Individual denominations developed by negotiating with one another's understandings of their shared inheritance of two centuries of medieval religious reform. The early modern bride of Christ fits this model closely—confessionalizing the bride was a slow process whereby Protestants and Catholics disentangled their theologies and communities from one another through social control and education campaigns.

As part of this process, medieval books on the bride of Christ were reissued in the sixteenth century as propaganda, university textbooks, and devotional reading. To give just a few examples, in Cologne, the Carthusian Laurentius Surius (1522–78) translated the vernacular writing of Ruusbroec, Tauler, and Suso into Latin and

---

[41] The most concise articulation of the confessionalization thesis in English is Wolfgang Reinhard, "Reformation, Counter-Reformation, and the Early Modern State a Reassessment," *The Catholic Historical Review* 75, no. 3 (1989): 383–404. Heinz Schilling, *Religion, Political Culture, and the Emergence of Early Modern Society: Essays in German and Dutch History* (Leiden; New York: E.J. Brill, 1992); Schilling, *Konfessionskonflikt und Staatsbildung: eine Fallstudie über das Verhältnis von religiösem und sozialem Wandel in der Frühneuzeit am Beispiel der Grafschaft Lippe* (Gütersloh: Gütersloher Verlagshaus Mohn, 1981); Schilling, *Early Modern European Civilization and its Political and Cultural Dynamics* (Hanover, NH: University Press of New England, 2008).

20   *Marrying Jesus in Medieval and Early Modern Northern Europe*

promoted new devotional works by Catholic women authors like Maria van Oosterwijk and the anonymous author of the *Evangelical Pearl* as part of a media campaign to reestablish the spiritual heritage and credibility of the Roman church. The Flemish Franciscan Frans Vervoort published the first edition of his *Bruygoms Mantelken* [*The Bridegroom's Cloak*] in Antwerp, a meditation on Christ's passion from the perspective of the bride, which incorporated the writings of fifteenth-century Flemish Prioress and bride of Christ Alijt Bake.[42] In Catholic Bavaria, new editions of Henry Suso's *Exemplar*, Hendrik Herp's *Mirror of Perfection*, and Otto von Passau's *24 Elders* would be printed for use in universities and among religious orders. Late medieval pamphlets, which promised that Christ's love remitted sin and predicted baptisms (in blood or water) signified the wedding between Christ and the Soul signaled the beginning of the End Times, were reissued by Protestants. In the seventeenth century, the Société des Bollandistes, an organization dominated by Jesuits, began gathering manuscripts from across Europe and publishing information about the lives and cults of Catholic saints. Their criteria for inclusion in the *Acta Sanctorum* still influence the study of medieval and early modern hagiography. In the Spanish Netherlands and Southern Germany, Catholics turned to late medieval literature about the bride of Christ when defending and reforming monasticism and the cult of the saints. In Spain and Italy, as well as in the Catholic colonies of the New World, the nun's identity as a bride of Christ was central to reforming convents, and a number of new manuals on living and serving as a bride of Christ were commissioned. In the Spanish Netherlands and the Catholic regions of Germany, virginity was resurrected as an ideal for female piety, and the role of bride of Christ was largely restricted to nuns and saints.[43] Teresa of Avila's transverberation and reception of Christ's marriage ring dominated late baroque iconography.[44] Perhaps in response to the imposition

---

[42]   Frans Vervoort, *Bruygoms mantelken, vanden inwendighen nauolghen des leues en des cruycen ons liefs Heeren Ihesu Christi* ([Antwerp?]: Godefridi, Petrus Ghelen, Jan van, 1554).

[43]   The situation in Germany has attracted far more comment, on both sides of the confessional divide. Joel F. Harrington, *Reordering Marriage and Society in Reformation Germany* (Cambridge: Cambridge University Press, 1995); Ulrike Strasser, *State of Virginity: Gender, Religion, and Politics in an Early Modern Catholic State* (Ann Arbor: University of Michigan Press, 2004); Cornelia Niekus Moore, *The Maiden's Mirror: Reading Material for German Girls in the Sixteenth and Seventeenth Centuries*, vol. Band 36 (Wiesbaden: Otto Harrassowitz, 1987).

[44]   On this development in art, both sacred and secular, see Carolyn Diskant Muir, "Art and Religion in Seventeenth-Century Antwerp: van Dyck's 'Mystic Marriage of the Blessed Hermann-Joseph,'" *Simiolus: Netherlands Quarterly for the History of Art* 28, no. 1/2 (2000); Marilyn Aronberg Lavin and Irving Lavin, *The Liturgy of Love: Images from the Song of Songs in the Art of Cimabue, Michelangelo and Rembrandt* (Lawrence: Spencer Museum of Art, University of Kansas, 2001); H. Rodney Nevitt, *Art and the Culture of Love in Seventeenth-Century Holland* (Cambridge: Cambridge University Press, 2003). On nuns in Golden Age Spain, I depend on Jodi Bilinkoff, *The Avila of Saint Teresa: Religious Reform in a Sixteenth-Century City* (Ithaca: Cornell University Press, 1989); Barbara Louise

Portraits of the Bride of Christ

of strict enclosure following the Council of Trent, late sixteenth-century convent manuscripts emphasize nuns' obligations as brides of Christ in ways medieval manuscripts did not. For instance, the only two surviving copies of Johannes Nider's *Spiritual Marriage* [*Geistliche Gemahelschaft*] come from sixteenth-century personal prayer books once owned by women religious.[45] The later copy, Karlsruhe Landesbibliothek Cod. St. Georgen 103, dating to 1572, also contains a *Rule for Marrying Eternal Wisdom* [*Ordnung wie du dich der Ewigen weisshaitt sol vermechelen*], likely a late copy of the *Brotherhood of Eternal Wisdom*.[46] In the late seventeenth century, sister Elizabeth Silvoorts of Mariendaal in Antwerp recopied fifteenth-century visions, letters, and other documents pertaining to the spiritual reforms inspired by Jacomijne Costers, perhaps, as Wybren Scheepsma proposed, to inspire solidarity among a community challenged on all fronts by war and religious dissent.[47] And a fifteenth-century manuscript translation of Mecthild of Hackeborn's *Book of Divine Grace* manuscript from the Bridgettine community of St. Mary of the Vineyard remained in use into the eighteenth century, when it was assigned for use to "Sister Maria Magdalena Bedycx, Jesus' Bride, professed on November 11th, 1714."[48]

These early modern interests directly influence which medieval texts survive, which ones are now easily available for modern study, and, consequently, have guided modern scholars to associate the medieval bride of Christ almost exclusively with enclosed women religious. They also have created a false perception that convents were isolated from the secular world. This explicit equation of chaste nun and bride of Christ in sixteenth- and seventeenth-century Catholic sources closely resembles the marital union between celibate male and female religious and Christ which historian Jo Ann McNamara once called "castimony."[49] Unlike the early Christian authors who informed McNamara's concept of castimony and

---

Mujica, *Sister Teresa: The Woman who Became Saint Teresa of Avila* (Woodstock, NY: Overlook Press, 2007); Mujica, *Teresa de Avila, Lettered Woman* (Nashville: Vanderbilt University Press, 2009).

[45]   Nider's "die giestliche gemahelschaft" survives in two sixteenth-century manuscripts from women's communities. His *24 Harps* [*24 Harpfen*], which borrows significant passages from the writing of Otto von Passau and Henry Suso, had wide lay vernacular circulation. He also wrote and preached for lay audiences as well as instructing clergy in hearing confession and preaching. Nider's *Sermon on the 7 Sacraments* makes an elegant case for the good of marriage. Margit Brand, *Studien zu Johannes Niders deutschen Schriften* (Institutum Historicum Fratrum Praedicatorum Romae. Dissertationes Historicae 23, Rome, 1998), 21–2n79.

[46]   Brand, *Studien Johannes Niders*, 174–5.

[47]   Wybren Scheepsma, "De Helletocht van Jacomijne Costers (d. 1503)," *Ons Geestelijk Erf* 70 (1996): 164.

[48]   Oxford, Bodleian Library MS Douce 44, inscribed on endpapers. "[T]ot gebruyck van suster Maria Magd. Bedycx, Jesus Bruydt, geprofessit 1714 den 11 november."

[49]   Jo Ann McNamara, *Sisters in Arms: Catholic Nuns through Two Millennia* (Cambridge, MA: Harvard University Press, 1996), 2, 43–5, 154–9.

the early modern women defending their religious vocations against criticism from Protestants, many fourteenth- and fifteenth-century convent documents prioritize everyday interactions between Christ and the sisters over guarding physical and spiritual purity.

Despite the enforced enclosure of women religious following Boniface VIII's decretal *Periculoso* (1298), enclosure was infrequently enforced and sometimes forcefully resisted.[50] A sixteenth-century Dutch folk song about a young knight in love with a newly professed nun shows that in the medieval imaginary, enclosure could be penetrated by male voices and passed through by young nuns. He rides to her convent hoping to visit his lover but is turned away—"[T]he newest little nun cannot come out. She must serve Mary and be Jesus' bride." "Oh, is she Jesus' Bride? May I still see and talk with her a little while?" he asks. The young nun comes to the speaking grille to send her knight away; eight days later, she finds his corpse by a spring and mourns his death.[51] Though marriage to Jesus in the form of monastic vows supersedes the love between this young nun and her knight, the knight's verses recognize the potential for negotiation. He can visit the convent, and she travels outside its walls to find his corpse. Though women's communities were protected and sometimes enclosed, they were not islands.

Medieval nuns were not just brides of Christ by virtue of their religious profession; they, like all other Christians, recognized that embracing Christ as a spouse required far more than a spoken vow. Sisters were the owners, copyists, readers, and even authors of many of the devotional books and objects I shall discuss, as well as the interlocutors of many authors and preachers who instructed others in marrying Christ. Communities were also in conversation with one another and with family members and spiritual friends outside convent walls, and taught those who visited them how to pray, repent, and become brides of Christ.

The media campaign to introduce marriage to Jesus to lay Christians originated no later than the last half of the twelfth century and endures in the twenty-first. The theological basis for this development can be traced back to the third century. As most histories of the bride of Christ note, exactly 200 years before Gertrud listened and wept during the Strasbourg sermon, and 400 years before Luther wrote *On Christian Freedom*, the Cistercian abbot Bernard of Clairvaux (1090–1153) delivered a series of exegetic sermons on the *Song of Songs* to the celibate men of his community. Despite his oft-cited warning that the *Song* was appropriate only for the most advanced students of Christian mysteries, in manuscript form, these sermons and their imitators would be read by the very women, novices, and

---

[50] Anne Winston-Allen, *Convent Chronicles: Women Writing About Women and Reform in the Late Middle Ages* (University Park: Pennsylvania State University Press, 2004), 152–61.

[51] Hoffman von Fallersleben's text is copied from a sixteenth-century manuscript. The song is also attested in several other manuscripts and would become part of the printed songbook known as the *Zutphen Leidbook*. Hoffman von Fallersleben, *Horae belgicae. Studio atque opera Hoffmanni Fallerslebensis* (Hannoverae: C. Ruempler, 1836), vol. 2, 76, http://www.dbnl.org/tekst/hoff004hora01_01/. Hereafter HB.

Portraits of the Bride of Christ   23

recent converts Bernard found dangerously unqualified to understand his words.[52] There is little theological distance between the bride of Christ known to Gertrud von Ortenberg in the fourteenth century, Jerome Müller in the fifteenth century, or Martin Luther in the sixteenth century, but a chasm separates them from Bernard of Clairvaux. In the four centuries separating the religious and cultural renewal of twelfth-century France from the reforms of sixteenth-century Germany, marriage to Jesus had ceased to be the private pursuit of the Latinate and celibate—if it ever was. Luther had not invented the idea that marriage to Christ was a transaction in salvation, only repeated a belief familiar to university professors as well as widows, wives, and burghers across fifteenth- and sixteenth-century Germany. How had Bernard's often-cited assertion that marriage to Christ was for the celibate and well-studied religious become a certainty that marriage to Christ sifted the saved from the damned?

As early as the third century, exhortations to virginity and guides to female comportment certainly addressed consecrated virgins as "bride," and early ceremony for consecrating Christian virgins mimicked contemporary Roman and Jewish marriage rites.[53] In this period, marriage to Christ also explained the sacraments of baptism, the symbolic baptism of blood that befell martyrs, and the ritual and then sacramental ceremony of holy orders, marked with the crowning tonsure or head shaving.[54] In a fourth-century sermon addressing adult catechumens (converts preparing for baptism), John Chrysostom described the transformation and redemption accompanying the sacrament of baptism as an intimate union between Christ as husband and the catechumen as wife, a joining so complete that "thereafter they are not two but one."[55] According to Chrysostom, the marriage of baptism is a beautiful moment which breaks worldly bonds to friends, family, and even personal identity. Early Church fathers also explored God's multiple genders to explain how different the creator is from his creations. For instance, the third-century ascetic and exegete Origen of Alexandria wrote that even though bridegroom and bride are gendered, and "the 'Word' of God is of the masculine gender in Greek, and neuter with ourselves, yet all these matters with which this passage deals must be thought of in a manner that transcends masculine and neuter and feminine and everything whatever to which these words refer. And this applies not only to the 'Word' of God, but also to His Church and the perfect soul, who

---

[52] The line famously appears in sermon 1, paragraph 12. Several English translations are available, most accessibly, *Bernard of Clairvaux: Selected Works*, ed. G.R. Evans (New York: Paulist Press, 1987), 215.

[53] For a discussion of the integration of secular marriage practices into the rituals for consecrating virgins, see René Metz, *La consécration des vierges dans l'église Romaine: Étude d'histoire de la liturgie* (Paris: Presses Universitaires de France, 1945), 50–51.

[54] Giles Constable, "The Ceremonies and Symbolism of Entering Religious Life and Taking the Monastic Habit from the Fourth to the Twelfth Century," in *Segni e riti nella chiesa altomedioevale occidentale* (Spoleto: Presso la sede del Centro, 1987), 788.

[55] John Chrysostom, *Baptismal Instructions*, trans. Paul W. Harkins (Westminster, MD: Newman Press, 1963), 18.

24 *Marrying Jesus in Medieval and Early Modern Northern Europe*

likewise here is called 'the Bride.'"[56] In Homily 59, John Chrysostom addressed the problem of whether the bride was espoused to the Father or the Son: "Why then is not the bride said to be espoused to Him, but to the Son? Because she that is espoused to the Son, is espoused to the Father. For it is indifferent in Scripture that the one or the other should be said, because of the identity of the substance."[57] Both Origen and Chrysostom explained these ideas in sermons, public speech-acts addressed to the theologically naïve. As Jerome comments in his introduction to the translated Homilies on the *Song of Songs*, Origen wrote "for those who were still like babes and sucklings."[58] Origen and Chrysostom were likely influenced by Paul's wording in challenging the circumcision party's hindrance to Jewish law in Galatians 3:27–8: "As many of you as were baptized into Christ have clothed yourself with Christ. There is no longer Jew or Greek, there is no longer slave nor free, there is no longer male or female; for you are all one in Christ Jesus." While these passages cannot be directly linked to any of the medieval texts I discuss, they testify to an early tradition of teaching sacramental theology to the laity through the metaphor of marriage to Jesus and wearing the spouse as a spiritual garment.

In the twelfth century, more than 30 Latin commentaries on the *Song of Songs* would be written, all drawing on a range of patristic and scientific sources. Several of these commentaries used the fluid genders and interchangeable body parts of bride and groom to reconnected marriage to Jesus with personal salvation.[59] In a commentary on Joel, Richard of St. Victor describes the groom as Christ, who has taken on the qualities of wisdom, even as he grants the power of grace to his bride. He also described the sensation of union with the bridegroom as "a thing which anyone can feel" in a commentary of Psalm 30.[60] William of St. Thierry interpreted the bride's black skin as a sign of her sinfulness, erased only when she turned away from her past life.[61] In *On Loving God*, Bernard of Clairvaux mentioned that there were seats at the wedding banquet for souls who fell short

---

[56]   J. Christopher King, *Origen on the Song of Songs as the Spirit of Scripture: The Bridegroom's Perfect Marriage-Song* (Oxford: Oxford University Press, 2005), 201.

[57]   Chrysostom, Homily LXIX on Matthew XXII. Translation from Augustine, John Chrysostom, and Philip Schaff, *A Select Library of the Nicene and Post-Nicene Fathers of the Christian Church* (hereafter NPNF), vol. 10 (Grand Rapids, MI: Eerdmans, 1974), 403.

[58]   Philip Schaff, ed. *The Principal Works of St. Jerome*, NPNF Second Series (New York: Christian Literature, 1893), 485.

[59]   Eloe Kingma, *De mooiste onder de vrouwen: een onderzoek naar religieuze idealen in twaalfde-eeuwse commentaren op het Hooglied* (Hilversum: Verloren, 1993); Friedrich Ohly, *Hohelied-Studien: Grundzüge einer Geschichte der Hoheliedauslegung des Abendlandes bis um 1200* (Wiesbaden: F. Steiner, 1958).

[60]   Richard of St. Victor, *Selected Writings on Contemplation*, trans. Clare Kirchberger (New York: Harper Brothers, 1957), 234–5.

[61]   William and Jean Déchanet, *Exposition on the Song of Songs* (Spencer, MA: Cistercian Publications, 1970), 10. The expanded meaning of this relationship and the ways the bride may win love and grace are the subjects of his reading of *Song* 1:4. Ibid., 43–9. This reading is briefly discussed by Ann W. Astell, *The Song of Songs in the Middle Ages* (Ithaca: Cornell University Press, 1990), 10.

Portraits of the Bride of Christ

of becoming brides, describing a threefold banquet in heaven.[62] Rupert of Deutz (1070–1130) read the bride as Mary, but glossed the groom's good looks with references to the two adulterous sisters Israel and Judah in Ezekiel 23, painting Jesus in vivid detail for the interior eyes of a meditative soul: "Ooliba opened her eyes to see men, images of Chaldeans in the polychrome frieze [on the wall before her], to see their belts, their crowns, and their figures, so now open your own eyes, your interior eyes, to see this Beloved one, to see his golden head, his sparkling eyes, his awe-inspiring cheeks, his glorious glossy lips, his hands wrought like gold, his ivory belly inlaid with sapphires, thus it is said of him 'taste and see that the lord is good.'"[63] Here, Rupert has superimposed the groom's attributes from *Song 5:14* onto the exterior beauty of the painted Chaldean soldiers, the object of Ooliba's adulterous desire. Rupert guided his male readers' inner eyes over Christ's body so that, just as Ooliba was aroused by paintings of the Chaldean warriors' colorful garments and the bride by her sculpted spouse, they too would become infatuated with an image of this dangerously handsome man. These and other Latin exegetes normalized the belief that Jesus was an object of desire, that marriage was a path to salvation, and they introduced the use of illustrations and richly described textual passages to draw readers to their spouse.

In addition to these exegetical innovations, the twelfth century witnessed the composition of instructional treatises for nuns framed as dialogues between Christ and the Soul, two of which I shall discuss in Chapter 3. In this same period, the Lateran Councils (1119–1215) instituted the catechetical instruction of the laity. As early as the 1140s, soon after the First Lateran Council had formalized social and sacramental distinctions between clergy and laity, the lay brides of Christ appeared in books written by and for the celibate religious. In 1215, the Fourth Lateran Council institutionalized firm distinctions between lay and professional Christians, codifying clerical celibacy and introducing new expectations of religious literacy and liturgical participation for the laity within every parish. In the thirteenth century, Christian renewal centered on cities, driven by women's participation, and dependent on vernacular preaching, devotional images, and meditative prayer. The image of Christ as spouse to every soul was not a regional variant peculiar to Germany and the Low Countries. The *Early English Bestiary*, dated to 1220, glosses the dove as representing the soul wed to Christ: "Each Christian man / chooses Christ for his mate at the / church door / He is our soul's spouse, and we / ought never to forsake him … Let us take no new love."[64] A fifteenth-century

---

[62]   Evans, *Bernard of Clairvaux: Selected Works*, 198–9.

[63]   Rupert does not note or is not aware that the original Hebrew includes euphemisms for the penis in the description of the painted warriors. Both Ezekiel and Rupert are describing a painted or enameled relief frieze. Note that modern translators and biblical editions usually spell her name Oolibah. Rupert of Deutz, *Ruperti Tuitiensis Commentaria in Canticum canticorum*, ed. Hrabanus Haacke (Turnholti: Brepols, 1974), 130.

[64]   Richard Morris, *An Old English Miscellany Containing a Bestiary, Kentish Sermons, Proverbs of Alfred, Religious Poems of the Thirteenth Century, from Manuscripts in the British Museum, Bodleian Library, Jesus College Library, etc* (London: N. Trübner, 1872), 21, lines 716–28.

26 *Marrying Jesus in Medieval and Early Modern Northern Europe*

Portuguese law code, issued during the reign of Alfonso X, prescribed death for Jews who had sexual intercourse with Christian women because, it claimed, "[I]f Christians who commit adultery with married women deserve death on that account, how much more so do Jews who have sexual intercourse with Christian women, who are spiritually wed wives of Our Lord Jesus Christ because of the faith and the baptism which they receive in his name?"[65] Marriages to Christ, often symbolized by the gift of a ring, only entered the iconography of virgin saints in the thirteenth century, and occurred far less frequently in art than in hagiographies even in the early modern period.[66] For instance, though hagiographies addressed her as a bride of Christ, paintings of Catherine of Alexandria receiving a ring from Jesus first appeared in late thirteenth-century Tuscany, perhaps in response to a developing iconographic tradition for the marriage of Francis of Assisi to Lady Poverty.[67]

This urban piety correlates with the exponential increase in depictions of the bride of Christ in the early thirteenth century and reproduction and adaptation of those images in the fourteenth and fifteenth centuries. The late medieval Church was deeply conflicted about who could or should be called Christ's elect spouse. Marrying Jesus involved accepting a theological perspective and using devotional tools that were themselves novel and sometimes suspect, and self-identified brides of Christ often met significant resistance and suspicion from church authorities. Looking across Europe in the fifteenth century, it might seem as if Church leaders were advocating the very same practices they also persecuted, so that marrying Jesus originated from within the same organization that was attempting to forcibly regulate brides of Christ.[68] Realistically, distinguishing between true and false brides of Christ was a low priority for the late medieval Church. Male theologians were also constantly evaluated for the whisper of heresy or contamination and some of the very same male authors who accused fifteenth-century women also wrote advice on becoming a bride of Christ. Heinrich von Langenstein and Jean Gerson, who modestly supported some female brides of Christ, initially condemned the Flemish hermit Jan van Ruusbroec's *Geestelijke Bruiloft* [*Spiritual Espousals*].[69]

---

[65] Robert Ignatius Burns, *Underworlds: The Dead, the Criminal, and the Marginalized,* trans. Samuel Parsons Scott (Philadelphia: University of Pennsylvania Press, 2001), 280.

[66] Though published too late to inform my own study, Carolyn Diskant Muir's discussion of the iconography of mystical marriages also argues that depictions of marriages are late and rare for saints whose hagiographers portrayed them as brides of Christ. Carolyn Diskant Muir, *Saintly Brides and Bridegrooms: The Mystic Marriage in Northern Renaissance Art* (London: Harvey Miller, 2012).

[67] My thanks to Misty Mullin for drawing my attention to this citation. Millard Meiss, *Painting in Florence and Siena after the Black Death* (Princeton: Princeton University Press, 1951), 108.

[68] Dyan Elliott addresses this scenario in the seventh and final chapter of *The Bride of Christ Goes to Hell*, 233 ff.

[69] Geert Warnar, *Ruusbroec: Literature and Mysticism in the Fourteenth Century,* trans. Diane Webb (Leiden: Brill, 2007), 2–3.

Portraits of the Bride of Christ 27

The fifteenth-century Dominican Johannes Nider, whose witch-and-devil-filled *Formicarius* warns against misguided women falsely believing themselves to be brides of Christ, also authored a German-language treatise on marrying Jesus. His *Geistliche Gemahelschaft* [*Spiritual Marriage*] was addressed not to nuns, daughters, or maidens but to "kinderen" [children].[70] These cases show that the singling out of individual brides of Christ for possible heresy originated not from rampant misogyny but rather from a need to enforce doctrinally sound theology. In the fifteenth century, the councils of Basel and Constance were called to negotiate questions of sacramental theology posed by university-trained theologians such as John Wycliffe and Jan Hus, biblical translation, and lay ministry, as well as settling the break with the Eastern Orthodox churches and resolving the issue of competing papal seats of authority in Avignon, Rome, and Pisa. If the cardinals gathered in Constance and Basel discussed marriage to Jesus or condemned the biblically supported claim that each individual could become a bride of Christ, they did not publish those conversations.

In the sixteenth century, as war spread across Europe and the medieval church fragmented into the Protestation and the Church of Rome, debates over theology frequently descended into arguments over whose church was the "true" bride of Christ. In 1562, the 22nd Session of the Council of Trent concluded that their Church was Christ's own beloved spouse [*dilectae sponsae suae*] in a passage validating the Catholic understanding of salvation through the sacrifice of Crucifixion and the sacramental meal of communion. This certainly did not stop Protestant denominations from claiming the bride of Christ for themselves, but it reflects a change in Catholic thinking. Though Trent carefully outlined reforms for religious orders and advocated a more strict observance of enclosure for women religious, nothing in the Council's decrees referred to the professional religious, whether male or female, as espoused to Christ.[71] Nor did the Council's careful defense of infant baptism describe that sacrament as a marriage, instead using the language of "putting on Christ." By the last quarter of the sixteenth century, both Catholic and Protestant artists and rhetoricians had made the story of the bride of Christ entirely their own.

Only in the seventeenth century would Protestants and Catholics produce understandings of marrying Jesus which moved past medieval models. Some of these baroque innovations transcended denominational boundaries. The soul's marriage to God became part of an alchemy of salvation comprehensible only to those steeped in hermetic science. In Saxony and the Protestant Netherlands, Jakob Boehme and his followers, among them the poet and engraver Jan Luyken, elaborated on the master narrative of Christ's courtship with the soul to teach moral living and guide readers to salvation. Luyken and Boehme's books remained

---

[70] Brand, *Studien Johannes Niders*, 238–42.

[71] James Waterworth, *The canons and decrees of the sacred and ecumenical Council of Trent, celebrated under the sovereign pontiffs, Paul III, Julius III and Pius IV* (London: C. Dolman, 1848), 153–4.

in use among Anabaptist, Lutheran Pietist, and Rosicrucian communities into the nineteenth century. At the same time, among Catholics in the Spanish Low Countries, serving as a bride of Christ became an important social and communal identity for lay women missionaries known as "geestelijke maagden" [spiritual maidens]. The seventeenth century witnessed the reintroduction of Jesus as an equal partner in worldly marriages in England, Germany, and then in Early America. In England, married women declared themselves brides of Christ—among them, the apocalyptic prophetesses Anne Wentworth and Mary Gadbury. In Germany, Nikolaus von Zinzendorf and other Pietists voiced the fervor of their religious revivalism in the language of sex with and marriage to Jesus. By the eighteenth century, these new versions of the bride of Christ had arrived in America with German-, Dutch-, and English-speaking immigrants. Though late medieval concepts of the bride of Christ were reevaluated in the sixteenth and seventeenth centuries, the bride of Christ remained relevant across confessions. With new technologies of communication and the relative availability of international travel, the bride of Christ was exported to the colonies even as she was being reconstructed in Continental Europe. Boehme's supporters produced print editions of his books in Dutch, German, and English, operating out of Amsterdam and London as well as the relatively new city of Philadelphia. The first female Catholic saint of the New World, Rose of Lima, was revered as a crucified bride of Christ, as were the *beatas* and visionaries in colonial convents.[72] In contemporary America, the bride of Christ remains a meaningful expression of Jesus's personal love for creation, a warning against the end-times, and a subversively sexualized subject for mass-market media.

On the eve of the Reformation, medieval Christians regularly encountered invitations to wed Christ. Such invitations are reissued with only minor revisions by both Catholics and Protestants to the present day. Like the fourteenth-century Strasbourg preacher and the widowed beguine Gertrud von Ortenberg, the fifteenth-century scribe Jerome Müller, and the sixteenth-century Augustinian professor Martin Luther, many late medieval and early modern Christians saw Christ as a husband and lover. This did not supplant other medieval understandings of marital union with the divine, such as the symbolic marriages in convent profession and baptism, or the metaphoric unions between Christ and the personified Church, or Christ and the Virgin Mary. Instead, like the overlay of polyphony onto plainchant in organum, late medieval forms of marriage to Jesus elaborated on and responded to a much older theme. I use this musical metaphor to acknowledge a lacuna in my own retelling of the bride's story—the exclusion of music, including the exceptionally intricate musical settings of *Veni Sponsa Christi* by composers as disparate as the sixteenth-century Palestrina and the twentieth-century composer Daniel-Lesur's *Cantique des Cantiques*. Mine is only the most recent restatement of those same familiar notes—neither the last, nor the most comprehensive, but

---

[72] Frank Graziano, *Wounds of Love: The Mystical Marriage of Saint Rose of Lima* (Oxford: Oxford University Press, 2004).

Portraits of the Bride of Christ 29

one which strives to acknowledge both the form of the original plainchant and subsequent elaborations on that theme. For each name I have recovered, there may have been thousands more who once were called brides of Christ but have since been forgotten by history. Their desire to master the mysteries of creation and salvation encoded in that wedding was shared, to echo a refrain from the thirteenth-century lay poet Brun von Schönebeck's elaborate retelling of the *Song of Songs*, by both clerics and the laity [*die pfaffe und der leie*].[73]

---

[73] "Daz wizze der pfaffe und der leie." Brun von Schönebeck, "Das Hohe Lied," *Bibliothek des Litterarischen Vereins in Stuttgart*, 198, ed. Arwed Fischer (Stuttgart, 1893), 335, 48, 880.

Chapter 2
Any Body's Bridegroom

Whatever a person is, be he man or woman, young or old, worldly or spiritual, married or single, who desires to be a loving retainer of Eternal Wisdom, this person should industriously receive what stands written out here, which is thus meted out fairly so that it is neither too hard nor too difficult. Thus each and every person who wishes to may bring this to completion, whether worldly or spiritual, married or single, because Eternal Wisdom will form no alliance nor promise nor set out any vows unless it is in a new fashion … And it is also to be known that this spiritual spouseship[1] should take place not only in a person's interior heart and soul by reason of ever more great and ardent devotion, without also being brought forth by as many exterior exercises as he may privately perform.[2]

—*The Brotherhood of Eternal Wisdom*

---

[1] I have translated this passage from the first printed edition; however, the title "brotherhood or spousehood" is present only in manuscript copies. The A1453 copy produced in Nuremburg is titled "Von der bruderschaft oder mahelschaft d[er] ewige[n] weißheit vn[d] wie sich halten sullen die Iunger d[er] ewigen weißheit" (BSB CGM 405), 107r. The same heading appears in Karlsruhe Badische Landesbibliothek (hereafter BLB), MS Lichtenthal 99, dating to 1469.

[2] "Wer der mensch ist er seÿ man oder frau jung oder alt weltlich oder geistlich an der Ee oder ledig der begert sein ein minnsamer junger der ewigen weisheit die sol fleissiklich behalten das hernach geschrieben stat daz also gemessen und gewegen ist dass daran kein hertikeit noch beschwaerd ist. Also das ein Jeklich mensch es wol volpringen mag et seÿ weltlich oder geistlich an der Ee oder ledig wann die ewÿg weißheÿt wÿl dar mit den menschen keyn bünttt nuß noch kein antheÿsse noch gelübd auflegen Sunder allein ein neüue weiße da mit der mensch der biß her träge und sämig ist gewesen an andacht ein ursach hab sich selb czewecken ze geistlicher übung und andacht und wer der ist der sich an dem als hernach geschriben ist mit fleß und mit andacht üben will der hůt wol unnd loblich, aber der es nichtt thůt der s:undet damit nich sen. Zů dem ersten vn[d] vor allen dÿngen sol der iunger der ewigen weysheit meyden und lassen leiplich vnnd weltlich lieb, ob er sÿ hab, unnd sol im czü eyner er geystlichen gesponsen nemen die edelen vnd claren vnd ewigen weÿsheit des hÿmlelischen vatters. Wäre aber das et war als größlich vnnd krefftigklich gebunden und betricket wär mit sunder vnnd unordenlicher lieb, das in gedeüucht es wäre im hört vnnd schwär als bald sölich liebe abprechen vnnd meiden, Der habe doch goutten willen vnnd vürsacz das er sich davon ziehen wölle mit gotes hilff so er aller bel dest müge. Aber die dÿe mit lieplicher lieb nichtt bestricket seind, vnnd doch bis her träg vnd ablässig od[er] sanng gewesen synd in göttlicher minne, Dye söllent dÿe gÿstlichen gesponsen die ewÿgen weysheit in von neüue gemahelen vnnd sich an irer liebe vnnd mÿnne mit eÿner neüuen andacht er nüueren vnnd erczaigen…. Es ist auch zewissen das dise geistliche gemahelschafft durch grösser vnnd inbrunstiger andachte wegen sol nicht allein in des menschen sel und hercze inwendig beschehen sunder auch mit ausser ubung doch als vil er mag heimlich." Henricus Suso, Rulman Merswin, and Henricus

32   *Marrying Jesus in Medieval and Early Modern Northern Europe*

It is a mistake to assume that because treatises like *The Brotherhood of Eternal Wisdom* depict Christ as Bridegroom, they were intended for "brides of Christ," that is, nuns. By the fifteenth century, the bride of Christ was literally a popular cultural icon—widely understood, internationally reproduced, yet localized to the needs and vocabularies of individual communities. This popularity did not follow the publication of one important book, the promotion of a single saint's cult, or the edict of any church leader. Instead, it unfolded simultaneously in dozens of cities across Europe as Latin texts about the bride of Christ, likely written for monks and nuns, were adapted for local audiences. Suso's invitation to wed Christ as Eternal Wisdom, no matter one's gender or vocation, which introduces the late medieval *Brotherhood or Spousehood of Eternal Wisdom* [*Bruderschaft oder mahelschaft der Ewigen Weisheit*], characterizes this process. Extracted from a fourteenth-century Latin book designed by the fourteenth-century Dominican Henry Suso, arguably for the professional religious, elaborated on and reworked for the laity, reproduced by professional scribes and trade printers, marketed to pious book collectors, the *Brotherhood*'s textual history defies dualisms of "high" and "low," "literate" and "unlettered," or "lay" and "religious." This modified text provided rules for an informal community of strangers joined in brotherly marriage who were to perform synchronized prayers lifted from book 2, chapter 7 of Suso's *Wisdom's Watch Upon the Hours* [*Horologium Sapientiae*].[3] In his original Latin work, Suso made allowances for those unable to live celibately, created alternate prayers for the illiterate and those whose work obligations interfered with devotions, and prescribed special obligations for the professional religious and clerics, but nothing in his surviving writing or the cult developing after his death suggests his involvement in establishing a prayer confraternity. Suso soon lost control of his carefully crafted persona as others transformed his devotional writing into a regimen of prayers and meditations capable of wedding the full spectrum of humanity to Christ. In the fourteenth-century Low Countries, Geert Grote, the founder of a new lay religious movement known as the *Devotio Moderna*, transformed Suso's Latin *Horologium* into the *Hours of Eternal Wisdom* [*getijden van eeuwige wijsheit*] for use in Dutch books of Hours. The German *Little Book of Eternal Wisdom* [*Buchlein der Ewigen Weisheit*] and its Latin counterpart,

---

de Herph, *Hie seind geschriben die capitel des büchs d[as] do der Seüsse heisset ... Vita; Büchlein der ewigen Weisheit; Büchlein der Wahrheit; Briefbüchlein. - Merswin, Rulman: Neunfelsenbuch. Mit Kap. 60 aus dem Spieghel van Volcomenheit von Henricus Herp* (Anton Sorg: Augsburg, 1482), 103v–04r, MDZ, http://daten.digitale-sammlungen. de/~db/0003/bsb00031701/image_1.

[3]   The Latin, as translated by Colledge, begins "Therefore whoever desires to become a loveable disciple of Eternal Wisdom, whatever may be his condition or state or sex or order or even his religious life, he should diligently observe these matters which follow, which are so moderated that they need not bring with them any difficulty, and everyone should be able to carry them out with no prejudice to his profession and state of life." Henry Suso, *Wisdom's Watch Upon the Hours*, trans. Edmund Colledge (Washington, DC: Catholic University of America Press, 1994), 319.

Any Body's Bridegroom 33

the *Horologium Sapientiae,* were reproduced in illustrated omnibus sets and excerpted into small, undecorated prayer books. The earliest manuscript copy of the *Brotherhood* dates to 1418 and was produced within the circle of Wurzburg's bishop Johann von Brunn, contemporary with and possibly initiated by reforms introduced at the Council of Constance.[4] A fifteenth-century copy once owned by the Dominican sisters of St. Margaretha in Strasbourg describes the "geistliche Bruderschaft" [Spiritual Brotherhood] as espoused to Eternal Wisdom rather than adapting the text for sisters and brides of Christ.[5] A 1452 copy once owned by the male Dominican community of Wessobrun in Nuremburg, titled the "bruderschaft oder mahelschaft" [Brotherhood or Spousehood], explicitly addresses Jesus as the male devotee's spouse.[6] Anton Sorg's 1482 print edition, from which I quote above, introduced some uniformity. A 1512 edition printed in Augsburg reproduces Sorg's text closely, only modernizing the spelling. In 1518, a Basel merchant financed an elaborate illustrated adaptation, *The Little Prayer Book of Eternal Wisdom* [*Betbüchlein der Ewigen Weisheit*], which included a calendar and astrological tables indicating the prayers Suso had prescribed for each day's devotion.[7] Suso's authorized books and appropriations like the *Brotherhood of Eternal Wisdom* defy the modern expectation that professed nuns uniquely identified with the role of Christ's spouse. These changes reflect a fifteenth-century media machine creating, but also powering, the wedding-Jesus industry.

The late medieval Jesus was so available for marriage that one story circulating in German and Dutch songs and printed books presents him seducing, kidnapping,

---

[4] Dresden Landesbibliothek, MS M 277, 89v–106r. Digital facsimile: http://digital.slub-dresden.de/ppn279351666. Werner J. Hoffmann, *Die deutschsprachigen mittelalterlichen Handschriften der Sächsischen Landesbibliothek - Staats- und Universitätsbibliothek (SLUB) Dresden,* vol. 132, 462.

[5] Gebet-und Betrachtungsbuch, Karlsruhe Badische Landesbibliothek St. Peter pap. 9, 1451, f. 26v. Digital facsimile: http://digital.blb-karlsruhe.de/urn/urn:nbn:de:bsz:31-8328.

[6] For example, "den edeln namen seiner gesponsen Ihesus" [the noble name of his Bridegroom Jesus], BSB CGM 405, 1452, f 109v, MDZ, http://daten.digitale-sammlungen.de/bsb00064470/image_1.

[7] Heinrich Seuse, "Diess Buch begreifft in sich viel gütter geistlicher leeren, wie der Mensch, so er sich gewendet hat von Gott zu der Creatur, ainen widerker soll thun zu seinem ersten ursprung der da got ist / und wie er sich haben sol in sein selbs vnd aller creatur gelassenhait vnd absterben aller fröd, begirlichait, wollusts vnd gemachs diser welt vnd seins aignen leibs Gott vor augen haben/ in süchen vnd über alle ding liebhaben / sein leiden betrachten / vnd sich selb vnderwürflich in rechter demut geleichförmiklich halten in tun vnd in lassen in lieb vnd laid vnd vil ander kostlich underchtungen die da ainem anfahenden widereinkeren den menschen zu mal fürderlich vnd nüz sein / so es auff merklich gelesen vnd betracht wirt. Es gibt och gütherzigen vernünfftigen menschen lichtreiche weissung zü göttlicher warhait / und ainen richtigen weg z er aller höchsten säligkait" (Augsburg: Othman, 1512), bb ii r, MDZ, http://daten.digitale-sammlungen.de/~db/0001/bsb00018923/image_1; *Bethbüchlein der ewigen weißheit* (Basel: Jacob von Porzheim, 1518), MDZ, http://daten.digitale-sammlungen.de/~db/0002/bsb00020406/image_1.

34   *Marrying Jesus in Medieval and Early Modern Northern Europe*

and eventually wedding the daughter of a Muslim Sultan.[8] The popular devotional practices which formed the religious culture of the laity were indistinguishable from the elite culture of the clergy—at least insofar as they strove to enact marital unions with Jesus. Nor was this cultural movement limited to one gender, social class, or religious organization. In this chapter, I explain how my claim that late medieval Christians believed Jesus was espoused to every person, male and female, Christian and Muslim, and Latinate, is possible in light of current understandings about medieval gender roles and mystical theology. This is borne out by the fragmentation of narratives of the bride of Christ in fourteenth-century art and sermons, fifteenth-century print media, and visual depictions of Christ marrying male brides. The history of the bride of Christ is entangled with the history of mysticism through the nineteenth-century German construction of "brautmystik" [bridal mysticism] and the related categories of "minnemystik" [mysticism expressed through tropes of courtly love] and "frauenmystik" [women's mysticism]—all postmedieval neologisms for union with God through a metaphoric marriage, which have informed fruitful discussions of gender roles, women's agency, and vernacular theology. For medieval and early modern Christians, the gendering of bride and groom did not conform to societal rules for gender and sexual pollution, nor do they exactly match our modern constructions of gender. Instead, these sex-like narratives were designed to interest and educate readers in basic elements of Christian theology. References to Jesus as spouse occur frequently in connection with the sacraments of baptism, holy orders, communion, and last rites. I propose that marrying Jesus should be understood as instruction in the "mysteries" of Christianity, that is, the sacraments, the history of Creation, and the nature of humanity and divinity.

The medieval bride of Christ comprised overlapping visual and theological codes that engaged viewers' emotions through images painted onto manuscript pages, conjured before the mind's eye, or revealed to the soul's gaze. The narrative elements of Christ's marriage to the soul operated much like devotional images so that each attribute simultaneously held several equally valid meanings. This art historical understanding of image and viewer, spanning overlapping spheres of sacred and profane, grants equal appreciation for each element of a composition and each complimentary meaning any detail signifies. I apply it here to *written* images in addition to illustrations and icons. Like visual devotional media, this iconographic narrative operated as a technology of salvation.[9]

Remarking on illustrations designed by theologians to support their explanations of the trinity, Bernard McGinn recently proposed that "theological

---

[8]   The German variants are known as "Die Sultanstochter im Blumengarten," the Dutch as "Soudaensdochter." At least six manuscript copies and two print editions are known. Gerrit J. Boekenoogen, *Een suverlijc Exempel, hoe dat Jesus een heydensche maghet een soudaens dochter wech leyde, wt haren lande naar den Delftschen druk van Frans Sonderdanck uit het begin der 16de eeuw* (Leiden: Brill, 1904).

[9]   I draw this language from John Decker's *The Technology of Salvation and the Art of Geertgen tot Sint Jans* (Burlington, VT: Ashgate, 2009).

Any Body's Bridegroom 35

iconographers were not really trying to depict what is by essence unimaginable ... they were trying to give fitting praise to the mystery that was the foundation of their faith."[10] Written and visual images of the bride of Christ are prayerful praise but also illustrations which focused devotion and led to new comprehension. Imagistic vernacular sermons, the rich iconography of Gothic art, the intense realism of renaissance paintings, and the hand-colored outlines of early printed images are scattered shards of belief which most Christians would have comprehended. If this iconography is opaque to the modern viewer, it does not mean that even the poorest lay Christian could not have accessed multiple meanings from an artifact with the assistance of a sermon or a devotional image.[11] Medieval viewers shared a visual and theological vocabulary whose meanings they could instantly apprehend, and whose meanings it is now our task to reconstruct.

Wedding Pictures

Images of the bride of Christ taught theology through gestures, clothing, gazing, blood, and male and female bodies. Following visual cues (clothing, hairstyle), medieval and early modern viewers could identify a bridal pair as male- or female-acting; reconstructing these cues in period art shows that illustrations of Christ and the bride were not consistently male-female pairings. In addition to depictions of the bride as female and Jesus as a young handsome man, John the Evangelist, the "beloved disciple," was sometimes portrayed as Christ's spouse and lover, the bridal soul was sometimes depicted as a young man in courtly attire or with a tonsure. Christ was often bearded but sometimes appeared as a beardless youth or a feminized Man of Sorrows nursing souls with his blood or in the guise of Sophia/Lady Wisdom.[12] These unstable elements of gender performance were a

---

[10] Bernard McGinn, "Theologians as Trinitarian Iconographers," in *The Mind's Eye: Art and Theological Argument in the Middle Ages*, ed. Jeffrey F. Hamburger and Anne-Marie Bouché (Princeton: Princeton University Press, 2006), 202.

[11] David S. Areford, *The Viewer and the Printed Image in Late Medieval Europe* (Burlington, VT: Ashgate, 2010), 65–7.

[12] For a discussion of the iconography of the Man of Sorrows and the Virgin as a mediator, see Erwin Panofsky, "'Imago Pietatis,' Ein Beitrag zur Typengeschichte des 'Schmertzensmannes' und der 'Maria Mediatrix,'" in *Festschrift für Max J. Friedländer zum 60, Geburtstage*, ed. Max J. Friedländer (Leipzig: Verlag von E.A. Seemann, 1927), 261–308. On John as a *sponsa*, see Jeffrey F. Hamburger, *St. John the Divine: The Deified Evangelist in Medieval Art and Theology* (Berkeley: University of California Press, 2002), 2, 132–6. The feminized medieval Christ is a well-established visual trope in late medieval art and theology. See not least Caroline Walker Bynum, *Jesus as Mother: Studies in the Spirituality of the High Middle Ages* (Berkeley: University of California Press, 1982); Michael Camille, "The Image and the Self: Unwriting Late Medieval Bodies," in *Framing Medieval Bodies*, ed. Sarah Kay and Miri Rubin (Manchester: Manchester University Press, 1994); Barbara Newman, *God and the Goddesses: Vision, Poetry, and Belief in the Middle Ages* (Philadelphia: University of Pennsylvania Press, 2003), 190–224.

36 *Marrying Jesus in Medieval and Early Modern Northern Europe*

visual extension of the theological claim that Jesus and the bride reflected one another. Their converging, gender-blurred portrayals represented the individual's proximity to salvation, not necessarily the bride and groom's biological sexes.

Medieval exegesis and iconography exploited the spouses' fluid gender identities to press viewers to theologically complex understandings. Honorius Augustudonensis's *Expositio in Cantica Canticorum*, a twelfth-century commentary on the *Song of Songs*, introduced a pictorial tradition to the narrative of the bride of Christ in which the bride changes face and form in each illustration. Using gender-signifiers from clothing, hair styles, and posture, these artistic depictions argue against the gender markers in their texts by showing the *sponsa*, or "bride," as a beardless male youth. In a prefatory image, the *sponsa* is crowned and enthroned with the *sponsus*, the Shulamite woman rides in the chariot of Amindab, the Synagogue rides a camel, and the mandragora-Antichrist hangs, nude, androgynous, and decapitated, from Christ's hand.[13] The program survives in six extant illustrated twelfth- and early thirteenth-century manuscripts, including a copy from Beuerberg Abbey believed to have been designed by Honorius himself, and a fifteenth-century manuscript related to the Beuerberg manuscript. In each of these illustrated manuscripts, depictions of the bride's sinfulness and unstable gender identity reinforced Honorius's exegetical claims about four biblical epochs corresponding to four brides of Christ.[14] Three extant copies preserve a prefatory image depicting an enthroned *sponsus* with companion *sponsa* and the transformation of an individual person into the *sponsa* through reception of Christ's blood: the twelfth-century manuscripts from the Benedictine abbeys of Benediktbeuren and Tegernsee and the 1403 copy possibly related to a twelfth-century manuscript from Beueberg Abbey.[15] The fifteenth-century copy either preserves an alternate twelfth-century program or, more likely, updated the original sequence to match newer beliefs about the bride of Christ.[16] Each surviving prefatory image invited readers to visualize themselves in her role and

---

[13] His influence on the vernacular poetry of Brun von Schönebeck is briefly discussed in Anne Matter, *Voice of My Beloved: The Song of Songs in Western Medieval Christianity* (Philadelphia: University of Pennsylvania Press, 1990), 190–91.

[14] Honorius's writing has been the subject of extensive inquiry, and the program of images is of considerable interest to scholars of Romanesque manuscript art. As his theological program is summarized in full by Anne Matter, and his art historical program by Michael Curshman, I direct interested readers to their work. Michael Curschmann, "Imagined Exegesis: Text and Picture in the Exegetical Works of Rupert of Deutz, Honorius Augustodunensis, and Gerhoch of Reichersberg," *Traditio: Studies in Ancient and Medieval History, Thought, and Religion* (1988): 145–69. Matter, *The Voice of My Beloved*, 58–76.

[15] Curschmann does not list this manuscript in his discussion of the program of illustrations. Curschmann, "Imagined Exegesis," 154n23.

[16] This manuscript, previously owned by the J.R. Ritman Library, was sold at auction to a private bookdealer in 2003 and has since been resold to the Bavarian State Library, where it is now MS CLM. 30172. My thanks to Arcadia Fletcher of Sam Fogg Ltd. in London for assistance in tracking down the manuscript following its sale.

Any Body's Bridegroom 37

wed Christ by partaking of the sacramental liquid of his blood. The genders of *sponsa* and *sponsus* do not always correlate to the grammatical gendering of their titles. Instead, the bridal pair takes on each other's attributes as they gaze into one another's eyes.

In the Tegernsee copy, which dates to around 1200 (Figure 2.1), two beardless spouses in male courtly attire are enthroned, gazing at one another. The *sponsus* embraces the *sponsa* with his right hand and extends his left hand through the window of the enclosed throne room to a veiled woman in an exterior garden. His blood flows from a wounded hand down towards her. In the Benediktbeueren copy (Figure 2.2), dating to the third quarter of the twelfth century, the *sponsa* also holds an open book and scepter, her mantle held closed by a brooch or clasp. The pair is crowned and nimbed, the *sponsus* beardless and barefoot. The *sponsus'* hair flows loose in wavy locks down his back, suggesting perhaps a second female figure. This bridal pair is also enclosed within an architectural space, gazing at one another. The *sponsus* extends a bleeding hand out to drizzle a veiled woman with his blood. The 1403 manuscript (Figure 2.3) alters this arrangement in several ways. The female devotee joins an explicitly male bridal pair in their architecturally enclosed space, directly touching her spouse rather than his blood. The larger center figure is Christ in majesty, explicitly gendered male with short hair, curling beard, and cruciform halo. Christ is bearded, the male bride bare-cheeked, the female bride-to-be veiled. Christ wraps his arm around the bride and extends his other hand to touch the veiled woman's face. Near him is a scroll reading "*Dextera illius amplexabitur me*"—"his left hand embraces me." The woman presses one hand to her chest, the other clasps a scroll implying Christ has grasped and lifted her up "*leva eius sub capite meo*" (*Song* 5:4). The lower register shows a second scene that may echo the message of transformation implied in the spatial boundaries between garden and room in the twelfth-century manuscripts. Beneath the enclosed lovers, members of the church go about their business: a seated bishop flanked by two young men, one reclining and another striding past, seems to suggest the daily life of the physical world. Details lost during a cropping of the text block show an extended foot, perhaps of a dancer or acrobat. Above them in the heavenly palace, salvation is granted through Christ's love and blood.

Each manuscript's veiled woman seeking Christ's love has become a bride who almost exactly reflects the divine spouse. Text scrolls and accessories (shoes, cloak, brooch, crown) announce the bride's transformation. The two twelfth-century images show the *sponsa* and *sponsus* as nearly indistinguishable equals unknowable to the veiled woman in the garden, suggesting that *sponsa* and *sponsus* exchange identities and attributes through Christ's blood, while the fifteenth-century version eliminates all mediators save Christ's touch. These shifts certainly modulate the theological meaning written into each prefatory image, but Honorius's core message remains: Christ saves those he weds, transforming them with love and blood. This transformation is open to any person who requests Christ's embrace.

This message of personal salvation through marriage also appears in the twelfth-century *Mirror for Maidens* [*Speculum Virginum*], an illustrated dialogue

Figure 2.1   *Sponsa et Sponsus*, *Exposition on the Song of Songs*. Bayerische Staatsbibliothek München, CLM. 18125, 1v., c. 1200.

Figure 2.2 *Sponsa et Sponsus, Exposition on the Song of Songs*. Bayerische Staatsbibliothek München, CLM. 4550, third quarter of the twelfth century.

40   *Marrying Jesus in Medieval and Early Modern Northern Europe*

Figure 2.3   *Sponsa et Sponsus, Exposition on the Song of Songs*. Bayerische Staatsbibliothek München, CLM. 30172, 1403.

I shall examine in Chapter 3. Though the text claims to have been written for a young nun, surviving twelfth- and early thirteenth-century manuscript copies typically incorporate a tonsured male figure kneeling before an image of Christ in Glory at the opening to book 10 (Figure 2.4). The praying male figure is an interloper in the manuscript tradition—he appears in none of the other chapter illustrations and cannot represent either of the dialogue's interlocutors, the young nun Theodora, or her tutor, Peregrinus, who are sometimes pictured in surviving manuscripts as a young veiled woman and an older, bearded, tonsured male. This male figure gazes at Christ, his right hand open imploringly, his left hand passing through the frames of heaven and the rainbow mandorla of glory to grasp Christ's toes. Christ is surrounded by saints, including several virgins holding lilies, a visual reminder of the bridegroom's identity as a Lily of the Valley.[17] He represents a reader delivering the prayer which opens book 10, which narrates creation, Christ's crucifixion, and the soul's entrance into heaven as a bride. This version of the scene comes from a mid-thirteenth-century manuscript copy originally owned by the male Cistercian Abbey of Himmerod, which closely follows the program of the earliest surviving manuscripts, all now traced to male religious houses. In this context, the tonsured praying figure in the accompanying miniature should be read as speaking the prayer, and thus as a representation of a newly made bride of Christ who represents the reader.

As these illustrated manuscripts show, by the late twelfth century, the genders of Christ, the loving soul, and the intended reader had become profitably ambiguous. Theologically, textually, and sometimes even visually, the lovers' gender identities and sexual characteristics blurred as Christ and a Soul drew closer to perfect union. By the fifteenth century, this motion of Jesus and spouse drawing close and reflecting one another had become a powerful visual representation of the incarnation and the reflection of God in the created human's soul which guided viewers to experience Christ's suffering in their own body and imitate his virtues in their daily lives. The convergence of the lovers' identities through desire, shame, and violence is neatly condensed in a half-sheet hand-colored print produced in Ulm c. 1480–90 (Figure 2.5). This woodcut incorporates several components of the iconography of the bride of Christ: the vanquishing of the devil by Christ's death, the offer of bags of coins, the binding of bodies to a cross with a rope, the visualization of "drawing close" expressed with the binding of the soul and of Christ to one another with rope, the exchange of love, the submission of the soul's

---

[17]   The British Library's MS Arundel 44, believed to be an author's working copy, includes a similar tonsured figure as MS Walters 72, fol. 98 r. On the iconography of the manuscripts, see Arthur Watson, *The Early Iconography of the Tree of Jesse*, 1st ed. (London: Oxford University Press, 1934); Eleanor Simmons Greenhill, *Die geistigen Voraussetzungen der Bilderreihe des Speculum virginum; Versuch einer Deutung* (Münster: Aschendorff, 1962); Morgan Powell, "The *Speculum Virginum* and the Audio-Visual Poetics of Women's Religious Instruction," in *Listen, Daughter: The Speculum Virginum and the Formation of Religious Women in the Middle Ages*, ed. Constant J. Mews, The New Middle Ages (New York: Palgrave, 2001).

42   *Marrying Jesus in Medieval and Early Modern Northern Europe*

Figure 2.4   *Christ in Majesty, Speculum Virginum*, book 10. The Walters Art Museum, Baltimore, MS W 72, fol. 98 r.

Figure 2.5   *Jesus Attracting the Faithful to Heart*, 1480/1490. Courtesy of National Gallery of Art, Washington, Rosenwald Collection, 1943.3.853.

desire to Christ, the soul's nakedness, and even the pastoral setting suggested by the trees, hills, and grass.[18] Christ asks the one he loves to "gib mir din herz / den ich lieb hab" [give me your heart, because I love you]. The lover steps forward, his arms extended offering his heart in both outstretched hands, voicing his desire to be drawn close to the bleeding savior. The pair wear only matching loincloths; Christ's cloth extends in a flourish behind his legs, towards the pillar behind him.[19]

---

[18]   The localization to Ulm is based on the small coat of arms shield hanging from the tree. The image has been read as belonging to the visual sphere of bridal mysticism both for its depiction of the lovers and its citation of *Song* 1:3 in the male soul's desire to be "drawn to Christ." Peter W. Parshall and Rainer Schoch, *Origins of European Printmaking: Fifteenth-century Woodcuts and their Public* (Washington: National Gallery of Art, in association with Yale University Press, New Haven, CT, 2005), 282–4. This image is also discussed in Peter W. Parshall, *The Woodcut in Fifteenth-century Europe* (New Haven, CT: National Gallery of Art, Distributed by Yale University Press, 2009), 283.

[19]   I discuss the theological significance of nakedness in greater detail in Chapter 4. On nakedness, especially the nakedness of Christ and the soul, see Susan L. Smith, "The Bride Stripped Bare: A Rare Type of the Disrobing of Christ," *Gesta* 34, no. 2 (1995), 126–46; Leo Steinberg, *The Sexuality of Christ in Renaissance Art and in Modern Oblivion*, 2nd ed. (Chicago: University of Chicago Press, 1997). For a discussion of the theological

Christ is tied to the cross as he draws the lover closer with a pull of the rope. Christ's bleeding body and the pillar remind the viewer of his pre-crucifixion scourging; the switches directed to the male lover's unblemished skin anticipate a parallel scourging performed by first the devil and then Christ.

Recent scholarship on this image and other late medieval depictions of love between Christ and a soul have assumed the normativity of a heterosexual, consensual, and affectionate relationship between Christ and his human lovers. Violent love and ambiguous gender identities must be explained as unusual, transgressive, or theorized through modern concepts of gender and power.[20] But the medieval theological meaning of these violently interacting bodies is as clearly exposed as the lovers' limbs, and the shared masculinity of Christ and the Soul are an important part of that message. The soul is becoming Christ-like—his posture, his attire, and even his tonsure mimic the savior in a visual parallel emphasized by their similarly naked male bodies. The cross, drops of blood, and switches remind the viewer of Christ's sacrificial death. The lover's nakedness represents liberation from material goods, the soul's proximity to the divine, and his imitation of Christ's naked shame. The lovers gaze at one another, alluding to the promise of the beatific vision. Their love has defeated the diminutive devil. The text scrolls and instruments of the passion also remind the viewer that Christ's sacrifice does not remit all sins; the penitent soul must be scourged. And all dear sinners, as the angel's scroll warns, should avoid sin in fear of final Judgment. This mix of love and submissive penitence would draw the soul—and the viewer—closer to salvation, completing the covenant of Christ's love. This love scene offers a concise but exceptionally rich explanation of the mechanism of salvation through faith and love.

In 1550, Dutch engraver and Catholic humanist Dirck Coornhert and the mannerist painter Maarten van Heemskerck collaborated on *Jacob's Ladder* [*Jakobs ladder of de allegorie van de weg naar eeuwige zaligheid*], 14 engravings retelling a male Christian's conversion and eventual union with Christ.[21] Heemskerck was 24 years older, an established international artist, while Coornhert was just beginning a long career as an artist, author, and philosopher. Art historian Ilja Veldman has shown that the sequence's design and theology originated with Coornhert, while the images' depictions of naked male bodies derive from Heemskerck's visual theology of the incarnation. *Jacob's Ladder* illustrates the salvation of a human bound by sin. The sequence unfolds as a series of Petrarchan triumphs, the victor

---

meanings of nakedness in medieval religious art, see Blair Reynolds and Patricia Heinicke, *The Naked Being of God: Making Sense of Love Mysticism* (Lanham, MD: University Press of America, 2000).

[20] For instance, the recent catalogue accompanying this woodcut's display comments that "partly due to the dictates of the heterosexual paradigm of the Song of Songs ... although the woodcut's masculine soul may be unusual, it is not unprecedented." Parshall and Schoch, *Origins of European Printmaking*, 283.

[21] Ilja M. Veldman, *Maarten Van Heemskerck and Dutch Humanism in the Sixteenth Century* (Maarssen: G. Schwartz, 1977), 56–62.

Any Body's Bridegroom   45

of each image vanquished in the next as the soul draws closer to eternal bliss, each lightly glossed with abbreviated scriptural citations. The Latin inscriptions, the fine quality of engravings, and the relatively small size of the images suggest this series was designed for devotional use, perhaps to be pasted into a personal prayer book. The sequence's emphasis on ropes, harnesses, phallic crosses, and finely detailed naked male bodies closely resemble contemporary homoerotic art, but were intended to display artistic virtuosity appropriate to renaissance and mannerist aesthetics. Each detail of these compositions held theological significance. The first etching, *A Slave of Sin is also a Slave of Satan* (Figure 2.6), shows a naked man bound hand and foot, a bit and bridle in his mouth. A small winged devil holds his lead rope and the reins but cannot restrain him; rays from an unseen sun penetrate his bare shoulder, and his head turns to the light. This is the moment of conversion. Through God's mercy, suggested by the rays of light in the first image, the man is freed from his demonic master, dies to sin, contemplates himself in a mirror which inspires conversion (signified by a switch or flail), takes up his own cross in imitation of Christ, is strengthened by patience, finds knowledge of God, attains virtue, learns from Christ, and is at last united with God. The twelfth image depicts Charity holding two serving dishes of wounded hands and feet, reminding the viewer of Christ's death on the cross. In the thirteenth image, Christ displays his wounds. His left hand points to the gash on his side, a cruciform staff in the crook of his elbow, while his right hand supports the top of a large cross, appearing to thrust out of Christ's thigh. This is the soul's final lesson—Christ's humanity, masculinity, wounded muscular body, and the phallic cross now thrust behind him *are* salvation. Like the bowed male straining beneath his own cross in image 8, Christ's torso, thighs, genitals, and instrument of torture are in motion, and the figures' shared masculinity emphasize Christ's humanity and humankind's potential divinity. In the final image, a naked bearded Christ extends his left arm around the shoulder of the naked soul (Figure 2.7). Both are unequivocally male—the soul's bare penis and Christ's flamboyantly draped loincloth are at the center of the engraving, drawing the viewer's eye straight to the proof of their shared humanity. The soul looks up at Christ's face, his hands clasped in prayer, as Christ turns out to meet the viewer's gaze, his right hand raised in a gesture, as if inviting another to join their embrace.

These two naked male bodies bound in bliss can be read neither as advocating female chastity nor as a precocious gay icon—or at least not exclusively as one. As Veldeman stresses, the individual concepts and elements incorporated into this series were not novel.[22] Art historian Leo Steinberg's readings of Heemskerck's depictions of the Man of Sorrows with draping cloths and tumescent bulges in the 1520s and 30s may also inform the significance of the naked male soul. Steinberg proposed that Heemskerck had reversed the trope of the euphemistic use of "flesh" for "penis" to represent the "risen flesh as the roused sexual member."[23]

---

[22]   Ibid., 60.
[23]   Steinberg, *The Sexuality of Christ*, 83.

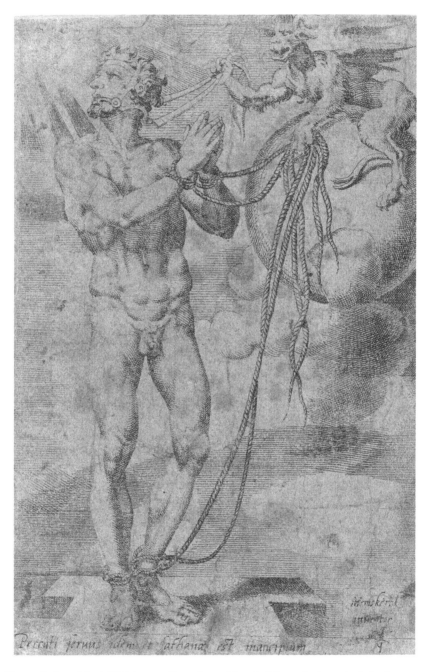

Figure 2.6   Dirck Volckertsz Coornhert, *Mensheid wordt door de duivel geketend*, 1550, after a design by Maarten van Heemskerck. Rijksmuseum, Amsterdam, RP-P-BI-6540X.

Any Body's Bridegroom 47

Figure 2.7 Dirck Volckertsz Coornhert, *Zaligheid wordt bereikt door een te worden met Christus*, 1550, after a design by Maarten van Heemskerck. Rijksmuseum, Amsterdam, RP-P-BI-6553x.

48   *Marrying Jesus in Medieval and Early Modern Northern Europe*

Following Steinberg, the draping of cloth and display of genitals in this sequence accentuate Christ's sexuality, the sexuality of the male soul, and through those bodily citations, their—and the viewer's—shared humanity. These images of naked male bodies drawn close to, and embracing, Christ as spouse invited viewers, whether male or female, to identify with the bride and become like Christ. Each viewer selected which role she might be playing—Mary, Ecclesia, the Soul, the penitent sinner saved through Christ's sacrifice.

When positioned in a chapel or before an altar, images of Christ and his spouse also guided the individual's participation in a theater of devotion when the communicant swallowed the host, perhaps while speaking prayers addressed to Christ as bridegroom.[24] The proliferation of devotional prayers associated with the Eucharist that address Christ as spouse supports this connection. Approaching the altar after reciting such prayers, the viewer's glance would fall first on the table's bread and wine, then look up to contemplate first Christ and the bride painted or sculpted behind the altar, then receive Christ as a spouse incarnate upon the tongue. The identity of "bride of Christ" in altarpieces and other interior church sculptures is assumed from contextual clues (crown, feminine long flowing hair, pairing with a crowned bearded man, elevation) that intentionally suggest multiple identities, allowing the female figure to easily be read as any number of women along a spectrum that included the historical empress and queen of heaven. This presumably was intentional, allowing viewers to read themselves in the figure while contemplating Christ's love and humanity. Those who partook of the Eucharist while meditating on Christ's passion might, in that moment of bodily union with the divine, join with their bridegroom like the brides in heaven.

The Ulm woodcut, the prefatory images to Honorius Augustudonensis's *Commentary on the Song of Songs*, the Heemskerck-Coornhert engravings, and the praying figure who appears in manuscript copies of the *Mirror for Maidens* all assumed viewers could distinguish between the corporeal and spiritual bodies of Christ and the human lover and step into the role of the (naked) soul. These bridal pairs were intricately humanized, inviting each observing "sinner" to take on the identity of the Everysoul, looking only at Christ, loving only Christ—not the material world—and imitating Christ while expressing loving pathos for his torments.

---

[24]   The crowned couple nested in the center of a double-winged altarpiece in the Pilgrim's Church of St. James the Greater in Göttingen (1402) arguably opens to show Christ with the bride. The composition urges the viewer to consider both human and divine identities of the enthroned couple while guiding the eye to the Eucharistic significance of Christ's death. The first set of exterior panels shows scenes from the Life of St. James and opens to reveal scenes from the life and passion of Christ. The most recent work on this altar is Bernd Carqué and Hedwig Röckelein, eds., *Das Hochaltarretabel der St. Jacobi-Kirche in Göttingen* (Göttingen: Vandenhoeck and Ruprecht, 2005).

Mystics, Mysteries, and Marketing

Depictions of marriage to Jesus in late medieval and early modern Christianity are, in essence, narratives of union with God. This two-becoming-one as the human dissolved into divinity [*unio mystica*] was understood by premodern readers as a Christian mystery, but has taken on the modern sense of mysticism. The distinction is important: reading marriage to Jesus as mystery rather than mysticism prioritizes lessons in theology given to entire communities of believers over experiences which can be neither replicated nor fully described. Neither "mysticism" nor "mystery" as conventionally defined is typically considered a popular religious phenomenon. The former depends on an advanced theological understanding and personal access to the divine; the latter suggests a top-down dissemination of knowledge from educated and ordained religious leaders to a homogenous gathering of believers. As Richard King notes, historians of western mysticism focus on doctrine and belief over practice, often overlooking the cultural specificity of mystical practices.[25]

Definitions of "mysticism" must encompass superficially similar phenomena across multiple religious traditions, including those without a concept of soul or deity, a fraught exercise which depends on similarities in language, meditative practice, bodily asceticism, and societal responses.[26] For western traditions, including Christianity, mysticism is usually provisionally defined as partially incommunicable utterances relating human encounters with God.[27] This definition reflects the influence of the early twentieth-century psychologist William James's four-part definition of mystical experiences as transient, ineffable, informative (noetic) and spontaneous (passive). Though James's work has been thoroughly supplanted for medieval and early modern Christianity by new formulations from Michel de Certeau, Bernard McGinn, Michael Anthony Sells, Grace Jantzen, and Amy Hollywood among others, "mysticism" is still typically conceived of as the receptive experience of an individual practitioner, and thus studied primarily through the words and bodies of the "mystic."[28] For de Certeau, "mystical

---

[25] Richard King, *Orientalism and Religion: Postcolonial Theory, India and 'The Mystic East'* (London: Routledge, 1999), 33.

[26] Michael Anthony Sells, *Mystical Languages of Unsaying* (Chicago: University of Chicago Press, 1994); Michael Kessler and Christian Sheppard, *Mystics: Presence and Aporia* (Chicago: University of Chicago Press, 2003).

[27] Michel de Certeau, *The Mystic Fable*, Religion and Postmodernism (Chicago: University of Chicago Press, 1992), 76; Amy M. Hollywood, *Sensible Ecstasy: Mysticism, Sexual Difference, and the Demands of History*, Religion and Postmodernism (Chicago: University of Chicago Press, 2002), 6–9. McGinn has continually refined his view of mysticism, most recently Bernard McGinn, "Mystical Consciousness: A Modest Proposal," *Spiritus* 8, no. 1 (2008): 44–63.

[28] William James, *The Varieties of Religious Experience* (Cambridge: Harvard University Press, 1985), 371. Modern alternatives include the corpus of Bernard McGinn's work as well as Grace M. Jantzen, "Mysticism and Experience," *Religious Studies* 25, no. 3 (1989); Hollywood, *Sensible Ecstasy*; de Certeau, *Mystic Fable*.

literature composes scripts of the body," an observation medievalist Amy Hollywood has adjusted to reflect the dichotomies of gendered experience, so that "mysticism (again, extraordinary experiences of divine presence or of union with God) is simply associated with femininity or with women and so denigrated, or a distinction is made between good and bad, acceptable and unacceptable, non-pathological and pathological forms of mysticism, with the first category in each case associated with masculinity and men and the second with femininity and women."[29] In the specific case of medieval texts describing a marriage to God, the narrative of love is understood as a metaphorical substitute for experiences which exceed articulation.[30] For Hildegard Keller, the phrase "secretum meum mihi" [my secret is mine] characterized declaring oneself a bride of God—"it demarcates the border between what can and cannot be said, and yet this border area can only be addressed through speech."[31] Bernard McGinn once characterized the exchange of ideas between male and female mystics as constituting a "community of discourse."[32] I extend that concept to encompass not just an author's interlocutors, but also readers, and anonymous individuals connected through practice and study in the centuries following a "mystic's" first utterance.

By appropriating the secret and acquiring the skill to reveal it to others, the bride of God transforms the unspeakable and experiential into a carefully scripted uncovering. Whether termed "love" or "bridal" mysticism [*minnemystik, brautmystik*], or, following Barbara Newman, courtly mysticism, or new mysticism, as Bernard McGinn would have it, accounts of marrying Jesus are repeatedly categorized within a strain of ecstatic experiential writing influenced by courtly culture, and characteristic of the new women's religious movements of the late twelfth and thirteenth centuries. But for medieval readers, Christ's spousehood framed a theological argument for the anthropology of the soul, the operation of the sacraments, and the true path to salvation that was a "mystery" of the Church, something comprehensible only with assistance.

Existing definitions of "mysticism" wrestle with a modern term's contested meanings in contemporary scholarly debates; only some of these meanings would have been relevant to medieval and early modern Christians. For scholars of "mysticism," the tortured language and artful reassembly of personal experience overshadows the "mystic's" students and readers. Even if "mystics" wrote for themselves—or to appease their demanding God—the pressure of experience could never account for the investment of material, time, and labor involved

---

[29] De Certeau, *Mystic Fable*, 81; Hollywood, *Sensible Ecstasy*, 7.

[30] For justification and analysis of this "apophatic" eroticism, see in particular: Denys Turner, *Eros and Allegory: Medieval Exegesis of the Song of Songs*, Cistercian Studies 156 (Kalamazoo, MI: Cistercian Publications, 1995); Grace M. Jantzen, "Mysticism and Experience"; Sells, *Mystical Languages of Unsaying*. And for an assessment of mystical expression, see Hollywood, *Sensible Ecstasy*, 198–202; de Certeau, *Mystic Fable*, 113–200.

[31] Keller, *My Secret Is Mine*, 1.

[32] Bernard McGinn, *Meister Eckhart and the Beguine Mystics: Hadewijch of Brabant, Mechthild of Magdeburg, and Marguerite Porete* (New York: Continuum, 1994), 4.

in producing and translating their books. The available evidence regarding the circulation of codices within and across late medieval convents suggests that manuscripts depicting Jesus as bridegroom were part of a widely collected genre of vernacular devotional literature. Of course, this information is partial, derived from surviving manuscripts, early print books, and fragmentary library catalogues and inventories, but the proportion of surviving evidence supports general assumptions about textual transmission, the popularity of some genres over others, and how, when, and why some treatises might be translated or abridged.

Several hundred written works on the bride of Christ would be printed, translated, and adapted for lay audiences between 1140 and 1780. Many of these books circulated alongside one another, quoted extensively from one another, or were bound together in manuscripts and pamphlet collections. A single manuscript codex originally owned by a secular family might later be donated to a religious community, fall again into private hands during the Reformation, and at last enter a public library's collection in the nineteenth century. For instance, Einsiedeln Stiftsbibliothek Codex 710 (322), an illuminated miscellany containing an illustrated copy of Suso's *Exemplar*, included a copy of the *Brotherhood of Eternal Wisdom*, the illustrated poems *Christ and the Loving Soul* and *Love Bears a Cross*, and other German-language texts on loving God. The manuscript is now in a nineteenth-century binding, and may have been altered at any point during the last five centuries. It once belonged to the married lay couple Heinrich Ehinger and Margaretha von Kappel, who donated it to the Dominican sisters at St. Peters in Constance. It likely was acquired by the Abbey of Rheinau after the sisters of St. Peters dispersed during the Reformation, and arrived at the library of another male monastic institution, the Benedictine Abbey of Einsiedeln, sometime in the eighteenth century.[33] It has been owned by a married couple, by nuns, by two different communities of monks, and is now available to read for free on the internet. Few of these previous owners have left us records of how they used the book or why they protected it, and there is not any evidence-based reason to connect this manuscript with a hypothetical "medieval women's mysticism."

According to book ownership records, learning how to become a bride of Christ was considered an appropriate subject for every Christian person, and volumes on the topic were listed in several lay collections. The fifteenth-century noble laywoman Elisabeth von Volkenstorff owned copies of the bible, psalter, apocalypse of John, and lives of the Apostles in German translations, as well as numerous prayer books, law books, and copies of Henry Suso's *Little Book of Eternal Wisdom* and Honorius's *Lucidarius*.[34] The fifteenth-century Colmar burgher Iohannes Schedelin owned an extensive library of devotional manuscripts

---

[33] Amy Gebauer, *"Christus Und Die Minnende Seele": An Analysis of Circulation, Text, and Iconography* (Wiesbaden: Reichert Verlag, 2010), 33–45.

[34] Ann Marie Rasmussen and Sarah Westphal-Wihl, eds., *Ladies, Whores, and Holy Women: A Sourcebook in Courtly, Religious, and Urban Cultures of Late Medieval Germany* (Kalamazoo, MI: Medieval Institute Publications, Western Michigan University, 2010), 106–8.

52 *Marrying Jesus in Medieval and Early Modern Northern Europe*

often associated with the Dominican observant reform movement.[35] Additionally, an epitaph for fifteenth-century Nuremburg patrician Ursula Schürstab (d. 1480) cited lines from a woodcut depicting Christ's marriage to the soul.[36] Nor were convents interested in only sacred books. One southern German convent owned a 1477 incunable copy of a German translation of the *Decameron*, another held a manuscript copy of Jean Gerson's *Tractatus de nocturniis polutionibus*, a treatise on male nocturnal emissions, and one surviving copy of *Christ and the Loving Soul* was commissioned by a laywoman and donated to a relative at the Dominican convent of St. Nicolas in Undis.[37] These glimpses into fifteenth-century libraries demonstrate that Elizabeth Lehfeldt's observation about early modern Spanish convents also pertains to medieval women's communities: convents were permeable spaces through which words, bodies, and objects flowed.[38]

Medieval and early modern descriptions of marriage to Jesus survived because they explained mysteries—religious truths attainable and comprehensible not through reason or observation but only through divine revelation. An author's identity, sanctity, and experiential authority were secondary to a text's utility. For instance, brief anonymous poems recorded in the pseudonymous *Book of Perfection* are treated just as authoritatively as passages attributed to university-trained theologians like Meister Eckhart and Hugo von Ripelin, or visions now traced to holy women like Mechthild of Magdeburg. The *Book of Perfection* unfolds as a series of discrete theological images, most easily spoken in a single breath. One verse reads:

> God blooms beneath the soul like a loving little flower and opens up around the soul like a light and enters the soul like a swelling fountain and merges into the soul like a loving Bridegroom. Thus the soul perceives and recognizes God's wisdom and his goodness to all created things, [and] thus God rises up beneath the soul.
>
> But just as the person lives virtuously, so that all those who long for it will be improved from this, thus God rises up around the soul.

---

[35] Balázs J. Nemes, "*Dis buch ist iohannes schedelin.* Die Handschriften eines Colmarer Bürgers aus der Mitte des 15. Jahrhunderts und ihre Verflechtungen mit dem Literaturangebot der Dominikanerobservanz," in *Kulturtopographie des deutschsprachigen Südwestens im späteren Mittelalter. Studien und Texte*, ed. Barbara Fleith and René Wetzel (Berlin: De Gruyter, 2009), 157–214.

[36] Sabine Griese, *Text-Bilder und ihre Kontexte: Medialität und Materialität von Einblatt-Holz-und-Metallschnitten des 15. Jahrhunderts* (Zürich: Chronos, 2011), 90.

[37] Florian Sepp, Bettina Wagner, and Stephan Kellner, "Handschriften und Inkunabeln aus süddeutschen Frauenklöstern in der Bayerischen Staatsbibliothek München," in *Nonnen, Kanonissen und Mystikerinnen: Religiöse Frauengemeinschaften in Süddeutschland*, ed. Eva Schlotheuber, Helmut Flachenecker, and Ingrid Gardill (Göttingen: Vandenhoeck and Ruprecht, 2008), 320, 327.

[38] Elizabeth A. Lehfeldt, *Religious Women in Golden Age Spain: The Permeable Cloister* (Burlington, VT: Ashgate, 2005), 175–83.

Any Body's Bridegroom 53

So then you, soul, think about how God came down from heaven and became a person and suffered death; thus God rises up into the soul like a swelling fountain.

But thus when the soul should come out of suffering, then God comes like a loving bridegroom and leads her into the eternal life and lets her drink from the abyss of his love.[39]

This poet delights in the multiple meanings of the verb "gehen," to rise up, to go under, to bloom, to embrace, creating a sense of constant motion. Like a bridegroom, God embraces the soul, grows in the soul, changes the soul, each motion a reaction to the devotee's bodily actions. This brief passage represents a widespread late medieval belief that the divine spouse was available eternally for every person contemplating the mysteries of creation, incarnation, and resurrection.

Medieval readers prized books which would guide them down the path of salvation to find their own celestial spouse, and early printers advertised their products accordingly. A book on the bride of Christ which appeared on the inaugural Index of Banned Books marketed itself to "allen goeden Christen menschen" [all good Christian people]. Augsburg's prolific printer of illustrated books, Anton Sorg, marketed a book on the bride of Christ now catalogued as "Geistliche gemahelschaft"—that is, "Spiritual Spouseship"—as "The book of Art, through which the worldly person may become spiritual." Even if these printed books were adapted from convent manuscripts, their invitations to "Christian people" were not necessarily late additions. The preface to Suso's German-language *Exemplar* invites

anyone who would like to become a good and blessed person and share special intimacy with God, or whom God has singled out by severe suffering—which he is accustomed to do with his special friends—such a person would find this book to be a comforting help. Also, for well-disposed persons it lights the way to divine truth and for thoughtful people it points out the right path to supreme happiness.[40]

---

[39]   God der get under den selen uf alz ein minneclichú blůme und get umb die sele uf alz ein lieht und get in den seln uf alz ein quellender brůnne und get ob den seln uf alz ein minneclicher brútegam. So die sele market und erkennet gotes wisheit und sin güte an den creaturen, so get got under den selen uf.

So aber der mensche alz tugentlichen lebt, daz alle die dovon gebessert werden, die ez sehent, so get got uf umb die sele.

So denne dú sele gedenket, wie got von hymel kam und mensche wart und den tot leit, so get got uf in der sele alz ein quellender brunne.

So aber die sele usser dem ellende sol, so kumet got alz ein minneclicher brútgam und füret sie in daz ewige leben und lat si do ertrinken in dem abgrunde siner minne.

Pseudo-Engelhart von Ebrach, "Das Buch der Vollkommenheit," in *Das Buch der Vollkommenheit*, ed. Karin Schneider (Berlin: Akademie Verlag, 2006), 93.

[40]   Unless otherwise specified, I have used Tobin's translation of Suso's *Exemplar*, which follows Bihlmeyer but has been updated when readings are more plausible in variant manuscripts. *Henry Suso: The Exemplar, with Two German Sermons*, ed. and trans. Frank J. Tobin (New York: Paulist Press, 1989), 59. This prologue has been generally accepted as authentic, though perhaps a later addition to the *Exemplar*.

54 *Marrying Jesus in Medieval and Early Modern Northern Europe*

Suso was not alone in inviting readers to identify with and imitate his service to a celestial spouse.[41] "Mystical" treatises are infused with an urgent desire to inspire others to seek God. This information was especially important to the laity, novices, and other spiritual beginners who sought to wed Christ by inviting God into their own souls. In the specific cases I analyze in this book, the spousal couple's embraces were carefully designed pedagogic illustrations appropriate for guiding spiritual beginners to grasp the full implications of religious conversion and devotional exercises, not the last resource of emotionally overwhelmed mystics grasping after slippery words. Medieval authors and scribes often identified their books as manuals in the arts of devotion, or lessons in learning to love and serve God. As manuscripts first written for convent audiences were adapted to meet the needs of the laity and a new market for printed books, readers and listeners on both sides of cloister walls were reassured that Christ's love saved all sinners.

Sexing (Up) the Bride of Christ

Medieval authors and artists explicitly describe the bride's fluid gender identity as unrestricted by the biology of human bodies. Henry Suso's books relate the experiences of his authorial avatar, the Lover (*Amandus*) or Servant (*Diener*), who was not exactly Suso himself, but instead "represent[s] everyone who is like him." Interactions between the disciple and wisdom are staged for entertainment, rather than exactly as the author had experienced them.

> As teachers do, sometimes he [the servant] speaks as he were a perfect man, and then as one who is imperfect, sometimes as if he were one who loves Christ with all his heart and has given himself in marriage to him in faith and love, then later as a sinner, pitifully begging God to pardon him his excesses. And so the style changes from time to time, to suit what is then the subject. Sometimes the Son of God is presented as the spouse of the devout soul; then later the same Son is introduced as Eternal Wisdom, wedded to the just man.[42]

Though the author was a celibate man, his authorial persona, the Servant of Eternal Wisdom, was neither exactly male nor explicitly celibate. Suso the only man to take on the role of exemplary bride—as Virginia Burrus has argued, the fourth-century translator, exegete, and theologian Jerome adopted the bride's role in his 22nd letter addressed to the virgin and bride of the Lord, Eustochium.[43] Late medieval depictions of the bearded crucified bride of Christ *Kümmernis/*

---

[41] For a discussion of the four headings typical of medieval scholastic prefatory comments, which also guide these devotional works' prologues, see Nigel F. Palmer, "Das Buch als Bedeutungsträger bei Mechthild von Magdeburg," in *Bildhafte Rede in Mittelalter und früher Neuzeit: Probleme ihrer Legitimation und Funktion*, ed. Wolfgang Harms and Klaus Speckenbach (Tübingen: Niemeyer, 1992).

[42] Suso, *Wisdom's Watch Upon the Hours*, 55.

[43] Virginia Burrus, *The Sex Lives of Saints: An Erotics of Ancient Hagiography* (Philadelphia: University of Pennsylvania Press, 2004), 20.

Ontcommer/Wilgefortis also emphasize the transformation of a female body into a fully hirsute Christ-analogue.[44] The bride's gender also fluctuated in manuscript copies, as well as throughout the body of single copies. Extant manuscripts of Hendrik Mande's (c. 1360–1431) *Loving Complaint* rarely agree on the gender of the bride or the groom—some use "hoers/hoer" [her/she], others "his/him," and others still the plural and gender neutral inclusives "mijn/sijn/dijn" [mine/yours]. Though medieval scribes seemed comfortable with shifting the gender of the bride and groom, in his critical edition of the *Loving Complaint,* Thom Mertens normalized all pronouns to suggest a female bride and male groom, to match what he considered to be the more conventional characterizations.[45] Similarly, the anonymous *Spouseship of Christ [Gemahelschaft Christi mit der gläubigen Seele]* differentiated between the "sy" [she] of the individual bride and the generic "er" [he] of potential brides. Most medieval texts I shall cite in this book alternate between the female-gendered "bride" and the male-gendered "person" in the grammatical gendering of their original languages. None of these switches in any way correlates with contemporary English words to mark gender fluidity, performativity, or transition such as trans-, drag, third sex, or intersex. Rather, they signify beings whose sex, sexuality, and gender identity were perpetually in flux.

Sex That Saves

Depictions of naked bodies merging in blissful union may seem pornographic rather than pedagogical—but for medieval readers, sex could be a sacred act. In the 1340s, Christ told Bridget of Sweden (1303–73), "[W]hen a couple comes to bed, my Spirit leaves them … but my mercy can still be with them if they are converted, for I lovingly place a living soul created by my power into their seed."[46] Nonetheless, illustrations of union with God are frequently read as sexual. Because scholars invented the subgenre of "bridal mysticism," experiential erotic literary accounts of personal encounters with God are typically read as apophatic mysticism, a way of describing in comprehensible images an experience that exceeds rational vocabulary. Simply, the mystic *cannot* say what he or she truly has experienced, and uses seemingly erotic language to recount a personal sensation of rapture or a sublimation of sexual desire. Though his recent work on Julian of Norwich acknowledges the skillful theological lessons encoded in medieval mystical writing, Denys Turner previously remarked that "Mediaeval monks … seem to be happy. They *like* sexual imagery, … he *knows* what he is

---

[44] The most recent discussion of *Ontcommer* in art is Ilse E. Friesen, *The Female Crucifix: Images of St. Wilgefortis since the Middle Ages* (Waterloo, ON: Wilfrid Laurier University Press, 2001).

[45] Hendrik Mande, *Een minnentlike claege,* ed. Thom Mertens (Erftstadt: Lukassen, 1984), 21, 31.

[46] St. Birgitta of Sweden, *The Revelations of St. Birgitta of Sweden,* vol. 2: *Liber Caelestis,* books 4–5, ed. Bridget Morris, trans. Denis Michael Searby (Oxford: Oxford University Press, 2006), 93–7.

56   *Marrying Jesus in Medieval and Early Modern Northern Europe*

doing, he *intentionally* denies to himself a genital outlet for his sexuality and *deliberately* transfers his sexual energies upon a spiritual object."[47] This agency has sometimes been denied female authors, who are reduced to their bodies and their utterances when they channel God's voice. Feminist psychoanalyst Luce Irigaray characterized women's forays into this subgenre as "the only place in the history of the West in which woman speaks and acts so publicly ... it is in order to speak woman, write to women, act as a preacher and confessor to women, that man has usually gone to such excesses ... mimicking them ... to the point when he can no longer find himself as 'subject' anymore and goes where he had no wish to follow."[48] Irigaray was neither a medievalist nor even weighing in on the historical situation of the women she mimicked, but her perception that the mystic's performance of taking in and loving God is inherently female, feminizing, and violently, reductively somatic guides many readings of bridal mysticism.[49] Nearly two decades ago, Barbara Newman observed that these sex scenes made theologians into apologists, elicited "older critics to diagnose psychopathology," and distressed feminist readers who must reconcile their delight at finding women's voices with their dismay at the impulsive self-destruction women voiced.[50] In the intervening decades, the theological innovations of male and female mystics remain somewhat obscured by the commonplace that "bridal mysticism" is a (female) visionary's experience of overwhelming love and peace during the moment of union with God which can only be explained through the analogy of erotic love. This modern "bridal mysticism" makes a male author's union with his male God into an autoerotic or hypersexual exhibition of gender-bending designed for a voyeuristic (female) listener, or a female author experiences the sexual fantasies of her lustful amanuensis-confessor. As I shall show in Chapter 4, descriptions of kissing, longing, embracing, and loving were not the last resource of emotionally overwhelmed mystics grasping for words to describe the indescribable. These so-called bridal mystics had carefully designed these images to inspire religious conversions and guide devotional exercises. Neither the author nor the audience was necessarily the bridal soul, but these passages were often explicitly marked as teaching texts.

Descriptions of marriage to Jesus abound with body parts, nakedness, longing, and tumultuous emotions that inspire scholars to imagine intertwining bodies and lovers' moans—to read medieval images as our own sexual fantasies. Medieval and early modern Christians, based on what they left us to know them by, did not think about sex in the same ways as modern semisecularized western scholars. They created bawdily comic images of naked genitalia but also left us hauntingly erotic passages about intermingling and pleasures that could never be set into words. Consider the depiction of Christ naked in bed with a female soul, from

---

[47]   Turner, *Eros and Allegory*, 17–18.

[48]   Luce Irigaray, *Speculum of the Other Woman* (Ithaca: Cornell University Press, 1985), 191–2.

[49]   Hollywood, *Sensible Ecstasy*, 203.

[50]   Newman, *From Virile Woman to WomanChrist*, 159.

Any Body's Bridegroom 57

Wolfgang Schenck's 1499 print of *Christ and the Loving Soul* (Figure 2.8). Both are naked, though the Soul wears her crown in bed. The pair gaze into one another's faces as the soul leans over to embrace Christ—she is on top. An urban landscape appears outside the bedroom window. Christ says "Ich bin dein vnnd du bist mein / Wir wollen nun ewig bey einander sein" [I am yours and you are mine / We shall now eternally be with one another]. Considered alone, this woodcut may be the most explicit depiction of sex with God produced by any fifteenth-century artist. But the image is surrounded with printed text that praises God's saving love and pleads for forgiveness for sins through Christ's death and red blood. Without these contextual explanations, the two naked bodies in bed are lovers distinguished from scenes in the *Decameron* or the *Roman de la Rose* only by their halos and crowns. The text and iconography mark *this* sexual union as a visual representation of human salvation.

To illustrate my point, I turn to a frequently quoted passage on the Eucharist written by a thirteenth-century Antwerp beguine known as Hadewijch of Brabant (d. 1248). Following Caroline Walker Bynum's influential discussion of Hadewijch in *Holy Feast* nearly two decades ago, Hadewijch—in English translation—has attracted significant academic interest. Bynum once warned against misinterpreting Hadewijch: "[T]his meeting with God reads like a description of a sexual orgasm (and it is only our modern sensibility that makes the suggestion a shocking one)."[51] Bynum's parenthetical aside entices the audience to recognize the pleasure-filled mingling of human and divine as analogous to orgasm and implies that medieval readers would have thought that an appropriate way to write about God. But Bynum's disclaimer has invited others to insist that Hadewijch is both pornographic and sadomasochistic.[52] Hadewijch's poetry and letters appear to blend violent ecstasy with God's love in a virtuosic mastery of poetic form. In the original Dutch, in her historical context, Hadewijch is, above all, a consummate teacher.

In *Letter 9*, the exiled beguine describes an insistently physical intermingling of two beings becoming one, their bodies pressing against and then passing into one another to teach the "dear child" to whom she writes the lessons *he* (God) imparted to the body with which he blends:

> Dear Child, God will teach you who he is…. From this [joining] he shall teach you what he is and how wonderfully sweetly one love dwells in another, and through this dwelling within one another neither can know his or herself apart from the other. But they mutually consume one another.
>
> Mouth in mouth, heart in heart.
> And body in body.
> And soul in soul.

---

[51] Caroline Walker Bynum, *Holy Feast and Holy Fast: The Religious Significance of Food to Medieval Women* (Berkeley: University of California Press, 1987), 156.

[52] Bart Vandenabeele, "Strelend wonden helen: over Hadewijch, erotiek en esthetiek," *Uil van Minerva (De): Tijdschrift voor Geschiedenis en Wijsbegeerte* 13, no. 2 (1996–97).

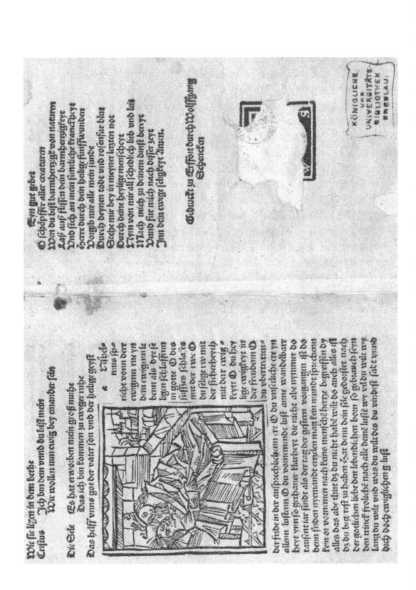

Figure 2.8 Unknown artist, *Eternal Embrace and Closing Prayer*, *Von der ynnigen selen wy sy gott casteyet vnnd im beheglich mach*. Erfurt: Wolfgang Schenck, 1499. Biblioteka Uniwersytecka we Wrocławiu, XV.Q.329 d iii v–d iv r.

Any Body's Bridegroom 59

And a sweet godly nature flows through them both, and they are both one as they pass through themselves. And both also remain individuals. And they truly shall remain [joined yet distinguishable in this way].[53]

As the boundaries between self and God dissolve, Hadewijch learns, and the dear child—and any others who have read the letter over the centuries may yet learn—the nature of God through the sweetness of his love. Hadewijch's stated intention is both to arouse a desire for God and to assure the "dear child" and her community that they can recreate this encounter through their own devotional practices. Though the passage describes two bodies, two hearts, two mouths, it is not describing sexual intercourse. Instead, Hadewijch has made her personal encounter with the divine into a roadmap to heavenly salvation for her students.

Partially because of outdated critical editions and poetic flourishes from English translators, medieval texts like Hadewijch's ninth letter have sparked a decades-long argument among critics—can Hadewijch (or Bridget, or any other author) actually be writing about sex as a path to salvation? Are these women sublimating sexual desire? Amy Hollywood, Denys Turner, Nancy Partner, and Hildegard Keller recognize an authorial impulse to eroticism where Bynum insisted on pure theology.[54] Amy Hollywood has compellingly linked the mystical gaze to the modern film genres of pornography and snuff that stage violent anti-feminist sexual encounters for male entertainment and sexual gratification. Though Hollywood's argument persuasively explains the relationship between violence, viewer response, and the consumption of mystical literature in the past and the present, I think it is vital to recognize that medieval readers would have responded to such passages as modern viewers do not to true pornography but to other contemporary genres like "food pornography." Unlike commercial pornography, in which actors perform sexual encounters to arouse, entertain, and enliven viewers' fantasies, but generally are not instructing viewers in how to conduct their own sex lives, food pornography is usually didactic. These highly sensual displays of edible commodities, coupled with stylized performances of licking, pleasurable moaning, and swallowing, simultaneously elicit desire and, crucially, instruct viewers to recreate the performer's experience, whether by following the same recipe, eating at the same restaurant, or settling for a far less sublime rendition of

---

[53] Van Mierlo suggests that "si ghebruiken onderlinghe" is a marker of the time during which the divine and human flow into one another, though I have rendered it as mutual consumption. Hart, in a note, suggests that the "heart in heart" refers to the Sacred Heart, but this seems out of place in the passage. Hadewijch, *The Complete Works*, trans. Columba Hart (New York: Paulist Press, 1980), 66. I have provided my own translation which more closely follows the original, always using "and" rather than "but" for *ende* and "passes through" rather than "interpenetrates" to indicate the overlapping of beings. Hadewijch, *Brieven*, ed. J. van Mierlo (Antwerp: Standaard-Boekhandel, 1947), 79.

[54] I shall return to Turner and Keller's claims in Chapter 4. Nancy F. Partner, "Did Mystics Have Sex?," in *Desire and Discipline: Sex and Sexuality in the Premodern West*, ed. Jacqueline Murray and Konrad Eisenbichler (Toronto: University of Toronto Press, 1996), 301–2.

60   *Marrying Jesus in Medieval and Early Modern Northern Europe*

the desirable dish.[55] Like the swallowing of an oyster or the dipping of a banana into chocolate, Hadewijch's phrases appear to be sexual and she intentionally uses language overlapping with love poetry, but her writing is not pornographic in either the modern sense of an erotic display designed to arouse the viewer to (sexual/spiritual) pleasure or the medieval sense of depicting copulating naked bodies (for humor/arousal). Like the celebrity chefs of food pornography, Hadewijch has provided clear directions for anyone who hoped to recreate this scene.

Medieval readers had a very different set of metaphors for describing orgasms than modern viewers of pornography. As Bynum stressed, most would not have read sexual pleasure in Hadewijch's account. The bedroom scenes modern readers sometimes find erotic were meant to evoke a lust for salvation, titillating readers with glimpses of heaven. Even when naked newlyweds blissfully intertwine in their bedchamber, modern and medieval assumptions about sex should be separated. For me, the more interesting question is not "Were they having sex?" but "What is this suggestion of sex trying to sell medieval readers?" Hadewijch's description of two bodies blurring into one is not just mysticism—the meeting of human and divine—or a mystery—the revelation of secret knowledge. It is also the exhibition of a private encounter between two beings exchanging love and pleasure, and a replicable lesson in devotional practice. This two-becoming-one is a common motif of the "mystical eye," shared by medieval Christian and Muslim authors, which expresses the union of two intact beings.[56] Hadewijch's pacing and punctuation break the encounter into sensual actions. The mouths meet in a kiss and then enter one another, chests press against one another so closely that skin can no longer separate heart from heart. The bodies are not just *in* but *through* each other as knowledge of self dissolves into knowledge of the beloved other. Is this interpenetration about spiritual union or sexual intercourse with God? Or both? As I document in Chapter 4, intimate encounters with God, especially nakedness and intermingling, were a theologically rich explanation of creation, the incarnation, and the Eucharistic wafer. The impulse to import sexual desire *into* Hadewijch and other female authors and draw theology out of the words of men like Meister Eckhart originates in our own reading practices. If we are shocked to see sex where we hoped to find salvation, we may have overlooked the theological significance these images held for medieval and early modern Christians.

This is not to say that joining Luce Irigaray in reading St. Theresa while gazing at Bernini's sculpture and concluding that both he and she were describing an

---

55   Hollywood, *Sensible Ecstasy*, 42–4. Although the concept of food pornography is fairly novel, I find it a useful comparison—I draw here in particular on the work of food writer and chef Anthony Bourdain, who has extensively and ironically commented on the pornographic handling of food in contemporary culture. See especially *Anthony Bourdain: No Reservations*, "Food Porn," episode 67, first aired on February 9, 2009, by the Travel Channel, and *Anthony Bourdain: No Reservations*, "Food Porn 2," episode 93, first aired on April 19, 2010, by the Travel Channel.

56   Bernard McGinn, "The Problem of Mystical Union in Eckhart, Seuse, and Tauler," in *Meister Eckhart in Erfurt*, ed. A. Speer and L. Wegener, Miscellanea Mediaevallia 32 (Berlin: de Gruyter, 2005), 540.

Any Body's Bridegroom 61

orgasmic experience of the divine is a modern mistake.[57] But we are not thinking about sex in the ways that medieval and early modern Christians did. Medieval authors and artists were unabashedly explicit when detailing sex, body parts, and orgasms, but they did not always, or often, equate genitalia and intercourse with eroticism.[58] Though some medieval authors made courtship a sexless dance of blind admiration, in fabliaux, minnesang, and even manuscript marginalia, sex was bawdy, lewd, and delightfully entertaining. Sexualized nuns abounded, even brandishing, buying, and chasing after penises, as in the widowed manuscript artist Jeanne de Montbaston's lewd depictions of the religious fornicating in the margins of a *Roman de la Rose* or the story of a disembodied penis roaming a convent in the anonymous fifteenth-century *Nonnenturnier* [*Nuns' Tournament*].[59] Some pilgrimage badges, possibly from brothels, imitated religious icons but depicted human genitalia like winged penis-beasts wearing leashes.[60] Vernacular medical texts like the *Mirror of Coitus* focused on bodily signs to identify orgasm and cultivate pleasure to achieve conception, courtly poets like Chrétien de Troyes and Wolfram von Eschenbach lingered outside the bedroom chamber, recognizing the privacy of pleasure, then looking away again to the next plot element.[61]

---

[57]   Irigaray, *Speculum of the Other Woman*, 201.

[58]   On the shift in viewing breasts and genitals as sexual, see Steinberg, *The Sexuality of Christ*; Margaret R. Miles, *A Complex Delight: The Secularization of the Breast, 1350–1750* (Berkeley: University of California Press, 2008).

[59]   These scenes are well known through Camille's work on marginal art. One even appears on the cover of Nicola McDonald, ed., *Medieval Obscenities* (Woodbridge: York Medieval, 2006). The manuscript can be viewed online: Bibliothèque nationale de France, fr. 25526, http://romandelarose.org/#read;Francais25526.163v.tif. The sequence begins on 106r and reappears intermittently through 140r. In the *Nonnenturnier* a knight's penis leaves him to go adventuring in a convent. The nuns fight over it fiercely. Thomas Cramer, *Maeren-Dichtung* (München: W. Fink, 1979), 164–72.

[60]   A full catalogue and analysis of these obscene pilgrimage badges is Sarah Blick and Rita Tekippe, *Art and Architecture of Late Medieval Pilgrimage in Northern Europe and the British Isles* (Leiden: Brill, 2005), 493–510, figures 232–57.

[61]   For instance, Michael R. Solomon, *The Mirror of Coitus: A Translation and Edition of the Fifteenth-Century Speculum al Foderi* (Madison, WI: Hispanic Seminary of Medieval Studies, 1990), 29–42. I am thinking here of scenes like Lancelot and Guinevere's night together in the barred turret and Parzival's first night with Condwiramurs. In both cases, the author alludes to pleasure but leaves the couple in privacy. Chrétien de Troyes, *Le chevalier de la charrette*, Éd. Bilingue by Catherine Croizy-Naquet (Paris: H. Champion, 2006); Wolfram von Eschenbach, *Parzival*, ed. Karl Lachmann and Bernd Schirok (Berlin: De Gruyter, 2003). The erotic in courtly literature and its implications for medieval gender and sexuality is an enormous topic. Peter L. Allen, *The Art of Love: Amatory Fiction from Ovid to the Romance of the Rose* (Philadelphia: University of Pennsylvania Press, 1992); E. Jane Burns, *Courtly Love Undressed: Reading Through Clothes in Medieval French Culture* (Philadelphia: University of Pennsylvania Press, 2002); Albrecht Classen, ed., *Discourses on Love, Marriage, and Transgression in Medieval and Early Modern Literature* (Tempe: Arizona Center for Medieval and Renaissance Studies, 2004); Karma Lochrie, Peggy

Consequently, sex-like scenes between Jesus and his brides *must* be read within their historical, physiological, and theological contexts.

In the medieval secular world, sex regulated property transactions by notarizing marriages or violating and invalidating them—even vows of abstinence, the absence of sex, legally regulated property and family by removing the abstinent from a marriage economy.[62] In a religious setting, as shown in canon law, studies of the penitentials, and by historians of sexuality, sexual relationships might better be considered by degrees of sinfulness.[63] Which bits went into whom, how often, with what motivation, and in which location were important details for assigning penance, but the body parts themselves did not always evoke eroticism as they do in modern pornography. Within medieval thinking about sex and marriage, marriage to Jesus and related copulations with the divine and pregnancies stemming from those unions mark the extreme end of a sin spectrum. Sex with the divine spouse was the one form of copulation that erased, rather than created, sin. Even as early as the third century, John Chrysostom marveled that marriage to God was a "new and strange event! With us marriage destroys virginity, but with God marriage hath restored it. With us she who is a virgin, when married, is a virgin no longer: with Christ she who is a harlot, when married, becomes a virgin."[64] Any married couple dedicated to God who entered a church and approached the altar could become spiritual spouses, to whom God acted as "their third companion." Marriage itself did not trap men and women in sin, or force their eyes eternally away from God's face. Whether or not their worldly husbands welcomed Christ into their beds, many late medieval couples had remade their marriage beds to accommodate a heavenly husband.

Something Both the Church and the Layfolk Knew

Images of the bride of Christ guided what we now consider to be affective meditation by making the devotee a participant in the drama of a scene, eliciting emotional responses and altering the spiritual state of the viewer. But where had viewers acquired the theological and visual literacy required to enter such a state?

McCracken, and James A. Schultz, eds., *Constructing Medieval Sexuality* (Minneapolis: University of Minnesota Press, 1997).

[62]   The literature on marriage in medieval and early modern Europe is extensive. The distinctions I am drawing follow Emma Lipton's *Affections of the Mind: The Politics of Sacramental Marriage in Late Medieval English Literature* (Notre Dame, IN: University of Notre Dame Press, 2007). Georges Duby, *Medieval Marriage: Two Models from Twelfth-Century France*, trans. Elborg Forster (Baltimore: The Johns Hopkins University Press, 1978).

[63]   The most concise summary of this way of reading sex along a sin spectrum is the interactive diagram provided in James A. Brundage, *Law, Sex, and Christian Society in Medieval Europe* (Chicago: University of Chicago Press, 1987), 162, figure 4.1.

[64]   Chrysostom, Homily II, NPNF, series 1, vol. 9, 256. Christian Classics Ethereal Library, http://www.ccel.org/ccel/schaff/npnf109.xv.iv.html.

Any Body's Bridegroom 63

Secular courts, city cathedrals, and women's religious communities were central to the production and distribution of vernacular advice on marriage to Jesus. Most medieval Christians learned about marriage to Jesus through sermons and art, and those able to master the intricacies of Latin theology brought this cultural literacy to their reading of biblical commentaries and other specialized books. In the thirteenth-century, a Saxon layman known as Brun von Schönebeck penned a verse commentary on the *Song of Songs* that presents the knowledge shared by trained theologians and commoners.[65] Brun read Bernard of Clairvaux, cited John Chrysostom of the Golden tongue, evoked Honorius of Augustodunensis's readings of the *Song of Songs*, and shared the book with Heinrich von Huxerre, a Franciscan lector and preacher whose spiritual authority sanctified the poem.[66] Brun was a receptive reader who ruminated over Latin treatises, an active redactor and transmitter of theology, and an original poet transferring the techniques of a secular discipline to a sacred study. His poem mingles courtly and spiritual modes of love.

Brun derived from Latin authors the bride's multiple identities as Mary, Church, and individual Christian. For Brun, "di sele si gotes brut / got ir brutegom und trut" [the soul is God's bride / God is her bridegroom and darling].[67] God elected brides from "the good," whose ranks included widows and widowers Brun likens to the Virgin Mary.[68] Across the span of the poem, Brun describes the sinful and sick nature of the bride which will melt away in Christ's blood until the sinner's heart is joined to God.[69] His gloss on the opening lines of the *Song, osculetur me osculo oris sui*, compares the kisses exchanged between Christ and the bride and Christ and Judas. Judas's kiss fell far to the side of the bridegroom's lips and dropped him into hell, but kissing the bridegroom on the mouth erases the curse of death brought on by Adam's sin.[70] The bride is dressed and wed to a starkly naked groom [*nacket und bloz*]. As Christ sets a gold crown on the bride's head, Brun explains that this coronation signifies the bride's faith and the power of prayer.[71] Brun's poetry alternates between Latin and German and his interpretations of the *Song*

---

[65] Though Brun wrote for a lay audience, the *Hoheleid* survives in only one complete manuscript and a few fragments. For recent discussions of Brun in English, see Sara S. Poor, "Mechthild von Magdeburg, Gender, and the 'Unlearned Tongue,'" *Journal of Medieval and Early Modern Studies* 31, no. 2 (2001): 213–50; D.H. Green, *Medieval Listening and Reading: The Primary Reception of German Literature, 800–1300* (Cambridge; New York: Cambridge University Press, 1994), 103; Matter, *The Voice of My Beloved*, 190.

[66] Brun comments that he read Bernard and Jerome, frequently references Augustine, cites the Vulgate, quotes Chrysostom on spiritual nakedness, and cites several readings from Honorius, especially the reading of the bride as the mandragora-Antichrist. For instance: Brun von Schönebeck, "Das Hohe Lied," *Bibliothek des Litterarischen Vereins in Stuttgart*, 198, ed. Arwed Fischer (Stuttgart, 1893), 314, 25, 46, 94–5, 72.

[67] Ibid., 221.

[68] Ibid., 160.

[69] Ibid., 236.

[70] Ibid., 362–3.

[71] Ibid., 385–6.

64   *Marrying Jesus in Medieval and Early Modern Northern Europe*

draw on so many sources that the poem elicits a "hermeneutic confusion."[72] But his seemingly disorganized verses encompassed a comprehensive explanation of the nature of creation, creator, and the power of God's love that encompassed the fullness of Christian history.

An apocryphal tradition about the fourteenth-century Dominican preacher Johannes Tauler explains how information about marrying Jesus circulated through conversations between clerics, townsfolk, and nuns. The account survives in printed editions of Tauler's work and manuscript copies of the *Meisterbuch* [*Book of the Master*], a dialogue between a Master of Holy Scripture and a layman identified only as the "Friend of God from the Bernese Highlands." The pair are often identified as the Dominican preacher Johannes Tauler, and his spiritual son and companion of the fourteenth-century merchant, religious convert, and theologian Rulman Merswin.[73] In most chapters the layman [*leie*] instructs and corrects the cleric [*pfaffe*], an antiecclesiastical tone common to late medieval books about the bride of Christ. In one chapter, the Master delivers a sermon to a cloister on the reading "Look, the bridegroom comes, Go out to meet him" (Matt 25:6). Explaining that he will be speaking in German, rather than in Latin, as only the clergy would understand Latin, the Master preaches, "Dirre brútegoume ist Cristus und menschliche nature ist die brut. Ach lieben kint, nuo heissent wir alle Cristus brute.... Lieben kint, sider wir nuo alle brute geheissen sint, so ist es guot das wir nuo ettewas sagent wie die brut tuon sol das sie dem brútegoume engegene

---

[72]   Annete Volfing, "Middle High German Appropriations of the Song of Songs: Allegorical Interpretation and Narrative Extrapolation," in *Perspectives on the Song of Songs. Beiheft zur Zeitschrift für die alttestamentliche Wissenschaft*, ed. Anselm Hagedorn (Berlin: De Gruyter, 2005), 303.

[73]   Authorship of the book was once attributed to Nicholas of Basel, though subsequent scholarship has posited that Rulman Merswin himself compiled the *Meisterbuch* to chronicle the founding history of the Friends of God movement. I have translated from Karl Schmidt, ed., *Nicolaus von Basel. Bericht von der Bekehrung Taulers* (Straßburg, 1875), 28–35. Early print editions of Tauler's work included the *Meisterbuch* and presented it as being about Tauler. At least 37 manuscript copies of the *Meisterbuch* survive. An extremely problematic nineteenth-century English paraphrase is available in Frances A. Bevan, *Three Friends of God: Records from the Lives of John Tauler, Nicholas of Basle, Henry Suso* (London: J. Nisbet, 1887). Bevan's bias cannot be understated, so let me quote directly: "We must remember also, that the nuns in the convent, to whom the Master was to preach, were not in his eyes, as in ours, poor misguided women, who were building up a tower of their own righteousness, and neglecting their natural duties. On the contrary, the Master really in his heart regarded them as persons who had professedly chosen the better part, and who belonged to God accordingly, in a special manner." It is not clear whether the sermon was preached to the women's community rather than the Dominican men's cloister. He had spent the previous day visiting brothers at the Dominican schoolhouse and invited a student preacher to attend the following day's sermon at a "closter,"—later, a "mensche" or person cries out—the sermon seems to have been delivered outside the church, whether the church of the men's or women's community, as the master then goes into the church to speak mass ["do gie derm meister in die kirche und sprach zuo stunt messe"].

gange" [The bridegroom is Christ and human nature is the bride. Ah Dear child, we are all called Christ's brides, ... dear child, because we are all called brides, it is good that we should say a little about how the bride should go out to meet the bridegroom]. The sermon details the qualities of the bride and groom and presents a dialogue between the two spouses. After the bride receives jewelry [*cleinoeter*] and gifts of suffering, the bridegroom asks her to commit fully to meet him in every fashion by receiving suffering and sorrow. The bride responds with terror [*erschricket die brut*] that she hopes her spouse will not be angry with her, and that she will be obedient and suffer gladly with his help. As the bridegroom prepares her for a martyr's death, the bride submits entirely to her spouse's desire, meets God the Father, and receives great gifts and uncontainable love. The preacher concludes that every person should prepare for their own coming wedding, pray to the Trinity, and find pleasure and comfort in the Holy Ghost.

According to this account, the preacher's sermon was dramatically disrupted and subsequently dissected by the congregation. As the preacher speaks the words, "The pleasure which the bride received from the most high bridegroom is so truly great that she can never grasp or attain it with reason," a person in the congregation shouted out loudly, "It is true, it is true, it is true!" and fell to the ground, just as if he were dead. The sermon is briefly interrupted by the commotion, until the preacher uses the drama to remind the congregation to prepare to meet their own spouse at death. After the sermon ends and the preacher says mass, a group of 12 or so, including Rulman's companion, and a nun [*closterfrouw*] returned to the courtyard to discuss the sermon. Even if the entire scene were a work of theological fiction, meant to bolster the reputation of the Friends of God, it idealizes how a sermon might move an entire community. To consider a convent an island, a sermon a static text, and a bride of Christ a quietly listening nun is to overlook the conversations and communities which centered around the courtyards of religious communities and the public squares outside cathedrals.

In fourteenth- and fifteenth-century Germany and the Low Countries, laymen and women encountered Jesus-as-bridegroom in devotional art, sermons, and books designed for or shared with women religious, and through sermons and public art, marrying Jesus reached even the illiterate and irreverent. Through the copying of books and manuscripts and the solicitation of sermons, the religious renewal of the convents became a religious renewal of the streets. The anonymous *Spiritual Spouseship* [*Gemahelschaft Christi mit der gläubigen Seele*] which only survives in manuscripts from women's communities, answered the question of which souls might wed God simply: "[T]he soul is a spouse for God and God a spouse for the soul."[74]

---

[74]   BSB CGM 516, 21rb –va. DMZ, http://daten.digitale-sammlungen.de/~db/0003/bsb00035383/images/, "hie ist ein frage ob got aller sele gesponsun seij vnd alle selen sein gesponsi sein ... Von der bewertten sach das die sele seij ein gesponns gottes vnnd got seij ein gespons der sele."

Chapter 3
Transmedia Stories of Jesus and the Loving Soul

> Therefore I ask that you, dear soul, and all of God's friends, spiritual and worldly, noble and common, women and men, or whoever they may be, who better themselves through this book's lessons: pray at the last most earnestly to God for a humble brother Otto of Passau, whether he is living or dead.[1]

The late medieval "Loving Soul" was a composite of the bride of the *Song of Songs*, the bride of the Lamb in *Revelation*, and the protagonists of courtly romance, who came to represent an individual Christian convert. In the last half of the twelfth century, a new genre of devotional books emerged which packaged essential information about creation, theology, and salvation within the loving Soul's marriage to Christ. By the fourteenth century, a relatively uniform master narrative had emerged: the "Loving Soul" is invited (by Christ or an angelic messenger) to marry Jesus, then learns how to serve her spouse while preparing for a wedding in heaven. This narrative mixed dialogue from the biblical books of *Psalms* and the *Song of Songs*, episodes from Christ's life, and passages from *Revelation* and the letters of Paul to build a mnemonic frame relating the bible to human morality. Undressing the bride, redressing her in a fine gown, crowning and placing a ring on her finger, and even the use of rope to bind the lovers together paralleled the closely related rituals of monastic initiation and secular marriage, and also recalled Christ's death on the cross. The bride of Christ became a pedagogic device for training new members of religious communities in twelfth-century Germany. By the fifteenth century, fragments from this narrative migrated to print, painting, song, and fashion. From these fragments, I first shall outline and then use the medieval master narrative of the bride and groom's courtship to reconstruct the

---

[1] "Dair nae so bydde ich mit allen vlijſſe vnd begerte mit allen mynen crafften dat du lieue sele vnd alle godes vrunde geystleichen vnd werltlichen, edel vnd onedel, vrouwen vnd man off wye sy synt die sich der lere dyß boichs gebeſſeren moegen endelich vnd ernstlich got oug mich bidden wyllen ich sy leuendich off doyt vur eynen oitmodelichen broder Otten van Passouwe ſent franciscus ordens wyllent leſmeyster zo Basel." Otto von Passau, *Die vierundzwanzig Alten, oder Der goldne Thron* (Cologne: Johann Koelhoff the Elder, May 26, 1492), A iii v. The same plea is present in most of the extant manuscripts. Wieland Schmidt, "Die vierundzwanzig Alten Ottos von Passau," *Palaestra*, no. 212 (1938): 28–9. It appears in one of the earliest extant manuscripts, numbered 24 in Schmidt's study, which was owned by Strasburg Dominicans and is now Hamburg University Library, MS theolog. 105. It also appears in the final chapter of the first Dutch print edition, *Boeck des gulden throens of der XXIV ouden* (Utrecht: [Drukker met het monogram], March 1480).

68 *Marrying Jesus in Medieval and Early Modern Northern Europe*

bride of Christ's transformation from virginal nun to lay sinner. Transmediation—the movement of a story or image from one media platform to another—occurred as teachers and marketers adapted the story of Christ's wedding for new audiences. I understand fixed details of the narrative to preserve a developing medieval consensus about Christ's wedding to the bride and idiosyncratic personalizations as responses to popular culture.

The static iconography of the crowned woman who simultaneously represented Ecclesia, the Virgin Mary, an individual saint, or a bridal soul recalled the bride's acquisition of those garments: the soul removed worldly clothing and was given jewelry and a fine dress to wear to her wedding. At the ceremony, she received a crown from her spouse. These sartorial items simultaneously evoked the real-world wedding dress, the iconography of the Virgin Mary, the tattered rags and fine jewels of the bride in the *Song of Songs*, and the celestial dress of the Woman of the Apocalypse. In the context of religious communities, this also evoked the change of clothing that accompanied monastic profession. The loving soul infrequently wore monastic habit in illustrated texts; more often, she or he was dressed in courtly attire.

Like the polysemous elements of a devotional image, each moment from this narrative conveyed multiple meanings. The static iconography of the crowned woman who simultaneously represented Ecclesia, the Virgin Mary, an individual saint, or a bridal soul recalled the bride's acquisition of those garments: the soul removed worldly clothing and was given gifts of jewelry and a fine dress to wear to her wedding. At the ceremony, she received a crown from her spouse. These sartorial items simultaneously evoked the real-world wedding dress, the iconography of the Virgin Mary, the tattered rags and fine jewels of the bride in the *Song of Songs*, and the celestial dress of the Woman of the Apocalypse. In the context of religious communities, this change of clothes also evoked the monastic habit received at profession. The religious habit sometimes appeared on the loving soul in a single copy of an illustrated manuscript, but the bride typically wore secular courtly attire. The garden was an enclosed convent, the paradise of heaven or the site of Christ's crucifixion on Calvary. Wine signified Christ's blood, a wedding toast, or the onset of spiritual drunkenness, the palace either the heavenly kingdom of Jerusalem or the soul's body. The bride's nakedness recalled the Disrobing of Christ before his death (or the nakedness of baptism or monastic profession ceremonies), her crown his crown of thorns, so that her spiritual exercises combined and the crucifixion with preparation for an ascent into heaven. At the end of lessons, the loving soul was dressed in new beautiful garments, bedecked with jewels, led by the hand before the throne of God, kissed, crowned, given a ring, and wed to the bridegroom. The couple embraced so that Christ's left hand was beneath the Soul's head or chin and his right arm embraced her, acting out *Song of Songs* 2:6, and spoke words echoing, "my beloved is mine and I am his" (*Song* 2:16). Following this marriage, the loving soul might be apportioned a share of her spouse's kingdom in heaven, enjoy a celebratory

Transmedia Stories of Jesus and the Loving Soul

feast (often with Eucharistic and Apocalyptic implications), or consummate the wedding.

Typical of this genre is Otto von Passau's *24 Elders or the Loving Soul Before the Golden Throne of God* [*Die vierundzwanzig Alten, oder der goldene Thron der minnenden Seele*], an illustrated theology textbook which assumed readers could situate the Soul's experiences within absent elements of a much larger narrative. Otto's book invites readers of every worldly station to take on the role of the "Loving Soul," a late medieval representation of the bride of Christ. Completed in German in 1386, perhaps for the Poor Clares of Königsfelden, the *24 Elders* invited discursive meditative reading. Regarded as one of the most widely transmitted German-language works of the medieval period, the *24 Elders* remained in print well into the nineteenth century and was read both within religious houses and among the laity.[2] Even the earliest manuscript copies include indices, tables of contents, and other aids for cross-referencing, and illustrated copies typically depicted the soul kneeling before a series of enthroned men. The "24 elders" and the "golden throne of God" reference the biblical books of *Ezekiel* and *Revelations*, connecting the book's lessons to the destruction of creation and the potential for humanity's eternal salvation. Each chapter opened with the soul meeting a new Elder, who explained a core principle of Christian thought with translated excerpts of Latin theology and Greek philosophy. Most of the 145 surviving manuscript copies and all print editions of Otto von Passau's *24 Elders* include the author's hope that those who use his book will be better able to pray for his soul. The book's content and structure, including its author's plea for prayers, remained intact in manuscripts designed for mealtime reading in religious houses, illuminated manuscripts for wealthy book collectors, and printed folio volumes. The first Dutch and German imprints appeared within 20 days of one another in 1480, both with woodcut illustrations. Yet the *24 Elders* offered little more to bind its chapters' excerpts from Latin theologians together than subheadings noting the Soul's position before a given Elder's throne.

Instructions in prayer techniques, sacramental theology, and biblical history often used familiar moments from a widely known master narrative about the courtship between Jesus and the Soul to create new edifying stories. Because audiences already knew the story well, authors could easily reinterpret

---

2   Schmidt identified 135 copies, seven of which have been lost since the Second World War. Several more manuscripts have since been identified. No tally of early printed editions is available. Very little provenance information is available for the print editions, although John Van Engen notes that one copy of the Dutch 1480 edition was owned by a lay sister of the Augustinian canoness house of Diepenveen, the founding female house of the Windesheim Congregation, the monastic branch of the *Devotio Moderna*. John H. Van Engen, *Sisters and Brothers of the Common Life: The Devotio Moderna and the World of the Later Middle Ages*, Middle Ages Series (Philadelphia: University of Pennsylvania Press, 2008), 33n9. *Die Deutsche Literatur Des Mittelalters: Verfasserlexikon*, ed. Wolfgang Stammler, Karl Langosch, and Kurt Ruh, 14 vols. (Berlin: De Gruyter, 1978–2008), vol. 11, 1153. Hereafter *Verfasserlexikon* or VL.

70   *Marrying Jesus in Medieval and Early Modern Northern Europe*

characterization and theology or add novel elements. For instance, the fifteenth-century *Christ and the Loving Soul* [*Christus und die minnende Seele*], an illustrated verse dialogue used by wealthy nuns and lay women, discouraged materiality with references to luxurious clothing and tables set with lavish feasts. Another fifteenth-century text, known as the *Spouseship of Christ* [*Gemahelschaft Christi mit der gläubigen Seele*], was used primarily in monastic communities where fasting and vegetarianism were common practices. In this text, feasting is a reward Christ served the bridal soul a rich feast of roast beef and grilled onions as part of her education; at the close of lessons she prepares a feast reenacting the Last Supper. In the late fifteenth century, widespread political and religious instability in Europe and the threat of the Ottoman army were viewed as portents of impending judgment, inspiring authors like Henry Pomerius to present celebratory meals as the apocalyptic wedding feast of the Lamb.

The books, paintings, songs, and images I discuss in this chapter demonstrate how marriages between Christ and the Loving Soul were typically catechetical, designed to teach basic theology to spiritual beginners. Of course, other medieval books about the bride of Christ were incomprehensible to anyone without extensive Latin and theological learning, but I focus here on examples which were demonstrably of interest to both lay and religious readers, and have been largely overlooked by historians of medieval Christianity. These sources show that between the twelfth and fifteenth centuries, medieval authors used a widely known master narrative about the bride of Christ to transmit preliminary lessons in serving and loving God to those newly converted to piety. Though they share storylines and protagonists, these texts differ significantly. While twelfth- and thirteenth-century authors were most interested in proscribing behavior, after the mid-thirteenth century, lessons increasingly focused on imitation of and empathy for the crucified Christ. By the fifteenth century, more manuals also linked the wedding itself to the end-times, often warning their readers to prepare their souls for an imminent judgment. Each depiction of the courtship and marriage between Christ and the soul reflected contemporary devotional trends, and respected a monastic tradition of instructional entertainment invented in the twelfth century.

Because the sources I discuss in this chapter are primarily undated anonymous works with very similar titles, I have listed those which have been translated, abridged, or significantly reformatted in a brief textual history in Table 3.1. In my discussion, I shall compare these diverse narratives to examine how specific moments such as dressing the bride develop to take on multiple equally valid theological meanings.

Table 3.1   Uniform Titles and Descriptions of Treatises About Christ and the Loving Soul

Abbreviated English title	Original Title(s)	Earliest dated copy (if known)	Brief Description
24 Elders	*Die vierundzwanzig alten oder der guldin Tron der minnenden seelen* (German, Manuscript and Print) *Boeck des gulden throens of der XXIV ouden* (Dutch, Manuscript and Print)	May 14, 1383, Karlsruhe Badische Landesbibliothek, cod. St. Georgen 64. Possibly originally from Freiburg im Breisgau? *erassimus hemelig hant genant von rotwil* (f. 226r)	Attributed to the Franciscan Otto von Passau. Compilation and commentary of approximately 100 Latin classical and theological works ranging from Cicero and Socrates to Augustine and Aquinas. Presented as a series of 24 chapters/lessons given by "Elders" to a "Loving Soul." Many copies are illustrated, including 41 extant manuscripts and all print editions published prior to 1500. Translation to Dutch c. 1448. First print edition: 1480; last known printed edition: 1836.
Art of Spiritual Living	*Buch der Kunst, dadurch der weltlich Mensch mag geistlich werden* (German Print editions only); *Büchlein von der geistlichen Gemahelschaft* (Manuscript copies only); *De Gheestelycke Bruyloft Tvsschen Godt Ende Onse Natvre, Verclarenden Hoe Seer Dat Ons Van Noode Is Het Cieraet Der Liefden, En Alle Deuchden, Om Tot De Bruyloft in Te Gaen*		A 6,525 line poem in rhyming couplets composed—according to an attribution in a prose print adaptation—by Konrad of Spitzer (perhaps of the Franciscan community of the Holy Cross in Vienna). The verse version is dated to between 1365 and 1385 and probably addressed a lay courtly audience. The prose version was probably created between 1418 and 1430, as part of an observant reform movement centered on the Benedictine house of Melk. Both versions teach sacramental theology, sins, the biblical narrative, and acts of grace through an allegorical account of a young woman preparing for marriage to god. An illustrated prose version appeared in the last quarter of the fifteenth century in both print and manuscript. Nine manuscript copies survive, dating between 1386 and 1517. The print edition was dedicated to the humanist author and dowager empress Eleonora of Scotland. An illustrated print edition was issued four times before 1500 in Augsburg. A Dutch translation was printed in 1657 by Jan van Gorcum.

Table 3.1 *continued*			
Book of Perfection (ps. Engelhart von Ebrach/ Engelhart of Eberbach)	*Das Buch der Vollkommenheit*	c. 1350, BSB CGM 181 or BSB CGM 172, both mid-fourteenth century	A compilation of 250 numbered short sayings, legends, and religious poems, including excerpts from the writings of Meister Eckhart, Berthold of Regensburg, St. Bernard of Clairvaux, Ambrose of Milan, Thomas Aquinas, Jerome, and Mechthild of Magdeburg. The collection was attributed to a brother Eberhart or Engelhart of Eberbach. As many as 109 copies survive from the fourteenth and fifteenth centuries.
Christ and the Loving Soul	*Christus und die minnende seele*	Mainz, Stadtbibliothek, MS I 221, third quarter of the fourteenth century	An illustrated dialogue between Jesus and a Soul in which the soul is disciplined, crucified, and then pursues and binds Jesus prior to their final unitive kiss. Several versions survive, including an illustrated picture cycle with brief rhyming couplets, a Latin version, and a long illustrated poem. The longest verse version borrows from a satirical anti-marriage poem known as the *Teufels Netz*. The dialogue survives in manuscript, single sheet woodcut, and printed book. Three of the four surviving manuscript copies originate in fifteenth-century Constance, although print editions from the same period were produced as far north as Erfurt.
Exercises on the Pater Noster	*Exercitium Super Pater Noster*		A Dutch and Latin meditative lesson on the lines of the *Pater Noster/ Our Father*. The treatise has been attributed to Henricus Pomerius/ Hendrik vanden Boemgaert, who likely designed the image sequence for the blockbook versions after writing longer Latin and Dutch prose works on the prayer. Two blockbook editions survive from Netherlandish workshops, the second of which is attributed to Vrancke van der Stockt. There are also single-sheet woodcuts, including one in German.
Garden of Devotion	*Le Jardin amoureux*; *Thoofkijn van devotien*	BNFr MS Français 1026, mid-fifteenth century	The story of a wandering female soul who finds an Abbey and is educated by personified virtues and Christ as Wisdom. Probably written between 1410 and 1420 by Pierre d'Ailly; French and Dutch print editions were commissioned by the Bruges courtier and book collector Lodewijk van Gruuthusein, who also likely owned an illuminated manuscript copy, BNFr MS F1026. The Dutch printed books are illustrated with 16 woodcuts.

Table 3.1 *continued*			
Love Bears a Cross	*Kreutztragende Minne*; *Jesus und die Braut*; *Nonnenlehre*; *Die Innige Seele*		A loosely related group of fifteenth-century verse dialogues between Jesus and a Soul who is reluctant to be crucified. The southern version, known as *Kreutztragende Minne*, survives in middle high German, and a second group, known as *Jesus und die Braut* in middle low German and middle Dutch and was sometimes set to music. The middle high german version was reworked into the *Nonnenlehre*, a 20-strophe poem about cloister life, as well as into *Die Innige Seele*, an 18-strophe adaptation. *Jesus und die Braut* is a 9-part dialogue between the pair which would be translated into Dutch and Middle German. Several surviving copies are illustrated; most depict Jesus and the female Soul walking together, each carrying a cross. In some images, the soul is dressed as a lay woman, in others as a nun.
Mirror for Maidens	*Speculum Virginum, Maechden Spieghel, Spieghel der Maechden, Jungfruspegel, Jungfrauspiegel, Jungfrauwen-spiegel*	British Library Arundel 44, c. 1145	An illustrated dialogue explaining theology, history, philosophy, and classical literature. Some early copies also include an antiphonal choral work. Claims to have been written by a confessor for his nieces. Translated into Swedish, German, Dutch, and Low German. Remained in print until the seventeenth century. 36 Latin, 13 Low German, 6 middle Dutch, and 1 middle Swedish manuscripts survive. Most surviving manuscripts date to the fifteenth century.
Mirror of Perfection	*Spieghel der Volcomenheit, Spiegel der Vollkommenheit, Directorium Aureum contemplativorum*	Leiden University Library, LTK 1129, c. 1462.	Originally written in Dutch by Hendrik Herp (OFM), translated into German, Latin, Italian, and Spanish. First printed in 1501, first Latin edition 1513.
Spiritual Loveletter	*Den gheesteliken minnenbrief die Jesus Christus sendet tot synre bruyt*		Survives in at least three sixteenth-century manuscripts and several print editions from print shops in Antwerp, Leiden, and Delft. All have been tentatively dated to between 1486 and 1496 but it is not clear which one is the earliest. The earliest known manuscript, Edinburgh University Library MS 65 f.017r-029r (dating to c. 1516), was copied from an incunable.

Table 3.1 continued			
Spiritual Melody	Geestelijke lied; Die Gheestelicke Melody	Leiden University Library, Ltk 2058 c. 1470	A Dutch and Low German song cycle on the soul's marriage to God and Christ's life and crucifixion. Some of the surviving manuscripts are illustrated. Several of the songs would be reproduced in printed books into the seventeenth century. Some copies of the cycle include the Low German version of "Love Bears a Cross."
Spiritual Spouseship	Gemahelschaft Christi mit der gläubigen Seele	Harburg, Fürstliche OEttingen-Wallersteinische Bibliothek cod. III. 1.2 * 5. 1413	Chapters on catechism, exegesis, virtues, and cloistered living; frequently references the bride of Christ. Most surviving copies date to the second half of the fifteenth century and were owned by women's religious communities. This anonymous text was probably composed between 1379 (the year of the founding of the Bridgittine order) and 1413, the date of the earliest manuscript. The latest copy dates to 1664 (BSB CGM 3853) At least 16 copies survive from the fifteenth century.
Trudpert Song of Songs	St. Trudperter Hohes Lied	Nuremburg, Germanisches Nationalmuseum 42518 (2 leaves) First half of the twelfth century	A mid-twelfth-century German verse commentary on the Song of Songs presenting itself as written by a confessor for a women's community. Cites Honorius Augustodunensis and William of St. Thierry. Incorporated into Dutch and German sermon cycles in the thirteenth and fourteenth centuries.

Where a scholarly convention exists already for a nontranslated text, as in German texts entered in the *Verfasserlexikon*, I have translated that title into English, only substituting a different title when a simple translation might cause confusion. Thus *Christ and the Loving Soul* [*Christus und die minnende Seele*] but *The Art of Spiritual Living* [*Büchlein von der geistlichen Gemahelschaft / De Gheestelycke Bryyloft Tysschen Godt Ende Onse Natvre / Buch der Kunst, dadurch der weltlich Mensch mag geistlich werden*], to differentiate between this book and the *Spiritual Spouseship*. In cases where a text is known by different titles in different languages, I have opted to translate the title into English even if scholarly convention has been to use the Latin (e.g. *Mirror for Maidens* rather than *Speculum Virginum*). I do not include texts with a single known author or title, even when they have been translated and adapted to other media (such as the writing of Henry Suso or Mechthild of Magdeburg).

Transmedia Stories of Jesus and the Loving Soul 75

This ensemble of distinct texts with near-identical titles creates an illusion of homogeneity and enormous potential for confusion. Karin Schneider stresses in an entry in the *Verfasserlexikon* that the *Büchlein von der geistlichen Gemahelschaft* attributed to Konrad von Spitzer is entirely different from [*vollig verschieden von*] the near-contemporary *Gemahelschaft Christi mit der gläubigen Seele*.[3] This confusion—not just between the two books she addresses, but the surviving corpus of songs, books, and poems about Christ marrying a loving soul—has been partially created by cataloguing practices and exacerbated by the sheer number of distinct medieval narratives about Christ and the loving soul. Artists and authors adjusted depictions the soul's marriage to Christ for particular audiences; each variant reflects regionalized contemporary religious trends.

Transmediation in Monastic Devotion Manuals

Across northern Europe in the late twelfth and early thirteenth centuries, clerics composed instructional literature intended to guide and to protect women religious. These manuals typically explained communal obligations and behavioral expectations through the narrative of a protagonist-soul's training and progress from spiritual beginner to bride in heaven. Though most of these twelfth-century books were particularly concerned with female chastity, following the reforms of the Lateran Councils, this narrative was adapted to teach the laity about sin, salvation, and sacramental theology. Barbara Newman argues that this formational literature, written by men for twelfth-century women religious, used antifeminist constructions of female piety and sexuality. By placing a disproportionate value on intact virginity, most of these authors advertised Christ as a better husband than anyone a "nubile virgin" might find on earth.[4] Two south German books belonging to this group were more interested in theological and moral education than chastity. They introduced the use of the soul's marriage to Christ to explain the individual's position in creation and would be read and adapted for lay use into the sixteenth century. Composed between 1140 and 1160 in the Black Forest region of southern Germany, the *Mirror for Maidens* [*Speculum Virginum*] and the *St. Trudpert Song of Songs* [*St. Trudperter Hohes Lied*] both purport to have been written by men for women, though their manuscript traditions, illustrations, and content complicate the gender(s) of author, protagonists, and audience. Both texts acknowledged that

---

[3]   VL, vol. 2, 1190.

[4]   Newman, *From Virile Woman to WomanChrist*, 31. This development may also be related to a push to produce vernacular translations of the *Song of Songs*. An Old French reworking of the *Song of Songs* also dates to this period, but its provenance and relationship to the German adaptations or the Latin commentaries are uncertain. It was probably but not definitively written by a lay poet for use at court. Cedric Edward Pickford, *The Song of Songs: A Twelfth-Century French Version* (London: Oxford University Press, 1974). Anne Savage and Nicholas Watson, *Anchoritic Spirituality: Ancrene Wisse and Associated Works* (New York: Paulist Press, 1991); Vera Morton, *Guidance for Women in Twelfth-Century Convents* (Rochester, NY: Boydell and Brewer, 2004).

76   *Marrying Jesus in Medieval and Early Modern Northern Europe*

chastity was not the best or only path to salvation by making the courtship between Christ and the Soul into a form of *imitatio Christi* that taught the history of creation. By explaining the obligations of monastic life and the central mysteries of Christian thought through the domestic rituals of contemporary lay society, the *Mirror for Maidens* and the *St. Trudpert Song of Songs* created an educational device that would influence readers far beyond the convents of southern Germany.

Both books are multimedia (using different narrative techniques and mediums to tell a story) and transmedia (adapted, excerpted, and reformatted as their stories were adapted to new media platforms). The Latin *Mirror for Maidens*, an illustrated dialogue between Peregrinus, the male teacher, and his always-questioning student, Theodora, used novel musical techniques, complex diagrams, and references to classical literature to explain not just the obligations of a bride of Christ but the full history and theological significance of the created universe. The Middle High German *Trudpert Song of Songs* is a verse exegesis, commentary, and vocal performance of the lines of the *Song of Songs*. Both the *Mirror for Maidens* and the *Trudpert Song of Songs* are dialogues blending prose, poetry, and song, and both developed liturgical applications: portions of the *Trudpert Song* would be used in Dutch and German sermon collections, while the *Mirror for Maidens'* choral *Epithalamium* perhaps was performed during ceremonies of religious profession.

In recent studies, the *Mirror for Maidens* is presented as a protofeminist work concerned with the education of women, while the *Trudpert Song of Songs* is typically read as an erotic meditative piece performed by choir nuns.[5] Both are linked to the vibrant women's monastic communities associated with the twelfth-century Hirsau reform, an observant movement of the Benedictine order which supported women's houses and double monasteries. The *Mirror for Maidens* may be the work of Conrad of Hirsau, a musician, poet, and instructor of novices at the Benedictine abbey of Hirsau.[6] Written within 15 years of the *Mirror for Maidens*, the *Trudpert Song* was once attributed to the abbess Herrad von Hohenburg, but

---

[5]   The two works are sometimes paired as representative of the mid-twelfth-century *curia monialium* or pastoral care for women religious. See especially Urban Küsters, *Der Verschlossene Garten: Volkssprachliche Hohelied-Auslegung Und Monastische Lebensform Im 12. Jahrhundert*, Studia Humaniora, Bd. 2 (Düsseldorf: Droste, 1985); Hildegard Elisabeth Keller, *Wort und Fleisch: Körperallegorien, mystische Spiritualität und Dichtung des St. Trudperter Hoheliedes im Horizont der Inkarnation* (Frankfurt am Main; New York: P. Lang, 1993); Constant J. Mews, ed., *Listen, Daughter: The Speculum Virginum and the Formation of Religious Women in the Middle Ages*, The New Middle Ages (New York: Palgrave, 2001); Regine Hummel, *Mystische Modelle im 12. Jahrhundert: St. Trudperter Hoheslied, Bernard von Clairvaux, Wilhelm von St. Thierry* (Göppingen: Kümmerle, 1989); Matthäus Bernards, *Speculum Virginum; Geistigkeit und Seelenleben der Frau im Hochmittelalter*, 2.unveränderte Aufl. ed. Beihefte Zum Archiv Für Kulturgeschichte, Heft 16 (Köln: Böhlau, 1955).

[6]   The fifteenth-century humanist abbot Johannes Trithemius first attributed the *Mirror for Maidens* to Conrad of Hirsau, but authorship for both books remains unresolved. Jutta Seyfarth, ed., *Speculum Virginum*, Corpus Christianorum Continuatio Medievalis (hereafter CCCM) (Turnholti: Brepols, 1990), 33–7. Küsters, *Der Verschlossene Garten*, 60.

Transmedia Stories of Jesus and the Loving Soul   77

has since been linked to the literary and scribal center of the double monastery of Admont. Its name is borrowed from an early manuscript copy from the Hirsau-affiliated abbey of St. Trudpert in Munstertal. Neither text explicitly follows the master narrative's trajectory, but both cite elements of that narrative not found in the *Song of Songs*, such as the bride's use of the mirror, the wedding gift or dowry, and the teacher's letter to his student.

An introductory epistle to the *Mirror for Maidens* explains, "I have sent you a little book as a kind token of mutual love. In it you may exercise your mind [and] grow in the grace of the eternal bridegroom."[7] The closing epistle to the *Trudpert Song* identifies the commentary as "a lesson in the recognition of God. The bride of the almighty God should have this book as her mirror, and diligently keep her gaze on it [the mirror], so that she can please her bridegroom, because he is always gazing on her with loving eyes ... from this letter you should learn to recognize the Spouses of the Almighty God, that they have this [these characteristics] or that they eagerly strive to obtain them."[8] Both brides gather flowers, experience Christ's crucifixion, then journey to heaven to receive kiss, crown, and wedding gown before the throne of God.

Although few manuscripts contain the complete 12 chapters of the book with concluding epithalamium, the intact conclusion to the *Mirror for Maidens* is a perfectly choreographed narrative of the Soul's marriage to God. At the close of the dialogue's final chapter, Theodora proposes a song to celebrate the union of bride and bridegroom.[9] The wedding song or *Epithalamium*, which survives in three twelfth-century manuscripts originating in male religious houses, takes the form of a call and response between two choirs which juxtapose the bridal pair's violent battle during the Apocalypse with their luxurious preparations for a marriage in the heavenly kingdom. As the A choir describes the preparations of a rosy-pink eternal palace of heaven, the B choir's bride is at war. The two choruses' narratives overlap only during the description of the bride's wedding dress, when each contributes details about color, fabric, and accessories. The A Choir's couple then enters their new home: at its center is a burning fire of love, from which flows a stream of mercy. There, Christ lays out a new set of treasures, intended for the city dwellers who had been lost to him until the moment he wed his new bride. The B choir sings: "The heavenly choirs rejoice for the virgin who will be made rich with this wedding gift," human salvation.[10] The bride is strewn with flowers, presented a laurel wreath signifying her many victories in battle, and festively

---

[7]   When available and accurate I have used Barbara Newman's translations in *Listen, Daughter*, 269–96. I have otherwise translated from Seyfarth's Latin critical edition, hereafter abbreviated SV. I note Newman's translations where I have used them as Newman, SV, and when I have translated from Seyfarth's edition, I cite Seyfarth, SV. Seyfarth, SV, 2; Newman, SV, 270.

[8]   Friedrich Ohly and Nicola Kleine, *Das St. Trudperter Hohelied: eine Lehre der liebenden Gotteserkenntnis* (Frankfurt am Main: Deutscher Klassiker Verlag, 1998), 306, 13. All translations from this edition are based on the Middle High German.

[9]   Seyfarth, SV, 364.

[10]   Ibid., 366–7.

adorned with jewels and fine clothing made of muslin dyed in saffron, among the finest luxury fabrics brought back from the crusades.[11] The A Choir's loving couple consummates their wedding as the B Choir's bride arrives in a paradise, as gentle winds blow through the grass of a paradise garden, and a chorus of virgins welcomes her into the kingdom of her beloved. The B choir describes the story of the bride's battles against sin after she joins Christ the lamb and rides out to the War of the Apocalypse against the A choir's account of Christ's preparations for the bride, their marriage, and their union, through which Christ will gain his bride's kingdom. The written verses also spell out acrostic messages praising the Virgin Mary and paraphrasing the Vulgate's setting of the *Song of Songs*. These choral exchanges superimposed the salvation narrative of Christ's battle with the devil and future Judgment onto the daily struggles of individuals, tempted into sin before being welcomed into heaven, and the collective challenges of the Church against the sins of the world.[12]

According to musicologist Catherine Jeffreys, this choral setting represents a twelfth-century innovation in psalmody which served distinct liturgical purposes in each of the monastic houses to which a manuscript can be traced.[13] The closing chorus draws together every possible interpretation of the bride of Christ: she is each chorist, the dialogue's Theodora and Peregrinus, the reader, the bride of the Apocalypse, the Virgin Mary, the church in glory, and its newest converts. As an individual sinner, the bride battles against evil in the world and aids the cause of heaven in the cosmic battle with the devil. As an elect lover of the King of Heaven, she brings to her own people a special gift of salvation. In her role as the Church, she foretells the salvation of the community of burghers in the heavenly kingdom. As Mary, she gives birth to the hope of salvation, and in her guise as bride of the Lamb, she helps bring about the eternal heavenly Kingdom. Those seeking to marry Jesus ensured their personal salvation and helped redeem their other believers. These verses would also have reminded monastic choirs of their own vows of profession.

In the *Trudpert Song*, the bride's first crowning banishes the devil and relieves her from all suffering.[14] Later, the bride is redeemed by Christ's death on the cross.[15] In addition to jewels and clothes signifying virtue and protection, Christ transfers a portion of divine power through the groom's gift, explicitly identified as a *morgengabe* or dowry. The *Trudpert Song* also records an "andere brûtlouften"

---

[11]   Ibid., 368–9.

[12]   Ibid., 365–76. I cite the A choir's use of *civibus*, SV, 367, strophe 30; 370, strophe 63.

[13]   Catherine Jeffreys, "'Listen, Daughters of Light': The *Epithalamium* and Musical Innovation in Twelfth-Century Germany," in *Listen, Daughter*, ed. Constant J. Mews, The New Middle Ages (New York: Palgrave, 2001), 138–41.

[14]   Ohly, *Hohelied-Studien*, 132–3.

[15]   In a gloss on the Chariots of Amindab, the *Trudpert Song* reminds the spouse that obedience to Christ and gratitude for his death and the vanquishing of the devil will warm every heart and purify even the most polluted. Ohly and Kleine, *Das St. Trudperter*, 220–23.

Transmedia Stories of Jesus and the Loving Soul 79

[second wedding], the "aller beste brûtloufte" [very best wedding] when the bride receives dowry, crown, and a portion of Christ's saving power:

> Just as when a rich man weds a wife he grants her his worldly wealth, even if she is poor and noble, she arouses his pity, [so] he sends her his gifts, and thus it is with our own Spouse. He knows well how noble our soul really is. He knows very well how poor she is. For you he redeems her. He sends her his wedding treasure [*mahelschatz*].

With this gift, the devil is vanquished and the bride's heart is filled with faith. Bound to Christ "like man and wife," her mind's eye sees the Throne of the Most High. Filled with fear, she turns herself over to holy matters.[16] Following the second wedding, the bride, elected by God, enlightened by the son, adorned by the Holy Spirit, comforts souls lost to sin. Christ leads her through the desert of the world, a desert of iniquity, mirroring his own hermetic exile and the wandering years of the Exodus. She guides home the banished and enslaved, consoling the humble and the weeping, calling the hopeless back again, freeing the fettered of their chains, standing alongside the sinners, bringing joy to those who sorrow, and suffering with those in agony. She, like Christ, is guilty with the sinners and becomes absolution for the penitent. Her fragrance fills the desert of the world, and, as the verse concludes, *this*, her fragrance, her saving power, is the special assistance God grants souls he elects to wed.[17]

The *Trudpert Song*'s final act of courtship depicts a moment of communal redemption following the bride's liberation from bodily desires (as if in death). After converting to and learning to accept the sensation of God's presence, the bride truly learns the nature of her lover:

> ... when the flesh begins to cool
> and the spirit begins to warm.
> That is to say: when the wanton love cools in you
> and the love for eternal life heats you up,
> As hot wrath cools within you
> then love for your neighbor is kindled in you;
> Just as the heat of unchastity cools in you,
> And your love of God's spirit, your one true spouse [*karle*], burns intensely in you.
> That true husband is
> Your creator
> Your redeemer
> Your lover.[18]

The bride's body falls into irrelevance as her soul inflames with love, and the heat of passionate love for Christ culminates in the realization of the Beloved's nature:

---

[16]   Ibid., 42–7.

[17]   I have summarized, rather than translating the verses. Ibid., 102–5.

[18]   Ibid., 307–8.

Figure 3.1 *God sends his messengers, Buch der Kunst, dadurch der weltlich Mensch mag geistlich werden*. Augsburg: Johann Bämler, 1477, a 4 r RB 85766. Reproduced by permission of The Huntington Library, San Marino, California.

He redeems those he has created with his unstoppable cleansing love. Redemption depended only on the love of Christ, the true spouse whose love triumphs over bodily desires.

By using the exegetic identities of the bride of Christ as Church, Virgin Mary, and Human Soul to inspire individuals to merit their betrothals to God, the *Mirror for Maidens* and the *St. Trudpert Song of Songs* introduced the possibility that education and devotional practices could make brides of Christ. Within the limited definition of "successful" measured by manuscript circulation, translation, and uncredited reproduction, these books and their notion that study, rather than chastity, made brides of Christ would remain influential across Northern Europe into the sixteenth century. Transposing the practices of biblical exegesis onto monastic instructional literature had several unintended consequences in the late medieval period: the courtship of Christ and the Soul was now part of the history of creation, and thus also of Christ's own life and message, and the history of every person, living and dead. The love and longing of the bride and bridegroom would merge with the love and sacrifice of Christ on the cross and the human's desire for rest in a heavenly paradise, making marriage to Jesus an integral part of personal salvation.

The twelfth-century *Mirror for Maidens* and *Trudpert Song of Songs* introduced a new mode of Christian education appropriate for readers of all social stations. Their dialogue format, melodic elements, and promise that every reader could become a bride of Christ would be recreated in dozens of Dutch and German works authored between the twelfth and fifteenth centuries.

Citing the Master Narrative

In the twelfth century, the courtship between Jesus and the Soul became a tool to entertain and educate. As examples from the *St. Trudpert Song* and the *Mirror for Maidens* show, this master narrative blended elements from the *Song of Songs*, scriptural citations to books of the New Testament, and medieval courtship practices. These elements remained so central to the bride's story that references to mirrors, letters, and other elements external to the *Song of Songs* still reminded readers of the bride of Christ. For instance, mirrors became visual references to the bride's story in illustrated fifteenth-century books. In Konrad Spitzer's *Art of Spiritual Living* [*Büchlein von der geistlichen Gemahelschaft / Buch der Kunst, dadurch der weltlich Mensch mag geistlich werden*], the soul views the story of creation through a mirror, and the fifteenth-century Dutch printed book *The Garden of Devotion* [*thoofkijn van devotie*] depicts the soul contemplating Christ's death on Calvary through a mirror. Viewing God through a mirror or glass also alluded to 1 Corinthians 13 and, by the thirteenth century, also signified the relationship between human and divine, created and creator.[19]

The master narrative also borrowed from secular medieval romances and marriage practices, including the exchange of love letters, ritual bathing, dancing, feasting, the adorning of the bride, and gifts presented to the bride following the marriage ceremony. The *Trudpert Song* and the *Mirror for Maidens* had included a letter from their authors inviting the reader to apply the book's lessons to self-betterment and depict the bridegroom reaching out to his chosen spouse, singling her out among many others for her special beauty. By the late fifteenth century, introductory letters represented an individual's renewed commitment to their Christian faith. Konrad of Spitzer's *The Art of Spiritual Living* opens as an enthroned God the Father charges his angelic messengers to travel his kingdom with sealed letters inviting virgins [*iunckfrawen*] to join him as spouses in heaven (Figure 3.1). Six young women reject God's invitation and meet unfortunate fates. When the angelic messengers ask the seventh virgin if she is willing to love God above all things, her pious "yes" is amplified by an illustration of the failed brides falling into hell. The seventh virgin soon appears at church to hear a sermon

---

[19] The mirror also signified vanity and was associated with the exchange of gifts in secular courtship. Camille, *The Medieval Art of Love*, 45–7.

Figure 3.2   *The Soul at the altar with Christ as Man of Sorrows, Buch der Kunst, dadurch der weltlich Mensch mag geistlich werden.* Augsburg: Johann Bämler, 1477, c 8 v RB 85766. Reproduced by permission of The Huntington Library, San Marino, California.

and begin her lessons. There she is guided from the altar through a gate of grace [*gnaden einfarrt*] by her spouse, Christ, who appears and embraces her as the Man of Sorrows (Figure 3.2).[20] This mediated communication between the soul and her divine spouse establishes the tone of the treatise. This bride will be prepared by angels and other brides of Christ before at last meeting God.

Angelic messengers blended biblical and secular references, citing the iconography of the Annunciation, and the letters and "complaints" sent by a lover to his lady via an emissary in courtly romance. A fifteenth-century Dutch letter addressed by the crucified Christ to a wayward bride interested in worldly suitors blends these motifs in the prefatory image to its print editions. The *Spiritual Loveletter* [*Den gheesteliken minnenbrief die Jesus Christus sendet tot synre bruyt*] may be related to a Middle High German letter addressed to God's Lover,

---

[20] *Buch der Kunst, dadurch der weltlich Mensch mag geistlich werden* (Augsburg: Johann Bämler, 1477).

Transmedia Stories of Jesus and the Loving Soul

catalogued as *sendbrief: ach ir gottes minnerin*. The opening lines of the text suggest the soul has broken her gaze away from Christ: "Jesus Christ, King of Heaven and Earth sends my bride the loving soul friendly greetings," the letter begins, but Christ soon turns to serious matters. "Your heart is turning again to transitory things," he scolds, "but no man will ever feel as much love for you as I do, I always have my eyes on you." As Christ watches the bride, he sees how unfaithful she has been and laments, "[B]ecause of this I am miserable ...!"[21] He requests she invite him back into her soul and take up her own cross again by attending mass daily, saying the hours, and reading only that which is "good for her soul" (not secular love letters). The letter closes with a warning and a comforting reminder: the apocalypse approaches, but Christ will come in an instant if his beloved shouts his name.

Govert van Ghemen's 1496 imprint and Christian Snellaert's 1491 imprint of the *Loveletter* both include a prefatory woodcut depicting a recipient of the letter in a garden kneeling in prayer before a Christchild framed by the branches of a dry tree or thorn bush (Figure 3.3).[22] A copy of Govert van Ghemen's edition now held by Cambridge Library has been colored in green, red, and brown, likely by the original owner. The prefatory image poses the bride as intently focused on her prayer to a beaming Christchild the very moment she receives her spouse's letter. The Christchild blesses her and shows his wounds, as if he were not the bitterly disappointed author of the letter. Instead, the prefatory image's prioritizing of the bride's demure prayer, her knees touching the earth in a display of humility, and the Christchild's tranquil gesture of forgiveness seem to show the end and the beginning of the story at once, as if to reassure the reader that the letter's cause for complaint will be quickly corrected. As these illustrated books show, only a few narrative cues could transform a devotional lesson into a story about the bride of Christ.

---

[21] "Ihesus cristus coninc des hemels ende der eerden seyndt mijnder bruyt der minnender zielen vriendelike groete. Hertelike gheminde dochter wt groter begheerten uwer salicheyt scrive ick nu tot u want al spreke ic v dicwijls toe int heymeliken, ghi en achtes niet vele, oftoeck ghi en houdt mi gheen sprake. Mij dunct dat u herte al meer geneycht is tot wtweyndighen dinghen ende tot quader ghenoechlijker vrientscap van creaturen dan tot mi. Ic en can u niet verbergen die heymelike vrientscap die ick tot u hebbe. Noyt mensche en mocht so grote minne ghevoelen tot synen kijnderen magen ofte vrienden als ic tot u dragen. Waer ghi gaet oft sy oft wat ghi doet, altijt dae ick mijn oghen op u Och dan mishaget mi alte seere al sic yersye aen u dat onghetrouwe schijnt te mij waerts ..." (aiir–v). "Want ic scamel ben ende daer omme so scame ick mi bi u te comen als ghi mit wtwendighen dingen of mit eenigerhande ydelheit becommert syt meer dan u bevolen is" (aiir).

[22] Snellaert's artist depicts the bride holding the letter, van Ghemen's shows an angel flying down from heaven to deliver the message, and neither cut is clearly copied from the other or from a shared exemplar. The thorny frame maybe related to the seal of the Confraternity of the Dry Tree, which depicts the Madonna and Christchild in a dead tree, as in Petrus Christus's *Madonna of the Dry Tree*. Hugo van der Velden, "Petrus Christus's Our Lady of the Dry Tree," *Journal of the Warburg and Courtauld Institutes* 60 (1997): 89–110.

Figure 3.3   Title page, *Den gheesteliken minnenbrief die Jesus Christus sendet tot synre bruyt*. Leiden: Govert van Ghemen, c. 1495, a i r. Cambridge University Library Inc.6.E.102[3117].

Becoming Jesus

In the fourteenth and fifteenth centuries, Christ's life was interpolated into the bride's story, so that the bride experienced Jesus's execution, and Jesus's biography sometimes ended with his marriage in heaven. The illustrated early fifteenth-century vernacular poem *Christ and the Loving Soul* [*Christus und die minnende Seele*] begins in a bedroom, where the soul prays for guidance: she is in love with a man and considering marriage. As her guardian angel looks on, she announces that should she come to rue her earthly marriage she will redevote herself to God. In the middle of the night, Christ wakes her from bed to explain that he would be a far more pleasant groom. At the close of this chapter, the soul at last concedes that marriage to Christ would be preferable to the life of suffering and servitude that is, apparently, earthly marriage.[23] But as she falls back into sleep, Jesus warns the soul that she will have to "take up the cross and learn to die ... to enter the Holy Spirit's realm," foreshadowing her long and sometimes painful lessons in self-martyrdom.[24] In subsequent chapters, the soul will learn hard lessons in love, experiencing extreme physical brutality before becoming pure enough to wed Christ. Four surviving manuscript copies depict Christ standing by the soul's bedside in a teaching pose, while the same scene in the heavily abridged printed book and blockbook versions represent the soul's difficult path visually. In Wolfgang Schenck's 1499 printed edition of *Christ and the Loving Soul*, which replaces almost all of the poem's narrative with theological commentary, a woodcut illustration shows Jesus pulling the naked crowned soul's hair as she reclines in bed (Figure 3.4). The exaggerated violence of Jesus's gesture preserves the violence accompanying the soul's transformation absent in the accompanying text. Medieval readers would have understood these illustrations without explanatory text—they had already internalized the theological certainty that Christ's love, which cleansed sin, was available to every penitent who accepted his hand in marriage. But the path to that wedding was laborious, and no bride traveled it alone.

When Christ dressed a bride for marriage, the change of clothing might be an intimate striptease, or an embarrassing assault recreating the Disrobing from the Passion. In the *Trudpert Song*, Christ in the guise of the Gardener (John 20:15) dresses the bride with jewels of virtues and clothing cut from scripture, replacing her fleshly girdle with a spiritual girdle of praise, making the worldly bride into a spiritual Christlike being.[25] The *Spouseship of Christ* similarly proposed that the

---

[23]   On the relationship between these lines and the satirical *Teufel's Netzt* see Romuald Banz, *Christus und die Minnende Seele: zwei spätmittelhochdeutsche mystische Gedichte* (Hildesheim: G. Olms, 1977), 124–40; Hildegard Elisabeth Keller, "Die minnende Seele in des Teufels Netz. Geschlechterpolemik kontrafaziert," in *Text im Kontext: Anleitung zur Lektüre deutscher Texte der frühen Neuzeit*, ed. Alexander Schwarz and Laure Ablanalp (Bern: Lang, 1997), 109–26.

[24]   Banz, *Christus und die minnende Seele*, 267.

[25]   Ohly and Kleine, *Das St. Trudperter*, 260.

Figure 3.4 *Christ wakes the Soul, Von der ynnigen selen wy sy gott casteyet vnnd im beheglich mach.* Erfurt: Wolfgang Schenck, 1499, a iii r. Biblioteka Uniwersytecka we Wrocławiu, XV.Q.329.

soul would take on Christ's qualities as he dressed her in kingly clothes.[26] The soul is first arrayed before the throne of God; several chapters later, the allegoric meaning of her attire becomes clear. Christ first wrapped the soul in a triple cloth [*dreyerley claider*] of labor, shame, and grace.[27] This was covered with another layered garment of guiltlessness and chaste living covered with a long dress woven from humility. Finally the soul was granted a cloak of virtues which protected against evil, "vnd mit dem wurt er xpi gelich" [and with this he was like Christ].[28]

The bride's change of clothing often involved nudity or shame. Wearing an invisible garment made of virtues or of Jesus himself exposed both skin and soul.

---

[26] I transcribe this passage from the 1499 manuscript copied by Johannes Ruff of Inglestadt for the Cistercian sisters at Neuberg (f. 319ra: *von mir Johannes Ruff die zeitt wonnhaft zw Inglstadtdie zeitt wonnhaft zw Inglstadt*), now owned by the Bavarian State Library. BSB CGM 7241, MDZ, http://daten.digitale-sammlungen.de/~db/0003/bsb00034597/images/.

[27] "Wie die sele got geleich sol werden mit der gezürde der claider von den claidern der sele ... Unnd darumb sol sie haben dreyerleii claider das ist das ein claid der arbait das ander ein claid der scham das dritt ein claid der zürdtt." BSB CGM 7241, 88r, *Von der Gemahelschaft Christi*, 1499, MDZ, http://daten.digitale-sammlungen.de/~db/0003/bsb00034597/images/.

[28] BSB CGM 7241, 92v (the *er* is present in all manuscript copies I have been able to consult, and refers to the *mensch* or person).

As clothing fell away, the shame of human sexuality was replaced with the purity of pre-Fall Eden in unmediated contact with God. In the twelfth century, the *Mirror for Maidens'* Theodora objected to wearing Christ as an invisible garment: "I keep wondering to myself how a Virgin of Christ can be clothed in Christ, how Christ can conform himself to our bodies like well-fitting clothing." Peregrinus explains that "this garment must be thought of in a spiritual sense, because even as invisible clothing is provided, it shall be accepted as invisible clothing," which is "uncorruptable, unchangeable, tearproof, fixed, eternal, … covers up every sin." As the explanation concludes, whoever "is dressed in God, what should they fear of cold, embarrassment, or nudity?"[29] In the fifteenth-century German poem *Christ and the Loving Soul*, Christ threatens to undress the soul before she is ready to submit to his request. In the sequence as Romuald Banz presented it in his 1910 edition of the poem, Christ first commands the soul to undress and pray at home in her kitchen, to abandon her rich clothing, makeup, and the approving gaze of townsmen at church. The soul perceives this to be an unreasonable punishment. Christ commands, "You must go naked." The soul attempts negotiations, explaining that she cannot attend church undressed, offering to wear an "old grey dress" and exclaiming "Ja, die wil mocht ich wol gon sterben!" [Yes, well I would rather die!]. Christ points out that he goes barefoot and does not attend church. The soul decides that she would rather hang than go naked. In the next scene, she is dressed and suspended from a gallows. After dying like Christ, the soul drinks from a chalice filled with Christ's love—a gesture blending Eucharistic imagery with the love philter of courtly romance—becomes intoxicated, and takes off her dress to put on a heavenly garment.[30]

In *Christ and the Loving Soul*, disrobing and execution allow the soul to share Christ's suffering on the cross and become worthy of his love. Her crucifixion and intoxication thus parallel the ritual of Mass.[31] An illustration of this narrative from a pair of images cut out of a 1455 imprint and pasted into devotional manuscript belonging to the male Benedictine house of Mondsee makes Christ and the Soul into loving collaborators in both her nakedness and her crucifixion (Figure 3.5). In the first image (the cycle reads from right to left), a gently smiling Christ looks into the soul's eyes as he helps remove her dress; her nipple is clearly defined in the original block, emphasizing nudity. In the second image, Christ places his hands on the soul's clothed body as if to support her weight as she dangles above the earth from a beam. In both scenes, the pair gaze into each other's eyes. That some artists' interpretations of these moments of nudity emphasize the soul's perfect submission, while others focus on the necessary use of force to initiate her transformation may originate in condensing narrative elements into printed

---

[29] Seyfarth, SV, 111–12.

[30] Banz, *Christus und die Minnende Seele*, 304–5, 342.

[31] On the iconography see KdiH and Amy Gebauer, *"Christus Und Die Minnende Seele."* Though ownership of the incunables is uncertain, one copy has remained in the possession of the Marktkirche of St. Cosmas and St. Damian in Goslar.

Figure 3.5 *Christ undresses the Soul/Christ hangs the Soul, Christus und die minnende Seele.* Albertina, Vienna, DG1930/198/6–7.

images divorced from explanatory text, rather than the transition from manuscript to print.

By the fifteenth century, whether through the influence of authors like Mechthild of Magdeburg and Henry Suso, or trends rooted in now-lost artifacts, Christ's execution and the bride's parallel torture and crucifixion would become an important subplot in the master narrative. The bride became Christlike by suffering like the Man of Sorrows. Fifteenth-century depictions of this moment combined the concept of being wounded by love in courtly romance with the wounding of Christ's body and the agony of the violated lovers in the *Song of Songs*.[32] This might be acknowledged briefly as a piercing wound, or more elaborately through the bride's imitative crucifixion and martyrdom. The illustrated prose version of Konrad of Spitzer's *Art of Spiritual Living* shows a sequence of assaults with bow and arrow: the bridal soul is first shot by one of the virtues and later pierces God's body with an arrow provided by her teachers (Figure 3.6). This composition incorporates the wounding (in the background) with a depiction of the soul enthroned in heaven in a paired wounding that references the soul becoming Christlike through the bolt of love and the wounding of Christ on the cross.

Parallel wounding or crucifixion was a central theme in fifteenth-century illustrated texts about Christ and the Soul. *Christ and the Loving Soul* and the poems and songs catalogued as *Love Bears a Cross* [*Kreutztragende Minne*] share an iconography of the bride on the cross. Despite their differences in tone, each version teaches the devotee that Christ's brides sacrifice bodily health and pleasure, submit to another's will, and take up the cross in imitation of the groom. In *Christ and the Loving Soul*, the bride's reluctant crucifixion effects a spiritual transformation and infuses her with love for Christ. Both finally acquiesce to martyrdom; by accepting the cross the bride becomes worthy of marriage.[33] Both books voice Christ's command that the soul accept her cross, the soul's protests, and Christ's comparison of the two crosses—his is the harder.[34]

In a south German version of *Love Bears a Cross*, the bride voices the dilemma of loving a tender but strict partner: "du bist mir so hart / und bist doch gar minneclich zart" [Oh Lord, you are so hard on me and yet you are so lovingly sweet]. In a northern variant the soul laments: "Waenstu in den rosen te baden / du moetste eerst door die doornen waden" [if you want to bathe in roses, you must first wade through thorns].[35] The southern version's soul embraces crucifixion as a

---

[32] On the motif of the bow and arrow in these images see Jeffrey F. Hamburger, *The Rothschild Canticles: Art and Mysticism in Flanders and the Rhineland Circa 1300* (New Haven, CT: Yale University Press, 1990), 72. Keller, *My Secret Is Mine*, 231–63.

[33] For instance, "Du müst mir min marter gelten" [you must be made into my martyr]; "Oh herr, was du wilt, das wil ich och" [what you want, I want that too]. Banz, *Christus und die minnende Seele*, 308–9.

[34] "der sol sin crútze uff sich nemmen," Banz, *Christus und die minnende Seele*, 253, or "Heffe op dijn cruce, mijn alreliefste bruut," HB, vol. 9, nr 81.

[35] I give the transcription from HB, vol. 9, 166–7, which includes a partial transcription of the text on the Coblenz panel painting.

Figure 3.6 *The Soul enthroned with her Attendants and Wounding Jesus, Buch der Kunst, dadurch der weltlich Mensch mag geistlich werden.* Augsburg: Johann Bämler, 1477, m 8 r, RB 85766. Reproduced by permission of The Huntington Library, San Marino, California.

ransom for Christ's love.[36] This version closes with the crucified soul's lament that "Liden is mijn naeste cleit, een mantel van liden is mi bereit" [Sorrow is my most intimate garment, a robe of sorrow is prepared for me].[37]

The soul's crucifixion was a well-known theme in fifteenth-century theology, art, and music. Two fifteenth-century Dutch examples, the *Loving Complaint* [*Een mynlike clage der mynnender zielen tot horen gemynden*], attributed with some certainty to the Windesheim canon Hendrik Mande (c. 1360–1431), and the *Ardent Desire* [*Een Mynlike vuerighe begerte der ynniger zielen tot horen Ghemynden Here*], once considered inspired by Mande, if not authored by him, unfold as conversations between a bride who compels Christ to return her love and learns she must first accept his suffering. Mande's *Loving Complaint* voices the frustrations of a soul abandoned "alone in my bedroom," imploring Christ to embrace and

---

[36] Banz, *Christus und die minnende Seele*, 258.
[37] HB, vol. 9, 167.

Transmedia Stories of Jesus and the Loving Soul 91

desire the soul. The soul begs, "[O]h eternal truth, come light up the depths of my interior with yourself and lead me on the right path and give me the strength and the fortitude to accept whatever you, my dear, will make happen to me." As soon as she or he relinquishes her own desires and willingly submits to the Lover's whims, Christ flows into the soul, transmitting his own agony.[38] The soul of the *Ardent Desire* also invites God into its heart. There, God teaches the soul three ways to be remade with love. This lesson culminates in the soul's willing crucifixion: the soul faces Christ's crucifixion in Calvary and senses rays of love. As Christ's soul breaks with burning hunger, limbs desiring death, the soul lights up, comprehending with love what no one can understand through learning. As Christ weeps, the soul weeps for him, until they become one another. When the soul's desire is finally satisfied, Christ whispers that he has never met a soul incapable of experiencing this perfect overwhelming union or of making their body into God's temple.[39] The *Spiritual Melody* [*Gheestelijke Melodie*], a cycle of fifteenth-century Dutch songs recorded in manuscripts and reproduced in early modern printed books, set fragments of this narrative to the tunes of popular secular music. A manuscript version of this collection originally owned by a leprosarium in Roremond contains a variant of *Love Bears a Cross*. The songs share the experiences of a loving soul weary with the world, who struggles to submit to her lover's will. Christ's crucifixion and the soul's acceptance of his cross are recurring themes. The songs were part of a cycle: performed or read together, they narrated the soul's relationship with Christ, the crucifixion, the wedding, and the salvation. One lament is voiced by a nun regretting her vocation, who at last rejoices as she tastes Jesus.[40] Another singer wonders who will cuddle with Jesus, promising: "Ic wil mijn hertken breken af / mit hameren ende mit tanghen, / ende senden dat Jesu in sijn coninclike sael, / ic hope hi salt vriendelic ontfanghen" [I will break off my heart / with hammer and with tongs / and send it to Jesus in his kingly hall / I hope he shall receive it kindly].[41] Another begs Christ the gardener to plow the garden of her heart, where he already hangs on a cross and runs as a child over a stream. He kneels to kiss her red mouth while she begs him to join them eternally through love and the crucifixion: "So biddic u, lieve here, door dine sware pijn, so verenighe mi in dijnre minnen" [Thus I ask you, dear Lord, through your terrible pain, join yourself to me in your love].[42] In each song, the lovers speak for one another, telling only small pieces of a story their singers must have known in its entirety.

---

[38]   Hendrik Mande, *Een minnentlike claege*, 15, 16, 17.

[39]   Gerard Visser, "Een Mynlike vuerighe begerte der ynniger zielen tot horen ghemynden here," *Nederlands archief voor kerkgeschiedenis*, Band 1 Heft 3 (1902), 257–67.

[40]   For a recent discussion of these songs in their manuscript context see Thom Mertens, "*Die Gheestelicke Melody*: A Program for the Spiritual Life in a Middle Dutch Song Cycle," in *Women and Experience in Later Medieval Writing: Reading the Book of Life*, ed. Anneke B. Mulder-Bakker and Liz Herbert McAvoy (New York: Palgrave Macmillan, 2009), 123–48. HB, vol. 9, 146.

[41]   Ibid., 156.

[42]   Ibid., 188–9.

92 Marrying Jesus in Medieval and Early Modern Northern Europe

Gender, Enclosure, and Bibliographic Evidence

Though enclosed gardens often signified convents or the intact purity of the Virgin Mary, not every walled-in lawn marked out a convent. The fifteenth-century blockbooks *Exercises on the Pater Noster* and *Spirituale Pomerium*, both tentatively attributed to the fifteenth-century Flemish canon Henricus Pomerius, offer two entirely different versions of the courtship between Christ and the soul. Both books are multimedia lessons in prayer, and both depict the soul as a bride of Christ and end with her soul's entrance into heaven. The *Exercises on the Pater Noster* was reissued by the same workshop that produced the *Spirituale Pomerium*.[43] The *Exercises on the Pater Noster* exists in four known formats: Dutch and Latin prose treatises, two blockbook editions with several different accompanying text commentaries, in both Latin and Dutch, and two distinct single-sheet woodcuts with accompanying German prayers, while the *Spirituale* survives in a single xylographic copy, pasted into a manuscript with accompanying Latin explanations. Both feature carefully composed images correlating to explanatory text. The *Spirituale* focuses on the narrative of creation and the passion, while the *Exercises* offer a commentary on the geography of heaven and hell, with contrasting images of the path of the virtuous and the path of the damned. Both end with weddings. In the *Spirituale*, the female soul is dressed in a gown, crowned and blessed by Christ in a paradise garden, while the *Exercises* concludes with a tonsured naked male joining other brides of Christ in a postapocalyptic kingdom of Heavenly Jerusalem. In the *Spirituale*, Jesus personally instructs a young virgin to pray while contemplating a series of 12 spiritual trees. By the second lesson, he has already offered her a wedding ring. In contrast, the tonsured soul of the *Exercises* is guided through a series of visions by a messenger [*bode*].[44] Despite these differences in tone and theological message, most retellings of the story of Christ and the Loving Soul closely followed the same master narrative and addressed their lessons to (or were appropriated by) a mixed audience of lay and religious Christians.

In manuals like the late medieval *Christ and the Loving Soul*, deception and force propel the lovers to eventual union. In other works, one or both protagonists

---

[43]   On the dating of the text through clothing in the oldest surviving blockbook, see Adrian Wilson and Joyce Lancaster Wilson, *A Medieval Mirror: Speculum Humanae Salvationis, 1324–1500* (Berkeley: University of California Press, 1984); Paul Kristeller, *Exercitium Super Pater Noster, Nach Der Ältesten Ausgabe Der Bibliothèque Nationale Zu Paris, in 8 Lichtdrucktafeln* (Berlin: B. Cassier, 1908); Hector Marie Auguste de Backer, *L'Exercitium Super Pater Noster; Contribution À L'histoire Des Xylotypes* (Mons: L. Dequesne, 1924); Barbara H. Jaye, *The Pilgrimage of Prayer: The Texts and Iconography of the Exercitium Super Pater Noster* (Salzburg: Institut für Anglistik und Amerikanistik Universität Salzburg, 1990).

[44]   The second xylographic recension labels this figure *Oratio*, a personification of prayer. For a discussion of these distinctions, see Jaye, *The Pilgrimage of Prayer*, 36–8. The longer prose manuscript, which Jaye was not aware of, describes the brother's soul being guided by two angels.

might wed a series of figures. For instance, Pomerius's soul in the *Exercises on the Pater Noster*—visually represented in the printed versions as a tonsured male—observes weddings between the divine lover and first Mary; the personified Church, Ecclesia; and, in some versions, saints; while preparing himself for his own union with the Godhead in the heavenly city of Jerusalem. In the late fourteenth-century *Art of Spiritual Living*, seven maidens are invited to wed God; only one succeeds. This bridal soul is then prepared for marriage by the personifications of the Seven Virtues, each also a bride of Christ. The six rejected brides who refused the King of Heaven's invitation to become his bride instead wed the devil in hell. Rather than distracting from the ultimate union between Christ and a soul, or even imitating a biblical polygamy, these serial marriages and gender changes represented moments in an individual's spiritual progress, or in cosmic history. This representation of the bride's identity as not-just-a-virginal-nun in treatises addressed to virgins is present not only in the *Mirror for Maidens*, for which there is reason to believe the Latin version was designed to be used by male confessors. The Middle High German *Trudpert Song of Songs*, which addressed a female audience, would subsequently influence the *St. George Sermons* and the Dutch *Limburg Sermons*—both also vernacular collections. Surviving copies of these related texts were also owned by and adapted for male religious houses and lay audiences.[45] What might it mean that men wrote, financed, printed, and purchased books which so closely conform to our current preconceptions of what a book written by and for women religious might look like?

In the fifteenth century, the *Song of Songs* was translated from a collection of love songs into an image cycle. Jeffrey Hamburger's study of the Rothschild Canticles showed that as the *Song of Songs* was adapted for personal contemplation, its iconography accreted elements of Christ's own life and a devotee's personal interests. In the fifteenth-century Dutch and German prints known as the *Xylographic Cantica Canticorum*, the story of Christ's life and death, the individual's battle against sins, the coronation of the Virgin, fifteenth-century prayer and labor, and the soul's marriage to Christ become a new backdrop for verses from the *Song of Songs*. This image sequence was also closely related to mid-fourteenth-century murals within the Cistercian convent of Chełmno on the Vistula.[46] As murals became picture books or manuscripts transformed into

---

[45] The Limburg sermons also exhibit clear influences from Old French sources. Regina D. Schiewer, *Die St. Georgener Predigten* (Berlin: Akademie Verl., 2010); Wybren Scheepsma, *The Limburg Sermons: Preaching in the Medieval Low Countries at the Turn of the Fourteenth Century*, ed. and trans. David F. Johnson (Leiden: Brill, 2008); Ohly and Kleine, *Das St. Trudperter*.

[46] Nigel F. Palmer and Andrew Honey, "Cantica Canticorum," in *A Catalogue of Books Printed in the Fifteenth Century Now in the Bodleian Library, Oxford*, ed. Alan Coates (Oxford: Oxford University Press, 2005). This blockbook also derived some of its sequences from contemporary altarpieces: Todor T. Petev, "Spiritual Structures in the Netherlandish Blockbook *Canticum canticorum*, ca. 1465," *E-magazine LiterNet* 15, no. 3 (2008), http://liternet.bg/publish17/t_t_petev/spiritual_en.htm.

94 *Marrying Jesus in Medieval and Early Modern Northern Europe*

songs, altarpieces, books, or broadsheets, the essential features of a sequence's iconography remained fixed. Whether blockbooks, with their focus on images, were intended for a broader lay audience than incunables or manuscripts remains contested. Certainly murals and altarpieces addressed a viewing public. These sequences incorporated biblical glosses into a relatively uniform corpus of images. The use of Latin text and the fine artistic details of the *Cantica Canticorum* blockbooks suggests that they would have been of interest primarily to the upper echelons of medieval society.[47] Though printers altered the text or had the blocks recut, the visual sequence, and thus the narrative theology, of these xylographic reproductions remained consistent. Surviving prints consistently link the bride to salvation by depicting her praying before the crucifixion and later displaying Christ's bleeding crucified body as an example to a young uncrowned woman in an adaptation of the iconography of the *Gnadenstuhl* [Throne of Mercy], where God the Father holds the Crucified Christ. These blockbooks also incorporated late medieval Christians into the scenes, showing monks harvesting wheat and making wine, pious Christians praying before the altar, and mounted knights at war.

Because each scene was carved into a unique block of wood, the illustrations were not limited to retelling the story of the *Song of Songs*. The fifteenth-century Zwolle printer Peter Os used half of a block from a Netherlandish printing of the *Cantica* sequence (c. 1465) for the title page of his edition of Johannes Mauburnus's *Rosetum exercitiorum spiritualium et sacrarum meditationum*, issued in 1494 (Figure 3.7). Mauburnus's *Rosetum* was a large Latin compendium with several custom-designed woodcuts and intricately typeset tables and diagrams. It contained songs, theological material, and numerous Marian devotions, and would directly inspire Ignatius of Loyola's *Spiritual Exercises*. For his title page, Os reused a woodcut which had opened the *Cantica* sequence. The scene shows the nimbed crowned bride, her two female companions, and a beardless Christ with cruciform halo walking from the kingdom of heaven towards an open gate. Christ seems to lead the group of women forward as he speaks. Across the fence, a group of tonsured men harvest wheat and make beer. Christ's text scroll begins "Veni mi ortum meum soror mea sponsa" [come into my garden my sister my bride], while the words embracing the two women following the bridal pair utter the opening lines of the *Song of Songs*: "osculetur me osculo oris sui quia meliora sunt verbera tuo vino" [kiss me with the kiss of your lips, your breasts are sweeter than wine]. Considering the amount of care and technical expertise demonstrated by the book's layout and the skill demanded of its compositor, Os's reuse of a half-block designed for another book was probably not a cost-saving measure. Rather, this image complemented the other promotional elements of the title page.[48]

---

[47] See, for instance, Nigel F. Palmer, "Woodcuts for Reading: The Codicology of Fifteenth-Century Blockbooks and Woodcut Cycles," *Studies in the History of Art* 75 (2009): 91–118.

[48] On marketing practices and the advertisements worked into late fifteenth- and sixteenth-century title pages, see Yves G. Vermeulen, *Tot profijt en genoegen: motiveringen voor de produktie van Nederlandstalige gedrukte teksten, 1477–1540* (Groeningen: Wolters-Noordhoff/Forsten, 1986), 27–37.

Figure 3.7   Title page, Mauburnus's *Rosetum exercitiorum spiritualium et sacrarum meditationum*. Zwolle: Peter Os, 1494, RB 104186. Reproduced by permission of The Huntington Library, San Marino, California.

96   *Marrying Jesus in Medieval and Early Modern Northern Europe*

With the assistance of Mauburnus's prayers and songs, the reader will be able to sing the bride's part in the *Song of Songs*, even while laboring each day as the tonsured brothers do in the picture. That this particular copy was owned by the men's Benedictine Abbey of Tergensee adds an important reminder that male viewers also identified with the role of *Sponsa*.

Other male book owners participated in the bride's story through inscriptions, meditation, and touching and kissing books. A rare complete copy of Hans Sporer's 1477 German xylographic edition of the *Biblia Pauperum* [*Bible for the Poor*], which was once owned by the male Cistercian house at Heilsbronn and is now part of Princeton's Scheide Library, preserves statements of profession from two male novices, each beneath an image of the Virgin Mary.[49] Their inscriptions respond to a design element in Sporer's layout that invited viewers to identify with the role of bride while reading Christ's life. The *Biblia Pauperum* was an anonymous treatise comprised of images and text juxtaposing events from the Hebrew Bible and New Testament to set the Life of Christ alongside prefigurations and prophecies. In its manuscript tradition, these typological readers were spread across an opening, allowing the reader to move from left to right, from past to future, contemplating the meaning of each image and gloss both vertically and horizontally. Blockbook adaptations like Sporer's compressed this format into a single page, requiring the reader to follow the narrative between interlocking frames of image and text. Sporer's edition incorporates the story of Christ's bride into these already intricate exegetic images more fully than other variants, making the story of the Bible into the history of the bride. His three brides, Mary Magdalene, the Virgin Mary, and the Soul, each interact with Christ after his crucifixion.

The final leaf introduces a scene unique to the *Biblia Pauperum* tradition. Sporer depicts Christ's wedding to the soul, the coronation of the virgin, and the wedding of the Lamb at the End of Time, harmonizing Christ's life and the narrative of all creation with the marriage between Christ and the soul (Figure 3.8). In the left frame, a kneeling woman is crowned, a soul who the reader is instructed to praise as the spouse of the Lord. In the center frame, a nimbed Christ crowns another kneeling woman, this one wearing a mantle, her hands clasped to her chest in a posture of humility borrowed from the iconography of the coronation of the Virgin. The far right panel depicts a nimbed, bearded saint, possibly Isaiah, blessing a barefoot youth in a loose belted robe. Beneath this pair, the carved text reads, "Ich wvrd dich mich vermechelen inn ewigkeit" [I will espouse myself to you for all eternity]. The top left text reads, "Der herr ist ußgangen als der spons von seiner schlaffkamer" [The Lord has gone out like the spouse from his bedroom]. The right text reads, "Er hat mich gezieret mit der cron als der gemahel" [He has crowned me and adorned me with the crown as the spouse]. A gloss on Ezekiel in the lower left register explains that Christ is the spouse of the immaculate soul ("der gemahel und spons ist cristus die gespons ist die sel die da

---

[49] *Biblia Pauperum* (Nuremburg: Hans Spörer, 1477), http://arks.princeton.edu/ark:/88435/ht24wj49c.

Transmedia Stories of Jesus and the Loving Soul 97

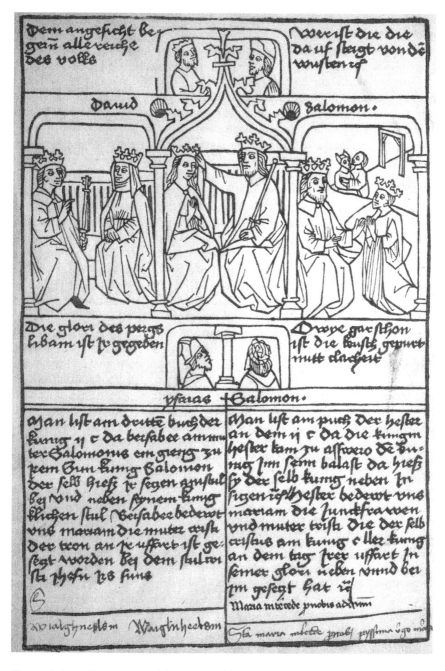

Figure 3.8 *Coronation of the Virgin* with profession statements, *Biblia Pauperum*. Nuremburg: Hans Sporer, 1471–75, 36. Courtesy of Scheide Library, Princeton, NJ.

98   *Marrying Jesus in Medieval and Early Modern Northern Europe*

ist on mackel"), and a reading from the Apocalypse explains that the pure Lamb will wed the sinless soul.

This final image shifts the traditional focus of the *Biblia Pauperum* from the story of Christ to the story of human salvation (Figure 3.9). As the narrative of Christ's life, death, and resurrection unfolds, so too does the story of the bride. She first appears after the crucifixion and harrowing of hell, but before the resurrection, weeping as she walks away from two images of graves. The text in the top registers reads "er sol suchen den herre en so man in finden mag" [whoever seeks the Lord shall find him], and a lower register commentary cites the *Song of Songs*, book 4, counseling that the one who came seeking her love and could not find him is the same spouse and bride who is Mary Magdalene seeking Christ ("ist die selbs gemachel vnnd gespons bedeut mariam magdalenam als sie cristum den herren suchet"). The next sequence centers Mary Magdalene in the garden with Christ as gardener, with textual references rejoicing at their reunion. Several pages later, a postulant named William has written his profession on a page that depicts three enthroned couples: in the left frame, David blesses Bathsheba, in the center frame, God crowns the Virgin, and in the right frame, Esther kneels before King Ahesureus. The layout of the page conveys the desire each person feels to contemplate the face of God, but also the prefiguration of Christ's story in the love of David and Bathsheba. Beneath a gloss on Second Kings' story of Bathsheba, who represents Mary, the mother of Christ, the postulant has written his name; beneath the reading of Esther, another hand has recorded a votive offering requesting prayers and protection from the Virgin Mary, to whom all Cistercian houses were dedicated. The postulant's decision to select this page over other pages depicting the Virgin suggests he may have associated his own monastic profession with the coronation of the virgin and of the bridal soul—a connection traditionally considered limited to use by nuns. The inscribed prayer, "Maria intercede pro nobis ad deum" [Mary, intercede for us with God], responds to the overlay of Marian identity on the crowned Esther, who pleads with a Persian king. Even without the notes left in this book, Sporer's edition of the *Biblia Pauperum* prioritizes the soul's relationship with Christ as bride as a crucial part of Christ's own life story, and the ultimate conclusion to the story of humanity. But these profession statements also demonstrate how important the bride's story had become for communities of readers who could decipher complex biblical cross-references. These readers did not question the prefiguration of the bride in biblical queens, or the promise of the individual's spouseship at the end of the world. Rather, they interacted directly with these brides as they participated in Christ's life, assuming the brides role as witness while the passion unfolded on printed pages.

Though the Heilsbronn brothers' notations in Sporer's blockbook leave little information about how this book informed their devotional practices, Sporer's rendition of the *Biblia Pauperum* represents a late fifteenth-century trend to conflate the story of the bride with the Life of Christ. This closely relates to the contemporary trend of the bride becoming like the crucified Christ, in works like *Christ and the Loving Soul* and *Love Bears a Cross*, and to viewers responding to

Transmedia Stories of Jesus and the Loving Soul 99

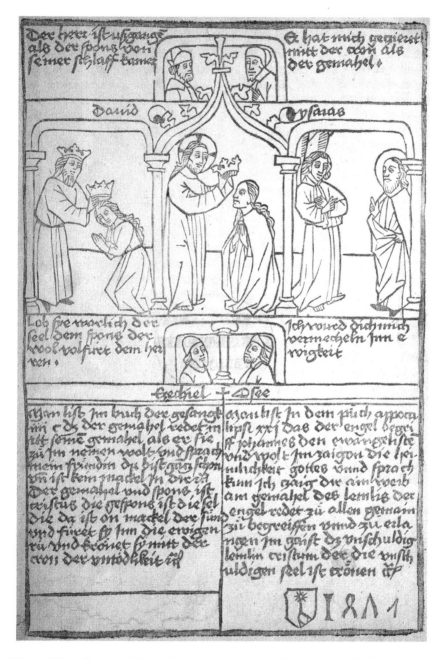

Figure 3.9   "er hat mich gezieret mitt der cronen als der gemahel" [He has adorned me with a crown as the bride], *Biblia Pauperum*. Nuremburg: Hans Sporer, 1471–75, 40. Courtesy of Scheide Library, Princeton, NJ.

100   *Marrying Jesus in Medieval and Early Modern Northern Europe*

and participating in illustrated scenes from Jesus's life. As Deborah Rose-Lefmann and William Werner-Krapp have shown, the fifteenth-century Nuremburg widow Katharina Tucher's diary records several visions which closely follow fifteenth-century devotional images and books about the bride of Christ. Katharina's renditions differ slightly from surviving manuscript copies, but may reveal how late medieval lay readers internalized narratives about the bride of Christ.[50] Several visions cite what may be a version of *Christ and the Loving Soul*, one seems to refer to a vision from the *Revelations of Bridget of Sweden*, and Entries 24 and 25 of Katharina's diary are closely related to *The Spiritual Hunt* [*Geistliche Jagd*] and the *Spiritual Dice Game* [*Geistliche Würfelspiel*]. In entry 24, Katharina describes hunting a stag with Jesus; in entry 25 she stakes her hand in marriage on a dice game with Jesus. Jesus calls to the soul, "Ah dear soul, turn your face to me, we will fly to my city of Jerusalem—I want to teach you how to fly ... we will go fishing and have our pleasure [*wollust haben*]."[51] They begin a game of dice. In the first round, the soul rolls a four, the Lord a two. In the second round, the soul rolls a three, the Lord a five. Following the rules of this game, the Lord has won and will wed the soul: "Drew avgen sein mein krevtz, daz scholtv tragen. Fvnf avgen sein mein bvnten, die wil ich in daz krevtz drvcken" [Three pips are my cross, which you shall carry; five pips are my wounds, with which I was struck on the cross].[52] The soul is crowned, clothed, given beautiful jewelry, and introduced to God, her new Father in Law. The Lord's allegorical gloss on these dice rolls closely resembles the *Spiritual Dice Game*, a commentary on a vision received by a "geistliche Tochter" [spiritual daughter] who diced with Christ the bridegroom. A manuscript copy once owned by a Cistercian abbey includes several

---

[50]   Visions 24 and 25, Katharina Tucher, *Die "Offenbarungen" der Katharina Tucher*, ed. Ulla Williams and Werner Williams-Krapp (Tübingen: M. Niemeyer Verlag, 1998), 42–3. I have only been able to compare her vision to one digitized copy of the *Geistliche Minnejagd* and one copy of the *Geistliche Würfelspiel*; the hunt sequence may also be related to the *Geistliche Minnejagd*, Williams and Williams-Krapp have extensively documented the connections between Katharina's diary and the blockbook tradition of *Christ and the Loving Soul*. On the *Geistliche Jagd*, see VL, vol. 2, 1164; VL, vol. 11, 504, and Einsiedeln Stiftsbibliothek Cod. 278 (1040): e-codices, http://www.e-codices. unifr.ch/de/list/one/sbe/0278. On the *Geistliche Minnejagd*, see VL, vol. 11, 505–7; on the *Geistliche Würfelspiel*, VL, vol. 11, 510. Heidelberg, Universitätsbibl., Cod. Sal. VIII, 77, http://digi.ub.uni-heidelberg.de/diglit/salVIII77. Werner Williams-Krapp, "Bilderbogen-Mystik: Zu Christus und die minnende Seele. Mit Edition der Mainzer Überlieferung," in *Überlieferungsgeschichtliche Editionen und Studien zur deutschen Literatur des Mittelalters. Kurt Ruh zum 75. Geburtstag*, ed. Konrad Kunze, Johannes G. Mayer, and Bernhard Schnell (Tübingen: Niemeyer, 1989).

[51]   "'Ach sel, avf dein gemvt zv mir, wir wollen fligen in mein stat Iervssalem. Ich wil dich wol lern fligen.' Der her spricht: 'Hor vnd merck, wir wollen fischen, wollust haben, wan dam it ist dir wol.' Ez wahs ein schon, lavter, grosz, flissent waszer, vnd ez wahs vol fisch." Tucher, *Offenbarungen*, 42.

[52]   Thanks to Ann Marie Rasmussen, Johanna Kramer, and Jennifer L. Welch for their help deciphering the rules to these dice games. Ibid., 43–4.

Transmedia Stories of Jesus and the Loving Soul   101

pen-drawn illustrations of three dice and a bag and gives different meanings to the possible rolls.[53]

A panel painting depicting the bride with a cross, part of a group of poems, songs, and images catalogued as *Love Bears a Cross* [*Kreutztragende Minne*] (Figure 3.10 and Figure 3.11) directly related the viewer's observation of the Crucifixion to the bride's participation in it.

Love Bears a Cross retained its integrity across media through rhyming couplets and its depiction of a female figure carrying a cross. The female might be dressed in courtly attire or a religious habit, bound to Christ with a rope or weighed down by a demon, but each iteration narrated Christ urging the loving soul to take up the cross, suffer for his love, and become his bride. This close connection between Christ's bloody execution and the bride's submissive love emphasized the relationship between love and self-martyrdom. The 1420 panel painting may have been part of a diptych or triptych commissioned by the Poor Clares of Coblenz and was later owned by the male Cistercian motherhouse of Camp in Boppard. The front depicts the Descent from the Cross; a variation of *Love Bears a Cross* appears on its reverse. In the Descent, Joseph of Arimathea and Nicodemus lower Christ's dead body, displaying his dripping side wound, the nails in his feet, and the open wounds in his hands. Christ wears only a sheer white cloth worked with pearls or lace and flecked with drops of blood, which lightly obscures his genitals and draws the eye to the curving lines of his navel, reminding the viewer of his humanity and incarnation. At the base of the cross, a fainted Mary, the mother of Christ, is supported by two female saints as John, the beloved disciple, twists his neck sharply away from Mary, his gaze following the blood dripping from Christ's left hand. Three men in fifteenth-century clothing comment on the scene. The reverse shows the resurrected Christ walking through a landscape with his cross hoisted on his back. He wears his crown of thorns, and droplets of red blood flow down his exposed hands and wrists and along his bare right calf. His naked body is covered with a black belted robe, probably a Franciscan habit, as he turns his head back over his shoulder as if to speak to the woman walking behind him. She is bent low by the cross slung over her right shoulder. As the dialogue beneath this image reveals, she has not yet embraced her own martyrdom. The panel's two sides teach the viewer that when the lover climbs onto her own cross, she will both consummate her union with her spouse and perfect her imitation of him. If this had been part of a multiwing moveable altar, the relationship between Christ's sacrifice, love, and personal salvation would complement the performance of the Mass and the viewer's reception of the host.

This personal engagement with viewing Christ's life and death as a bride of Christ was also performed daily on an individual's body. An iconographic ring etched with a garland of leaves and roses, excavated at Godstow Abbey near Oxford in the nineteenth century, suggests the private embodied devotional practices marrying Jesus might entail. The ring was initially believed to have belonged to

---

[53]   Heidelberg Universitätsbibl., Cod. Sal. VIII, 77, f. 98v–103v. This manuscript copy includes three illustrated dice throws.

Figure 3.10 *The Descent from the Cross* (front), c. 1420. Panel, 62 × 30 cm. Inv. Nr. 268.a. Museo Thyssen-Bornemisza, Madrid, Spain. Photo credit: Scala / Art Resource, NY.

Transmedia Stories of Jesus and the Loving Soul 103

Figure 3.11   *Christ bearing the Cross* (reverse), c. 1420. Panel, 62 × 30 cm. Inv. Nr. 268.b. Museo Thyssen-Bornemisza, Madrid, Spain. Photo credit: Scala / Art Resource, NY.

104   *Marrying Jesus in Medieval and Early Modern Northern Europe*

Rosamund, mistress of King Henry II, but more recently has been dated to the fifteenth century. It seems unlikely that such an expensive piece of personal jewelry would have been permitted in a convent, and the ring's dimensions suggest it may have belonged to a man or been designed to wear over gloves.[54] The seeming contradiction between the ring's exterior display of piety and the statement of love inscribed inside its band highlights the difference between the function of rings in modern and medieval societies. Iconographic rings depicting saints or images of Christ were a widespread form of personal devotion in fifteenth-century England, and poesy rings or love rings, bands inscribed with brief verses of love, were often exchanged as love tokens between betrothed couples. A poesy ring typically was inscribed on the outside of the band, while iconographic rings rarely bear inscriptions. This ring combines devotion and romantic commitment, in a form of perpetual devotion daily that had both private and public components.

Viewed on the wearer's hand, the ring depicted the Trinity as the Throne of Mercy [*Gnadenstuhl*], the Virgin Mary holding the baby Jesus, and an unknown nimbed male. Each devotional image is framed in a diamond outline emerging from blossoming rose branches. These frames recall the three nail-wounds left in Jesus's flesh, the flowering branches the purity of the incarnation (Figure 3.12).

On the interior, etched in thick gothic script, read the words: "Most in mynd and yn myn herrt Lothest from you ferto departt" (You are always in my mind and in my heart and I am reluctant to depart from you). Though its colored enamel has now worn away, the ring evokes the intersections of pious display, personal love, and luxury goods. The garlands carved on the outer band closely resemble depictions of fifteenth-century bridal souls' floral crowns, while the inscription is an utterly secret personal reminder to the ring's first owner that both mind and heart should be focused constantly on the figures of love depicted on the ring's exterior. Whether owned by a nun, a mistress, a careless scholar, or a wealthy merchant, the ring represents a blending of contemporary cultural trends, personal devotional interests, and the symbolic gestures of worldly marriage with the iconography of Christ's life and death which had broken away entirely from the confines of books and paintings.

Students of the School of Love

Many of the dialogues I have discussed in this chapter include visual depictions of the loving soul with clearly marked sexual traits which reveal less about authorship and audience than the content of a book and its textual history. When information about authorship, audience, and patron is available, as for two late fifteenth-century printed Dutch accounts which depict the loving soul's lessons unfolding within a garden, widely assumed connections between the bride of

---

[54]   The ring's diameter of 19.6 mm (0.76 in.) suggests it may have belonged to a man, been worn over a wealthy woman's gloves, or belonged to a nun with very thick fingers or a fondness for secular fashions.

Figure 3.12   Iconographic finger ring from Godstow Abbey, early fifteenth century. Depth: 11.3 millimeters, diameter: 19.6 millimeters, weight: 15.448 grams. British Museum, Inv. Nr. AN287704001. Copyright of the Trustees of the British Museum.

Christ and chaste female readers and the enclosed garden and the convent become less certain. *The Garden of Devotion* [*'t Hoofkijn van Devotie*] depicts the soul as a woman, the *Exercitio Super Pater Noster* (*Exercises on the Pater Noster*) as a man; both are dialogues set in gardens, during which the protagonist learns to pray, meets with Jesus, contemplates the crucifixion, and travels to heaven. Based on these elements, some scholars have concluded that *The Garden of Devotion* addresses an enclosed women's community, and the *Exercises on the Pater Noster* was written for a male religious house, perhaps to assist with pastoral care. Yet significant bibliographic evidence reveals that *both* books were intended for use among lay readers. *The Garden of Devotion* was written by the fourteenth-century Dominican Pierre d'Ailly, who spent his career at the University of Paris teaching philosophy and astronomy. He would be promoted to Cardinal and attend the Council of Constance, after which he began composing ascetic and spiritual treatises. Print editions of *The Garden of Devotion* in French and Dutch, as well

106   *Marrying Jesus in Medieval and Early Modern Northern Europe*

as a fifteenth-century illuminated manuscript copy, were commissioned by Bruges bibliophile Lodewijk van Gruuthusein, who had close ties to the Burgundian court. Though this soul is visualized as female and the use of an enclosed garden occurs in several of the images, all evidence links this book to men with no documentable interest in women's piety.[55] Similarly, though historians of Dutch literature have speculated that the Augustinian historian Henry Pomerius designed the blockbook version of his *Exercitio Super Pater Noster* [*Exercises on the Pater Noster*] for training pastors, Kees Schepers's examination of surviving copies' watermarks and codicological settings revealed that the blockbooks represent a mature adaptation of the author's earlier scholarly tract on the same subject, originally composed in 1444. Pomerius was clearly obsessed with praying on the Our Father for much of the last half of his life, and designed images [*picturen/ figurae*] to assist with his prayer practice.[56] Schepers's analysis of the surviving blockbooks also shows that whatever Pomerius's intention may have been, the books were cut apart and reused by later collectors who likely had no relationship with the author's religious community at Groenendaal. It was also adapted into a German-language broadsheet version with a heavily abridged image sequence and less explanation of the text's prayers.

The Garden of Devotion opens with an illustration of a woman who discovers a path *into* a Garden, the *Exercises* with a tonsured brother's departure from a garden.[57] This directional difference may subtly comment on the different religious vocations of their respective protagonists—the female enclosed, the male travelling in service of the church—but the garden walls represented far more than the division between secular and sacred space. Both male and female lovers transit from the material world to an interior space through the garden gate. The tonsured brother's body remained in his garden while his soul traveled with angels, just as the soul of *The Garden of Devotion* met angels, virtues, saints, and Jesus within a garden her body could never enter. Both lovers are taught to pray and drink from the fountain of Love. In *The Garden of Devotion*, the soul discovers a "garden of high contemplation laid inside an abbey of a devout religious institution in the desert of the world" by following a path of penitence and prayer.[58] There she studies (and becomes the subject of) a series of images [*picturen ende beelden*] intended to reform her devotional practices. The Soul, guided by the virtues, Faith, Hope, and Love (each modestly veiled), kneels before a cross and learns to see

---

[55]   P.-Y. Badel, "Pierre d'Ailly, auteur du 'Jardin amoureux,'" *Romania* 97 (1976): 369–81; Kees Schepers, *Bedudinghe op Cantica Canticorum*, vol. 1 (Leuven: Peeters, 2006), 59–60.

[56]   Kees Schepers, "A Very Old Fly in *Exercitium Super Pater Noster II* in the Bibliothèque national de France," *Quarendo* 29, no. 2 (1999): 83.

[57]   Jaye argues that the swan, stream, and hart signify the sacrament of baptism, while the hart and the fence also are citations of the *Hortus conclusus* and the *Song of Songs*. Jaye, *The Pilgrimage of Prayer*, 38–45.

[58]   "in die abdye van devoter religion ghesticht inde woestine deser werelt," *Hier beghint een sueuerlijck boecxken ghenoemt thoofkijn van deuotien* (Antwerpen: Gheraert Leeu, 1487).

God reflected in the mirror (Figure 3.13). The arrow piercing her body evokes her experience of the passion—which the viewer must sense entirely through viewing the soul. The cross stands alongside a flowing fountain; Christ's body can only be seen by those holding the bride's mirror, and the fountain's drink can only be tasted by those who have first seen Christ through a glass. Her hair is loose and unbound, as the three virtues direct her to look at and contemplate the cross. In her hands she holds a carved rose crown, and her body is pierced through with an arrow. The text explains that she is kneeling before and is embraced by the loving beloved, who had always been in front of her, nailed to a cross erected within her garden. As she contemplates Christ's sacrifice, she laments the pain piercing through her heart.

This image prioritizes the soul's transformation over Christ's suffering: prayer leads to virtue, allowing her to see the true pain of Christ's death, and receive a measure of his suffering. Once that transformation is completed, the soul meets her groom and drinks deeply from a chalice filled from the fountain running with the flaming love of Salvation (Figure 3.14). She learns from Christ and Eternal Wisdom, for whom she plays a serving wench [*dienstdeerne*]. These professionally colored images, now part of the Library of Congress's Rosenwald collection, come from the 1487 imprint commissioned by Gruuthuisen, in a copy previously owned by the Duc d'Arenberg, another wealthy courtier.

Pomerius's *Exercises on the Pater Noster* opens with the Soul kneeling in a garden and later viewing Christ's crucifixion and drinking from the fountain of life. The opening image of the brother, kneeling in prayer, in an enclosed garden would come to symbolize the book itself, as it was recut to illustrate German translations of the prayers in single-sheet woodcuts. In each scene in the blockbooks and the longer manuscript treatises, the soul is transported by angels through heaven, earth, and to the future to realize the deeper meaning of the short prayer of the Our Father. The angels transport the brother from his abbey to kneel before the throne of heaven—naked in the manuscript treatise, clothed in the surviving blockbooks. There, he and Christ clasp their hands in prayer and begin saying the Our Father. Only the prose version records the response to their prayers: "[B]ecause all [people] have likewise lost both the knowledge of the rosary and the hours" it had been too long since they received the Eucharist, and they could not attend the wedding of the bride and bridegroom in heavenly Jerusalem.[59] To prepare for this wedding, the brother will have to relearn how to pray. With each line of the Our Father, the brother learns an important lesson about vice, virtue, or a sacrament. In imitation of Christ's life on earth, he first meets the Virgin Mary, then descends to earth, where he looks down to see the Jews, Pagans, and Heretics

---

[59]   The prose treatise refers to a series of "figures," the first of which describes the Virgin Mary's desire to conceive the baby Jesus. Most correlate with images in the blockbook tradition. KBR MS 4328–33 f. 162r. "Nu es hir noch ten derden male in hemelrijc te merken der zielen begheerte die dair worden vader knelende al naect om hare begheerte van hem te ewighen Dats hair gloriose lichamen te aentweerden Want al hebbense haren wese lijken loon die bijder rosen ende horae betekent is ontfaen so verlanget hon noch daer toe seere te hebben hare gloriose lichamen om darre mede ghenert te comen ter brulocht Ter comen van der brudegome ende der bruyt Ten tijden als die schone sint van ihrlm volcomelijc."

Figure 3.13   "vanden boome des leuens. Dat is dat ghewarighe heylige cruys" [On the Tree of Life, that is that true Holy Cross], Pierre d'Ailly, *Hofkijn van devotien*. Antwerp: Geerard Leeu, 1487, 12 r. Courtesy of the Library of Congress, Incun. 1487. A393.

Figure 3.14 "Vanden fonteynen ende vanden loopenden wateren die inden seluen hof springhen: ende vander grooter lusticheyt die de siele ontfanghet vanden vogelkens die doer den hof vlieghen al singende" [On the Fountain and the Running Water which springs forth in that same Garden, and on the great desire which the soul receives from the birds who fly through that garden singing], Pierre d'Ailly, *Hofkijn van devotien*. Antwerp: Geerard Leeu, 1487, 22 r. Courtesy of the Library of Congress, Incun. 1487. A393.

110   *Marrying Jesus in Medieval and Early Modern Northern Europe*

in hell, souls rising out of purgatory, and the realm of earth with good Christians receiving blessings from heaven in a sacramental chalice. The angel then leads the brother to two feasts: at the first, Grace serves; at the second, death attends and disrupts a party of sinners. They also see hell and the kingdom of heaven, where the brother's naked soul is at last welcomed by Christ.

Henry Pomerius's depiction of the soul's reception of the Eucharistic drink shares many elements with *The Garden of Devotion*.[60] In the 1445 version (Figure 3.15), the tonsured brother clasps his hands over his chest, while the angel holds his hands in prayer. The two observe the "School of Charity," which combines the iconography of St. Gregory's Mass with the Fountain of Life. Christ as Man of Sorrows stands on an altar before a cruciform triptych. Blood pours in a stream from his side into a deep trough or font. Around the fountain, three men fill cups with blood. A crowned woman (Caritas) wearing a red mantle and a blue dress lifts a chalice in the center; above her, God the Father looks on; his hand makes a gesture of teaching. Across from the altar, three men beg Caritas and Pietas for forgiveness. Each represents a type of sin: commission, omission, or carelessness.[61] Caritas holds an empty chalice, Pietas two pitchers.[62] As the words "forgive our debts" move from the brother and his angel companions, Caritas announces that her cup "intoxicates and delights," Pietas that "with the same measure shall you be measured." A kneeling brother holds his empty chalice up to Caritas and Pietas, saying, "We offend in many things." Each surviving version of the School of Charity teaches how true penitence earns forgiveness for sins: through love and grace, Christ's blood will cleanse the soul. The Dutch prose treatise describes a much more complex medieval reading of the iconography. This version may either refer to a now-lost print version or have been the inspiration for the printed versions. In the description of the figure, the three brothers came together to pray for mercy and were guided by Caritas, who commands them to "merct mijnen kelc" [Look at my chalice] while she explains forgiveness through references to scripture. The brothers learn the importance of converting and praying for others. Caritas concludes her lesson by warning the brothers against mortal sins and the inevitability of death, and urging them to pray for their own forgiveness "because it shall soon be as the prophet said [when we die] we shall be like children of the grain [who] are accessories to the wedding of the lamb. It is for this purpose that

---

[60]   This is image 5 in the blockbooks and "Die viide figure" (image 7) in the KBR manuscript, KBR MS 4328–33, f 172v–173r. Both blockbook versions use this iconography. In the 1445 copy, which is hand-colored, the Eucharistic references are clearer. The later version omits the line of blood from Christ's wound to the font.

[61]   "Want die eyn en heft niet lusterlijc ghescept wer met gheneicht heiden van vroemden beelden. Dats inden latin Commisione. Dander met roekelosheiden ende versumelicheiden dats Omissionie ende die derde met lauwucheiden ende trachtheiden dat is remissionem ... soe comen sie te samen ende bidden gnade."

[62]   The Dutch manuscript describes the "eyn ionghe maghet met twee potkens dan eyn meerder dan dauder in hair hant" [young maiden with two little pitchers and one more than the other in her hand], suggesting the maiden should be holding both pitchers in one hand, rather than two pitchers in two hands, as in the blockbook versions.

Figure 3.15 *The School of Charity, Exercitium Super Pater Noster*, 1460. Courtesy of Bibliothèque nationale de France, Xylo 31.

112   *Marrying Jesus in Medieval and Early Modern Northern Europe*

Christ has given you these prayers to say."[63] When read alongside the image it describes, the lesson of the School of Charity gives new meaning to the actors in the scene. The path to penitence requires converting others, and its destination is a wedding in heaven. The recitation of prayer is meant to prepare each penitent for that wedding.

Drawing from information offered only in Pomerius's longer prose treatments, Caritas is transferring Christ's love to the world and helping prepare others for the wedding of the Lamb. Her iconography is atypical. She wears a crown, a mantle, a robe, and a belt, and in her hand she holds a chalice. If not for the label of "Caritas," she would be indistinguishable from near-contemporary Flemish depictions of the loving soul or the bride representing the sacrament of marriage in the border of the Triptych of the Redemption, which, like the second recension of the *Exercitium*, is attributed to Rogier van der Weyden's successor Vrancke van der Stockt. In the Dutch manuscript, her name alternates between "caritas" and "minne" and this may mean that Caritas, along with Gratia, who also appears crowned, with robe and belt throughout the *Exercises*, should also be recognized as Christ. The crowned Caritas performs the role of the bride by teaching others the mystery of Christ's love: prayers spoken with understanding, under the guidance of virtue, sinners into contact with Christ's love and forgiveness.

In both the *Exercises on the Pater Noster* and *The Garden of Devotion*, the loving soul cannot drink from Christ's fountain of love until she or he has gazed on and come to understand the meaning of his death on the cross. *The Garden of Devotion*'s soul is female and has been identified by some art historians as a nun or postulate according to her textual location as on the threshold of a cloister. The *Exercises* depicts a tonsured brother and has similarly been linked to a male religious community from that detail. Yet these seemingly significant gender differences have little bearing on the protagonists' experiences. Both souls are educated by virtues before a fountain and a cross to warn readers of the urgent need to repent and turn to Christ. Each penitent can find this path with training, becoming another bride of Christ. The use of a garden as the backdrop for the soul's encounters with Christ cited the pastoral setting of the *Song of Songs*, but, by the fifteenth century, the "garden" had taken on alternate meanings.[64] The enclosed garden, marked visually by a wattle fence or a brick wall bounding

---

[63]   "Want dan oic gheschien moet dat die prophete seit weer dat quat ende bitter es van gode verscheiden te sijn Om dit quaet ummer ten lesten te verhueden vanden kinderen der granen die der brulocht van ihrlm toebehoeren. Soe heeft u Christus dese bede aldus ten letsen geleert te seggen." KBR MS 4328–33, f. 175v.

[64]   Several other devotional works featuring a soul in a Garden were produced in the fifteenth century. Dietrich Schmidtke, *Studien zur dingallegorischen Erbauungsliteratur des Spätmittelalters: am Beispiel der Gartenallegorie* (Tübingen: Niemeyer, 1982). For a discussion of the garden as an allegory for monastic enclosure, see Winston-Allen, *Convent Chronicles*, 161–2. And for a close reading of many of these images in the context of the *Song of Songs* and late medieval devotional practices, see Reindert Leonard Falkenburg, *The Fruit of Devotion: Mysticism and the Imagery of Love in Flemish Paintings of the Virgin and Child, 1450–1550* (Philadelphia: John Benjamins, 1994), 20–49.

Transmedia Stories of Jesus and the Loving Soul   113

grassy fields filled with flowers, is traditionally read as a strictly enclosed convent. In the fifteenth-century iconography of the Virgin Mary, especially in the *virgo inter virgins* [the Virgin among Virgins], it also came to represent the miraculously intact chastity of the Mother of God. That both books were read outside religious communities only underscores the importance of reading past the visual depiction of the loving soul as male or female, religious (tonsured, in a habit) or lay (in a gown, with long flowing hair).

Transmediation of the Bride of Christ

In the first chapters of this book, I proposed that the transmission of images of the bride of Christ in medieval and early modern devotional media was analogous to contemporary convergence culture, in particular to the practice of transmedia storytelling. As individual authors reworked the story of the bride of Christ for new audiences and media platforms, they took advantage of cultural familiarity with each narrative moment—the bridegroom's gifts of gown and ring, the wedding invitation, the couple's kiss. When an author's original work was disassembled and repurposed, as in the case of Suso's *Brotherhood of Eternal Wisdom*, readers interpreted that fragment of the story through an internalized narrative of the Bridal pair's courtship, speaking unspoken lines, anticipating unwritten endings, and responding emotionally as they participated in remaking that story. The adaptation of the master narrative of Christ's marriage to new media formats testifies to the diffusion of the story of the bride of Christ across medieval Europe. Some of these adaptations were precipitated by moves across the boundaries of the cloister, others were accelerated by the new technologies of paper and handpress. These transmedia narratives functioned because the bride of Christ had become part of late medieval popular culture.

Fifteenth-century Christians participated in marriage to Christ in ways which harmonized secular and sacred by mingling together elements of daily life (harvesting, courtship), the techniques of popular poetry, and the symbols of Christ's passion. Scattered pieces of the story of Christ's courtship with the soul contain the flavor of civic piety in the midst of transformation. Though this master narrative likely originated in formational literature composed for use within twelfth-century monastic communities, by the fourteenth century, the loving soul was no longer simply a good nun. For instance, in the extant corpus of Dutch and German copies of the *24 Elders*, only six illustrated print and manuscript witnesses depicted the loving soul as a nun or a female stigmatic; only two of the extant illustrated manuscript copies and none of the surviving print copies depict the loving soul as a nun in German copies of *Christ and the Loving Soul*, and a single German manuscript copy of Konrad von Spitzer's *Book of Art* depicted the loving soul as a nun.[65] As I explained in the previous chapter, the twelfth-century

---

[65]   The stigmatic soul appears in several manuscripts and in the woodcuts of Anton Sorg's 1480 print edition. No more than four manuscripts depict the soul in the persona of

114   *Marrying Jesus in Medieval and Early Modern Northern Europe*

Mirror for Maidens, which explicitly addresses nuns, includes a tonsured male soul praying to wed Jesus. On the level of textual detail, descriptions of the bride's adornments transformed marriages between bodiless souls into replicas of aristocratic weddings on earth. The bridal gown often followed the most expensive contemporary fashions. Even in 1690 the bride dressed in contemporary fashion in the title of Flemish Carmelite Gabriel à S. Joanne-Baptista's *Christina the Bride of Christ, Clothed after the Fashions of Paris ... [De Bruydt Christi Christina ghekleedt naarde mode van Parijs]*.[66] These allusions to luxurious fashion reinforced the distinctions between spiritual and material worlds but also explained complex theology through analogies to familiar elements of daily life.

By the last quarter of the fourteenth century, loving God, becoming God, and experiencing Christ's torments on the cross were interconnected with marrying Christ. As Otto von Passau wrote in the *24 Elders*, to love God meant understanding and receiving the sacraments, partaking of confession, detaching from the material world, and dwelling deeply on Christ's death on the cross. The eighth elder teaches the soul why and how people should love God and Mary, his mother: "Love is a beginning and a middle and an end to all Virtues ... without love no one can truly please God, with love, no one may displease God, with love no one can sin.... Love conquers all."[67] He goes on to gloss a passage from Zephania, translating "Daughter of Zion" as "spouse," rewriting the meaning of that biblical book into a prefiguration of the Christian sacraments. Drawing together the saving power of Christ's blood, the love of God for humanity, and the obligation of each Christian to seek that love, Otto writes: "You are my spouse whose blood is truly in this holy sacrament, [and] all sacraments of holy Christendom which absolve all sins."[68] For Otto, as for every author I have discussed in this chapter, Christ's love, Christ's death, and Christ's body all signified the potential for personal salvation, and the bride's story was the image best suited to explain these mysteries.

Between the twelfth and fifteenth centuries, the love story of Christ and the bride had become a container within which theologians might pack different pieces of information about salvation, virtuous living, and the nature of the universe.

---

a male or a child. For a comprehensive discussion of the iconography in these manuscripts and the provenance of most known copies see the KdiH, vol. 1, 1–560.

[66]   Gabriel à Sancto Joanne-Baptista, *De bruydt Christi Christina, ghekleedt naer de mode van Parys en paradys, betoonende aen alle maeghden hoe sy heden-daeghs naer siel ende lichaem konnen verciert gaen* (Antwerpen: Augustinus Graet, 1690).

[67]   Otto von Passau, *Diß Buch ist genannt die Vier und czwentzig Alten, oder der güldin Tron, geseczet von bruder Otten von Passowe* (Augsburg: Anton Sorg, 1480), 32r–33r. "Mynne ist ein beginnen ein mittel und ein beschliessen aller tügenden ein stercke und ein uberwynden alles streites und anfechtunge ein vertreiben. Mynne itst den saligen ein verdeinung ein ursach und eÿn volbringen alles loues. On mynne mag nyemant got wol gefallen mit mynne mag nymant got mißfailen, mit mÿnne kan noch mag nyemant sünden ... Liebe uberwinnct alle ding vnd alle sachen seind on liebe unverfangen."

[68]   Ibid., 53v. "Du bist mein gemahel des blůts in disem heyligen blůte seind bestätiget alle sacrament der heyligen cristenheÿt die alle sünd abnymet."

Transmedia Stories of Jesus and the Loving Soul

The same storyline could prepare readers for convent life, explain the creation of the universe, bring to life the story of Jesus's sacrifice, or teach prayer techniques. Collectively, these manuals voice many of the conflicting priorities of late medieval Christians. Chronologically, they track developing beliefs about the bride of Christ. The adaptation of the bride's story from monastic manuscripts to mass media originated in a theological revolution that introduced private meditative prayer in place of monastic chastity as the preferred path to marrying Jesus.

Chapter 4
Created to Be a Bride

> The bridegroom is our Lord Jesus Christ, we are the bride, your soul and my soul, we are all called and invited, and all things are prepared for the time of union between God and the loving soul, with his bride.[1]

One Saint Cordelia's day (October 22) in the late fourteenth century, Dominican Johannes Tauler delivered a sermon on Jesus's Parable of the Wedding Banquet, a feast the King of Heaven prepares for his son (Matthew 22:1–14). From its references to the bride of Christ and external information about Tauler's service preaching to the seven Dominican women's communities and the dozens of beguinages around Strasbourg, this sermon is presumed to have been preached to a community of women religious or novices preparing for profession. But Tauler, even in the Adelhausen manuscript, does not equate the bride with a celibate woman, much less a Dominican nun, and this sermon also appears in manuscripts owned by lay families and every early print edition of Tauler's German works. In each surviving copy, Tauler uses explicitly gender-inclusive wording to represent the bride's transformation into a "nuwen menschen der nach Christo gebildet ist" [new person fashioned after the image of Christ], explaining that the bride is remade after the image of Christ through marriage, just as Christ takes on the appearance of humanity through incarnation. Tauler unequivocally asserts that Christ is a spouse to every soul from the instant of creation to the end of the universe, a perspective that first emerged in the late thirteenth century among mendicant friars and beguines offering catechetical instruction in urban communities. Their surviving texts addressed a universal community of brides for whom marriage to Christ

---

[1] "der brútegoûme daz ist unser herre Jhesus Christus. Die brut daz sin wir: din und min sele, wir alle sin geruffet und geladen, und alle ding sint bereit zů male in der vereinunge Gotz mit der minnender selen, mit sinre brut." All translations are my own from Vetter's edition of Freiburg University Library MS 41, against which I have compared Conrad Kachelofen's 1498 print edition. Johannes Tauler, *Predigten*, ed. Ferdinand Vetter (Dublin: Weidmann, 1968), 431–3. Vetter's manuscript came into possession of the Dominican convent of Adelhausen no later than 1410, and may have been copied there as early as 1359. It is one of two extant manuscripts dating to Tauler's own lifetime. According to the Freiburg catalog records, the manuscript was first owned by a lay family, and also contains an ownership note on 144v: "Diß buch höret Ketrinen von Hall vnd Gretlin von Hall ze Friburg" [this book belongs to Ketrin and Gretlin von Hall of Freiburg]. The Kachelofen edition only modernizes spelling. Johannes Tauler and Rulman Merswin, *Sermon des gross gelarten in gnade erlauchten doctoris Johannis Thauleri predigerr ordens, weisende auff den nehesten waren wegk, yn geiste czu wandern durch uberschwebenden syn, vnour acte von geistes ynnigen vorwandelt i deutsch manchen menschen zu selikeit* (Leipzig: Conrad Kachelofen, 1498).

118   *Marrying Jesus in Medieval and Early Modern Northern Europe*

was the only path to human salvation and the key to understanding the history of creation. As I shall explain, Tauler's exegesis related depictions of union between Christ and the bride to teach an anthropology of the human soul. Reconsidering the marriage between Christ and the soul within that theological framework recasts seemingly erotic depictions of union to Christ as explanations of creation and salvation. This theological message has been obscured by the invention of the category of "bridal mysticism" and the subsequent experiential-erotic discourse to which some medieval authors—especially women—have been subjected.

As a male cleric possibly preaching to celibate women whose religious profession made them brides of Christ, Tauler's assertion that he, as well as their friends and family, were also wed to Christ, evokes the inequity of medieval women's religious opportunities, the inefficacy of sexual abstinence for spiritual salvation, and the queerness of a Christian community that is all, whatever their biology, female on the inside. Reading Tauler this way, Carolyn Bynum once argued that Tauler was at best ambivalent about women religious.[2] But Tauler's sermon on the bride of Christ was neither meant for nor restricted to professed celibate nuns. Though Jesus recounts a wedding guest expelled for inappropriate attire and concludes his parable with the warning that many are called but few chosen, Tauler describes a wedding at which every guest is a bride. Even those dressed in tattered garments, representing the expelled guest from Jesus's parable, are washed and clothed by their celestial spouse. Tauler explains that loving God is a lifetime commitment of at least 20 or 30 years' effort to break away from worldly attachment, turn inward, and invite God into the heart. This lifetime labor may take place either in the cloister or in the world. In this sermon, Tauler presents women as fully equal to men, laity equal to religious. Each person who transformed into a bride of Christ would be stripped of filthy clothes, washed clean, and adorned in fine clothes like "die erste brúte" [the first bride]. Tauler, like many of his contemporaries, considered celibate women religious to be part of a larger community of brides of Christ. He uses gender-inclusive language like "kinderen" [children] and "menschen" [people] (paired with the masculine pronoun "er") in place of "daughters" or "brothers." The divine bridegroom's universal availability remained acceptable to leading fifteenth-century Dominicans, who revived, translated, and even printed Tauler and his contemporaries as part of their effort to reform their community in response to the Council of Constance. These fifteenth-century copies likely influenced early Protestant theologians, not least Martin Luther.

I focus here on the beguine Mechthild of Magdeburg (c. 1207–94), the Franciscan David of Augsburg (OFM c. 1200–72), the Dominicans Johannes Tauler (OP c. 1300–61) and Henry Suso (1295–1366), the priest and hermit Jan van Ruusbroec (c. 1293–1381), and the married layman Rulman Merswin (1307–82). This circle of authors agreed that God the Father and Christ the Son reflect one

---

[2]   Bynum is, to the best of my knowledge, the only person who has published on this particular sermon in English. She groups it with several other sermons cited as evidence of Tauler's ambivalence to the women in his care. *Holy Feast and Holy Fast*, 107.

Created to Be a Bride 119

another perfectly and comprehend each other entirely, while humans could only comprehend this relationship through representative images. They used details from the widely disseminated master narrative of Jesus's marriage to the soul as representative images to explain the history of creation and teach how, through a lifetime of pious acts, each soul might perform to become Christlike and cleansed of sin. In the last quarter of the thirteenth century, founding members of the new mendicant orders like the Franciscan David of Augsburg and semireligious women like Mechthild of Magdeburg used the wedding between Christ and created souls to explain creation, incarnation, and the sacraments. During the fourteenth century, writers like Jan van Ruusbroec, Rulman Merswin, and Henry Suso incorporated this sense of marriage to Christ into comprehensive treatises designed for both women religious and lay readers. Within this circle, marriage to Jesus directly correlated with personal redemption. Though this idea originated in a thirteenth-century apostolic movement, by the early fifteenth century, these disparate authors often appeared in excerpts alongside one another, often anonymously (or pseudonymously) in devotional miscellanies compiled for personal use, and by the last quarter of the fifteenth century, the understanding that *each* individual Christian was espoused to Christ was also transmitted widely in print media.

Viewed through the very practical concerns of spiritual advisors and those who purchased, commissioned, recopied, or printed their books, I propose that descriptions of the soul's union with Christ through marriage were primarily pedagogic, rather than erotic, public rather than private. Tauler had met Suso, Merswin, and Ruusbroec;[3] Ruusbroec read and was inspired by Hadewijch; Merswin's books were often recopied or printed with the writing of Tauler and Suso; Herp's *Book of Perfection* first appeared in print in German in an edition of Suso's and Merswin's writing.[4] Excerpts from Mechthild's *Flowing Light* circulated with Suso's (Budapest, Nationalbibl., Cod. Germ. 38) and Tauler's (Karlsruhe, Landesbibl., Cod. St. Georgen 78).[5] The German Friends of God, a

---

[3] Wilhelm Rath, *Der Gottesfreund vom Oberland; sein Leben, geschildert auf Grundlage der Urkundenbücher des Johanniterhauses "Zum grünen Wörth" in Strassburg* (Stuttgart: Verlag Freies Geistesleben, 1955).

[4] Hendrik Herp, *Spieghel der Volcomenheit*, OGE, vols. 1–2 (Antwerpen: Uitgever Neerlandia, 1931); Deborah A. Rose-Lefmann, "Hendrik Herps 'Spiegel der Volkommenheit' in deutscher Sprache: eine überlieferungsgeschichtkiche Edition" (Princeton, NJ: Princeton University Press, 1998); Suso, Merswin, and Herp, *Hie seind geschriben die capitel des büchs d[as] do der Seüsse heisset* ... (Augsburg: Anton Sorg, 1482).

[5] I draw this information from the bibliographic information and manuscripts listed under each author's name in handschriftencensus, http://handschriftencensus.de; Medieval Manuscripts in Dutch Collections, Koninlijke Bibliotheek, http://www.mmdc.nl; Bibliotheca Neerlandica Manuscripta Universiteit Leiden, http://digitallibrary.leidenuniv. nl/V/?func=native-link&resource=LDN10306; and the Incunabula Short Title Catalogue, The British Library, http://www.bl.uk/catalogues/istc. On the textual history of Mechthild's book, see Sara S. Poor, *Mechthild of Magdeburg and Her Book: Gender and the Making of Textual Authority* (Philadelphia: University of Pennsylvania Press, 2004), 138–40.

120   *Marrying Jesus in Medieval and Early Modern Northern Europe*

circle to which Tauler and Merswin belonged, translated Hadewijch and Ruusbroec into German in the fourteenth century.[6] David of Augsburg was copied with Suso and Ruusbroec (e.g. Beuron, Bibl. der Erzabtei, 8° MS 42).[7] The earliest copy of Henry Suso's *Exemplar* (Strasbourg Univ. Bibl. MS 2929), dating to 1370, belonged to the library of the Order of Sankt Johann in Jerusalem at Grünenwörth, a community financed by Rulman Merswin since 1367. Johannes Tauler helped Merswin negotiate a death absolution for Merswin's wife from pope Clement VI. Merswin's *Buoch von den fürkomenen gnoden* [*Book of Forthcoming Grace*] lifted heavily from Ruusbroec's *Geestelijke Bruiloft* [*Spiritual Espousals*], and there was a vibrant interest in translating and circulating the works of Ruusbroec and Hadewijch among the South German Friends of God.[8] In the fifteenth century, Alijt Bake, prioress of Galilea in Ghent, Anna Ebin, prioress of Pillenreuth in Nuremberg, Anna Jack, prioress of Inzigkofen in Strasbourg, and the fifteenth-century Nuremburg widow and tertiary Katharina Tucher, all working in monastic scriptoria, recopied these items for communal use alongside woodcuts, their own theological teachings, and visions.[9]

These social and textual connections demand scholars abandon longstanding assumptions about the use, audience, and authorship of vernacular treatises depicting union with Christ as a marriage. Even *if* these theological treatises originated in autobiographical moments of semi-pornographic mystical ecstasy or were designed for use by women religious, the codices in which these texts are copied document collaborations between nuns, friars, and laypeople.

Anthropologies of Spirit and Flesh

In the thirteenth century, the first mendicants arrived in Germany. Among them was the Franciscan David of Augsburg, who had arrived in Germany in 1221 with Berthold and Lamprecht of Regensburg to establish a foothold for the Franciscans. David of Augsburg had served as master of novices for the Franciscans, was involved in the inquisition of Waldensians in 1256 (during which time he wrote a treatise on the inquisition of heretics) and also served as a preacher and papal

---

6   Gregor Wünsche, "Hadewijch am Oberrhein: Niederländische Mystike in den Händen der sogenannte Gottesfreunde," in *Kulturtopographie des deutschsprachigen Südwestens im späteren Mittelalter: Studien und Texte*, ed. Barbara Fleith and René Wetzel (Berlin: De Gruyter, 2009), 83–98.

7   "Jan van Ruusbroecs 'Brulocht' in oberdeutscher Überlieferung: Untersuchungen und kritische textausgabe," in *Münchener Texte und Untersuchungen zur deutschen Literatur des Mittelalters, Bd. 22*, ed. Wolfgang Eichler (München: Beck, 1969); Wolfgang Eichler, *Van den blinckenden Steen in oberdeutscher Texttradition by Jan Van Ruusbroec* (München: W. Fink, 1968).

8   Gregor Wünsche, "Hadewijch am Oberrhein," 84–8.

9   For English summaries of these women's scribal activities, see Cynthia J. Cyrus, *The Scribes for Women's Convents in Late Medieval Germany* (Toronto: University of Toronto Press, 2009), 65, 70; Winston-Allen, *Convent Chronicles*, 113–14, 78.

Created to Be a Bride 121

representative for the visitation of canoness houses of Niedermünster and Obermünster in Regensburg. Each of these duties required carefully explaining orthodox doctrine in ways intelligible to nonexperts. His *Die Menschwerdung Christi* [*On the Incarnation of Christ*] or *Kristi Leben unser Vorbild* [*Christ's life as our Model*], one of the earliest vernacular assertions that every created human was espoused to God. Though perhaps originating in a sermon addressing novices or adult catechumens, this treatise also appears in fifteenth-century devotional manuscripts. In *On the Incarnation of Christ*, David of Augsburg explains the sacrament of the Eucharist, the history of Creation, and the relationship between humanity and God through marriage. Using the imagery of reflecting mirrors and torn cloths, David of Augsburg explains that every aspect of creation contributed to a wedding in heaven.[10]

On the Incarnation of Christ teaches that turning inward to contemplate the reflection of God while receiving the Eucharist will wash away sins because this sacrament reenacts the wedding of creation that gave birth to humans who perfectly resembled a God who is both God himself and his own spouse. Thus God (and God's spouse) is reflected within each human through the act of creation and accessible to each created human (as God's spouse) through contemplation and communion. In that moment of swallowing, the individual's eternal soul is one with God and can grasp the incomprehensible. Looking inward to find the reflection of God, learning from that reflection the true meaning of the incarnation, and then swallowing the Eucharist ripped through the barriers between God's bread-as-body/burial-shroud around Christ's corpse and the packaging material of the human body. Summarized so succinctly, David's understanding of creation is almost nonsensical. Through the imagery of mirrors and weddings it becomes both elegant and intelligible.

David begins:

> The Lord of Heaven had a spouse. Who is this? She is his Wisdom, the one in whom the son Jesus Christ was within in eternity and in whose dwelling [he] is eternally born. Like a painter who has made a beautiful image, which is not opaque with pigments, but instead is brushed with them so that people can see the form and know what it is, it is also like this with the outline of humanity in the Godhead. It is not totally filled with flesh, in such a way that humans could see or know it, but only God the father knows exactly what it has been

---

[10] Very little has been published on David of Augsburg's German writing since Pfeiffer's edition, which contains several transcription errors. I base my translation on Pfeiffer's edition, though I have also referred to BSB CGM 183, 71v–86v, and BSB CGM 176, 105r–122r, from which Pfeiffer made his edition. Franz Pfeiffer, *Deutsche Mystiker Des Vierzehnten Jahrhunderts I. Bd., Hermann von Fritslar, Nicolaus von Strassburg, David von Augsburg* (Göttingen: Vandenhoec und Ruprecht, 1907), 398–405. Francis Mary Schwab, *David of Augsburg's 'Paternoster' and the Authenticity of his German Works* (München: C.H. Beck, 1971). Bert Roest, *Franciscan Literature of Religious Instruction before the Council of Trent* (Leiden: Brill, 2004), 242, 383. Johanna Kramer generously corrected an earlier translation of this text, but all remaining mistakes are my own.

122   *Marrying Jesus in Medieval and Early Modern Northern Europe*

filled in with. The son is and was a mirror for the father. How? Then it was and it still is that his Godhead is so bottomless that it can never be known except by himself.[11]

Through the analogy of the gouache painter mixing pigments to wash color over the outlined form of a human figure, David translates the mystery that no one other than God (the artist) can fully know the process of creating humanity or the contents of God's depths (the pigments). The act of creation was a marriage whose consummation birthed salvation (Christ's incarnation). After this, Christ and God created humankind by consummating another marriage: "[T]hen came a time when the child should be born, that is, when humanity should be created with his spouse, who is wisdom, [his mother and himself] ... then the father was not only the father but also the son but the son was not only the father." From the Son, humans inherit transitory bodies, and from the father they inherit eternal souls.

As humans learned to love one another and to procreate, they passed along their Christlike bodies and their Godlike souls to each generation, interacting with the incarnate Christ with human bodies and with God through their eternal souls. David explains this through the image of a shattered mirror, darkened by sin, which nonetheless reflects God in each filthy shard. However many generations removed from creation, each human body still contains an image of God's face. Those who sin will see only death in a mirror darkened by their own fleshly actions, but if the person rues sin, confesses, and receives the Eucharist, the glass of the mirror becomes clear. Should that penitent being look within the mirror of its own body and soul, the face of the Godhead will appear. When human sin is washed away entirely, humanity perfectly reflects the face of the Godhead, for which we were created to be a mirror.[12] According to David, there are as many mirrors as there are people in this world. Whenever an individual received a cleansing sacrament, such as baptism or reception of the Eucharist, the mirrors aligned perfectly, each level of flesh and spirit passing into the creator it was made to reflect.

A new marriage took place during the consecration of the Eucharist when Christ's body returned to earth to touch and transform the bodies he had helped create. Just as God clothes his reflection (Christ) within a layer of flesh, because he loves *their* reflection (humankind), when Christ's reflection (the human body), winds around Christ's body by swallowing the Eucharistic bread, the layers of flesh separating each reflection are torn away:

> He is wrapped in the bread as he had been wrapped in his humanity; it is as if a person had been wrapped in a white linen cloth [a burial shroud], in this way is God wrapped in the bread. Look, when then the priest, or you, or any person,

---

[11]   Pfeiffer, *Deutsche Mystiker*, 398.

[12]   Ibid., 403–4. Though David of Augsburg does not explicitly state it here, he also anticipates the Eckhartian concept of the birth of God in the soul: if humans reflect God, this also means that the eternal birth of Christ through the consummation of God's marriage to Wisdom is reflected in and continually unfolding within the soul of each human body.

Created to Be a Bride   123

receives God from the priest, it is as if one tears the linen cloth in the mouth, and the soul receives him, the one who is wrapped into the cloth, that is God, [the one] who was wrapped into the bread.[13]

In this closing image, each person, whether a priest or a communicant, tears away the layers of cloth and body between the created self and the eternal God, reenacting the weddings between God and Wisdom, between Christ and God, and between created and Creator. The sacrament cleanses the soul of the human mirror until it reflects God's face perfectly. This is a stunningly comprehensive explanation of the acts of creation, crucifixion, and the redemptive power of the sacraments through the actions of soul-containing-bodies loving, copulating, bleeding, birthing, dressing, and eating. David of Augsburg has taught his audience—not a priest among them—that humans have the potential to be cleansed of sin and rejoined to the Creator through a marital union initiated by penance and consummated during communication (drawing Christ's body into their own).

David's use of mirrors and marriages to explain the relationship between creation, incarnation, and interpenetration of human and divine spouses was not uncommon in medieval sacramental theology. This imagery is frequently sexualized by modern readers, but, as a number of medieval texts show, the interpenetration of divine and human in a marital embrace was one of a series of standard images authors used to describe the sacraments. "Dits wie der mensche in gode blift ende got in heme" [How the person dwells in God and God in him], which circulated in the anonymous so-called "Limburg Sermon" collection, explains how humans alone among creatures were given a soul which reflected the nature of God. According to the sermon, God dwells in humans, driving away the darkness of mortal sin just as the sun dwells in the atmosphere to dispel the dark night. And the sensation of God dwelling in us is just like the way that fire melts and heats iron, so that humans are made beautiful and like radiant gold whenever

---

[13]   The passage poses some difficulties for translation in Pfeiffer's edition. I have provided a transcription of the passage from BSB CGM 176, f. 121r–122r, from which I translated this last section. "Ia ich ^wol wanne du spracher selber zu dinen *iungern* Er sprach daz brot daz ich ir hie gib daz ist min fleisch da du selbe uf erder gienge. Und du dich gechleidet hetest vz wendich mit der menscheit do heiz man dich einen menschen also mugen wir ouch uz den auzzern chleidern wol gesprechen zu dir in einer bezeichnusse daz brot sich also ist er gewunden in daz brot. Als er sich in die menscheit ver wunden here zegleicher wiser als da sich ein mensch ver wunden in ein wizzez lilachen also ist got ver wunden in daz brot, sich swenne denne der brister oder du oder ein ieglich mensch got von dem briester enpfahet sich so zerret man daz lilachen in dem munt vnd enpfahet diu sel den der in daz lilachen gewunden was daz ist got der in daz brot gewunden was sich do diu menscheit gezerret wart an dem cruce ob der gotheit do must das irdische werden der erde daz was sin lichname also muz daz lilachen daz ist daz brot enpfolhen werden dem libe vnd got selber der sele zu einer losunge aller gebresten vnd zeiner hilfe aller er zein ersten di menscheit uber sinen gotlichen schin zie hen muste daz wir in gesehen mohten mit menslihen ougen daz ist uns ein schonnu bechantnusse wan also must er uns zeglicher weise...."

124   *Marrying Jesus in Medieval and Early Modern Northern Europe*

we are illuminated by that fire.... When God flows into a person, sins are purified. This is because God has created two stamps or seals for himself, one after his own godly image [*gotliken bilde*] and another for the salvation of humankind. Consequently, each soul is just as strong as it is filled with god—the more full of God, the less space for evil spirits.[14] These same images were used by the fifteenth-century Franciscan Hendrik Herp in his widely translated and reproduced *Mirror of Perfection* [*Spieghel der Volcomenheit*]. For Herp, recognizing that humans desire eternal union with God was an essential first step in daily devotion.[15] Herp describes the soul's eyes opening as she wakes from a deep sleep and is lovingly united with her beloved God, a spiritual being [*God is een geest*] who can neither be viewed nor made of images. Citing Bernard of Clairvaux's image of water dissolving into wine, Pseudo-Dionysius the Areopagite's concept of God as unformed love from which all beings are created, Aristophones's counsels on love, and the experiences of Egidus (Giles of Asissi), the third disciple to follow St Francis of Assisi, Herp elaborates on the human mirror. According to Herp, human souls are a likeness of the formless God who have been animated through the foodstuff of love. The one and the other (God and the human) are like wine into which a drop of water dissolves and loses its nature entirely, its savor and its strength overwhelmed. When God flows through the soul and body of a created human, the two become of one seamlessly joined body containing one soul, and one essence. Whenever the soul is remade with the Godhood, the soul matches his dimensions. To understand this, Herp advises a person to set "two mirrors against one another, so that each mirror receives the image of the other mirror, in which is imprinted the image of itself reflected in the other mirror. And thus what is like eternity with these intellectual mirrors, it is also with the eternal reflection of God in the heart of men, bringing to fruition the words of the *Book of Love*: My Beloved is turned to me and I am turned to him."[16] God illuminates the soul, who receives an image of perfect glory and an image of the eternal and utterly incomprehensibly bright Godly mirror with which its soul is joined, just like a "drop of water which falls clearly into a jug of wine, or like a spark which flies in an extraordinarily large fire." Both Herp and the anonymous Limburg sermon cite the soul's marriage to God as part of a lesson in spiritual anthropology—the nature of the human soul, the relationship between creator and created, and the path to salvation. In their writing, as in David of Augsburg's, the human's marriage to God is explicitly pedagogic and sacramental. This unbreakable connection between the human and divine realms, if fully comprehended, could unlock the individual's

---

[14]   I paraphrase from Kern's edition, which is also available through the DBNL, http://www.dbnl.org/tekst/_lim003limb01_01/_lim003limb01_01_0037.php. In his study of the Sermons, Wybren Scheepsma discusses the positioning of this sermon in the manuscript tradition and its relationship to the St. Georgen Sermons. *De Limburgse sermoenen*, ed. J.H. Kern (Leiden: A.W. Sijthoff, 1895), 423–26; Scheepsma, *The Limburg Sermons*, 108.

[15]   I have condensed and paraphrased from Herp, *Spieghel der Volcomenheit*, vol. 2, 193–7.

[16]   Ibid., vol. 2, 195.

potential for redemption. This theological foundation in spiritual anthropology underpins the imagery of so-called bridal mystics.

For instance, in his *Spiritual Espousals*, the fourteenth-century priest and recluse Jan van Ruusbroec also explained the relationship between humanity and divinity using the images of evaporation and reflection in a two-sided mirror:

> But a person is like a double mirror, which receives images on both sides. For in his higher part, a person receives God with all his gifts, and in his lower part, he receives sensible images from the senses. Now he can turn inwards whenever he wishes, and practice justice without hindrance. But a person is changeable in this life. And therefore, he often turns outwards and exercises himself in the senses without need, and without the bidding of enlightened reason, and he falls into daily faults. But in the loving inward turning of the just person, all daily faults are just like a drop of water in a blazing oven.[17]

Here, Ruusbroec describes the two parts of the human, spiritual and physical, which interacted differently with God. Looking at the reflection of God vaporizes sin, but seeking virtue through actions of the body is futile. In every moment, the double-mirror, which is the created human, is constantly pulled by the body towards images, and by the soul to God's gifts. For Ruusbroec, this experience is open to every person because humans are mutable, while God is fixed. Accepting this model for the human's relationship with God and creation made each day into a battle. Though not always expressed as a consummation of marriage, the experience of discovering the spark of God within the soul could not have existed without love, a mutual affection flowing between the spirit of the Godhead and the soul of the individual that was an underlying principle of the universe.

Like David of Augsburg, Ruusbroec understood Christ's incarnation as a marriage and proposed that the history of creation was a series of weddings. The first coming of Christ the bridegroom was his birth, life, death, and ascent into heaven, the second coming is the "present coming of Christ our Bridegroom daily in our soul."[18] This second wedding is the practice of virtue by any living person, and the reception of sacraments. The third marriage "is at the judgment or in the hour of death," as the soul pulled away from the body.[19] The fourth and final union followed the discarding of body, manifesting as an unmediated encounter between the human and Christ. When a person "offers all his life and all his works to God's honor and to God's praise and is intent on God and loves him above all things [he will think often of Christ's sacrifice and the sacraments]," arousing a desire to "see and to know Christ his Bridegroom as He is in Himself: even though he knows Him in his works, that, he thinks, is not sufficient."[20] Those made receptive to the

---

[17]   All citations to the *Spiritual Espousals* are from the Brepols CCCM Opera Omnia edition, which is volume 3. Unless otherwise specified, I have used Helen Rolfson's translation. Jan van Ruusbroec, *Opera omnia*, vol. 3 (Turnhout: Brepols, 1989).

[18]   Ruusbroec, *Geestelike Brulocht*, 190–92.

[19]   Ibid., 196–8.

[20]   Ibid., 272–4.

126   *Marrying Jesus in Medieval and Early Modern Northern Europe*

power of God's love through daily exercises will sometimes glimpse God's face. With each new brushing up against God, souls detached more from the body and plunged deeper into the abyss of God.

The relationship between the reflection of God in creation and the notion that humans had been created to wed God is most succinctly explained in Rulman Merswin's *Nine Rocks* [*Neunfelsenbuch*]. The married merchant and leader of the Strasbourg Friends of God uses the form of a dialogue between the "der mensche" [the person] who played the part of (Merswin's) soul, and "die entwurte" [the answer], the voice of revelation. In the final chapter, the Person is utterly incapable of explaining his revelations in a way that would be useful for other beginners. After seeing the Source, that is the Creator, out of which all created things had been made, the person's soul experienced "an overwhelming joy surpassing gladness, that all created things are filled from that source, and that he alone, who created all creatures, was their spouse."[21] The creator had filled all creations with a portion of himself, and that same creator was the *gemahel*, spouse, for every person. Merswin's understanding of creation originates in revelation, is translated through divine exegesis, and articulated with a familiar analogy for explaining the relationship between creator and creation: all created humans are brides of Christ.

Simply put, these thirteenth- and fourteenth-century theologians believed the actions and experiences of the body were distinct from the actions and experiences of the soul. Created as pure souls within contaminated flesh, the sins of the body could at worst tarnish the divinity of the soul, and the body's good works could not wash that stain away without divine love. Humans, like the incarnate Christ reflected the spiritual divinity and carnal mortality of the imageless Godhead and turning inwards (focusing the interior eye of the soul introspectively to find God) meant drawing closer to the divine. By letting go of material images, humans drew close to God, and during communion, an individual's eternal soul blended with God's, until the interior self could no longer be distinguished from God. Consequently, the most worldly sinner might be closer to God than a monk or nun who had turned away from the Divine face by daily devotions.

Naked Mystic, Naked God

Each of the passages I have cited so far uses "the person" or "the one" in contrast to "the other" who is God to distinguish between the two entities who interlock, intertwine, and then blend together so perfectly that their identities are erased by love. This careful wording of the human's identity as neither male nor female may confuse modern readers who now see fetuses assigned to "team pink" or "team blue" based on ultrasound images. Medieval theologians understood human souls to be only as gendered as the formlessness of God the father and the form of

---

[21] Rulman Merswin, "Das Buch von den neun Felsen: von dem Strassburger Bürger Rulman Merswin 1352: nach des Verf. Autograph," ed. Karl Schmidt (Leipzig: Hirzel, 1859), 127.

Created to Be a Bride   127

the Incarnate Son. Merswin, Ruusbroec, and David of Augsburg describe mutable flowing bodies and souls molding to God's form and dissolving into his essence. These souls were not static genderless, intersex, or androgynous beings—they were becoming Godlike, so perfectly reformed to the other's shape that the reflection can no longer be distinguished from its source. Because these medieval theological images overlap with the illustrative examples of post-Freudian psychoanalysis, the one and the other's interpenetration and mirroring have been reinvented by Lacan, Irigary, and others as a sexualized couple, one dominating the other, but both exposed and utterly abject. As Amy Hollywood, Ulrike Wiethaus, Luce Irigaray, and others have artfully shown, the abject, subject, medieval female figure can become a spiritualized other, her naked wounds resonating with the ultrafeminized and bleeding Christ. Hollywood compellingly argues that mysticism and psychoanalysis are allied discourses; contemporary feminist readings of medieval mysticism influenced by twentieth-century psychoanalysis must not forget the real words and contexts of medieval authors.[22] Medieval women are still frequently imagined to be oppressed bodies subject to patriarchal violence and understood through a modern two-gender system documenting experiential and biological difference. Consequently, when a female practitioner becomes joined to the flesh and spirit of the Godhead, her account of stripping naked, kissing and then dissolving into the divine is marked as ecstatic, submissive, and sexualized even though she has used exactly the same images and taught the same theological principals as contemporary male authors.

The convergence of God and human and reflection of God in human represented a contested line between deification and pantheism in doctrinal debates of the fourteenth century. Going beyond being within God to claim to have *become* God would cause a good deal of trouble for Eckhart, Ruusbroec, and the beguine Marguerite Porete. Describing union with God invited accusations of subscribing to the so-called "Heresy of the Free Spirit."[23] With so much at stake, the interpenetration of God and Soul in fourteenth-century mystical writing demands gender parity for authors (what is recognized as "theological" in Ruusbroec must also be read as "theological" in Mechthild). The interflowing of God and human complicates the role of what we now call gender and perceive as erotic sexuality in accounts of marriage to Jesus. Medieval theologians described the lovers/spouses as alternating between male and female before the soul's gradual approach to and then dissolution into the Godhead *because* that exchange was one of the central idioms of medieval sacramental theology.

Mechthild of Magdeburg, a beguine who left her family around the age of 12 to live a semireligious life of prayer and labor, is both a gifted poet and a doctrinally

---

[22] Hollywood, *Sensible Ecstasy*, 7–9, 275–7.

[23] For a foundation in the distinction (in addition to sources cited elsewhere), see Auguste Jundt, *Histoire du panthéisme populaire au Moyen Age et au seizième siècle (suivie de pièces inédites concernant les Frères du libre esprit, maître Eckhart, les libertins spirituels, etc.) Paris 1875* (Frankfurt am Main: Minerva, 1964); Robert E. Lerner, *The Heresy of the Free Spirit in the Later Middle Ages* (Berkeley: University of California Press, 1972).

128   *Marrying Jesus in Medieval and Early Modern Northern Europe*

orthodox sacramental theologian. Since the rediscovery and publication of her writing in modern critical editions and translations, she has also become one of the most frequently cited examples of medieval female-authored mysticism (and of *Frauenmystik*).[24] Her *Flowing Light of the Godhead*, a collection of poems and visions compiled over decades, with assistance from sisters at the Cistercian convent of Helfta, references interpenetrative deification even in its title—the light flowing from the Godhead penetrates each human soul and draws individuals back into that abyss of divinity, until at last, personal identity dissolves. The passionate soul of the *Flowing Light*'s verses is very different from the self-taught theologian and evangelist Mechthild alludes to when she writes about herself, yet the two are dangerously conflated by post-Freudian readers.[25] Mechthild's allusions to nakedness beneath fabric may seem intensely sensual, bodily, or sexual, but differ significantly from bodily intercourse. No matter how deeply physical lovers penetrate each other, their union and their pleasure depends on distinct, intact bodies, while Mechthild's lovers are denied pleasure so long as they retain clothing and flesh. Though some readers project Mechthild's naked body into her poetry and assume that she writes as if she were having sex with God, theologically, her descriptions of nakedness and union with God are nearly identical to David of Augsburg's.

Though she explicitly describes naked bodies, Mechthild's use of nudity explains the soul's proximity to God. She also alludes to the dressing and undressing of the *Song of Songs* and to the washing of body and change of clothing which accompanied baptism, monastic profession, and other ritual cleansings of the medieval liturgy, reception of the Eucharist or the Incarnation (God taking human clothing), and being lit up by the divine spark (the glimmer of God within each human soul). In one verse, Mechthild describes God "clothing yourself with my soul / and you are her most intimate garment [*nehtes cleit*]."[26] Two non-bodies draw close, pressing against the naked flesh of the other in the comfortable intimacy of a brief embrace before parting again. Are they naked? Who is wearing whom?

---

[24]   On the discovery of Mechthild's manuscript and her rise as a universal representative for feminist studies, see Poor, *Mechthild of Magdeburg and Her Book*, 187–99. In addition to previously cited work on Mechthild by Amy Hollywood, Ulrike Wiethaus, who acknowledges Mechthild's theological innovations, uses Mechthild's bridal persona to inform modern constructions of gender and transpersonal psychology. Ulrike Wiethaus, *Ecstatic Transformation: Transpersonal Psychology in the Work of Mechthild of Magdeburg* (Syracuse: Syracuse University Press, 1996).

[25]   Bernard McGinn notes that Mechthild subtitled her book as a *bode*, message, or good news. Bernard McGinn, *The Flowering of Mysticism: Men and Women in the New Mysticism (1200–1350)*, vol. 3 (New York: Crossroad Herder, 1999).

[26]   I have used Frank Tobin's translations, noting where I have modified Tobin's wording. Citations list first Tobin's translation, the same passage in the German critical edition. Mechthild of Magdeburg, *The Flowing Light of the Godhead*, ed. and trans. Frank J. Tobin (New York: Paulist Press, 1998), 76; *Das fliessende Licht der Gottheit: Nach der Einsiedler Handschrift in kritischem Vergleich mit gesamten Überlieferung*, ed. Margot Schmidt (Stuttgart-Bad Canstatt: F. Frommann, 1995), 44. Hereafter FL.

Created to Be a Bride

This intimate garment implies a bodiliness shared by "the Soul" and "God." Mechthild returns to this idea of shared clothing again in another verse: "Lord, your blood and mine are one, untainted. Your love and mine are one, inseparable. Your garment and mine are one, immaculate [*unbevleket*]. Your mouth and mine are one, unkissed. Your breast and mine are one, not caressed by any man but you alone."[27] Again God and the Soul draw close, now wrapped within the same cloth, and into a single layer of skin which covers their shared mouth and chest. These naked bodies have drawn so close they can no longer caress. Their two mouths have become one mouth that does not kiss itself. God's pure blood of salvation pumps through their joined veins. For Mechthild, nudity is a prelude to removing the body itself, not a bodily pleasure.

Mechthild's understanding of nudity as a precursor to perfect union with God also shapes her descriptions of the soul's wedding dress and the bridal pair's consummation. In a chapter described as a "path of love" written for a "Dear friend of God," the soul wears a "soft slip of humility, so humble that it cannot bear anything underneath it. Over it comes a white dress of spotless chastity, so pure that it cannot bear anything in thought, word, or touch that might soil it. Then she puts on the cloak of her good name, which she has gilded with all the virtues."[28] The soul is invited to rock and suck the Christchild but insists, "I am a full-grown bride. I want to go to my Lover," even though her body and senses will be burned away as she drowns in him. She enters "the secret chamber of the invisible Godhead," where God, who is beyond humanity, commands that she "stay ... Take off your clothes ... you are so utterly formed to my nature that not the slightest thing can be between you and me." To which the soul replies, "Lord, now I am a naked soul and you in yourself are a well-adorned God." As the two surrender to their desire, we may assume that the naked soul and adorned God draw close enough to touch—but as the barriers of clothing suggest, they are not yet perfect reflections penetrating one another.

The superficial sensuality of this scene overshadows a profound theological argument. Elsewhere, Mechthild explains that with constant help and support from others, each "spiritual person," can dress in virtues and meet the heavenly spouse. She describes the bride and her wedding party's rich allegorical garments in another passage, omitting only details of the groom's body and attire, as if she could see only his embracing arms and crowning hands. Paired with the above passage, the bodies and clothing of bride and groom stand in for spiritual concepts, just like the clothing they wear. At the ceremony the bride receives a crown from her spouse which only "geistliche lute" [spiritual people] can wear.[29] The bride rides to her wedding on "a beast of burden ... the body," from which she will be

---

[27]   The last two lines are not present in the German manuscript editions and have been reconstructed from the Latin. Schmidt, FL, 95; Tobin, FL, 68.

[28]   Schmidt, FL, 27–31; Tobin, FL, 58–62.

[29]   Tobin translated this as "Religious people," 344n68. I have returned it to "spiritual," in keeping with this book's overall argument that the bride of Christ was not only for the professional religious. Schmidt, FL, 33–5; Tobin, FL, 63–5.

130   *Marrying Jesus in Medieval and Early Modern Northern Europe*

released as soon as her spouse summons her. As the two draw together, the bride casts aside her spiritual clothing and her physical body, and the bridegroom strips her naked, wraps her in his own clothing, and then pulls her even closer, until the two cannot be distinguished by barriers of flesh, bodily corruption and worldly sin are washed away by love.

Though they all use marriage, union, and nudity to describe joining with God, Mechthild's descriptions are far less sexually explicit than Jan van Ruusbroec and Henry Suso. In Ruusbroec's *Seven Enclosures*, casting off the worldly self and embracing Jesus in a change of clothing is explicitly a naked consummation: "[W]e disrobe ourselves, putting off the old man with his works and putting on the new, that is, Jesus Christ. He clothes us with Himself, with His life, His grace, and His affection. And when He has thus clothed us in His habit, with longing and with love, we live in Him and He in us.... And when the lover is united with the beloved in an enclosure of love, there is love consummated."[30] Ruusbroec's language is straightforward, lacking Mechthild's wordplay, but his meaning is no different. With each exchange of garments—the soul slipping out of the body and into God—clothing implies and announces nudity, bodiliness, and intimacy. Christ dresses the Soul in Himself, uniting the two in love. He has given "us" his "habit," the allegorical garment representing good spiritual living, just as "we" have cast off our old worldly clothes. Clothing is discarded before new clothing is put on, so that Jesus exposes himself in the same gesture which clothes the soul.

First nakedness, drawing close, then pressing against, and finally union. If Mechthild's nakedness is personal, intensely intimate, experiential, is Ruusbroec's any less so? If Ruusbroec's nakedness is simply an image standing in for a theological concept, is Mechthild's any different? If Mechthild's sensual poetry seems *more* erotic than Ruusbroec's explicit description of consummation, have we been aroused by a more artful writer? Are we projecting our own desire for sexually available women onto Mechthild, making her into a wanton lover of God even as we assume that Ruusbroec's sexual desire—if he has any at all—can be aroused only by demonic temptresses? Of course not. Even if Mechthild's "I" reveals personal experiences, while Ruusbroec's "we" is of an imagined perfect soul, both authors describe a *path* or way to finding God which allowed others to initiate their own spiritual transformations.

That nudity can be educational, not (only) erotic, becomes even clearer in the visual program which illustrated German manuscript and print copies of Henry Suso's *Life of the Servant*. Like Mechthild, Suso's writing is often read as gender-bending, violent, and erotic. Jeffrey Hamburger has linked Suso's self-presentation as a bride of Christ to devotional media he encountered in women's Dominican communities.[31] These close friendships with women led historian Caroline Bynum to label Suso's written works oriented "almost entirely toward women," but his

---

[30] Ruusbroec, *Opera Omnia*, vol. 2, 156–7.
[31] Jeffrey F. Hamburger, "The Use of Images in the Pastoral Care of Nuns: The Case of Heinrich Suso and the Dominicans," *The Art Bulletin* 71, no. 1 (1989).

Created to Be a Bride 131

self-help books attracted an international audience.[32] The dissonance between Suso's writing, which details the protagonist soul's nakedness and union with God as sensually as Mechthild's, and the pen-drawn images designed to illustrate the *Exemplar* reveal that medieval readers would have visualized these seemingly sexual passages as depictions of crucifixion, incarnation, and communication. The visual program repeatedly exposes wounded bodies of Christ and the Servant, emphasizing their shared wounds, total humiliation, and slow, unstoppable attraction. These painted images are carefully labeled diagrams with little sensuality. Their nude figures counter the illusion of eroticism in Mechthild's—or Suso's, or Ruusbroec's—written words.

Henry Suso's *Exemplar* is a compilation of five German-language books, including a spiritual autobiography titled *Life of the Servant* and the German version of his *Little Book of Eternal Wisdom*, which would also be translated into Latin as the *Horologium Sapientiae*. The *Little Book of Eternal Wisdom* and *Life of the Servant* give different, though related accounts of a pious friar's encounters with God. These same experiences may also be recorded in a third text ascribed to Suso, the so-called *Minnebuchlein* [*Little Book of Love*], which survives in a single manuscript copy. Only *Life of the Servant* is illustrated. Suso's naked union with God in the prose *Little Book of Eternal Wisdom* is far more sensual than the bare bodies illustrating *Life of the Servant*, and far less intensely personal than the interactions between God and the soul in *Little Book of Love*.[33] The differences in tone, wording, and language as the Soul encounters the Divine in these three books emphatically show that the intense imagery of some mystical texts was a form of word-painting which helped the reader construct mental diagrams.

Suso's Servant of Eternal Wisdom was a familiar figure across central Europe.[34] Portraits of the Servant guided viewers to match the actions of their own bodies to the experiences of the Servant's soul. Suso's corpus is a stunningly comprehensive adaptation of a single narrative to multiple media platforms. His *Little Book of*

---

[32] Bynum, *Holy Feast and Holy Fast*, 102. On the textual transmission of Suso's writing, see Karl Bihlmeyer, ed., *Heinrich Seuse, Deutsche Schriften* (Stuttgart: Kohlhammer, 1907), *3–*26; Hella Frühmorgen-Voss and Norbert H. Ott, "Katalog der Deutschsprachigen Illustrierten Handschriften des Mittelalters" (München: In Kommission bei der C.H. Beck'schen Verlagsbuchhandlung, 1986), vol. 4, 175–82 (hereafter KdiH).

[33] For a more recent argument for its canonicity and a partial reading of the text, see Peter Meister, "Suso's (?) Minnebüchlein," *Mystics Quarterly* 15, no. 3 (1989). All translations are my own, from Karl Bihlmeyer, ed., *Heinrich Seuse. Deutsche Schriften*, 537–54.

[34] For an overview of Suso's masculinity and his relationship with the female-gendered Christ, see Newman, *God and the Goddesses*, 206–22; Deborah Rose-Lefmann, "Lady Love, King, Minstrel: Courtly Depiction of Jesus or God in Late-Medieval Vernacular Mystical Literature," in *Arthurian Literature and Christianity: Notes From the Twentieth Century*, ed. Peter Meister, Garland Reference Library of the Humanities (New York: Garland, 1999); Sandra Fenten, *Mystik und Körperlichkeit: eine komplementär-vergleichende Lektüre von Heinrich Seuses geistlichen Schriften* (Würzburg: Königshausen and Neumann, 2007).

132   *Marrying Jesus in Medieval and Early Modern Northern Europe*

Eternal Wisdom described the marriage between Soul and God as a stripping-away of clothing, body, and worldly images, his *Life of the Servant* wrapped that marriage up again in pictures of bodies and clothing, his *Book of Love* [*Das Minnebüchlein*] performed the union between Loving Soul and Crucified Spouse as an agonizingly emotional conversation, and the *Brotherhood of Eternal Wisdom* replicated the Servant's prayer practices for potential brides of God. The Servant's performance as bride to God and groom to Lady Wisdom models breaking away from the material world mediated by images, even as the images illustrating his books transformed paintings of the Servant's exposed flesh into heaven's gate.

In each of these books, the Soul's marriage borrows from secular romance and troubles constructions of gender—as when, for instance, Wisdom scolds the newly knighted Servant for weeping "like a woman."[35] The Servant's life is often mistaken for Suso's own, but the Servant's body is no more Suso's than it is Christ's or the readers'. Suso's Servant is a young boy committed to religious life, educated by the Dominican Order, but hesitant to fully commit to his vocation. As the servant struggles against temptation, dedicates himself to suffering like Christ, and receives guiding visions, he comes closer to meriting marriage with his beloved wife, Wisdom. When his struggles against his pride become torture, he begins to comprehend the agony and wonder of Christ's death on the cross, until he becomes indistinguishable from his husband, Christ. As a spouse of Christ-Wisdom, the Servant models how individuals should respond to devotional media, including images but also sermons and counsel from teachers and spiritual advisors. He prays beneath painted cathedral walls, meditates before devotional images, carves Christ's name on his own body, and summons the apparition of Wisdom to shape reshape life. The Servant's betrothal to Wisdom in chapter 3 was inspired by a reading from the Book of Wisdom while sitting with other Dominicans in communal contemplation and consumption in the refectory. Later that evening, Wisdom appears to ask the Servant for his heart, but "more then was impossible for him."[36] The Servant was already a member of a religious order, receiving advice from God, and dedicated to daily prayer—enough to win only a smile from his new lover.

The *Little Book of Eternal Wisdom* relates a wayward soul's adornment and agonizing nudity as a bride: "[T]he heavenly Father [who] had adorned me more beautifully than all other corporeal creatures and had chosen me for his tender and lovely bride," but the soul succumbed to the temptation of the devil, who stole away his heavenly garments. The soul laments, "I have lost him. I have lost my only chosen Love ... I sit here naked. For my false lover, my true deceiver—oh the foulness of the deed—has left me deceived and wretched and has stripped me of all the belongings with which my only true love had clothed me."[37] Dressed by God, stripped by the devil, and now naked and weeping, this soul's nakedness is

---

[35]   *Henry Suso: The Exemplar*, ed. Tobin, 65.

[36]   Ibid., 67–70.

[37]   Ibid., 219.

Created to Be a Bride 133

shameful evidence of a fall from grace. God explains that when he gives himself "to a creature according to its capacity to receive me, I wrap up the brightness of the sun in a cloth and in human words give you spiritual meaning about me and my sweet love thus: I place myself tenderly before the eyes of your heart." This first part of the exchange can only be perceived with interior eyes. Once inner sight comprehends God's nature and reforms the individual, she or he is able to ask God to "clothe and adorn me in a spiritual manner, putting finery on me as you wish. Give me everything that can move your heart to special love (for me), delight, and full joy of heart. And this is absolutely everything that you, together with all men, can think up: form, adornment, grace; but in me all this is more lovely than anyone can describe." A person who has met God, clothed God, and perceived all things in the "pure, bright mirror of the naked Godhead" shall be embraced and carried into the kingdom of heaven. Clothed "with her external body," crowned with "the contemplative union of the soul with the naked Godhead [that leads the soul] into the simple nakedness of Being. Face to face with this it then finds fulfillment and eternal happiness … [plummeting into the abyss of God] where it is swept along, and to which it is so united that it cannot want otherwise than what God wants."[38] Suso's description here is even more elaborate than Mechthild's, more explicit than Ruusbroec's, and consonant with the use of mirror and marriage in the writing of other theologians. Even more than Mechthild, Suso insists that *he* is the soul of the story, and thus the bride face to face with and plummeting into God.

An illustration designed for Suso's *Life of the Servant* presents the servant in the process of stripping away clothing before the gaze of Christ. Its text scrolls, composition, and display of naked bodies closely correlate with the scenes I have paraphrased so far, yet little in the scene is easily sexualized (Figure 4.1). In a version of the scene preserved in a 1482 manuscript closely related to the print editions of the *Exemplar*, which belonged to the Benedictine Abbey of St. Ulrich and Afra in Augsburg, a tonsured male representing the Servant kneels at the base of a rosebush upon which the naked Christ has been crucified. Though sometimes titled "Das Kreuz als Rosenbaum des Leidens" ["The Cross as a Rosebush of Sorrows"], this manuscript copy does not include captions for images. Blood courses down from Christ's splayed arms, drizzling onto rose blossoms, down his side and over the drape of cloth banding his waist, and from the nail-pierced wounds of his contorted legs. Above, God the Father, male saints, and Angels observe the scene. A nimbed Christchild steps forward from the base of the cross to the kneeling figure, his hand on the stem of a rose, and behind him an angel grasps another rose by the stem. The Servant gazes up towards Christ, whose dead bloody face tilts towards him with heavily lidded eyes. Text scrolls explain the necessity of suffering with Christ, which will bring a devotee to God's peace. In this version of the image, which closely follows the first print edition, the Servant's robe falls open to expose his naked body. His navel curves in a perfect reflection of Christ's, as his hands pull back his robe to proudly display his naked torso to the naked Christ. A scroll

---

[38]   Ibid., 228.

Figure 4.1 *The Servant before the Cross as a Rosebush of Sorrows*, Henry Suso, *Exemplar*. Courtesy of Wolfenbüttel, Herzog August Bibl., Cod. 78.5 Aug. 2°, f 62 r, c. 1473.

Created to Be a Bride

proclaims that Jesus has wounded the Servant's heart right through so that the sign of Jesus now appears on its interior ["Jesus mein herze verwundet hat gezaichnet darin IESUS stat"]. A discreetly placed rose grows between the Servant's legs as if budding from his penis. Here a bride of Christ is undressing beneath the cross. Here Christ's naked body is on display, dead, bleeding, and evaluating the Servant's invisible wounds. Text scrolls proclaim the Servant's love, agony, and hope for redemption. The composition is antiseptic in comparison to Mechthild's passionate nakedness or Suso's heartrending prose. Without declarations of kissing and descriptions of naked bodies colliding to narrate the scene's actions, it is as if the Servant simply struck a pose. If Mechthild and Suso's prose evoke scenes so erotic, love so intense it verges on pornographic sexual ecstasy, the Servant's anatomically detailed naked body with its suggestively placed rose and proclamations of passionate love must be even more obscene. And if the Servant's display before the Rosecross is only a textbook illustration, Mechthild's sketches of naked abasement must not be read differently. For medieval audiences, each of these encounters was a scripturally supported lesson in salvation.

Suso, like Ruusbroec and Mechthild, paints naked interpenetrating bodies with his prose. But the artists who illustrated his texts emphasize that complete union with the naked God is possible only through God's love, Christ's incarnation, and the potential for each created being to become the bridal soul. In the *Little Book of Love* [*Minnebuchlein*], which survives in a single manuscript copy, the Loving Soul observes Christ's passion, watches the burial, and comes to understand the marvel that such a gruesome death could bring the promise of eternal life. The lovers draw closer, kiss, and undress, creating a dwelling place for Wisdom within the body's own heart. The soul and her spouse lovingly cuddle at the foot of the cross ["ein liepliches kosen der sele under dem crútze mit irem gemahel, dem abgelosten Christo"], and the loving soul expresses a desire to embrace her buried beloved. She seeks him, and finally finds him, splattered with blood, and begs to join Christ on the Cross: "I desire that all my strength die within you and all my bones be deadened with you, my soul hung up with you." The soul is invited to climb onto the cross and join him: "*consurge, consurge*, rise up my heart, and clothe yourself with God's strength" because she has her king before her and should never stray from him again.[39] What the visual program of Suso's *Life of the Servant* captured in a single drawing, this dialogue evokes with the loving soul's heart-wrenching insecurity and desire: To become the spouse of Christ, Eternal Wisdom, meant first fully experiencing Christ's suffering and death. When a soul pressed against and then passed through God, the one became the other, the bride became the groom. In a sense, then, encountering a naked God is just that—God without accoutrements, mediation, or distractions. Stripping also paralleled Christ's shameful disrobing and helped the naked bride identify with a naked crucified groom. Nakedness like this cited creation and incarnation—God's spirit and the human's soul have been dressed in flesh and clothing—and salvation. Whether painted or penned,

---

[39]   Bihlmeyer, *Heinrich Seuse. Deutsche Schriften*, 552–4.

136 *Marrying Jesus in Medieval and Early Modern Northern Europe*

these images inspired a longing for God and coached the viewer through spiritual exercises. Like the "every-soul" whose voice they adopted, the mystic's body became an "every-body," a teaching tool inviting the reader to identify with and share the experiences of the protagonist. Because women authors like Mechthild so skillfully articulated this anthropology of soul and body, love and salvation, it has almost naturally followed that medieval women's theological writing has been compared to their male contemporaries and been presented as more embodied, more affective, and more expressive as teachings authorized by the author's visions. And there is some truth in the notion that revelation created a space for physically female bodies to speak with religious authority in a world that honored Paul's warning against women teaching. But Mechthild must be understood as no more or less the bride than Suso the Servant, Merswin the Person, or Ruusbroec and Tauler the brides of their own books.

Marrying the Man of Sorrows

Henry Suso's Servant was a publicly available, accessible teaching body guiding viewers and readers to contract marriages with God through devotion to the crucified Christ. The visual program accompanying *Life of the Servant* presents the Servant's marriage to Wisdom several chapters after the related chapter. This illustration of wisdom giving the Servant a wedding ring and new clothes creates a second visual narrative.[40] In the image sequence, the Servant first marks his body with Christ's name, is tormented like Christ on the Cross, receives a vision of the Crucifixion, and then marries his heavenly spouse. After earning a wedding ring and heavenly garb, the Servant's robe falls open to reveal the bloody wound on his chest. He is Christlike as he at last is touched by Christ as the Man of Sorrows. This series of illustrations tracks a spiritual path from initial conversion to identification with Christ, in which marrying Wisdom is a moment of transformation, but not the final moment of perfect union.

The Ulrich and Afra manuscript's depiction of the Servant's knighting marks his body as the body of Christ and the body of the bride of Revelation. The Servant kneels, extending his hands up to heaven to receive a ring from a bearded Christ as angels deliver shoes, a rose crown, and a robe made of stars (Figure 4.2). By his knee are shield, helmet, and armor bearing the holy monogram IHS and the slogan "lauterkait" [honorableness]. A bearded Jesus with cruciform halo leans down from heaven to place a ring on the Servant's finger as angels hover with the "heavenly raiment." In this artist's rendition, a scroll wraps through the scene announcing that knightly clothing and honor shall be provided for an eternal person [*ewigclich minschen*] who suffers with God. This illustration conflates the seemingly courtly hyper-masculine action of spiritual warfare juxtaposing the armor bearing the crest IHS, the charging steeds with clothing marking the Servant as the bride of the Apocalypse.

---

[40] See especially the discussion by Jeffrey Hamburger, KdiH, vol. 4.

Created to Be a Bride 137

Figure 4.2 *The Servant's Marriage to Christ*, Henry Suso, *Exemplar*. Courtesy of Wolfenbüttel, Herzog August Bibl., Cod. 78.5 Aug. 2°, f 95 v.

These paintings of the Servant's exposed body reiterate the message of Suso's writing: marriage brought with it the experience of God's suffering through meditating on and recreating the crucifixion. Portraits of the Servant's scarred, bleeding body reminded the viewer that harsh ascetic practices were futile; only turning the soul's eye inward to gaze at the broken body of Christ would win the bridegroom's love.

For those who accepted that, salvation began with turning inward, abandoning the body, and experiencing Christ's crucifixion, which signified the redemptive power of *discarding* human flesh, the inverse and perfect reflection of Christ's

138   *Marrying Jesus in Medieval and Early Modern Northern Europe*

incarnation, not abject humiliation. With this reading, I return to book 1 of the *Flowing Light*, where Mechthild describes how a bride first follows Christ, then before her body dissolves into God:

> *How the beautiful bridegroom and how the bride shall follow the 23 grades of crucifixion*
>
> *Look at me, my bride.* See how beautiful are my eyes, how comely is my mouth, how on fire is my heart, how agile are my hands, and how swift are my feet. So, Follow me! You shall be martyred with me, betrayed in jealousy, hunted in ambush, taken prisoner in hate, bound in obedience, your eyes covered so that one will not tell you the truth, slapped by the rage of the world, brought to trial in confession, struck blows by penance, sent to Herod in derision, stripped naked by abandonment, scourged by poverty, crowned with trials, spat upon by disgrace, bearing your cross in the hatred of sin, crucified in voluntary withdrawal from all things, nailed to the cross by the holy virtues, wounded by love, dying on the cross in holy constancy, pierced in your heart by constant union, taken down from the cross in true victory over all your enemies, buried in oblivion, arisen from the dead in a holy end, and drawn up into heaven in God's breath.[41]

Mechthild's chapter teaches that the bride must be crucified, in perfect imitation of Christ, before she is drawn into God. Christ's exhortation to the bride is like a painted image cycle of the Passion, expanded with medieval accretions such as the crucifixion by the Virtues. Another passage again positions the soul in Christ's submissive posture during the scourging to receive shameful blows familiar through prayers and art: "Her eyes are bound with her body's baseness / because she is so utterly imprisoned in its darkness. She carries her cross on a sweet path / When she truly surrenders herself to God in all sufferings." Again, the chapter is written as if it were describing a painting. The soul's head is struck with a reed, and she suffers, thirsty, on the cross, until "her body is killed in living love / when her spirit is raised aloft above all human senses." Like Jesus, the soul is buried, and rises again on Easter and strives to teach her five senses the holy teachings, then ascends into heaven. This perfect identification with Christ is not for Mechthild alone, but for "every soul that in holy moderation of all her activity is truly permeated by genuine love of God."[42] For Mechthild, as for Suso, the bride's nakedness and painful humiliating death were intended to teach medieval Christians to turn away from material and bodily things: the absence of bodies is the theologian's ultimate goal, as the naked soul finally discards everything a body needs and wants. Even in that final naked moment, flesh and spirit are intimately related. If modern readers knew nothing of the historical Mechthild's career as a beguine, her retirement in Helfta, or her popularity as an author in the convents of southern Germany, these passages might never have been associated with a woman at all, nor invited speculation about the religious symbolism and feminist rhetoric

---

[41]   Tobin, FL, 54; Schmidt, FL, 22.
[42]   Tobin, FL, 117–19; Schmidt, FL, 89–91.

Created to Be a Bride 139

of superimposing a woman's body onto the crucifixion. But Mechthild's name and voice have become as important to understanding her book as she insists God's voice was in its composition. Has she become masculine through her martyrdom? Divinized through her suffering? Authorized through her role as a mouthpiece for the Divine? Had she feminized the Godhead with her own body? Or should we simply pretend that the historical Mechthild, who described herself as a woman and was welcomed by other women into a gender-segregated community, had neither a physical body nor a gender when she chooses not to mention it herself? I suspect some modern voyeurs forget to *read* the physical displays in medieval texts. We watch the fluid soul, gawk as male becomes female, body becomes spirit, and souls slip into and out of clothing while the Godhead slips into or out of them. And then, sometimes, we write only about the naked bodies and their imagined genitalia, forgetting that body, soul, gender, spirit, even human and God would never have been so formally separated by a medieval author who recognized that body and soul were connected by strong sinews, each acting upon the other, as they interacted with and reflected the flesh and spirit of the Godhead. By thinking so hard about the bodies behind our manuscripts—suffering, enraptured, engendered—we risk overlooking a far more profound lesson about souls in our medieval sources.

In the closing lines of the sermon with which this chapter opens, Johannes Tauler narrates the suffering of souls in purgatory, who have more pain than all the martyrs, and contemplates Christ hanging naked on the cross. Tauler warns his audience that they need only God, "and therefore many are naked in hand and foot, which are all their strength and like their patrimony, and those who are cast into the outer darkness, they will weep and gnash their teeth—Ah dear child, think of and love God [*meinent und minnent*] loudly, [in order] that he will lift us out of this true darkness and bring us into the true light, for that, God help us. Amen."[43] Using the same images of Christ on the cross, cosuffering, and nakedness which we now think feminized Suso and authorized Mechthild, Tauler has urged his audience to think of the danger of arriving for their wedding with God unprepared. Was Tauler positing a redemptive power that could be unlocked by stripping naked and crucifying the bodies of his own audience, or himself? Almost certainly not—neither were Mechthild or Suso when they depicted crucifixion as a prelude to the soul's marriage with Christ. Each was explaining the same doctrine of salvation, which depended on bodies (the incarnation, the divine spark within the human) and depended on love (the mutual love of God and the believer) but was available to every created person, impartially.

The moment the reader's or the author's eyes become the bride's eyes, she or he also sets aside the body and receives Christ's in its place, losing first the sense of sight, then the humanizing drape of clothing, then the motion of her limbs, the use of her own heart, and even the breath in her body. In the end, there is neither Mechthild/Tauler/Suso/Soul (bride) nor Christ (beautiful groom); there is no cross, no crown, no corpse. All that remains is the invisible, inaudible flow of

---

[43] Tauler, *Predigten*, 398–402.

140   *Marrying Jesus in Medieval and Early Modern Northern Europe*

God's breath. This division between body and soul, which eventually allowed the dissolution of body, name, and gender into the intangibility of God, meant every created human could follow Christ into torture, oblivion, and eternal union with God. To read these lines as a commentary on gender is to overlook their message about the hierarchy of creation: women, children, and tradesmen were just as qualified as the learned clerics who officiated the sacraments, because men and women both lost their bodily status when they melted into God.

Teaching Love and Salvation

Although their books, like many other medieval accounts of union with God have been categorized as "mystical" since the nineteenth century, Mechthild and Suso recorded their visions and personal experiences for the benefit of others and explicitly state as their goal of guiding the pious onto the surest path to salvation.[44] Through the persona of the Servant of Eternal Wisdom, Henry Suso guided readers across Europe to embrace Christ's suffering and crucifixion and become espoused to the Godhead. The prologue to Suso's *Exemplar* explicitly states that the collection will provide exercises for spiritual beginners. A similar statement opens Mechthild of Magdeburg's *Flowing Light*, describing the book as for all religious people, both bad and good.[45] Their shared anthropology of souls and theology of salvation developed into a program for abandoning the world and wedding Christ—not by entering holy orders, but by dedicating themselves to interior spiritual exercises while going about the tasks of the day. These collaborations are revealed both in the histories of individual manuscripts and in the anecdotes incorporated into devotional books.

Exchanges between self-taught lay practitioners and spiritual masters affirmed the fame of spiritual teachers and the importance of conversations with the laity. Chapter 22 of Suso's *Life of the Servant* relates two visions received by Anna, one of the Servant's confessants.[46] Anna's visions present the Servant as a member of two distinct communities—his brothers in religious orders, and the congregation he serves. The Servant's exceptional piety marks his body among a crowd of tonsured Dominicans and obscures his form entirely beneath the spiritual bodies of his congregation. In the second vision, Anna sees "in him and on him ... countless numbers of persons suspended, and each was different from the others.

---

[44]   See Kieckhefer and Bynum especially for the distinction between reverence for the lives of saints and the need for exemplary figures who any sinner might emulate. Caroline Walker Bynum, "Wonder," *American Historical Review* 102, no. 1 (1997), 1–17; Richard Kieckhefer, *Unquiet Souls: Fourteenth-century Saints and their Religious Milieu* (Chicago: University of Chicago Press, 1984).

[45]   McGinn suggests Mechthild's prologue positions the piece as evangelical, on a similar level with scripture. McGinn, *The Flowering of Mysticism*, 223–5.

[46]   The scenes are also typically included in the visual cycle; see KdiH, vol. 4. Bynum, *Holy Feast and Holy Fast*, 344n194.

Created to Be a Bride   141

The more each one possessed God, the more room each one had in him; and the more space was within him, and the more God turned to each one." God explains that these bodies belong to "those people who go to him to confession, who are taught by him, or, aside from this, who are particularly devoted to him."[47] Anna's vision shows that the Servant is inseparable from the community he served and entirely remade by that service.

Collaborations between pious layfolk and vision-gifted spiritual teachers were lifelong relationships, involving counsel on sin and comportment, as well as the exchange of books and updates about spiritual exercises. As a single example, Henry Suso's books reached the courts of Flanders and Paris, the towns of England, and the domestic spaces of the Low German and Dutch-speaking North. There, Geert Grote's *Hours of Eternal Wisdom* reminded readers that Suso had "loved Eternal Wisdom and sought her out from his youth, even as she sought him to take him as a bride—he was made worthy for this when the Lord created him, God be praised."[48] Daily recitation of the Hours reminded each devotee that all humans were God's brides.[49] Like Tauler, Ruusbroec, Mechthild, Hadewijch, and Merswin, Suso's lessons were designed to be put to use, interpreted sometimes through the lens of theological learning but more often through the guidance of divine interlocutors who encouraged their authors to translate their personal experiences into practical manuals on loving and serving God. As they appeared to share their own insecurities, setbacks, and fears, each also described the reassuring comfort that *every* soul had been created a bride, and walked the earth in a body that contained and reflected the image of their loving spouse.

The worldview created through this body-soul symbiosis extended well beyond the compilation of devotional miscellanies for use by lay Christians. It also gave rise to a genre of legendary accounts of worldly but wise self-taught Christians who corrected, educated, but also sought to learn from masters of theology. One of these legends, titled "The Master's Daughter," explained how a young woman arrived at the Dominican men's convent and introduced herself as "neither a girl nor a woman, nor husband nor wife, nor widow nor virgin, nor master nor maid nor manservant.... I am none of all these things, I am just a thing like anything else and go my way."[50] Through spiritual labor, this young woman had set aside

---

[47]   *Henry Suso: the Exemplar*, ed. Tobin, 105–7.

[48]   "Dese heb ic ghemint ende wtghesocht van mijnre ioghet ende hebse ghesocht mi tot eenre bruut tontfaen ende ic bin gheworden een minre hoerre formen. God si gheloeft." My translation, from the transcription in Helen C. Wüstefeld and Anne S. Korteweg, *Sleutel tot licht: getijdenboeken in de Bibliotheca Philosophica Hermetica* (Amsterdam: In de Pelikaan, 2009).

[49]   The *Hours of Eternal Wisdom* survive in several hundred manuscripts, some of which can be traced to lay readers or were produced into the sixteenth century. For example, Oxford BL Rawl Lit f8* was owned by Lucy Claes, a sixteenth-century married woman.

[50]   I have used the English translation in Meister Eckhart, *The Complete Mystical Works of Meister Eckhart*, ed. and trans. Maurice O'C Walshe, 4th ed. (New York: Crossroad, 2009), 581–2.

142 *Marrying Jesus in Medieval and Early Modern Northern Europe*

her gender, class, and status as an uneducated laywoman, becoming a qualified teacher for celibate male clerics. Other examples of conversation and collaboration between spiritual mentors and the visiting laity include Geert Grote's visits to Jan van Ruusbroec.

Medieval readers and scribes assembled new mosaic images of Christ and the bride out of fragments and verses broken out of longer mystical treatises. These miscellanies lacked the introductions and glosses necessary in modern editions. Readers had already internalized the complex theology in passages they lingered over; some had certainly selected favorite passages to include in their own private devotions. Manuscripts and printed books can never fully disclose their past owners' spiritual lives, but it is worth seriously considering their organization and marketing. Late medieval Christians read these complex "mystical" treatises and recognized passages on the bride of Christ as *useful*. Contemplating how best to fulfill an individual's role as Christ's bride was part of daily devotions and the reception of the Eucharist.

Where modern scholars have noticed visionary authority superseding restrictions of gender and class—making the sinful little woman an equal to the Latinate professor or preacher—medieval scribes instead located both themselves and their sources as members of a community. Though the blessed authors whose words merited inclusion in the book were more advanced in their journey to God, both the scribe and the readers of the manuscript were also part of a transgenerational group exercise in salvation. Thus Mechthild begged the Lord to give future scribes who copied her book a reward the like of which had never before been bestowed on human beings. Flemish Prioress Alijt Bake copied Tauler's sermons alongside her own visions, urging those who read her manuscript to pray for the woman who had written it.[51] These books were not like our critical editions—only a handful of manuscripts and early printed editions preserved entire treatises—but many remained in use well into the seventeenth century. The *Exemplar*, the *Flowing Light*, the *Nine Rocks*, the *Spiritual Espousals*, and sermons by David of Augsburg and Johannes Tauler were brought into dialogue with one another as devotees compiled manuscripts of spiritual exercises suited to their own needs. Their exhortations to wed Christ, which modern scholars find intimate, ineffable, erotic works of poetry, were actually practical daily exercises intended to prepare individuals for marriage to God.

Marriage to the Godhead initiated and explained unmediated unions with the divine. While the body labored, loved, or prayed, the soul could take an interior

---

[51] "dine schribere die das buoch na mir haben geschriben...." Tobin, FL, 69; Schmidt, FL, 98. The Bake Colophon reads:

Bidt voor diet maeete ende heeft gescr[e]uen /
Want zij arm door gode es bleuen / Doe men .M. vienhondert screef / na dat
ihesus ant tcruce bleef / en .xlvj. ofte daer omtrent / soe was dit eerst
ghemaeet te ghent / van zuster alijt der priorinnen / van galileen god wille
haer ziele gewinnen.

Created to Be a Bride

journey unfettered by its body's class, gender, or occupation. In fact, if legendary accounts of Meister Eckhart and Johannes Tauler are reliable, this style of devotion best suited the pious layperson. To become a bride of Christ, individuals only needed to understand the incarnation, the sacraments, and pray privately. Images derived from scripture guided spiritual beginners closer to the kernel of God within their own bodies—love, kisses, but also coal, ovens, flowing water, drops of water in wine, and mirrors—images which transcend our modern somatic vocabulary. The resemblance between the bodies and souls of humankind and the creator God's eternal spirit and his murdered incarnation, Christ, was the greatest mystery of the medieval Church. From the Alps to the North Sea, from the last decades of the thirteenth century to the late fifteenth century, these teachers and their copyists reiterated the promise that Christ was a groom for all Christian souls and that preparing for marriage was a path to personal redemption.

Chapter 5
Taking Jesus as a Second Husband

> This was in absolute truth, that she left the bed of the lord of her house who was called her bodily spouse with great weariness, and sought her tender lord Christ, who is the true spouse of her soul.[1]

Women who became brides of Christ while married to living men first stymied medieval hagiographers and now perplex historians of Christianity. These women's marital obligations to both physical and spiritual spouses potentially created domestic tensions and challenged dominant beliefs about the importance of celibacy. Some medieval hagiographers, as in the above verses from Middle High German adaptation of Dietrich of Apolda's life and miracles of St. Elizabeth of Hungary (1207–31), valorized caring for both worldly and spiritual spouses as a sanctified domesticity. These married brides of Christ were practicing their religion in ways and in spaces appropriate for the laity. In response, some clergy began promoting marriage to Jesus to the laity guided relationships between married laywomen, their worldly husbands, and Christ. Married men and women across northern Europe encountered Jesus as a bridegroom in art, sermons, and devotional books, knew the same master narrative, and believed they could step into the role of bride without entering a religious order. Pious medieval housewives would even provide inspiration and admonishment for the professional religious, who incorporated domestic piety into their communal life. Though some women sought chastity after a spiritual experience, either persuading their husbands to a celibate marriage, or *Josephsehe*, modeled on the marriage between Mary and Joseph, or emulating Judith by becoming holy widows, their religious conversions did not end marriages, they merely complicated them. Confession and the Eucharist were only available following periods of abstinence. Childbirth and pregnancy kept women temporarily out of church. The hours of the liturgical day conflicted with housework and childcare, the liturgical night with sleep and sex. Remarrying Jesus required careful negotiations with spouses and confessors, but those who managed to balance religious vocation and family obligation inspired subsequent generations of married Christians and celibate religious to live in the world as brides of Christ.

Both medieval and modern audiences realized that inviting Jesus into the marriage bed potentially disrupted a couple's sex life. For pious medieval Christians like Elizabeth of Hungary, the intimate space of the marriage bed was

---

[1] "daz was in rechter warheit / der frauwen gros otmüdeckeit / daz sie irs wirtes bette liz / der lipliche ir mahel hiz / unde suchte ir zarten herren Crist / der war ir selen mahel ist." Max Rieger, *Das Leben der heiligen Elisabeth, vom Verfasser der Erlösung* (Stuttgart: Litterarischer Verein, 1868), 106.

146   *Marrying Jesus in Medieval and Early Modern Northern Europe*

a place shared by the married couple and Jesus, their heavenly spouse. Most of Elizabeth's hagiographers promoted her as a tender, loving wife while emphasizing her chastity in the years following Ludwig's death, clarifying that the marriage between Elizabeth and Jesus exceeded the bond between Elizabeth and her worldly husband.[2] According to testimony in the saint's canonization proceedings, Elizabeth's worldly husband never objected to sharing his wife or his bed with Jesus, though Isentrud, the handmaid who woke Elizabeth each night for prayers, averred that Elizabeth struggled to tear herself from her "beloved husband" to pray each night.[3] A widowed lay sister who entered the Dominican convent of Kirchberg in Sulz with her daughter reportedly had often met with God while lying in bed alongside her worldly husband.[4] A fifteenth-century Basel beguine known only as the "Schererin," or Shearer's wife, dedicated herself to a life of penance following a vision she received while in bed with her husband.[5] The fifteenth-century anchorite, saint, and father of 10 Nikolaus von Flüe (1417–87) received two visions while lying in bed beside his wife Dorothea, the second of which inspired him to retire to a hermitage, leaving Dorothea to care for their newborn child.[6] Another sainted anchorite, the widow Dorothea von Montau (1347–94), irritated her husband by wearing a hair shirt to bed and sometimes

---

[2]   For a discussion of dynastic politics in the promotion of Elizabeth's cult, see Gábor Klaniczay, *Holy Rulers and Blessed Princesses: Dynastic Cults in Medieval Central Europe* (Cambridge: Cambridge University Press, 2002), 226–7; Kenneth Baxter Wolf, *The Life and Afterlife of St. Elizabeth of Hungary: Testimony from her Canonization Hearings* (Oxford: Oxford University Press, 2010), 60–63; Dyan Elliott, *Spiritual Marriage: Sexual Abstinence in Medieval Wedlock* (Princeton, NJ: Princeton University Press, 1993), 174; Ulrike Wiethaus, "Naming and Un-naming Violence Against Women: German Historiography and the Cult of St. Elisabeth of Thuringia (1207–1231)," in *Medievalism and the Academy*, ed. Leslie Workman, Kathleen Verduin, and David D. Metzger, Studies in Medievalism (Cambridge: D.S. Brewer, 1997).

[3]   Wolf, *The Life and Afterlife of St. Elizabeth of Hungary*, 60–61.

[4]   This passage is paraphrased and translated from F.W.E. Roth, "Aufzeichnungen über das mystische Leben der Nonnen von Kirchberg bei Sulz," *Alemannia* 21 (1893): 134–5.

[5]   Although she is never named a bride of Christ, the Schererin's biographer records undated visions in which Christ held her sleeping soul in his arms and dressed her in a white dress. Hans-Jochen Schiewer, "Auditionen und Visionen einer Begine: Die 'Selige Schereri,' Johannes Mulberg und der Basler Beginenstreit; mit einem Textabdruck," in *Die Vermittlung geistlicher Inhalte im deutschen Mittelalter: internationales Symposium, Roscrea 1994*, ed. Timothy R. Jackson, Nigel F. Palmer, and Almut Suerbaum (Tübingen: M. Niemeyer Verlag, 1996), 307.

[6]   Unfortunately, very little source material relating to Nikolaus von Flüe's visions and cult has been edited or digitized. I rely here on Werner Huber's transcription of a manuscript addition to an incunable copy of the *Leben der Heiligen Altväter*, now Luzern, Bibliothek des Kapuzinerklosters Wesemlin: Leben der heiligen Altväter, deutsche Inkunabel Kod. 32b (c. 1480), fol. 1r–3v. Werner T. Huber, "Visionsbericht Des Caspar Am Büel," *Bruder Klaus*, March 19, 2012, Web, September 2, 2012, http://www.nvf.ch/que_m.asp?num=bkq068#anf.

Taking Jesus as a Second Husband   147

falling limply into spiritual raptures next to him.[7] The fifteenth-century English mother of 14, Margery Kempe, also received visions of Christ in the marriage bed.[8] In each of these examples the phrase "in bed" indicates, at the very least, a private domestic location. Though accounts of purely nonsexual bed sharing, particularly between betrothed couples and childhood friends, also survive from fifteenth-century Germany, in some medieval dialects "in bed" implied sexual intercourse, much as "sleeping together" does in contemporary American English.[9] For instance, Margery Kempe negotiated to free herself from sexual obligations, and the Schererin's confessor cautioned against taking the Eucharist too often so that her husband would not have to go without sex. Dyan Elliott has pointed out that Dorothea von Montau's husband Adalbert suspected she used rapture to shirk wifely duties.[10] Other wives, like Elizabeth of Hungary, unabashedly took pleasure in the marriage bed.

Though filtered through Latin hagiographies infused with Christianity's deeply troubled relationship with human sexuality, these depictions of women resisting sexual intercourse with difficult and sometimes abusive spouses resonate with some feminist critiques of traditional marriage. Most scholarly examinations of married brides of Christ begin with the assumption that these women sought to recreate a lost virginal state. Sarah Salih and Dyan Elliot have argued that Margery, at least, conceived of her own vocation as partially imitating that of saintly virgins.[11]

---

[7]   All citations to the life of Dorothea von Montau are my own translations from the 1863 edition, which I have checked against the 1492 imprint. I have also given page numbers for Stargardt's translation. Johannes von Marienwerder, *Das Leben der heiligen Dorothea*, ed. Max Toeppen, in *Scriptores Rerum Prussicarum*, vol. 2 (Leipzig: Hirzel, 1863). Johannes de Marienwerder, *Das leben der seligen frawen Dorothee* (Marienburg: Jacob Karweysse, 1492), currently held by the National Library of Russia, St. Petersburg. Johannes von Marienwerder, *The Life of Dorothea von Montau, a Fourteenth-century Recluse*, ed. Ute Stargardt (Lewiston: E. Mellen Press, 1997).

[8]   Margery Kempe, *The Book of Margery Kempe: The Text from the Unique MS. Owned by Colonel W. Butler-Bowdon*, ed. S.B. Meech and Hope Emily Allen, Early English Text Society 212 (London: Oxford University Press, 1940), 6–7 (hereafter EETS Kempe). All citations from *The Book of Margery Kempe* are my own translations from EETS Kempe.

[9]   Gertrud Jaron Lewis, *By Women, For Women, About Women: The Sister-Books of Fourteenth-Century Germany* (Toronto: Pontifical Institute of Mediaeval Studies, 1996), 214. Corine Schleif and Volker Schier, *Katerina's Windows: Donation and Devotion, Art and Music, as Heard and Seen through the Writings of a Birgittine Nun* (University Park: Pennsylvania State University Press, 2008), 3–5.

[10]   Elliott, *Spiritual Marriage*, 259.

[11]   See especially Sarah Salih, *Versions of Virginity in Late Medieval England* (Rochester, NY: D.S. Brewer, 2001); Liz Herbert McAvoy, *Authority and the Female Body in the Writings of Julian of Norwich and Margery Kempe* (Woodbridge, Suffolk; Rochester, NY: D.S. Brewer, 2004); Katherin J. Lewis, "Model Girls? Virgin-Martyrs and the Training of Young Women in Late Medieval England," in *Young Medieval Women*, ed. Katherin J. Lewis, Nöel James Menuge, and Kim M. Phillips (New York: St. Martin's Press, 1999), 25–46.

148   *Marrying Jesus in Medieval and Early Modern Northern Europe*

More recently, Sarah McNamer has situated Margery and other married women's behavior within the practice of affective meditation, and Dyan Elliott has partially revised her view of married female saints, noting that Bridget of Sweden made this "potential weakness into a position of strength."[12] The perceived tension between personal religious vocation and obligations to husband and children continues to be presented as a problem to be overcome, not a path to piety.

Rather than refuting or restating these arguments over agency and female sexual autonomy, my interest in this chapter is documenting how the cults of married saints sanctified domestic spaces and marital routines and in reconstructing how married Christians responded to, embraced, and altered medieval perceptions about the bride of Christ. I examine the precedent-setting cases of the Swedish landowner Helena of Skövde (d. 1160) and the cult developing around the princess and tertiary Elizabeth of Hungary; Gertrud von Ortenberg and Bridget of Sweden, two near-contemporary aristocratic mothers; Margery Kempe, Dorothea von Montau, and the widowed diarist and scribe Katharina Tucher. Each woman describes her encounters with Jesus with vivid details from daily life—bedrooms, kitchens, and the experiences of birth, nursing, and changing diapers.[13] They also report near-identical encounters with Christ as a groom, from the clothes they wore, to their use of angels to travel to and from heaven, to the positioning of the bride and groom and wedding party. This does not mean that marrying Jesus was something only exceptionally holy wealthy women could achieve. Men like the hermit-saint and father of 10, Nikolaus von Flüe, and Rulman Merswin, who was married twice (though childless), followed similar paths. Married brides of Christ are also scattered across convent chronicles, biographies of saints, and unedited manuscripts. Some housewives also owned prayer books addressing Christ as a spouse, such as a 1523 volume owned by Mariken Hubrechts, wife of Ockair Sijmonszoon, now in the King Albert Royal Library in Brussels.[14]

Holy Housewives

The challenges of living with a bride of Christ should be readily apparent. For late medieval Christians, marrying Jesus was part of a spiritual program that might include regular prayer, giving away wealth to the poor, dressing in rags, eating the coarsest and most revolting foods, abstaining from sex, weeping, shrieking, and talking incessantly of Jesus. Husbands and children were not always supportive

---

[12]   Elliott, *The Bride of Christ Goes to Hell*, 219.

[13]   For instance, Katharina Tucher remarked that Christ was a baby who never needed washing and never cried. "Sie dorft mich niht paden. Ich wahs schon. Ich waint niht, als andrew kint." Tucher, *Die "Offenbarungen" Der Katharina Tucher*, ed. Ulla Williams and Werner Williams-Krapp (Tübingen: M. Niemeyer Verlag, 1998), 38.

[14]   KBR MS: II 5573 contains a number of prayers to Christ the bridegroom, including several intended for use in preparation for and after communion. The ownership note reads: "Mariken hubrechts ockair sijmon z. huijsvrouwe."

Taking Jesus as a Second Husband 149

or understanding—as John Kempe harshly told Margery, "[Y]ou are not a good wife."[15] When wives and mothers married Jesus, they disrupted home life, much like contemporary families are sometimes disrupted or destroyed by disagreements about faith, career, and morality.[16] While medieval hagiographers praised married women for their virgin-like chastity and their tender care for family, their families and neighbors judged wives for meeting their obligations to husband and family. These conflicting responses to married brides of Christ indicate that medieval society had very clear expectations: married women should care for their families, pray piously, go on pilgrimages, perform works of charity, but do these things only temperately. If a woman wished to spend every moment praying, she should first free herself of family obligations. When quiet prayer became loud weeping, making time for church left the husband hungry and the children unwashed, daily communion forced celibacy on an unwilling spouse, and ascetic practices endangered the family, both neighbors and local church leaders voiced concern. But, like the Virgin Mary and the thrice-married St. Anne, some married women became powerful intercessors through their capacity as wives and mothers.[17]

In response to societal pressure for pious living and widespread belief that private devotional practices could be performed during daily labor, married women found new ways to balance their religious vocation with family obligations. When hagiographers recorded their subjects' worldly husbands, their children, and their household chores, they transformed the daily lives of married women into examples of exemplary piety for the men and women, lay and religious, venerating those saints in future decades. The popularity of married saints and biblical matriarchs, among them Judith, Susannah, Mary, Anne, also testified that marriage never precluded spiritual vocation. Instead, raising a family became an important component of constructing and performing female sanctity, even more impressive than the pious prayer of the professional religious, whose days were free to devote to Christ.

This trend emerges in northern Europe in the late twelfth century, as represented by the rapid canonization of Helena of Skövde, and spread across Europe in the

---

[15] EETS Kempe, 23.

[16] On the troubled receptions of saints and the extraordinarily pious within their home communities, see Aviad M. Kleinberg, *Prophets in their Own Country: Living Saints and the Making of Sainthood in the Later Middle Ages* (Chicago: University of Chicago Press, 1992). And for the challenges of discerning sanctity, see especially Peter Dinzelbacher, *Heilige oder Hexen? Shicksale auffälliger Frauen in Mittelalter und Fruhneuzeit* (Zurich: Artemis and Winkler, 1995); Dyan Elliott, *Proving Woman: Female Spirituality and Inquisitional Culture in the Later Middle Ages* (Princeton, NJ: Princeton University Press 2004).

[17] On the cults of Anne and Mary and their role in promoting holy motherhood, see Ton Brandenbarg, "Heilig familieleven: Verspreiding en waardering van de historie van Sint-Anna in de stedelijke cultuur in de Nederlanden en het Rijnland aan het begin van de moderne tijd (15de/16de eeuw)" (PhD dissertation, University of Amsterdam/Universiteit van Amsterdam, 1990); Jennifer L. Welsh, "Mother, Matron, Matriarch: Sanctity and Social Change in the Cult of St. Anne, 1450–1750" (PhD dissertation, Duke University, 2009).

150   *Marrying Jesus in Medieval and Early Modern Northern Europe*

first quarter of the thirteenth century with the promotion of the cult of St. Elizabeth of Hungary. Though likely unknown out of Sweden, the twelfth-century saint was canonized within five years of her death, and was closely associated with Bridget of Sweden.[18] A pious wife and mother, Helena made a pilgrimage to Jerusalem following her husband's death. An exemplary wife and widow, she married her children off well and continued to manage her farm, traveling to visit neighbors and bring them to Christianity. Unfortunately, Helena's son-in-law died during a farmworkers' revolt. His kinsmen blamed the murder on Helena and her daughter and killed Helena to settle the blood feud.[19] Helena's promoters developed liturgies for her feast day describing her as a martyred bride of Christ and a pious matron. A fourteenth-century liturgy described Helena's perfect chastity and love for Christ through widowhood and martyrdom, explaining that she had dedicated herself to God after vanquishing marriage, and should serve as an example for others.[20] The second reading for Helena's Mass reminded the gathered "brothers" that Helena had wed God spiritually, following the example of Judith to do good works in marriage. In a response, the brothers praised Helena for surviving carnal marriage and celebrated all holy widows.[21] The liturgy's repeated references to Helena as *sponsa* wove praise with precedents for Helena's election as a married bride of Christ. This liturgy could plausibly have been heard by Bridget of Sweden, whose career as a sainted mother and mother of saints marks a midpoint in this history.

Like Helena of Skövde, during Bridget's lifetime, Elizabeth of Hungary, who had become the third most popular patron saint of beguinages as well as an important saint for pious wives, would be represented as the ideal wife for two distinct husbands.[22] Dietrich von Apolda's carefully structured *Life of Elizabeth* integrates the roles of princess, Landgrave's wife and bride of Christ into an exemplary piety marked by the attire and ceremony of a wedding. The *Life of Elizabeth* opens with Elizabeth marrying Ludwig and closes with her marrying Jesus. In both scenes, Elizabeth is a beautifully dressed young woman brought into a court and given rich gifts and a portion of her spouse's power. This double marriage made Elizabeth an important patron for both nuns and married women. Elizabeth's conversion predated her widowhood by several years, beginning with the arrival of Franciscans at court four years before her husband's death.

---

[18]   Bridget defended Byrnolf Algottsson, the author of Helena's liturgy and hagiography, after receiving proof of his holiness in a vision. St. Birgitta of Sweden, *The Revelations*, vol. 1, 171, 249–50. On Helena of Skövde, see Sven-Erik Pernler et al., *S:ta Elin av Skövde - kulten, källorna, kvinnan* (Skara: Skara stiftshistoriska sällskap, 2007). All references to the liturgy are my own translations from their edition. I thank Signe Cohen for her assistance with the Swedish text.

[19]   Johannes Vastovius's *Vitis aqvilonia* as edited in Pernler et al., *S:ta Elin av Skövde - kulten, källorna, kvinnan*, 237–42.

[20]   Pernler et al., *S:ta Elin av Skövde - kulten, källorna, kvinnan*, 191, 94.

[21]   Ibid., 198.

[22]   Walter Simons, *Cities of Ladies: Beguine Communities in the Medieval Low Countries, 1200–1565* (Philadelphia: University of Pennsylvania Press, 2001), 88.

Because her hagiographers wished to promote the influence of Franciscans, they could not postpone her acts of piety until the onset of widowhood. Instead, Elizabeth's status as a married bride of Christ was a crucial sign of her religious conversion, charity work, and relinquishing of honor and wealth.[23] Book two of the official Latin *Vita* would be dedicated to her "sanctimoniam matrimonii" [holy marriage] to Ludwig. Dietrich von Apolda's vernacular *Life* made Elizabeth a wife to two holy rulers. She became a mirror to teach the laity how to achieve purity, and both laity and clergy praised her as mother.[24]

Elizabeth's identity as a bride of Christ, princess, and queen, was visually signified through crowns; many fourteenth- and fifteenth-century artists depict her holding a large golden crown (or sometimes two crowns, one in each hand) while wearing a more modest celestial crown atop her veil. These crowns represent her renouncing the wealth of her father and husband, dedicating herself to acts of charity, and winning the love and wealth of a celestial father and spouse.[25] An idealized vision of Elizabeth of Hungary sanctifying domestic devotion appears in Petrus Christus's c. 1455 painting of a female donor (Figure 5.1). In this panel, a well-dressed woman kneels, her hands clasped in prayer. A devotional book rests open before her, its pages fluttering gently as if in a breeze, a curling colored woodcut of Elizabeth of Hungary is nailed to the wall behind her, but her gaze falls on neither page nor print. The painting has attracted significant attention for its depiction of a single-sheet woodcut in a domestic setting.[26] The woodcut is faded and blotched; a short prayer to Elizabeth appears in partially damaged gothic script. Elizabeth stands centered on a field of grass, crowned and draped in a red mantle. In each hand she holds a crown. Whether or not the painting accurately represents devotional woodcuts in fifteenth-century homes, it captures the flavor of fashionable fifteenth-century domestic piety, implicitly sanctioned by and modeled after the saint in the woodcut. Neither a queen nor a bride of Christ, the female donor's stylized devotional practice models the sort of domestic piety considered appropriate for fifteenth-century wives. Under Elizabeth's gaze, the female donor prays silently, alone in her home, her only spiritual guidance coming from the pages of her Book of Hours and the model of the saint on her wall.

Elizabeth also served as an inspiration for women religious. In 1481, the Poor Clares in Freiburg completed a small illuminated manuscript dedicated to the Franciscan tertiary and princess, St. Elizabeth of Hungary; it contained prayers

---

[23] Wolf, *The Life and Afterlife of St. Elizabeth of Hungary*, 204.

[24] For instance, Rieger, *Das Leben der heiligen Elisabeth, vom Verfasser der Erlösung*, 63; Pfeiffer, *Deutsche Mystiker*, 242–6.

[25] On the history of the cult and hagiography, see Klaniczay, *Holy Rulers and Blessed Princesses*, 209–90; Elliott, *Proving Woman*, 95; Elliott, *The Bride of Christ Goes to Hell*, 373–4n242. Barbara Helen Haggh, *Two Offices for St. Elizabeth of Hungary: Gaudeat Hungaria and Letare Germania* (Ottawa: Institute of Mediaeval Music, 1995); Wolf, *The Life and Afterlife of St. Elizabeth of Hungary*.

[26] For a discussion of the print as a representation of woodcuts in devotion, see Peter W. Parshall, *The Woodcut in Fifteenth-Century Europe*, 42–3.

Figure 5.1 Petrus Christus, *Portrait of a Female Donor*, c. 1455. Courtesy of National Gallery of Art, Washington, Samuel H. Kress Collection, 1961.9.11.

Taking Jesus as a Second Husband 153

addressed to or ascribed to Elizabeth, as well as Latin and vernacular biographies. The small size of the volume (5.8 in. × 4.1 in.), its decoration, and the design of the miniatures suggest that the *Elisabethbuch* was designed for private devotion and repetitive prayer.[27] The manuscript was created at a center of the observant reform movement sweeping the mendicant convents of medieval Germany, and the manuscript's scribe and artist were both active participants in the Observant reform.[28] Elizabeth of Hungary's conversion had become an international model for men and women, young and old, whatever their marital status.

Popularizing Praying at Home

The liturgies, lives, and iconographies of twelfth- and thirteenth-century married saints like Helena of Skövde and Elizabeth of Hungary helped create a new domestic piety centered on balancing family with devotion to God. In the fourteenth century, some pious married women emulated this model by seeking to balance a marriage to Christ with obligations to family. The most influential example of this generation is Bridget of Sweden, though many details of her life closely correlate with those of Gertrud of Ortenberg, the widowed mother of four whose life was recorded by her beguinage. Some, like the internationally popular saints Bridget of Sweden and Elizabeth of Hungary, would subsequently inspire and authorize the lifestyle of later married brides of Christ. Others, like Margery Kempe, Dorothea von Montau, and Gertrud von Ortenberg, were venerated locally. By the fifteenth century, married saints had sanctified marriage, making marriage to Jesus attainable for housewives who dedicate their days to prayer and penance.

Unlike their brothers and sisters in the convents, laywomen faced daily distractions from prayer and penance—jobs, children, parents to care for, food to procure, servants to deal with. Their ability to balance these competing demands while fully serving Jesus was not so much an updated domestic martyrdom as valued spiritual labor. Following the death of her husband, and against the wishes of her family, Gertrud had joined a beguinage in 1302 while greatly pregnant, leaving her two living children in foster homes. After giving birth, Gertrud entrusted God to look after the newborn and committed herself to living as a beguine: "[H]er heart, which God before made suffer in the world and in marriage, rejoiced. She was joyful to be taken out of the world ... [while in the world] she

---

[27] For a history of the manuscript, reproductions of the miniatures, and a discussion of the manuscript's position in the broader fifteenth-century cult of Elizabeth see Werner Heiland-Justi, *Elisabeth: Königstochter von Ungarn, Landgräfin von Thüringen und Heilige: "diese fröwe ist gewesen törlich wise und wiszklich torecht"* (Lindenberg: Fink, 2007). The manuscript is now held in Leipzig at the Deutsches Buch- und Schriftmuseum, Klemm-Sammlung I, 104.

[28] This manuscript's illuminator and miniaturist would also work together on Karlsruhe, Landesbibl., Cod. Donaueschingen 452, which contained the Töss Sisterbook and another copy of the German *Life of St. Elizabeth of Hungary* by Dietrich von Apolda.

wanted only to wed our lord; thus she gave that body and soul and heart and will and mind to wed our lord."[29] Gertrud's near-contemporary, Bridget of Sweden, also wed Jesus shortly after the death of her husband, Olof. In one passage, Christ described his marriage to Bridget as a pleasurable transaction in goods: "[S]ince you surrendered your will to me when your husband died.… In return for this great love of yours, it is only fitting that I should provide for you. Therefore I take you as my bride for my own pleasure, the kind that is appropriate for God to have with a chaste soul."[30] He later tells Bridget that he loves her "as a husband loves his wife … as a father loves his son, for I have given you discretion and free will. I love you, moreover, as a master loves his servant."[31] God asked to be wrapped in the arms of Bridget's soul, to take his rest in her embrace, "and your heart shall be my heart, for I am like a fire of divine love, and I want to be loved fervently there in your arms."[32] A passage from the *Book of Margery Kempe* closely follows Bridget's experiences. While in Rome, God the Father took Margery by the hand and stood with her in front of the Son and the Holy Ghost and pledged to take Margery "for my wedded wife, for fairer, for fouler, for richer, for poorer, in order that you be humble and obedient, doing each thing as I bid you. For daughter, there was never a child so kind to her mother as I shall be to you, both in good times and bad, to help you and comfort you. I swear this."[33] These closely related weddings from Switzerland, Sweden, and England represent an internationally familiar ceremony for weddings in heaven.

Gertrud von Ortenberg was memorialized by her beguinage as a good wife, an otherworldly friend of God, and a bride of Christ. She and Bridget of Sweden were both guided by sermons, devotional books, conversations with confessors, and their own revelations. Despite wearing fine clothes and being constantly pregnant, entertaining, and socializing "in the world," Gertrud maintained a regime of daily prayer and fasting in an effort to remain detached from materiality as a "guote andehtige frowe" [good devout woman].[34] Like Bridget of Sweden, Gertrud also used devotional tools such as prayer books and was inspired by the lives of other saints. Rather than simply imitating the hagiographies and devotional treatises they acknowledged reading, these women recorded distinctively personalized

---

[29]   "von hertzen fro wz dz dú got erlidiget hette von der welt vnd von der E doch wie fro sú wz dz sú der welte wz abkummen doch verlobete sú die welt gentzlich in irem hertzen kinnige vnd gronen wz ir alles in irem hertzen vnmers wenn sú wolte sich allein vnserm herren vermehelen also sú och det lib vnd sel vnd hertze vnd iren willen vnd gemüte gap sú," ibid., 13–14.

[30]   St. Birgitta of Sweden, *The Revelations*, vol. 1, 56.

[31]   Ibid., 83–4.

[32]   Ibid., 165.

[33]   EETS Kempe, 95. The vow uses many of the same phrases that would be standardized by the Book of Common Prayer, though God speaks many of the lines given to the bride.

[34]   Gertrud's years as a wife and mother are contrasted to her later spiritual elevation as an "otherworldly woman." Ibid., 9.

Taking Jesus as a Second Husband 155

courtships with Christ and intensely personal family challenges. As Emma Lipton has demonstrated, Margery Kempe's marital relationships with Jesus and her husband John Kempe should be understood within the contemporary English bourgeois model of sacramental marriage, an observation which should be extended to women from the continent.[35] Those who wed Christ participated in acts of devotion impossible for those confined to cloisters. Some, like the beguine Gertrud von Ortenberg or the Franciscan tertiary Elizabeth of Hungary, performed acts of charity. Others, like the twelfth-century Swedish Saint Helena of Skövde, her countrywomen Bridget and Catherine of Sweden, England's Margery Kempe, the Bavarian Katharina Tucher, and the Prussian Dorothea von Montau, went on pilgrimages. Some marriage visions originated in meditative prayer or devotional images. Others were brought on by spatial proximity to pilgrimage sites, inspirational sermons, or the sacrament of the Eucharist. Saints like Bridget of Sweden and Elizabeth of Hungary were inspired by and informed through the dissemination of mendicant penitence and the new theological emphasis on marriage to Jesus for the laity. Bridget read the *Mirror for Maidens*, prayed before devotional art, and took inspiration from sainted predecessors.[36] Margery Kempe commissioned a ring inscribed "Jhesus est amor meus" [Jesus is my love], an act rooted in the English tradition of iconographic devotional rings and poesy rings. Though they belonged to different social classes, different countries, and different centuries, each was inspired by what was then modern theology, and each had to reconcile her spiritual calling with obligations to family.

Even lesser-known married brides of Christ were represented *in* (not merely inspired by) media as examples for both lay and religious audiences. The Englishwoman Margery Kempe's visions would circulate in a heavily abridged form in two print editions, and the *vita* of Dorothea von Montau survives in both Latin and German manuscript and print. Katharina Tucher actively translated and transferred information about marriage to Jesus from secular Nuremburg to the convent she joined as a lay sister by donating her library, woodcut collection, and scribal labor. Copies of their lives survive in monastic libraries bound with lives of saints. The only surviving manuscript of the *Book of Margery Kempe* was once owned by the Carthusian monastery of Mount Grace in Yorkshire, the Dominican Simon Grunau promoted Dorothea von Montau in his 1522 *Prussian Chronicle*, and the only manuscript copy of the life of Gertrud von Ortenberg was owned by the Dominican convent of St. Nicolas in Undis. Married brides of Christ were also revered alongside virgin saints. Gertrud of Ortenberg's *vita* is bound with vernacular translations of the revelations of the virginal saints Gertrud of Helfta and Catherine of Siena. Henry Pepwell's 1521 printed *veray deuoute treatyse* combined excerpts from the *Book of Margery Kempe* with the writing

---

[35] Lipton, *Affections of the Mind*, 129–60.

[36] On Bridget's library and influences, see St. Birgitta of Sweden, *The Revelations*, vol. 1, 10–11. And on her use of the *Speculum Virginum*, see Powell, "The *Speculum Virginum* and the Audio-Visual Poetics of Women's Religious Instruction."

156   *Marrying Jesus in Medieval and Early Modern Northern Europe*

of Catherine of Siena, Walter Hilton, and Richard of Saint Victor.[37] Dorothea von Montau's *Life* circulated with the lives of Agnes of Prague and Clare of Assisi. With the exception of Katharina Tucher's diary, which may have been recorded for personal use, the hagiographies, edited visions, liturgies, and devotional art I discuss throughout this chapter were designed for public consumption, and to conform with contemporary assumptions about sanctity.[38]

Bridget of Sweden was herself influenced by Elizabeth of Hungary and, perhaps, Helena of Skövde. Bridget and Helena were often portrayed together in Swedish altarpieces and murals.[39] Margery Kempe justified her vocation through the examples of the early beguine Marie d'Oignies, the widowed Bridget of Sweden and Elizabeth of Hungary—whether or not the *Book* of Margery Kempe was actively seeking to conform to canonization documents, it insisted that nothing about Margery's lifestyle was atypical for married saints on the continent.[40] Bridget would also be an important inspiration to the Nuremberg widow Katharina Tucher.[41] Dorothea von Montau's confessor and hagiographer, Johannes von Marienwerder, cited Elizabeth, St. Hedwig, and "many other holy people" as precedents for Dorothea's "praiseworthy marriage" to both divine and

---

[37]   Margery Kempe, *Here foloweth a veray deuoute treatyse (named Benyamyn) of the myghtes and vertues of mannes soule, of the way to true contemplacyon, compyled by ... Rycharde of saynt Vyctor. (Dyuers doctrynes ... taken out of the lyfe of ... Saynt Katheryn of Seenes, etc.-A shorte treatyse of contemplacyon taught by our lorde Jhesu cryst, or taken out of the boke of Margery kempe ancresse of Lynne.-A deuoute treatyse called the Epystle of prayer.-A deuoute treatyse compyled by mayster Walter Hylton of the songe of aungelles.-A verary necessary Epystle of dyscrecyon in styrynges of the soule.-A deuoute treatyse of dyscernynge of sprytes, etc.)* (London: Henry Pepwell, 1521).

[38]   Anne Winston-Allen views Katharina's visions as self-censored and non-controversial, easily represented as dreams to stern confessors and church superiors seeking to quell heretical and spectacular women's religious writing. Winston-Allen, *Convent Chronicles*, 63, 164.

[39]   For a brief summary of her influences, see St. Birgitta of Sweden, *The Revelations*, vol. 1, 5–6. And on her cult and its relationship to Dorothea von Montau, see Cordelia Hess, *Heilige machen im spätmittelalterlichen Ostseeraum: die Kanonisationsprozesse von Birgitta von Schweden, Nikolaus von Linköping und Dorothea von Montau* (Berlin: Akademie Verlag, 2008).

[40]   Margery's citations and influences are well-documented, though the life of Elizabeth of Hungary in England was actually conflated with that of another Elizabeth, a sister at the Dominican convent of Töss. See, for instance, Karma Lochrie, *Margery Kempe and Translations of the Flesh* (Philadelphia: University of Pennsylvania Press, 1991), 117–19. These influences have also inspired scholarly editions of several of her sources: Julia Bolton Holloway, *Saint Bride and Her Book: Birgitta of Sweden's Revelations* (Newburyport, MA: Focus Texts, 1992); Sarah McNamer, *The Two Middle English Translations of the Revelations of St. Elizabeth of Hungary: ed. from Cambridge University Library MS Hh.i.11 and Wynkyn de Worke's printed text of ?1493* (Heidelberg: Universitätsverlag C. Winter, 1996).

[41]   Tucher, *Die "Offenbarungen,"* 32.

Taking Jesus as a Second Husband 157

worldly husbands.[42] In a vision, Jesus cited the precedent of Bridget of Sweden when urging Dorothea not to weaken her body through fasting: "Get up and feed your body, eat and drink! I also have called the holy Bridget to eat and drink and strengthen her body."[43] Katharina Tucher may have made a pilgrimage to Elizabeth's shrine, Dorothea certainly did, and Margery Kempe clearly knew of her cult, identified with the saint, and had been read to from her *Life*. Both Bridget and Margery visited Danzig, where Dorothea lived. Katharina learned of Dorothea von Montau when promoters of her cult visited Nuremburg. Even twelfth-century married saints whose first hagiographies had been patterned after virgins and martyrs had become fifteenth-century models for private prayer in the home.

Media networks running through these women's lives delineate how lay women's experiences were distinct from (yet related to and inspirational for) the celibate religious. For instance, several passages in the manuscript copy of Margery Kempe's *Book* express concern over sexual impurity, as when Christ promised that he would "also love wives ... I love you as much as I love any maiden in this world."[44] In contrast, in the version of Margery's book produced in 1501 by Dutch immigrant Wynken de Worde, Christ directly thanks Margery for praying for the married. He praises her for the "charity you have for all lechers, for your prayers and tears for them" and urges that she "be as gracious to them as I was to Mary Magdalene, and they may have as much grace to love me as she had."[45] Depictions of Bridget of Sweden's husband, children, and remarriage to Jesus evolved significantly after her canonization.[46]

In late medieval Europe the laity were urged at every turn to dedicate themselves to Christ; calls to repent saturated secular and sacred spaces, establishing a framework through which individual sinners could position their own lives in relation to Christ's, and the models offered by married lay saints were an integral part of this campaign. A late fifteenth-century church mural from Götene in Sweden depicts three married saints walking in procession, as if on pilgrimage (Figure 5.2). Bridget of Sweden is flanked by her daughter, Catherine, and her twelfth-century predecessor, Helena of Skövde, above a triumphal arch. Each holds a rosary in one hand, a staff in the other. They are all nimbed, their heads veiled. The three walk together towards heaven, or, perhaps, Jerusalem.

---

[42] Marienwerder, *Das Leben der heiligen Dorothea*, 218. Marienwerder, *The Life of Dorothea von Montau*, 57. Chapter 21 of book 1 is titled: "Von ire lobelichen ee" [on her praiseworthy marriage].

[43] This occurs on October 31, 1393, when Dorothea is tempted by a feast dish of fish cooked in cream and saffron. Marienwerder, *Das Leben der heiligen Dorothea*, 257–8; Marienwerder, *The Life of Dorothea von Montau*, 112–13.

[44] EETS Kempe, 48–9.

[45] "charyte that thou haste to all lecherous men & wymmen for thou prayest for them & wepest for them ... be as gracious to them as I was to Mary maudelyne & they might haue as moche grace to loue me as Mary Maudelyne had." Margery Kempe, *Here begynneth a shorte trystyse of contemplacyon taught by our lorde Jhesu cryste, or taken out of the boke of Margerie kempe of lynn* (London, Fletestrete: Wynken de Worde, c. 1500), iii r.

[46] Elliott, *The Bride of Christ Goes to Hell*, 218, 20.

Figure 5.2   Triumphal arch, Götene Church, last quarter of the fifteenth century. Photo courtesy of Lars-Olof Albertson.

The Götene saints are only one of many scenes painted on the arched portal, but they would have appeared at eye level as a devotee approached the Church's altar. Each viewer would be reminded that these three pilgrims, wives, and mothers, had lived within a day's journey of their own Church, raised families, walked through the world's holiest lands, prayed in their homes, and become brides of Christ. Facing scenes of Christ's passion panted above a fourteenth-century altar (whose corpus opened to show Christ as Man of Sorrows surrounded by saints), devotees might have felt they were traveling to Jerusalem in the company of local saints.

As the Götene mural shows, Bridget's visions and revelations were reproduced in art, translated widely, and rearranged to meet the needs of new audiences. By the late fifteenth century, Bridgettine communities commissioned woodcuts and printed books promoting her cult. The iconography of Bridget's role as visionary, pilgrim, wife, and bride of Christ was condensed tightly into many of these designs. Representative of this new scheme is a German print which closely follows those produced in the 1480s for the Augsburg printer Johannes Tortsch's abridged German edition of Bridget's *Revelations* (Figure 5.3). Unlike the Swedish mural, which positioned Bridget as one of three equally important local saints, each a pilgrim, the 1480 woodcut shifted references to Bridget's pilgrimage and Swedish ties to peripheral positions and promoted Bridget's roles as author, pilgrim, and bride of Christ. Bridget is seated in the distinctive habit of the Bridgettine order. Her writing desk contains a few reference works, though the saint gazes upward, her eyes fixed on a heavenly vision. An angel leans over Bridget, guiding her

Figure 5.3   *St. Bridget*, c. 1480. Courtesy of National Gallery of Art, Washington, Rosenwald Collection, 1943.3.593.

hand as she writes a line in her book. A tonsured figure, perhaps representing the viewer, kneels in prayer. Above, God the Father holds Christ as Man of Sorrows, Mary holds the Christchild, and the Holy Ghost in the form of a dove spreads its wings. Bridget's pilgrimages are noted with a pilgrim's staff, upon which is placed a badge, hat, and satchel. In this version of the block, her hat bears a pilgrim's badge of the Veronica, representing Bridget's pilgrimage to Rome, while other

160   *Marrying Jesus in Medieval and Early Modern Northern Europe*

contemporary compositions show the cockle of St. James for the pilgrimage to Santiago de Compostela. The Christchild reaches an arm out, as if to touch Bridget, while the Man of Sorrows lowers his fingers to the speech scroll, nearly dripping his blood on the words "O pater de celis Miserere nobis." Bridget's status as bride of Christ is marked by a crown hanging from the pilgrim's staff. Though it might at first seem as if Bridget's husband and children had been erased from the scene, the heraldic shields in each corner of the image anchored Bridget's reputation through her family, her service to the Swedish king, and her service to the papacy. In this image, as in the Götene mural, the *Elisabetbuch*, and Petrus Christus's *Portrait of a Donor*, the saint has been removed entirely from references to her historical life, yet her iconographer preserves subtle markers of domestic and familial piety.

Manufacturing Identical Weddings

As married brides of Christ, Bridget of Sweden, Margery Kempe, Dorothea von Montau, Katharina Tucher, and Gertrud of Ortenberg report many of the same details of kissing, courting, and wedding Christ which make up the medieval master narrative of Jesus's marriage to the soul. Rather than citing a particular scriptural passage or learned commentary, the veracity of their experiences hinged on resemblance to that existing narrative. Gertrud of Ortenberg and Katharina Tucher would be lifted to heaven by angels and led by Christ to marry God. Both Gertrud of Ortenberg and Margery Kempe would be brought by Christ to wed the Godhead. Both Katharina Tucher and Gertrud of Ortenberg were stripped naked before their spouse, and each detailed the gifts of clothing and jewelry they received from Jesus. As brides of Christ, these married women also were portrayed wearing crowns and brooches that marked that relationship.

This narrative's dominance introduced the iconography of Elizabeth of Hungary's three crowns and the way hagiographers and artists dramatically portrayed her renunciation of courtly attire as a moment of public nudity.[47] The sartorial elements which marked Elizabeth as a princess had been painstakingly allegorized by authors as diverse as Origen and Ruusbroec as the clothing of the bride of Christ. Returning to the verse retelling, while praying with her kinsmen at the church below the Wartburg, Elizabeth's eyes fell on an image of the crucifix. Taking in the crown of thorns and Christ's wounded hands and feet, she became conscious that she stood before the crucifix crowned with gold and jewels even as the cruel thorns pierced his head.[48] While many brides of Christ rejoiced to

---

[47]   I am thinking here of nineteenth- and twentieth-century depictions such as Philip Hermogenes Calderon's dramatic depiction of the scene in response to Charles Kingsley's "The Saint's Tragedy." Philip Hermogenes Calderon, *St. Elizabeth of Hungary's Great Act of Renunciation*, 1891, http://www.tate.org.uk/art/artworks/calderon-st-elizabeth-of-hungarys-great-act-of-renunciation-n01573.

[48]   "Waz gibet mir di sture, daz ich mit gulden sten iezu vor mines herren ougen nu Gechronet also schone unde doch ein durnen crone sin zartes houbet drucket? Auch sten ich

Taking Jesus as a Second Husband 161

be lovingly arrayed in rich samite and silk, adorned with jewels, and awarded a glittering crown, Elizabeth of Hungary was suddenly overcome by self-conscious terror at her royal dress. Her handmaids guided her back out the church door, calling for fresh air and water from the well to bring her to her senses. Alert but sodden, Elizabeth returned to the church to stand before Christ, "Ir brudegam" [her bridegroom]. As if to strengthen her resolve, contemplating a sculpture of Christ's naked wounded body, she began casting away her own golden ornaments. Much like the pious Francis, who stripped away his worldly clothes and renounced his family wealth, Elizabeth removed her jewels and publicly renounced the worldly trappings of her royal status.[49] Elizabeth's worldly attire corresponded in nearly every detail to the wedding gowns worn by Christ's brides. Her robe, mantle, rings, crown, brooch, jewels, and other ornaments signified not her spiritual accomplishments but, instead, her material attachments.

Other married women joined (or imitated) Elizabeth, stripping naked and then dressing in a celestial wedding gown, crown, brooch, mantle, robe, undergarments, and shoes whose allegoric significance varied. The Virgin Mary instructed Bridget of Sweden to clothe herself in new garments if she wished to return Christ's love: "Just as before you had an underbodice, then a bodice, shoes, a cloak, and a brooch upon your breast, so now you should have spiritual clothes."[50] As she dressed Bridget, Mary explained that the undergarment signified contrition, the shoes the intention of penitence and abstaining from sin, the spiritual bodice Bridget's hope in God, her two new sleeves God's mercy and justice. The cloak "covers everything and everything is enclosed in it, human nature can likewise comprehend and attain everything through faith." Bridget is to decorate her cloak with "tokens of [her] bridegroom's love," and close it with a brooch in "consideration of his passion," thinking of his pierced body as the pin pierced the cloak. Finally, Mary instructed Bridget to place a crown on her head, signifying her chastity. So long as she wore the crown, she should "rather endure lashing than be further stained."[51] When instructing Bridget on the bride's duties, Christ would again remind her to dress appropriately, wearing tokens of his favors and benefits on her breast.[52] In a later vision, Bridget would be recrowned by Agnes of Prague, who placed a seven-gemmed crown with ten allegoric meanings on her head.[53]

Dorothea von Montau was dressed by Christ in colorful items suggesting the variety of her virtues, and "her soul was adorned and dressed like the daughter of a mighty king ... arrayed like a bride ... adorned with gold, silver, and

---

hie gesmucket mit golde, mit samite, unde ist sin frone site verseret jemmerliche!" Rieger, *Das Leben der heiligen Elisabeth, vom Verfasser der Erlösung*, 117.

[49]   This passage is summarized from Rieger, *Das Leben der heiligen Elisabeth, vom Verfasser der Erlösung*, 115–19.

[50]   St. Birgitta of Sweden, *The Revelations*, vol. 1, 62.

[51]   Ibid., 63.

[52]   Ibid., 55.

[53]   Ibid., vol. 2, 210.

162   *Marrying Jesus in Medieval and Early Modern Northern Europe*

precious gems."[54] Christ described to Katharina Tucher his conception and birth as joining himself to Mary by wedding and dressing her soul: "I dressed her, I shod her, I girdled her, I gave her a brooch, I gave her beautiful treasure."[55] The vision then shifts to describe the miraculously well-behaved baby Jesus, who never needed bathing but loved to be suckled, before Katharina's naked soul can be cleansed, dressed, adorned, and crowned. While these changes of clothing suggest the casting off of impure worldly clothes in favor of spiritual garments, other scenes contrast the shame and filth of physical nakedness with the purity of spiritual nakedness. In one particularly terrifying vision, God commanded Gertrud of Ortenberg to divest herself of all worldly clothing. The Lord warned Gertrud that their next encounter would require total privacy. Gertrud instructed Heilke to come early and lock the house securely before going out to pray and get bread from the town. As soon as the door to the house was locked,

> the lord gave her to understand that all the things she possessed in her body, both great and small, good and evil, over-dress and slip, cloak ... her shoes, the socks and the lining of her shoes, and her girdle, and all that which belonged to her body, all of those things she should no longer have.

Gertrud trembled in horror as she began to comprehend that "Our lord wanted her to go naked." When her companion Heilke returned the next day, she found Gertrud near the bed, lifted her onto the bed, and sat next to her. During their conversation, Gertrud explained that Christ wanted her to give away all of her possessions, including the clothes on her body. Heilke interpreted Christ's command as "spiritual" rather than bodily nakedness. Both agreed that physical nakedness was an unreasonable expectation. The Lord soon admonished Heilke for cooling Gertrud's resolve. Contrite, Heilke returned to Gertrud and announced that she too would cast aside her clothes. She gave Gertrud her old cloak and a ratty old shift [*einen bösen vnder Rog*], though Gertrud continued to fret that Christ wanted her to go naked, not merely wear tattered clothes. Eventually, Heilke reassured Gertrud that the Lord would not really want her to remain naked when it clearly worried her so much; he only wanted Gertrud to give away her remaining material belongings. Dressing in castoffs would be a sufficient sacrifice.[56]

---

[54]   Marienwerder, *The Life of Dorothea von Montau*, 182–5; Marienwerder, *Das Leben der heiligen Dorothea*, 310–13.

[55]   Tucher, *Die "Offenbarungen,"* 37.

[56]   "Dar noch gap ir unser herre zů verstonde dz sú alles dz zů irme libe gehorte gewant klein vnd gros böse vnd gůt / öber röck vnder röck /mentel kúrsen böiltze sleger / ir schühe /. die söcke vnd die tücher in den schühen / vnd ir gúrtel / vnd alles dz zů irem libe horte dz sú do von nit so vil solte haben also einen einigen vaden vnd sú erschrag vnd enwuste wz sú tůn solte / ob unser herre wolte dz sú nackent ginge ... Vnd ob sú joch jungfrouw heilke nit also versorget hette so wer sú noch denn vnserm herren gehorsam gesin / wenn sú wuste wol dz er sú also versorget hette dz er sú nit nackent liesse gon / Sú hette alles dz enweg gegeben dz sú hette dz sú nit me hette denn einen hof von dem hette

The intense humiliation of public nudity recurs in an entry in Katharina Tucher's diary. Jesus leads a naked soul before the throne of God. She kneels naked before the divine throne to pray for eternal glory, as she has been commanded to do, but her appearance attracts divine rage: "The Lord said to the soul 'You are filthy, I want a beautiful woman. Now you are naked, and I want a woman who is richly clothed; I do not want you.'" Taken aback, she begs: "Dear lord, clothe me, make me beautiful." Christ took up a girdle, wrapping it around her waist as she stood before him.[57] In the next entry, the soul is punished by the Christchild for her inappropriate attire as the wedding guest had been in Matthew 22: "She has no wedding clothes. Bind her hand and feet, carry her away."[58] Christ also urges Bridget to make herself clean by focusing her thoughts on her sins, the cleansing sacrament of baptism, and Christ's support.[59] Dorothea constantly inspected her bridal dress for flecks of filth signifying transgressions, brushing each one way immediately, lest God be disgusted and turn away from her.[60] The association between clothing and spiritual state was absolute. As in baptism, only those cleansed of sin could wear wedding clothes.

These overlaps between spiritual and physical nakedness also appear in the biography of Eefce Neghels (d. 1423), a dying Sister of the Common Life, who tried to undress when the community's confessor, father Iohan Hoef, visited her. One of the attending sisters asked her, "'Sister Eefce, what do you mean to do? Will you make yourself naked while our father stands here?' She answered her directly saying 'A naked bridegroom desires a naked bride.' And when our father saw this, he was sympathetic to her action."[61] Eefce's desire to die naked, just like Gertrud's discomfort over destroying her clothing, show that many Christians knew Christ stripped his brides before marrying them. Though that nakedness signified a complete detachment from transitory goods and an unmediated experience with God, it was clearly not limited to spiritual nakedness. These physical acts of undressing simultaneously referenced the nakedness of the soul ascending to heaven, recreated the shame of Christ's disrobing and nakedness during the passion, and reenacted the nakedness at baptism and changing into the habit of a religious order.

Nakedness and receiving a wedding dress were often the penultimate steps before marrying God in heaven. Gertrud von Ortenberg was frequently transported

---

sú wol xl vieriel geltes dz stun dennoch also vnd lûgete sú ale zit wz vnser herre wolte dz sú do mit dete." Derkits, "Die Lebensbeschreibung Der Gertrud Von Ortenberg," 171–3.

[57]   Ibid., 43–4.

[58]   "Daz kindlein sprach: Sie hat kain hochziklich kleit. Pint ir hent vnd fusz, werft sie avsz." Tucher, *Die "Offenbarungen,"* 52–3.

[59]   St. Birgitta of Sweden, *The Revelations,* vol. 1, 55.

[60]   Marienwerder, *The Life of Dorothea von Montau,* 185; Marienwerder, *Das Leben der heiligen Dorothea,* 313.

[61]   Dirk De Man, *Hier beginnen sommige stichtige Punten van onsen oelden Zusteren: naar het te Arnhem berustende Handschrift met Inleiding en Aanteekeningen uitgegeven* (The Hague: M. Nijhoff, 1919), 57.

164 *Marrying Jesus in Medieval and Early Modern Northern Europe*

to heaven while praying in her bedroom through the night. On one occasion, her companion Heilke woke to find Gertrud immobilized in prayer and frozen through with cold. As Heilke warmed Gertrud's hands and feet, Gertrud recalled the experience of being dragged down into herself by a host of angels, stripped naked, and filled with ecstasy. In a gesture echoing the lovers' embrace in the *Song of Songs*, Christ took Gertrud's soul in his arms, his left arm supporting her weight as he lowered her to the ground in a long embrace. As they lay together, Gertrud was filled with peace and tranquility. Christ then lifted Gertrud and led her to stand with God the Father. God looked at Gertrud with his heavenly eyes as Christ explained that she had been prepared as commanded. Then God the Father drew Gertrud close. Christ stood between them and joined them together with the love of the Holy Ghost. After hearing this, Heilke asked what the marriage had been like. Gertrud replied, "it was a joining of the soul with god [ez wz ein ver einigung der selen mit gotte] who reveals himself in many ways."[62]

Domestic Piety and Holy Spousehood

Every aspect of married life offered a new opportunity to routinize piety and allegorize reality. Chastity was not the real problem—if it had been, worldly husbands would not have complained about absent meals and companionship, and Christ would not have reassured so many concerned wives to the contrary. Jesus revealed to Bridget of Sweden that he preferred "a devout and humble housewife" to a "proud and immodest virgin," as a "God-fearing housewife, who is in control of herself and lives according to the rule of her state, can win equal merit as a humble and modest virgin."[63] When Margery Kempe lamented her pregnancy and feared her sexuality would keep Christ from her, he reminded her that "I also love wives ... I love you as much as I love any maiden in this world."[64] Christ comforted Dorothea of Montau after a series of beatings, saying, "I have often drawn you away from your husband; the whole time he lived, believing that he owned you, I drew you to myself and I owned you."[65] Marriage also cleansed brides of their sins. In a vision, Christ promised Bridget that he would "commute [her] sentence to one of mercy and remit the heavier punishment in return for a small amount of reparation."[66] Margery Kempe was reminded by Christ that "even if he were a rich man and she a poor woman when he wedded her, they must go lie together and rest together in joy and peace."[67] Though Margery's vision is far more detailed, like Bridget, she heard Christ's voice urging her to wrap the arms

---

[62] Derkits, "Die Lebensbeschreibung Der Gertrud von Ortenberg," 108.

[63] St. Birgitta of Sweden, *The Revelations*, vol. 2, 129.

[64] EETS Kempe, 48–9.

[65] Marienwerder, *Das Leben der heiligen Dorothea*, 248–50. Marienwerder, *The Life of Dorothea von Montau*, 100–102.

[66] St. Birgitta of Sweden, *The Revelations*, vol. 1, 55–6.

[67] EETS Kempe, 90.

of her soul around her husband, and to think of their marriage as a cleansing of sin, an exchange of love for salvation.

This sanctifying of medieval marriage in the twelfth and thirteenth centuries and popularization of married brides of Christ in the fourteenth and fifteenth centuries overlaps almost exactly with the historical development of depictions of Christ as a groom for every Christian soul in the same period. Patristic authors, among them Augustine and Chrysostom, had long recognized a space for virtuous married Christians among the celibate saints. When defending marriage against the criticisms of the Manicheans, Augustine warned that the chaste and the married should both be judged for their virtues: "If you compare a drunken virgin with a sober married woman, who can doubt that ... marriage and virginity are two goods?"[68] In the twelfth century, the *Mirror for Maidens* warned that misbehaving virgins should not be ranked above married men and women. Both could find the bridal bed: "[T]hose who have lost their physical virginity, like those of the remaining believers who follow the Lamb, are not following Him wherever He goes (Rev. 14:4), but they are able to go where he has gone."[69] The late medieval *Spouseship of Christ* also warned that pious married women would fare better in the afterlife than many virgins. Through an allegoric reading of Leviticus 21 (regulating priestly purity by forbidding marriage to prostitutes), the author first establishes that Christ will wed any pure soul, regardless of sexual contamination. Citing Jerome and echoing Chrysostom, the treatise warns that Christ has no interest in tainted virgins. While bodily marriage robs one of purity, married souls are returned to a pure state so that widows who have had their souls destroyed by lust can, by wedding Christ, destroy their lust and purify their souls. In contrast, enclosed women who long for the world they have left are corrupted by sinful desires and shall be greatly shamed and eternally damned.[70] Worldly status bore no correlation to spiritual status: the shamed prostitute of Leviticus might have a pure soul, while her virginal counterpart was a spiritual prostitute.

Nuns and married women drove each other on with encouragement and competition and warned each other against haughtiness and complacency. A brief pseudo-Eckhartian exemplum known as *The 21-Year-Old Wife* tells the story of a young mother who inspires nuns and clerics with her piety. The housewife approaches a visiting spiritual master to discuss devotional practices. He disdainfully asks about her husband, family, and income, certain that it must be impossible for any Christian to achieve spiritual perfection while shackled to the world. To his amazement, every aspect of her devotional program tears her away from materiality. Her practice of inward meditation and "letting go," advocated by Eckhart and his followers, was exceptionally well-suited to domestic labor.

---

[68]   Augustine of Hippo, *De bono coniugali, De sancta virginitate*, trans. P.G. Walsh (Oxford: Oxford University Press, 2001), para. 29.

[69]   Seyfarth, SV, 272.

[70]   The passage goes on to describe the penitential practices required to make such a transformation, including tears, confession, sickness, and poverty. *Spiritual Spousehip* [*Gemahelschaft Christi*], f 166r–168r.

166 *Marrying Jesus in Medieval and Early Modern Northern Europe*

The young wife explains that her family and wealth do her no harm. In her meditations, she concentrates on losing herself in Christ's blood and suffering. Her daily devotions also include raising her children to be humble and praise God, living with her servants as if she were one of them, and breaking away from home to visit the local church. There, she found "a little place to stand just wide enough for both my feet, then I sink so deeply into God that I find that no one exists in that moment but Christ and me alone."[71] At last, weeping, the master begs the young wife for her prayers. The exemplum concludes,

> Now Behold! That was a young married woman in a city. Now you pay attention as well, you young maidens who have turned your hearts to worldly honor and goods. I know nothing more to write of the noble young married woman except this: let each married woman strive as best she can to improve herself in this manner. Such is my advice in all sincerity.

An alternate ending in a manuscript from the Dominican convent of Altenhohenau in Griestätt reminds sisters that they shared a desire for truth and eternal salvation with the young wife:

> She was a worldly married woman. Now mark you this well. This woman who tasted nothing but fleshly things nonetheless forced herself to savor spiritual matters ... and the spiritual person should seek the same thing. Because we all have the same desire for the Eternal Truth ... the highest grace of Godly love.[72]

Though the nuns could not emulate the young married woman's domestic piety in every aspect—raising children and minding servants—they certainly could have put into practice her inward and outward devotions, fixing their eyes on Christ as they performed mundane tasks.

By the fifteenth century, both the chaste religious and the sexually active married laity contemplated Christ while they worked. When nuns mixed contemplation with labor, envisioned themselves caring for the baby Jesus, and giving birth to spiritual virtues, they were imitating the domestic piety of worldly wives, who turned their eyes to heaven even when cooking dinner and changing diapers. This mode of living seems to have been broadly popular, appearing spontaneously across northern Europe. By marrying Christ, these women were allegorizing themselves, mixing theological meanings into daily activities in ways that sanctified both the actress and her world.

---

[71] I have used Ann Marie Rasmussen and Sarah Westphal-Wihl's edition except for the alternate ending preserved in the Altenhohenau manuscript. Rasmussen and Westphal-Wihl, *Ladies, Whores, and Holy Women*, 92–5.

[72] BSB CGM 1109, f 337v. MDZ: http://daten.digitale-sammlungen.de/bsb00035397/image_694. "daz wz ein weltliche frauw in der ee. Nun schawen sich die frauen dy nit anders smecken den fleischliche ding vnd auch dy geistlichen schein tragen von aussen vnd mit in der warheit vnd auch die geistliche man schauwen sich dy solch noch nie gesucht haben Daz wir alle begeiren nach der ewigen warheit zu leben des holff vns dy höchst genad der gotlichen lieb vnd bgegirt zu unsereewigen saligkeit der heiligen driualtigkeit Amen."

By the end of the fourteenth century, religious fragmentation and demographic disaster shifted the boundaries of authority to local ecclesiastical districts. Just as celibate visionaries like Mechthild of Magdeburg, Henry Suso, and Jan van Ruusbroeck were translating courtship with Christ into programmatic guides for the spiritual salvation of others, their lay contemporaries, not least Bridget of Sweden, publicized visions explaining the secrets of salvation to an international audience. During the late fourteenth and fifteenth centuries, the messy twilight boundary between medieval and modern, print flourished, and the streets were filled with preachers and penitents. And in the late fourteenth and fifteenth centuries, women and men across Europe made turning inward a daily exercise, seeking Christ's love while laboring. This shift from convent to household as a locus for ideal sanctity is typically thought of as a Protestant innovation. But the chaste bride of Christ was not primarily "Catholic," nor the holy housewife "Protestant." Though Lyndal Roper and other historians have established that domestic piety supplanted monastic piety as a model for Christian women in the sixteenth century, extant cases of married brides of Christ show that this shift significantly predates the Reformation.[73] Fourteenth- and fifteenth-century authors advocated domestic piety, insisting that family obligations should not stop Christians from seeking heaven. This gesture to incorporate Christian devotion into civic life and marriage was part of a broader social movement of religious renewal, expressed across Europe in the upsurge in confraternities, tertiaries, pious donations to religious organizations, and even the patronage of artists.

Both medievalists and hagiographers view these women's religious experiences as a struggle to compensate for lost chastity, to live as saints in a world where female sanctity sometimes equated with virginity. Medieval hagiographers uniformly confronted the "problem" of married and sexually experienced saints head-on by creating and promoting domestic piety as a superior Christian lifestyle. They also preserved accounts of local persecution—framed as testimony to a woman's sanctity via social martyrdom—that may reflect genuine discomfort with married women's religious vocations. But married brides of Christ were not simply fleeing bad marriages or mimicking heroic virginity. Moved by the tortured Man of Sorrows, penitent acts of worldly renunciation and charity, and the models of domestic sanctity offered by saints such as Mary and St. Anne, they wed Christ because they had learned that they could.

---

[73] Lyndal Roper, *The Holy Household: Women and Morals in Reformation Augsburg* (Oxford: Oxford University Press, 1989).

Chapter 6
Sisters and Brides of Christ

> In all manner of things we should be so decent, in sleeping and in waking up, in dressing and in undressing as chastely as if it were our very last day on earth, thinking of God's presence ... and remembering that we are Brides of Christ. Not only our souls, but also our bodies are consecrated to the king of maidens and the lover of purity.... Therefore our bodies are earthly vessels with which we carry all costly treasures for Jesus Christ, and our community are temples for the Holy Ghost. And that is a duty and a concern of a bride of Christ, that she be immaculate, pure, and chaste in both soul and body.[1]

The above excerpt from the dormitory regulations from the Augustinian canoness house of St. Agnes at Emmerich, a fifteenth-century women's community belonging to the monastic branch of the *Devotio Moderna*, typifies how medieval women's monastic vows initiated a lifetime spent preparing for a deathbed wedding and an eternity in heaven embracing a beloved spouse. Unlike the married women I discussed in the last chapter, these sisters or "mulieries religiosae" [women religious] received physical rings and new clothes during the rituals which began their monastic profession, liturgies which visually consecrated marriages between the bodies and souls of each vowed sister and Christ. In this interim period, dead to the world but not yet reborn in heaven, sisters worked, prayed, tended the sick, cooked their meals, and taught one another to beautify their souls for their heavenly bridegroom. Consequently, though women religious are often called—and call themselves—brides of Christ, their vocation entails far more than wearing a ring and veil while vigilantly guarding their chastity.

The ceremony that officially consecrated novices as brides of Christ varied considerably across Europe. As René Metz has documented, early rituals for

---

[1] "In alle onse manieren sullen wy wesen soo geschickt, in slapen te gaen ende op te staen, in cleden ende ontcleden soo eerbaer, of onse ouersten daer tegen woordich waren, denckende Godts tegenwoordicheijt ende van onsen heiligen engel, onsen behoeder, ende dat wij syn bruijden Christi, die niet alleen onse sielen, maer oock onse lichamen toe geheijlicht hebben den coninck der mageden ende en lief hebber der suiverheijt. Daerom seijt den heiligen apostel Paulus; Leert ende draeght Godt in u lichamen, ende dat een ijegelick sijn vat, dat is syn eygen licham, besitte in heijlichheijt ende in eeren ende niet mishandele nae die quade begeerlickheijt als die Godt niet en kennen. Dan onse lichamen syn eerde vaten, daer wij in dragen den alder costelicksten schat Jesum Christum, ende onse lidtmaten syn tempelen van den heiligen Geest. Ende dat is het eygen weerck ende becommernisse van een bruijt Christi, dat sij reijn, suiver, ende eerbaer sy nae siel ende lichaem." Anne Bollmann and Nikolaus Staubach, *Schwesternbuch und Statuten des St. Agnes-Konvents in Emmerich* (Emmerich: Emmericher Geschichtsverein e.V., 1998), 314.

170   *Marrying Jesus in Medieval and Early Modern Northern Europe*

consecrating virgins explicitly referenced secular Roman marriage rituals. While aristocratic and elite convents in Italy and Germany continued to use profession ceremonies paralleling secular weddings, in which new sisters wore elaborate gowns and received a ring from the bishop, observant orders in Germany and the Low Countries began simplifying the ceremony as part of a move to live more austerely.[2] This parallels late medieval German wedding customs; aristocratic weddings closely resembled the liturgically complex profession ceremonies for wealthy religious houses, while the austere ceremonies of observant houses and semireligious organizations more closely resembled the informal unions of the laboring classes. In late medieval Germany, secular marriage ceremonies were also far less elaborate, requiring only that couples articulated their consent to one another, often outside a church, though the rites of high society extended over several weeks or months.[3] Eva Schlotheuber has shown that some fifteenth-century German nuns dressed in fine aristocratic clothing, wearing jeweled rings and fashionable dresses as part of their perceived status as brides of Christ.[4] The chapter rule from Emmerich, for instance, does not specify the use of chants like *Veni Sponsa Christi* or the postulant's symbolic adornment with crown, veil, and ring. Each sister who was able should simply copy out her profession statement, kiss the foot of the cross behind the altar, then lay the statement down on the altar and be enclosed.

As manuscripts from medieval convent libraries reveal, women religious believed marriages to Jesus contracted through monastic profession could be broken or destroyed through sin, disobedience, or a love for material goods. Some convent authors contrast the suffering of respected deceased sisters in hell for false piety with virtuous laity rewarded in heaven with eternal union to Christ their spouse. Women religious also recorded lives of their confessors and their interactions with friends and spiritual students who visited the convents for guidance, among them men who married Christ. At the same time, perhaps as a response to the widespread success of sisters' lessons to lay audiences, skeptics within the church challenged some women's claims to be brides of Christ, arguing that redirecting erotic love to Christ was a perversion of Christian practice. At least in German and Dutch-speaking communities, women embraced, taught, and were some of the first to articulate the emerging mid-thirteenth-century understanding that every person had been created a bride of Christ. By the late fifteenth century, perhaps in response to accusations of heresy, demonic possession, and false teachings, women religious also less often presented themselves as brides of Christ.

---

[2] Kate Lowe, "Secular Brides and Convent Brides: Wedding Ceremonies in Italy During the Renaissance and Counter-Reformation," in *Marriage in Italy, 1300–1650*, ed. Trevor Dean and Kate Lowe (Cambridge: Cambridge University Press, 1999).

[3] Schleif and Schier, *Katerina's Windows*, 3, 20–35.

[4] Eva Schlotheuber, "Best Clothes and Everyday Attire of Late Medieval Nuns," in *Fashion and Clothing in Late Medieval Europe / Mode und Kleidung im Europa des späten Mittelalters*, ed. Regula Schorta and Rainer Christoph Schwinges (Basel: Joint publication of the Abegg-Stiftung, Riggisberg, and Schwabe Verlag, 2010), 139–54.

Sisters and Brides of Christ   171

Only during profession, at mass, or on their deathbeds were sisters particularly likely to describe one another as brides of Christ. Within women's communities, marrying Jesus was a lifelong courtship consisting of virtuous acts, frequent prayer, and total submission to Christ's love. Some sisters experienced marital union with Christ during communion, but several convent accounts present these experiences as available to anyone within a community, including men and lay women. Dissonance between convents' internal narratives and the ways male clergy perceived and sought to guide their spirituality anticipates a central debate of the early reformation: were nuns brides of Christ, brides of the devil, or concubines of God? In the fourteenth and fifteenth centuries, women's communities became a locus for teaching, adapting, and transmitting information about the bride of Christ to the laity. Only in the last half of the sixteenth century that the emerging confession of Catholicism would emphatically equate the identity of the bride of Christ and the chaste nun, while protestants slandered women religious as brides of the devil. Brides of Christ in medieval convents were sisters who lived and labored together, taught their neighbors as they taught those within their communities, and believed they would travel to heaven together to meet and wed Christ. No two sisters followed the same path to heaven, and some might never arrive there, but as they struggled against sin on earth, and so long as they suffered in purgatory, no sister was ever truly alone.

Collection Biases

The dissolution of monastic houses in the nineteenth and early twentieth centuries led to a terrible loss of manuscripts—only copies deemed culturally valuable were acquired by major state-owned libraries. This has meant, as Sara Poor stressed in her study of the textual transmission of Mechthild of Magdeburg's writing, that aesthetically interesting material was predominantly selected for editing and examination, and only women authors who mastered poetic forms were candidates for critical editions and scholarly consideration.[5] They often do not accurately represent the literary interests of medieval nuns. Manuscripts once owned by medieval women's communities typically bear signs of use and ownership marks dating to the seventeenth century. New copies of medieval convent texts were also made in the sixteenth, seventeenth and eighteenth centuries, and early modern religious orders sometimes bound medieval manuscripts within official histories of their orders. Most surviving manuscripts still traceable to medieval women's communities conformed to post-Tridentine models of female sanctity, were finely decorated, enticing seventeenth-century collectors of rare books, or contained copies of aesthetically important vernacular poetry, thus drawing the attention of historians and literary scholars.

Because contemporary scholarship on women in medieval Christianity depends on the writing for and about medieval nuns, these editorial and collecting priorities

---

[5]   See, for instance, Poor, *Mechthild of Magdeburg*, 39.

172   *Marrying Jesus in Medieval and Early Modern Northern Europe*

have disproportionately influenced the image of nun as bride of Christ. Like late medieval religious authorities who promoted some women as saints and teachers while condemning others as dangerous, we continue to present women's religious careers in terms of canonization or execution. Consequently, even recent historical reconstructions of women's communities continue to restate assumptions about chastity, vocation, and claustration that reflect postmedieval prejudices. Sources widely available in modern critical editions or anthologized for classroom use are typically selected for their theological innovation or stylistic beauty. But editors often select passages which conform to their expectations, rather than the spiritual concerns of actual medieval women or the collecting priorities of medieval libraries. For instance, Hildegard of Bingen's visions were available in English before her medical or musical compositions, and excerpts from Gertrud of Helfta's visions in the *Herald of Divine Love* were published for classroom use before her *Spiritual Exercises*. But medieval nuns—especially those eventually canonized—wrote about their vocation as honoring God, perfecting prayer, and guiding the souls of sinners closer to salvation. As surviving volumes traceable to women's communities demonstrate, sisters wrote for—and with the collaboration of—their communities, often without mentioning their status as Christ's brides at all.

Anne Winston-Allen's comprehensive study of German and Netherlandish convents during the fourteenth through early sixteenth centuries identifies at least 52 different women's communities engaged in producing their own historical documents. Cynthia Cyrus's recent survey of manuscripts traceable to German convents identified 3,195 manuscripts copied by 635 scribes, most of them undecorated vernacular devotional books intended for personal study and prayer.[6] Grouping together such a diverse body of devotional material as "of the convents" obscures the individual experiences of historical women behind a homogeneous identity of "nuns." German-language scholars continue to mark the cultural production of medieval convents as *Frauenmystik*, *Nonnenarbeit*, or *Nonnenliteratur* (women's mysticism, nuns' handicrafts, nuns' literature), even as they increasingly acknowledge that these are problematic categories. Singling out the material culture of medieval convents as something *by* and *for* women

---

[6]   Winston-Allen, *Convent Chronicles*, 2. Cyrus, *The Scribes for Women's Convents in Late Medieval Germany*, 5, 150. Recent studies of medieval nuns' reading habits and libraries include: Gertrud Jaron Lewis, *By Women, For Women, About Women*; Marie-Luise Ehrenschwendtner, *Die Bildung der Dominikanerinnen in Süddeutschland vom 13. bis 15. Jahrhundert* (Stuttgart: Steiner, 2004); Anne Bollmann, *Frauenleben und Frauenliteratur in der Devotio moderna: Volkssprachige Schwesternbücher in literarhistorischer Perspektive* (Groningen: Rijksuniversiteit Groningen, 2004); Wybren Scheepsma, *Deemoed en devotie: de koorvrouwen van Windesheim en hun geschriften* (Amsterdam: Prometheus, 1997); Erika Lauren Lindgren, *Sensual Encounters: Monastic Women and Spirituality in Medieval Germany* (New York: Columbia University Press, 2009); Siegfried Ringler, *Viten- und Offenbarungsliteratur in Frauenklöstern des Mittelalters: Quellen und Studien* (Zürich: Artemis, 1980).

Sisters and Brides of Christ 173

recreates the nineteenth-century ghettoizing of nuns. Contemporary critics are more cautious when discussing "the work of nuns," but still mark nuns' work as "different"—if no longer "inferior."[7] As the burgeoning study of the art and literature of nuns in Germany and the Low countries has shown, medieval convents were neither cultural backwaters nor socially isolated. Social interactions within convents, across generations, among family members in the secular world, and between living and dead sisters suggest medieval nuns considered teaching a vital part of their vocation and saw every spiritually inclined person as a sister-bride of Christ.

In light of the sheer number of surviving sources from German and Dutch women's communities, most still unedited and some still uncatalogued, I focus here on accounts of sisters teaching others to be brides of Christ drawn from manuscripts which were recopied for instructive use in other communities or remained in use during the early modern period. My discussion shall sidestep distinctions between religious orders, acknowledging only in passing regional variations in nuns' social standing, financial security, and pastoral support. Though these nuances are important, my intention here is to show that medieval women's communities collected practical lessons from and about sisters and that these communal experiences differed from the more often examined accounts of individual sisters who received visions of Christ as spouse. This aspect of convent devotion has been highlighted by early modern and modern inheritors of their books, who have prioritized revelation, asceticism, aesthetics, Catholic orthodoxy, and protofeminism, but are relatively rare occurrences in surviving convent manuscripts. The importance of this distinction becomes immediately apparent when comparing the available editions and manuscript histories of individual texts. For instance, Adelheid Langmann (1306–75) was a widowed Dominican whose piety, prayers, and visions were memorialized by her sisters at Engelthal.[8] Her *Revelations* appeared in a palm-sized late fourteenth-century manuscript perhaps originating with the sisters of Engelthal alongside German translations of the instructional devotional works of Ruusbroec; by the seventeenth century, it had passed into lay ownership. Langmann's *Revelations* survive in a fifteenth-century manuscript possibly used as table reading at the Augustinian canoness house of Inzigkofen, which was eventually transferred to the library of a male Benedictine community in Vienna. This manuscript, Wien, Schottenkloster, Cod. 308 (Hübl 234), also preserves the only surviving copy of the life of the Dominican

---

[7] On the value of using these antiquated terms in a less antifeminist way, see Jeffrey F. Hamburger, *Nuns as Artists: The Visual Culture of a Medieval Convent* (Berkeley: University of California Press, 1997), 3.

[8] Adelheid Langmann, "Die offenbarungen der Adelheid Langmann, klosterfrau zu Engelthal," ed. Philipp Strauch (Strassburg: K.J. Trübner, 1878), 26–7. On Langmann in her communal context, see especially Rebecca L.R. Garber, *Feminine Figurae: Representations of Gender in Religious Texts by Medieval German Women Writers 1100–1375* (London: Routledge, 2003); Leonard Patrick Hindsley, *The Mystics of Engelthal: Writings from a Medieval Monastery* (New York: St. Martin's Press, 1998).

174 *Marrying Jesus in Medieval and Early Modern Northern Europe*

confessor and bride of Christ Friedrich Sunder.[9] In 1878, Philipp Strauch published an edition of *Revelations* [*Offenbarungen*] which reorganized Langmann's visions into a rough chronological narrative built from visions and relegated the prayers she had written to a coda, typical nineteenth-century editorial practices. Strauch's version became one of the few widely available editions of medieval women's religious writing cited by contemporary scholars. Based on Strauch's edition, Bernard McGinn characterizes Adelheid Langmann's *Revelations* as reflecting "many of the best, as well as some of the worst, aspects of the mysticism of these monastic women. Above all, it is typical."[10] Whether or not Langmann's experiences were typical for fourteenth-century Dominican women, Strauch's editorial practices have certainly informed what contemporary scholars assume went on in medieval convents. In contrast, the life of Christina Retters (1269–91), a virgin and visionary who entered religious life at the age of six, was only edited in 1965, and remains obscure. Nonetheless, Retters was an important figure for her own religious house, and her experiences should be considered no more or less typical than Langmann's. Her visions survive in a composite manuscript preserving fifteenth- through eighteenth-century documents pertaining to the history of the Praemonstratensian order. The entry for Retters's biography was commented on by several later hands, among them perhaps Johannes Haas, prior of the Praemonstratensian house of Ilbenstad in the eighteenth century.[11] The experiences of medieval women like Christina Retters and Adelheid Langmann are thus necessarily mediated by the communal concerns of their confessors and sisters, as well as the political priorities of their religious orders and the historians who have worked with their surviving records. As these two examples show, every attempt to reconstruct how medieval sisters understood their obligations as brides of Christ is skewed by later collectors' concerns.

Espoused Before Profession

Twelfth- and thirteenth-century Latin treatises used marriage to Christ as one of many images when preparing novices for their profession. Some also made profession ceremonies relevant to older residents by reminding them of their obligations as sisters and brides of Christ. Many of these communal documents present both unconsecrated women and members of the community as brides of Christ, emphatically underscoring that the profession ceremony was neither the beginning of that marital relationship nor its most important aspect. As the thirteenth-century Benedictine St. Gertrud of Helfta instructed her sisters in the *Spiritual Exercises*, "In this way, you will celebrate the spiritual matrimony,

---

[9] Ringler, *Viten- und Offenbarungsliteratur in Frauenklöstern des Mittelalters*, 19–34, with a partial transcription on 391–447.

[10] McGinn, *The Flowering of Mysticism*, 316.

[11] Franz Paul Mittermaier, "Lebensbeschreibung der sel. Christina, gen. von Retters aus Ms. 324, fol.211 sequ. der bibliothèque nationale et universitaire de Strasbourg," *Archiv für Mittelrheinische Kirchengeschichte* 17 (1965): 226–7.

Sisters and Brides of Christ 175

the marriage of love, the espousal and coupling of your chaste soul with Jesus, the heavenly spouse, in the unbreakable bond of cherishing-love."[12] Following René Metz's foundational work on this ceremony, most scholars agree that the symbolic use of veil, ring, and vows in the ceremony for consecrating virgins must be read as intentionally mimicking late Roman marriage practices. The *Spiritual Exercises* is one of the earliest surviving female-authored manuals designed for use in monastic profession. Though Gertrud of Helfta's *Spiritual Exercises* closely follows the liturgy and music of the *Consecratio Virginum*, the official ritual process for transforming a lay girl into a professional woman religious, she incorporates gestures which recognize the communal importance of profession to sisters already within the community.[13] In addition to Gertrud of Helfta's *Spiritual Exercises* should be added Hildegard of Bingen's *Ordo Virtutem*, Herrad of Hohenburg's *Garden of Delights*, and Mechthild of Hackeborn's widely copied and translated *Book of Special Grace*.[14] These treatises were multimedia lessons beneficial to novices and senior sisters. Such teaching texts would have been particularly useful in twelfth- and thirteenth-century convents practicing child oblation—that is, allowing very young children to be placed at their communities in anticipation of a monastic career. Sisters might have learned the full significance of their vocation only years after making their vow.[15] By the fifteenth century, many communities insisted that novices be old enough to consent to their vocations. Though Christ's role as spouse is less prominent than a sister's obligations and vocational future

---

[12] Translated in Gertrud of Helfta, *Spiritual Exercises*, trans. Gertrud Jaron Lewis and Jack Lewis, Cistercian Fathers series, 49 (Kalamazoo, MI: Cistercian Publications, 1989), 40.

[13] Metz, *La consécration des vierges dans l'église Romaine*, 188. See especially Philipp Oppenheim, *Die Consecratio virginum als geistesgeschichtliches Problem, Eine Studie zu ihrem aufbau, ihrem Wert und ehrer Geschichte* (Rome, 1943); Columba Hart, OSB, "*Consecratio Virginum*: Thirteenth-Century Witnesses," *The American Benedictine Review* 23, no. 2 (1972): 258–74; Anne Bangall Yardley, "The Marriage of Heaven and Earth: A Late Medieval Source of the Consecratio Virginum," *Current Musicology* (1990): 305–24. McNamara, *Sisters in Arms*, 43–5, 154–9. More recently, the publications based on the 2005 exhibition of convent art, *Krone und Schleier*, used these symbolic items of monastic profession as an organizing principle. Jutta Frings and Jan Gerchow, eds., "Krone und Schleier: Kunst aus mittelalterlichen Frauenklöstern: Ruhrlandmuseum, die frühen Klöster und Stifte 500–1200: Kunst- und Ausstellungshalle der Bundesrepublik Deutschland, die Zeit der Orden 1200–1500" (München: Hirmer, 2005).

[14] For a discussion of how bridal imagery operates in each of these texts, see Fiona J. Griffiths, *The Garden of Delights: Reform and Renaissance for Women in the Twelfth Century* (Philadelphia: University of Pennsylvania Press, 2007), 183, 95–7; Barbara Newman, *Sister of Wisdom: St. Hildegard's Theology of the Feminine* (Berkeley: University California Press, 1987), 43–53.

[15] On changing practices of child oblation in the late medieval period, see Maria Lahaye-Geusen, *Das Opfer der Kinder: Dienst und Leben der pueri oblati im hohen Mittelalter. Ein Beitrag zur Liturgie und zur Sozialgeschichte des Mönchtums*, Münsteraner theologische Abhandlungen, no. 13 (Althenberge: Oros, 1991).

176   *Marrying Jesus in Medieval and Early Modern Northern Europe*

for these communities, several anonymous medieval manuscripts with convent provenances also use marriage to Christ as a framework for preparing young women for the peculiarities of life within a particular community, among them Park Abdij Heverlee MS 18, dating to the end of the fifteenth century, the Rule of St. Agnes, and Karlsruhe Badenstadtsbibliothek MS St. Georgen 98 (dated to 1582). The Rule of St. Agnes at Emmerich, with which I opened this chapter, prescribes that the *magistra novitiarum* [mistress of novices] should teach the novices to be affectionate towards the heavenly bridegroom and please him with their purity and simple obedience.[16] Novices were to be "industrious in their work, their prayer, and reading of the holy scripture ... and with fiery devotion to choose Our Dear Lord Jesus, our purifier and bridegroom."[17] These lessons may have resembled the illustrated instructional program found in Park Abdij Heverlee MS 18, a late fifteenth-century manuscript partially transcribed by Kathryn M. Rudy. The devotional book contains a short *Spiritual Bedroom* amidst readings for feast dates and several pasted-in, hand-colored engravings of Christ's passion. Rudy suggests the text was intended to prepare postulants in preparation for their profession. Using the pasted down images and richly detailed narrative, each devotee transformed herself and her surroundings into a bedroom for consummating a spiritual marriage to Christ by learning to care for sick patients.[18] Like Gertrud of Helfta, these late medieval convent authors ensured that new members recognized that professing as brides of Christ was not enough: sisters would have to work together their entire lives if they wished to join their divine groom in heaven.

The sense of community in these manuscripts and liturgies reappears in the biographies of late medieval nuns. In both contexts, nuns present becoming a bride of Christ as a communal process of penance and prayer, rather than a battle to protect chastity or visionary encounters with Jesus. Several authors describe sisters as espoused to Christ even before entering the novitiate. For instance, Christina Retters's biographer introduces her as a bride of Christ when she enters a Praemonstratensian community at the age of six, comparing her entrance and espousal to the marriage and crowning of the biblical Esther.[19] Fifteenth-century Clarissan Magdalena Beutlerin (1407–58), who joined a convent at the age of five, had been heralded as bride of Christ in visions received anticipating her birth. A letter dated just prior to her entrance to the convent also described Magdalena as

---

    [16]   Bollmann and Staubach, *Schwesternbuch und Statuten des St. Agnes-Konvents in Emmerich*, 321.

    [17]   Ibid., 322.

    [18]   Kathryn Rudy includes a description of the manuscript, its use of pasted-in engravings, and a transcription. Kathryn Rudy, "How to Prepare the Bedroom for the Bridegroom," in *Frauen—Kloster—Kunst: Neue Forschungen zur Kulturgeschichte des Mittelalters: Beiträge zum internationalen Kolloquium vom 13. bis 16. Mai 2005 anlässlich der Ausstellung "Krone und Schleier,"* ed. Jeffrey F. Hamburger (Turnhout: Brepols, 2007), 369–78, 505–6.

    [19]   Mittermaier, "Lebensbeschreibung der sel. Christina," 226–7.

Sisters and Brides of Christ

"a new daughter of the Heavenly Father and a Bride of the Son."[20] Sister Souke van Dorsten, the daughter of a prominent Friesen family, also wed Christ before formally professing at the Augustinian Canoness house of Diepenveen. Souke's story is noteworthy because she fled an arranged marriage to become a nun and was supported by her sisters as a bride of Christ before making her profession. According to her biographer, when Souke van Dorsten's fiancé's family appeared outside the community's wall demanding that she leave the convent to honor her betrothal to their son, one of the older sisters, moved to pity, shouted, "Oh bride of Christ, stride now forcefully, because God in the heavens and all His angels see your conflict. Life here [on earth] lasts but briefly, but eternity endures so long! If you leave, then you please the devil and make him snigger. Stay here with us and then you will make your guardian angel happy." Hearing these words, Souke turned her back on the world and her distraught family. Souke's uncertainty as to which of her two betrothals to honor disappears when she is called a bride of Christ.[21]

The importance of community, memory, and daily devotion to convent life also is present in surviving profession statements, written vows which sisters initialed or signed when they entered a community. Several profession statements survive, many from women about whom little more is known. Profession statements from Jacoba Custodis (Jacomijne Costers; c. 1490) and Katherina van Mispelteren (c. 1475) were used as endpapers in Jewish Theological Seminary MS NH108, a small (13.5 cm × 10.5 cm) manuscript when it was rebound in the sixteenth century. These formulaic texts stated the sister's vows, her obedience to the rule of the Second Order of Augustine, Christ, and the Virgin Mary, and the names of the head of her house and her order. Little is known of Katherina van Mispelteren, but Costers became an author and scribe whose visions inspired fervent observance at the Windesheim-associated house of Mariendaal in Antwerp, inviting a reconstruction of her work as a teacher through bibliography. This is one of three surviving manuscripts associated with Costers which remained at Mariendaal during the disruptions the Reformations brought to Antwerp. Like the JTS manuscript, the other two volumes show that Costers remained an important contributor to communal life even after her death. Belgian Royal Library MS IV: 50, a very small (10 cm × 6.9 cm) sixteenth-century devotional manuscript, was inscribed with Costers's name in the seventeenth century. The third, Austrian National Library Series Nova 12827, is a seventeenth-century volume which recopies lost medieval texts. Though the seventeenth-century manuscript contains

---

[20] Magdalena was a renowned stigmatic and prophetess who guided the convent of Saint Clara's in Freiburg into adopting the Observant reform. Translation of this line is from Karen Greenspan, "Erklaerung des Vaterunsers: A Critical Edition of a Fifteenth-century Mystical Treatise by Magdalena Beutler of Freiburg" (PhD dissertation, University of Massachusetts-Amherst, 1984), 23.

[21] Unfortunately, *The Life of Souke van Dorsten* has not been made available in a modern edition. I summarize and translate from the modern edition by Wybren Scheepsma, *Hemels verlangen* (Amsterdam: Querido, 1993), 161.

178   *Marrying Jesus in Medieval and Early Modern Northern Europe*

texts related to the convent's history as well as practical advice from Costers to her sisters, only fragments of her poetry and a description of one of her visions have been made available in a modern edition.[22] Costers's story differs starkly in the three surviving manuscripts which contain her name.

Only her profession statement is an unfiltered artifact of the moment Jacomijne Costers became a bride of Christ. The fifteenth-century manuscript containing Costers's statement of monastic profession is modestly decorated and contains excerpts from Thomas à Kempis's *Imitation of Christ* and Hendrik Herp's *Mirror of Perfection*, likely copied for personal prayer. Costers is literally tucked into the back of the book, either because the parchment she had marked was on hand and durable, or because her name held some value for the person who assembled the codex. The small Brussels devotional book begins with an excerpt from a middle Dutch translation of Thomas of Cantimpré's *De Bonum universale de apibus*, which addresses the state of virginity; the second, "How the Loving Soul Sought Her Beloved after She Had Lost him," is an anonymous dialogue; the third is another unknown spiritual tract discussing righteous love and the proper way to dedicate all daily work to wisdom and detachment from the material world. Read together, these three short tracts retrace a woman's monastic experience: first, understanding the obligations and rewards of chastity, then finding and loving Christ, and finally learning to live virtuously in the world. The inscription linking this volume to Costers is only partially legible, and does not explain whether Costers copied the texts, owned the manuscript, or gave it to someone else. Even if this attribution is spurious, Costers's name added meaning to an otherwise unremarkable book. Because only brief excerpts from her visions and poetry have been edited, Costers is best known to modern scholars as a nun whose visions reformed a lax religious community; the manuscript record shows that this community valued her practical teaching and scribal labor far more than her visions.[23] At Mariendaal, where Elizabeth Silvoorts recopied the Vienna manuscript in the seventeenth century, Jacomijne Costers's sensible advice first guided a community destabilized by reform, then inspired embattled sisters struggling to maintain their vocation. Each of these manuscripts reveals less about the historical Jacomijne Costers's perception of herself as a bride of Christ than ways she served her community.

Living sisters worked together out of love for their divine spouse, supported by the memory of the dead from whom they learned and for whom they prayed. In convent manuscripts, when a sister died, she embraced Christ as a spouse, but she never left her sisters behind. This bond of sisterhood which transcended death is elegantly represented in a vision revealed to Adelheid Langmann of Engelthal shortly after Good Friday Mass. According to the text of the *Revelations*, Adelheid saw 10 women gathered in a lushly fragrant garden, each a sister who had died in the previous year. Nine were dressed alike in humble clothing, the tenth was stunningly arrayed in the finest shimmering gold and green gown. She wore a golden crown on her head and jeweled shoes on her feet, as if she were the Queen

---

22   Scheepsma, "De Helletocht van Jacomijne Costers (d. 1503)," 164.

23   Ibid.

Sisters and Brides of Christ 179

of Heaven or a cleansed and clothed bride of Christ. "Tell me, are you in heaven?" Adelheid asked the beautifully dressed soul. "No," she replied, she was waiting to make that journey with her sisters. The spirit explained that the difference in the women's clothing signified the gap in their accomplishments while living at Engelthal. The crown represented the tenth sister's natural chastity, the beautiful shoes signified the speed with which she daily went to the choir stalls, the golden mantle marked her eager performance of the daily offices, the surcoat reflected the purity of her heart and all the sorrows she suffered, its fabric signified her religious order, and its decorative jewels her many good works and the accomplishments of the sisters within that order. Her chastity, obedience, and enthusiasm for daily prayer materialize as jewels and fine damask. Though the beautifully dressed sister's soul is arrayed like a princess and crowned like a bride of Christ, she waits for her sisters to join her with their enthroned groom. The recently deceased Sister Hiltegunt appeared to Mechthild of Magdeburg in similarly allegoric clothing to report about heavenly wonders.[24]

Perhaps the most comprehensive expression of communal living and death as a shared wedding occurs in a series of entries describing an outbreak of plague at the house of Diepenveen in 1443–45, which memorializes the tragedy as a "Great Wedding" predicted in a revelatory dream:

> Our Dear Lord had selected some portion of his beloved brides to be taken out and away with him to heaven. And so it happened that he sent a sort of sickness here [to Diepenveen] that afflicted one in the throat, the other in the side or often in the back or in the head and through all the sorrows caused by this sickness they would die. These were the exquisite, sweet, and elect brides who were very sweetly selected for their numerable virtues ... [the list of departed sisters then follows].[25]

In these short lines, a potential communal tragedy becomes a divine gift that rewards the most virtuous. The language of the *Song* is prevalent in the chapter which follows, as Diepenveen becomes Christ's vineyard and the dying sisters are both flowers and brides.[26]

---

[24]   Mechthild of Magdeburg, *Das fliessende Licht der Gottheit: Nach der Einsiedler Handschrift in kritischem Vergleich mit gesamten Überlieferung*, ed. Hans Neumann and Gisela Vollmann-Profe (München; Zürich: Artemis Verlag, 1990), vol. 1, 52–4. Langmann, "Die offenbarungen der Adelheid Langmann, klosterfrau zu Engelthal," 68–9.

[25]   Alijt Comhaers, a sister studying visionary techniques, predicted the pestilence while dreaming of "a very beautiful and long-lasting wedding" that would soon take place, in D.A. Brinkerink, ed., *Van den doechden der vuriger ende stichtiger susteren van Diepen Veen: ('Handschrift D')* (Leiden: A.W. Sijthoff, 1904), 281.

[26]   The last bride to join in the Great Wedding, Sister Barte van der List of Zwolle, died on December 28, 1452, becoming the nineteenth woman to succumb to this sickness. This final entry contains no bridal references, but the narrator does remind the readers that each of the 19 women were part of a "lengthy and holy wedding which was foretold by Sister Alijt Comhaers the holy widow, the like of which had never happened before since the beginning of this cloister." Ibid., 309.

180   *Marrying Jesus in Medieval and Early Modern Northern Europe*

The sixteenth-century manuscript which preserves the Great Wedding distinguished individual sisters according to the virtue which earned her deathbed wedding. The author sometimes disrupted chronology to group sisters alongside those they traveled with into heaven, rather than those with whom they had died.[27] These groupings reinforce the author's depiction of her community as sister-brides helping one another become worthy of a communal spouse. For instance, the author joins Griete Tasten and Griete ten Kolke in a single entry, then, after several brief undated entries, all lacking bridal references, pairs the deaths of Griete Koetgens and Griete des Vryen together. Sister Griete Tasten from Zutphen and Sister Griete ten Kolke, were close friends who worked together, died together, and were together with Christ, their shared bridegroom after death. According to the sisterbook, as the two lay together in the infirmary, Griete Koetgens would often ask Griete des Vryen if she would like to travel together to meet her heavenly bridegroom, and Griete des Vryen would always answer that she would do whatever her dear Lord decided he wanted her to.[28]

According to the author of this entry, even those who survived the pestilence desired to travel together to heaven with the dead. One anecdote describes a Sister Yutta Viel, who fretted that good health might cheat her out of death and her bridegroom because Christ was displeased with her. She "went to that grave and stood there and lamented actively to Our Dear Lord" until she too fell ill and could wait for "the arrival of her loving bridegroom" in the infirmary.[29] Writing about the Dominican sisters of Corpus Domini in Venice, historian Daniel Bornstein proposed that deathbed scenes followed a formulaic sequence for a good death.[30] In the Dutch and German sisterbooks, deathbed scenes emphasized a sister's particular devotional habits. Deathbed weddings were only one possible ending to a sister's life: some sisters were greeted by the vision of a deceased friend or died showing their devotion to a saint.[31] For instance, Gese Tijtes (d. 1425) called

---

[27]   Griete Tasten, Griete des Vryen, and Griete Koetgens all died in 1452, Griete ten Kolke early in 1453. While the dates of Griete Tasten's and Griete Koetgens's deaths are uncertain, Griete Koetgens must have died several weeks before November 22, 1452, and Griete Tasten could not have died much earlier than late October of 1452.

[28]   Griete des Vryen lingered on in the infirmary a while longer, and would die on November 22, 1452. Ibid., 289.

[29]   Yutte continues to fret that she will not actually die, but rejoices when reassured that her illness is fatal. Ibid., 295.

[30]   In his introduction to the translation of the chronicle of the Venetian community of Corpus Domini, Bornstein suggests the deathbed sequence was a formula signaling a sister's good death. Bartolomea Riccoboni and Daniel Ethan Bornstein, *Life and Death in a Venetian Convent: The Chronicle and Necrology of Corpus Domini, 1395–1436* (Chicago: University of Chicago Press, 2000), 15.

[31]   I have not included the individual entries in the "Great Wedding" chapter from Diepenveen when making this statement, nor have I included unedited manuscripts. While she does not count the entries, Martina Klug provides a list of every woman mentioned in each of the edited sisterbooks. Martina B. Klug, *Armut und Arbeit in der Devotio moderna:*

Sisters and Brides of Christ

out to St. Bernard of Clairvaux as if he had appeared to escort her to heaven, and Geertruijt Hoppen (d. 1484) met death boldly by emulating St. Francis.[32]

Community weddings also occurred during the performance of offices, during Mass, and when performing choral works describing marriage to Christ. An intricately designed fifteenth-century Dutch Song cycle, *The Spiritual Melody* [*Gheestelicke Melody*], has the choir and audience perform the role of a penitent Soul who eventually weds Christ. The song cycle uses tunes from popular secular music and was intended to be performed over a period of 40 days alongside devotional readings.[33] Each song advanced the soul's transformation from a fearful sinner into a bride filled with hope and love, and crowned in glory.[34] In a communal context, vocalists might have identified with the protagonist soul, reflecting on their own sins for which they were atoning through obedience, song, and communal prayer.

Some melodies were technically demanding; in the original secular songs to which these verses were reset, such lyric flourishes would have demonstrated artistic mastery. Transposed to devotional lyrics, these moving notes took on theological meaning. For instance, Song 15, which draws on the musical techniques of the Meistersingers, uses rising notes spanning over an octave to recreate the soul's actions in each verse.[35] The first phrases are a more elaborate, rhythmically complex anticipation of the sustained refrain: "Come, Come, Come, Come, [the singers repeat the same interval, imploring Christ with rising hope] Lord Jesus Christ, Come [a resting tone, a pause, the song continues] My Soul's Bridegroom." The rapid coloratura of the first musical phrase emphasizes key

---

Studien zum Leben der Schwestern in niederrheinischen Gemeinschaften (Münster: Waxmann, 2005), 277–98. There are 68 entries for Emmerich, 69 for Meester-Geertshuis in Deventer, and at least 40 for the convent at Diepenveen, if both surviving manuscripts are included. Fewer than 1 in 12 entries in the three edited Dutch sisterbooks contain bridal references.

[32] De Man, *Hier beginnen Sommige stichtige Punten*, 53. Bollmann and Staubach, *Schwesternbuch und Statuten des St. Agnes-Konvents in Emmerich*, 303.

[33] Two of the three surviving manuscripts are available in facsimile; one was directed to a male community, one clearly owned by a female community, and one incorporated into a devotional book, again associated with a female religious communities. No surviving copies contain exactly the same selection of songs. E. Bruning et al., *Het geestelijk lied van Noord-Nederland in de vijftiende eeuw. De Nederlandse liederen van de handschriften Amsterdam (Wenen ÖNB 12875) en Utrecht (Berlijn MG 8o 190)* (Amsterdam: Vereniging voor Nederlandse Muziekgeschiedenis, 1963). Thom Mertens argues that those who, through performance, identified with the soul would be spiritually transformed. Thom Mertens, *Die Gheestelicke Melody*. See also Kathryn Rudy, "An Illustrated Mid-Fifteenth-Century Primer for a Flemish Girl, British Library, Harley MS 3828," in *Journal of the Warburg and Courtauld Institutes* 69 (2006): 51–94.

[34] Some of the manuscripts were designed for reading as well as singing.

[35] This is also the only entry in the manuscript with a decorated initial, a bearded face in the initial D. See Bruning et al., *Het geestelijk lied van Noord-Nederland in de vijftiende eeuw*, 45–7.

concepts in every stanza. In the first verse, lilies, roses, love, and senses; in the second, Christ will stay with *us*, giving him*self* to us so that we can live with him in eternity. Christ is the singer's elect love, who, if implored, will unfetter the singers from sinful bodies. The last verses bring the soul to heaven's gate, singing loudly, "Sanctus Sanctus Dominus," while running to meet Christ. With each verse, the song begs Christ to return to the soul he has wed, yet he, unmoved, remains in heaven. Only by patiently repeating the refrain will the soul herself ascend into heaven, running to embrace her beloved like the running notes on the page. Read silently from a page, this song cycle loses much of its efficacy. But when these songs were performed daily before an audience, alongside sisters from the same community, those who listened, sang, or passed near the choir's windows might have felt that they were running alongside the soul to embrace Christ in heaven.

This sense of community also appears in a description of singing mass from within an enclosed choir stall in the biography of Christina Retters dated to the Feast of the Three Kings in 1289. Although her biographer focuses on Retters's experience of marriage during communion, the entry acknowledges a community of brides which consists of the priest officiating mass, the sisters present in the choir, and those in the main chapel. As the priest approached the choir with the "dear body of God," a light passed through the wall which separated the nuns' choir from the main chapel, filling her soul with honey-sweetness. Retters heard a voice in her soul say, "I forgive all your sins." She perceived a godly light touching each virgin; when she went forward to take the sacrament, she too was filled with a sweetness which transported her to the throne of heaven. There she saw a heavenly queen arrayed in roses, lilies, and violets, with burning eyes like a falcon's—this was God's true love, for whom he had sacrificed his body to forgive all sins. Christina was led into a palace, where God embraced her soul kindly and granted her peace and mercy and said, "[R]ejoice, my soul, you have received me so certainly within you as my mother received me in her pure virgin body. I live more happily in you than in my heavens."[36] Christina Retters's soul sinks into her divine lover's embrace as she swallows Christ, an experience she shared with every person touched by the light in the choir stall, the priest whose hands transported that light, and by those in the main chapel who partook of the Eucharistic host.

Teaching Others to Love God

Marriages between Christ and each nun were more than a replacement for the relationship of worldly marriage or a symbol of a lifelong vow of chastity—they challenged each bride to make herself worthy of her spiritual groom so that communities of sisters could all enter heaven together. As should by now be apparent, medieval nuns welcomed advice about preparing themselves for encounters with Christ, their shared spouse. They turned to their sisters for encouragement, and,

---

[36] Mittermaier, "Lebensbeschreibung der sel. Christina," 203–5.

Sisters and Brides of Christ

when necessary, for correction. As part of this communal quest to earn Christ's eternal embrace in heaven, some sisters also taught visitors the art of prayer and pious living. Other convent authors praised their male spiritual advisors and chaplains for having fulfilled the individual promise of Christ's eternal embrace.

The biographies of Henry Suso (c. 1295–1366) and Friedrich Sunder (d. 1328), two Dominicans who wed Christ while ministering to Dominican women's communities, have been identified as cases of male clerics imitating nuns, but are better understood as examples of sisters working alongside male supporters to guide an entire community of brides.[37] As remembered by "their" nuns, these weddings to Christ were brought about largely through their contributions to women's communities; their *Lives*, like the lives of sisters, were designed to guide younger members of religious communities to join their chaplains alongside the bridegroom in heaven.

According to a brief biography recorded by his confessants, Sunder's spiritual experiences and marriage to Christ are a reward for his collaborative service to Engelthal; his piety is framed through his service as confessor to the blessed sister Gertrud and as a spiritual advisor to the entire community [*geselschaft*].[38] Entries show Sunder welcomed as friend by a group of saints, receiving visions of representatives of religious orders alongside cardinals, and conversing with his confessant Gertrud. These scenes portray Sunder as a negotiator between the community of the saints in heaven and the community of potential saints in Engelthal. Celebrations of mass are acknowledged with phrases like "prister singn vnd lessen" [the priest sang and read], and notices that Sunder effected the salvation of souls in a way the sisters could not.[39] Sunder's marriage to the Christchild occurs during the celebration of Mass and brings a bridal gift of redemption to the community of Engelthal.

Sunder married Jesus around the feast day of St. Damien while performing mass. In the first chapter related to this marriage, a diminutive Jesus appears during mass to explain that he is Sunder's little brother, and that Sunder is the mother of Christ's soul: "I am not your child, I am your little brother [ich bin nit din kind: ich bin din brüderlin] ... [yet] I have two mothers, Mary is my bodily mother and you, my dear soul, are my spiritual mother [Nun han ich zwó müttran: Maria, die ist min lipliche mûtter, so bist du, liebe sel mine, min gaistliche mûtter]."[40] The little Jesus [*Jhesuslin*] then pulls Sunder into his crib and asks to suckle from his right

---

[37] Other male mystics have been read as feminized, but I focus here only on those whose lives were demonstrably of interest to women's communities. See, for instance, Carolyn Diskant Muir, "Bride or Bridegroom? Masculine Identity in Mystic Marriages," in *Holiness and Masculinity in the Middle Ages*, ed. P.H. Cullum (Cardiff: University of Wales, 2004), 58–78; Deborah Rose-Lefmann, "Lady Love, King, Minstrel." And, of course, Caroline Walker Bynum, *Jesus as Mother*. For a corrective reading of Sunder and Suso, see Jeffrey F. Hamburger, "Overkill, or History that Hurts."

[38] All references to Sunder's life are from my own translations of Ringler's edition. Ringler, *Viten- und Offenbarungsliteratur in Frauenklöstern des Mittelalters*, 391–447.

[39] Ibid., 412, for instance.

[40] Ibid., 412–13.

184   *Marrying Jesus in Medieval and Early Modern Northern Europe*

breast since Sunder had just fed on Christ's body during mass. The author carefully explains that suckling from two little breasts is not to be understood literally, but that some mysteries have to be explained with bodily images because it is not possible to comprehend the sweet exchanges between God and the soul which Sunder experienced at that moment.[41] In the following chapter, Sunder performs another mass and marries the little Jesus who lives in the cradle of his soul. The wedding begins when Sunder swallows Christ's body at mass. Christ requests that Mary prepare his cradle "for [him and his] dear spouse, where [he and his] most dear spouse can take [their] pleasure with one another." Mary arranges the cradle with flowers symbolizing Sunder's virtues and unites Friedrich's holy soul to the Christchild. The two embrace and kiss and laugh in loving pleasure while the saints of heaven marvel at the union.[42]

A literal or queer reading of Sunder and the Christchild consummating their marriage in a cradle raises several practical questions—how might a celibate man playing the part of a bride and an infant playing the part of a groom have sexual intercourse? Does this passage record same-sex desire between two men? Might it be a rare medieval example of female-authored homoerotic fantasy? This queer consummation depends on unstable gender identities and transgressive sexual acts—a mother arranging for a priest to have sex with her infant son would be grounds for a modern criminal investigation. The troubling resemblance between this union and homoerotic child pornography elicits cautious responses from the few scholars who have published on it. Hildegard Keller finds their embrace an asexual union between two infant spirits, concluding "a mother marries two children."[43] In contrast, art historian Jeffrey Hamburger reads this as an explicitly sexual union between two male bodies, remarking that "copulation and contemplation go hand in hand."[44] Despite these interpretations, the medieval author's own insistence that the image is not literal is supported by the range of texts examined in previous chapters, all describing reception of the Eucharist as an embrace and marriage. An educated medieval reader would have recognized that one meaning for these two male bodies blurring into tangled gender confusion was the temporary interlocking of heaven and earth, body and spirit, Jesus and communicant, during the reception of the Eucharistic wafer. As the little Jesus explains, "You shall know that for this wedding which just occurred between me and this soul many people will be particularly pleased, both those in the convent and others, and all the souls currently in purgatory shall be given respite from their pain."[45] Sunder's marriage brings salvation to the souls of those suffering in purgatory and to the religious community whose support had nurtured him.

---

[41]   Ibid., 414–15.

[42]   Ibid., 416–17.

[43]   Keller, *My Secret Is Mine*, 28.

[44]   Hamburger, "Overkill, or History that Hurts," 421–2.

[45]   Ringler, *Viten- und Offenbarungsliteratur in Frauenklöstern des Mittelalters*, 416–17.

Sisters and Brides of Christ   185

Nor was the transformation of male visitors to a convent into brides of Christ limited to celibate chaplains singing Mass. As an episode in the *Revelations* of Adelheid Langmann reveals, any man might study with the sisters and become a bride of Christ. In 1336, the exceptionally sinful knight, Eberhart Schutz of Hohenstein, and his beautiful but sinful aristocratic wife knew nothing of God—he did not pray and had never taken communion.[46] While riding through a forest Eberhart received a vision warning that the couple had a month to reform their lifestyles or they would both die. Deeply concerned, Eberhart begged a passing hermit for prayers. The hermit directed Eberhart to ride on until he came to Engelthal, where a sister "full of God's mercy" could pray for him and teach him how to pray for his own sins. At Engelthal, Adelheid Langmann saved his life. Eberhart's wife refused to reform and died within the month. After burying his wife, Eberhart returned to Engelthal to inquire whether he too would soon die. Langmann replied that he should wed "[t]he queen of Heaven, the Mother of God" and spend his days fasting and industriously praying. Jesus personally appeared on the Feast Day of the Circumcision to officiate a marriage between Eberhart and the Virgin Mary. This marriage finally elicited a heartfelt religious conversion, and Eberhart soon entered the community of Kaisheim. As Leonard Hindsley proposes, this scene was included in the *Revelations* to establish Langmann's reputation as a wise counselor. Eberhart's naïve sinfulness and heartfelt conversion would also have been instructive to convent readers: if even the worldliest of men could make a religious conversion simply by expressing a willingness to reform, how much more important was it for Christ's vowed brides to live virtuously? It also reveals that lay men and women respected enclosed nuns as teachers: over several decades of conversation, an enclosed widow instructed a layman in prayer, guided him to a second spiritual marriage, and inspired his monastic profession.

These accounts of male brides of Christ were recorded by nuns for use in women's communities and unfold much as if they had been written about sisters, rather than the men who visited them. Nuns transformed their confessors' experiences into instructive works to chronicle the distribution of salvation by brides of Christ to their communities. Friedrich Sunder, his near contemporary Henry Suso, and Eberhart Schutz set aside their bodies, not their masculinity, when they put on dresses, developed lactating breasts, and joined a community of brides of Christ. Each of these *Lives* taught that a resolution to repent and live virtuously was itself enough to win Christ's hand in marriage, but each warned that such unions required a lifelong commitment to labor in prayer. Whatever these marriages between men and Jesus may add to modern reconstructions of medieval masculinity, the nuns who wrote, read, and copied their stories recognized the men who worked alongside them as espoused to Christ, and thus as sisters.

---

[46] Langmann, "Die offenbarungen der Adelheid Langmann, klosterfrau zu Engelthal," 53–60. The scene is summarized and partially translated in Hindsley, *The Mystics of Engelthal*, 52–4.

186   *Marrying Jesus in Medieval and Early Modern Northern Europe*

Brides of the Devil and Concubines of God

Sixteenth-century accusations that nuns were prostitutes and that monastic profession was a form of adultery inspired by the devil himself likely originate in manuscript books produced in fifteenth-century women's communities. The late fifteenth century witnessed the first mass possessions of convents, and some fifteenth-century clerics sought to forcibly reform women's religious expression. But this does not necessarily mean that by the fifteenth century, there were too many brides of Christ, too many dangerous mystics, and too many religious women. Rather, as Moshe Sluhovsky has shown, women's religiosity had become subject to competing hermeneutics.[47]

The Dominican Johannes Nider reported several convent possessions in his *Formicarius*, including a possession in 1428 at the convent of St. Katharina's in Nuremburg, the same institution to which the widow Katharina Tucher donated her books and scribal services.[48] In 1455, the Windesheim Congregation, the monastic branch of the *Devotio Moderna*, banned all women's communities from composing or copying theological and mystical texts.[49] Even as male authorities attempted to exert control over women's communities perceived to have fallen into control of the devil, women *within* these communities found a different narrative frame for demon possession. The late fifteenth-century *Letter on the deception of devilish apparitions* [*Sendbrief vom Betrug teuflischer Erscheinungen*] purports to have been written by a confessor warning sisters in his care against demonic visions, but only one copy belonged to a male community, the Franciscans of Cheb.[50]

---

[47]   In this phrasing I am following the suggestion that demon possession was a "hermeneutic and labeling mechanism," Sluhovsky, *Believe Not Every Spirit*, 236. Peter Dinzelbacher explores the interpretive tools theologians used to differentiate between holy women and witches in the late middle ages. Peter Dinzelbacher, *Heilige Oder Hexen? Shicksale Auffalliger Frauen in Mittelalter Und Fruhneuzeit*.

[48]   Johannes Nider, *Formicarius* (Graz: Akadem. Druck-u. Verlagsanst, 1971), book 3, 3.

[49]   The connection was first drawn by Spaapen and subsequently discussed within the context of gender hierarchies by Scheepsma, Lie, Mertens, Bollmann, and Winston-Allen. Anne Bollmann, "'Being a Woman on My Own': Alijt Bake (1415–1455) as Reformer of the Inner Self," in *Seeing and Knowing: Women and Learning in Medieval Europe 1200–1550*, ed. Anneke B. Mulder-Bakker (Turnhout: Brepols, 2004), 94–5; Orlanda S.H. Lie, "Middelnederlandse Literatuur Vanuit Genderperspectief: Een Verkenning," *Tijdschrift voor Nederlandse taal- en letterkunde* 117, no. 3 (2001); Wybren Scheepsma, *Medieval Religious Women in the Low Countries: The 'Modern Devotion,' the Canonesses of Windesheim, and Their Writings*, trans. David F. Johnson (Woodbridge: Boydell Press, 2004); B. Spaapen, "Middeleeuwse Passiemystiek, III: De Autobiografie van Alijt Bake (Vervolg); IV: De Brief Uit De Ballingschap," *Ons Geestelijk Erf* 40, no. 1 (1967): 5–64; Winston-Allen, *Convent Chronicles*.

[50]   I translate from Ulla Williams and Werner Williams-Krapp, "Eine Warnung an Alle, Dy Sych Etwaz Duncken. Der 'Sendbrief Vom Betrug Teuflischer Erscheinungen' (Mit Einer Edition)," in *Forschungen Zur Deutschen Literatur Des Spätmittelalters. Festschrift*

Sisters and Brides of Christ 187

The *Sendbrief* constructed true and false piety within late medieval hierarchies of gender and consecration, stressing the reliability of consecrated submissive virgins over laywomen, especially widows who play witness to Christ's passion. Contrasting falsely pious widows who have been deceived by the devil to one of the author's confessants, an exemplary holy maiden [*heylig junkfraw*] and bride of Christ who has vanquished devils and truly experienced the revelations of God within her soul, the *Sendbrief* stressed that women's visions alone were not a legitimate basis for spiritual teaching.[51]

Another fifteenth-century convent manuscript, the *Schwesternspiegel* [*Mirror for Sisters*], relates the story of a Sister Agnes of Brabant who was possessed by a demon in 1439. In his edition of the text, Ekkehard Borries proposes that Agnes's possession modeled virtuous behavior for women religious because her devil painstakingly explains the consequences of sins.[52] Like the *Sendbrief*'s possessed widows, Agnes's possession warns against the misleading influence of demons disguised as heavenly visitors and cautions the professional religious against pride and complacency.

Unlike the manuals for hunting witches and banishing devils written by and for clerics, these accounts of demon possession teach readers humility, safe prayer practice, and constant oversight from spiritual superiors, all necessary practices to escape the devil's trickery while praying. Every surviving manuscript copy of the *Sendbrief* and the *Schwesternspiegel* date to the last half of the fifteenth century, and most to the years between 1450 and 1470, and all but one were owned by women's houses. Both warn that demons may appear as singing angels, the virgin Mary, the baby Jesus, the holy spirit, or even a bleeding Jesus inviting the contemplative to suckle from his wounds.[53] But these texts warn sisters against prideful confidence, rather than condemning women's visions or warning against women teaching theology. Agnes's demon explains clearly that curiosity and a desire for fine clothes would draw demons to enclosed women, the author of the *Sendbrief* blames incompetent confessors for failing women deceived by devils.[54] In the same period that these manuscripts were produced, printers first adapted treatises written by nuns for print, among them visions of individual sainted nuns, such as Bridget of Sweden and Hrotsvita of Gandersheim, but also accused

---

Für Johannes Janota, ed. Horst Brunner and Werner Williams-Krapp (Tübingen: Max Niemeyer Verlag, Imprint von de Gruyter 2003), 174–5. For a brief English-language summary of the text, see Werner Williams-Krapp, "The Erosion of a Monopoly: German Religious Literature in the Fifteenth Century," in *The Vernacular Spirit: Essays on Medieval Religious Literature*, ed. Renate Blumenfeld-Kosinski, Nancy Bradley Warren, and Duncan Robertson (New York: Palgrave, 2002), 253.

[51]   The letter describes two such widows: Williams and Williams-Krapp, eds., "Eine Warnung an Alle," 183, 186.

[52]   Ekkehard Borries, *Schwesternspiegel Im 15. Jahrhundert: Gattungskonstitution, Editionen, Untersuchungen* (Berlin: Walter De Gruyter, 2008), 23–4.

[53]   Williams and Williams-Krapp, "Eine Warnung an Alle," 180–82.

[54]   Borries, *Schwesternspiegel*, 146–7.

188 *Marrying Jesus in Medieval and Early Modern Northern Europe*

demoniacs and exiled dissenters like Magdalena Beutlerin and Alijt Bake.[55] This indicates that perceived lapses in humility were considered far more threatening than women's visions, uncontrolled speech, or sexual depravity.

Serving as a bride of Christ was a lifetime commitment, a series of small acts performed within a community. Demon possession, like the sale of sexual favors of nuns, represented a breakdown in the formation of women's spirituality—a system designed primarily *by* sisters for one another. As Dyan Elliott, Michel de Certeau, and Moshe Sluhovsky have demonstrated, the relationship between mystical experience and demon possession was understood differently for nuns, not just because sexual abstinence protected women's reputations even as it invited demonic temptation, but also because a single devil could quickly corrupt an entire community. Sluhovsky argues that demon possession was another form of "female monastic creativity ... express[ing] nuns' involvement in the reform movements of the period and demonstrat[ing] the earnestness of nuns' engagement in their personal spiritual well-being and—no less important—the well-being of the world at large."[56] Sluhovsky's point is that demon possession meant something very different for women's communities than it did for the men sent to examine them. In written accounts by and for women's communities, possession by demons and marriage to Jesus *both* demonstrated a community's proximity to God and taught sisters how to live faithfully.

These competing fifteenth-century narratives of brides of Christ and brides of the devil provided a meaningful vocabulary for reformers challenging monastic celibacy. The religious debates of the sixteenth century required each sister to reconsider her marriage to Jesus; some would decide a monastic marriage to Christ was adulterous or diabolical, others found inspiration in exemplary marriages of dead brides of Christ. As a representative example, the ex-nun Ursula of Münsterberg (who briefly resided with Martin Luther), published a pamphlet in 1522 attacking communal religious life. She recalls that reformers shouting over the walls of her former convent insisted that all Christian souls were already married to Christ in baptism. According to Ursula, weddings contracted between women religious and Christ were a "peculiar and fabricated spousehood," which adulterously violated the marital bond formed during baptism. In her pamphlet, she argues that she and her sisters had broken their marriage to God because:

> we have allowed ourselves to be glorified as brides of Christ and let ourselves even be lifted up over other Christians who we have regarded as unworthy of this ... [the] spousehood and alliance made between God and us through faith, publicly professed in baptism, is sullied and broken in this.[57]

---

[55] Rabia Gregory, "Thinking of their Sisters: Authority and Authorship in Late Medieval Women's Religious Communities," *Journal of Medieval Religious Cultures* 40, no. 1 (2014): 75–100.

[56] Sluhovsky, *Believe Not Every Spirit*, 242.

[57] Merry E. Wiesner, *Convents Confront the Reformation: Catholic and Protestant Nuns in Germany*, Reformation Texts with Translation (1350–1650), Women of the Reformation, vol. 1 (Milwaukee: Marquette University Press, 1996).

Sisters and Brides of Christ 189

From years of living as a nun, Ursula of Münsterberg felt singling nuns out as elect brides of Christ falsely glorified them above lay Christians.

Other nuns who heard the reformers' challenge but decided to remain faithful to their vows took special inspiration from their marital relationship to Christ. The pages of a late sixteenth-century prayer book from the dissolved Dominican convent of St. Nicolas in Undis in Strasbourg are covered with rubricated references to Christ as spouse. Dating to around 1570, this manuscript would have been produced at a time of relative stability for St. Nicolas in Undis, as sisters restored their reputation by performing their duties as chaste brides of Christ, eyes turned to heaven, voices raised in prayer. In 1592, following years of financial difficulty and the trial of several sisters for sexual debauchery and prostitution, the community permanently dissolved.[58] Portions of the library survive, including a personal prayer book given by Christina Seyczin to Sybilla Schaupin, both sisters at St. Nicolas.[59] As a manuscript given by one nun to another when their community was consistently defending their reputation for chastity and sanctity, this codex maintains continuity with the medieval practice of sisters helping one another learn and refine the art of prayer. Christina Seyczin, the donor, remained in the community's ruins until c. 1590; she was among the sisters tried for prostitution. When Schaupin received this book in 1592, interactions with townsfolk, and even with the male religious who provided confession and the sacraments, had become dangerous for the women at St. Nicolas in Undis.

Their prayer book is dedicated to the Eucharist, a sacrament rarely available to the last nuns of post-Reformation Strasbourg. Many of these prayers entrust the individual's protection to Christ and implore him to come to the penitent in his capacity as spouse. Some describe the soul's nakedness and clothing by Christ as groom, others are voiced by the loving soul [*mynnende seele*] or offer progressive exercises to prepare the soul for taking the Eucharist. Some passages retain medieval vocabulary, using *minne*; others used the modernized *leibe*. One prayer addressed to Christ, "mýn gott mýn aller bester liebhaber" [my God, my very best Lover], praises chastity as the devotee embraces her divine lover within the soul and the heart and receives the Eucharist. Some of these references come through excerpts from the writing of medieval figures like Henry Suso, pseudo-Bernard of Clairvaux, and Mechthild of Hackeborn; others have no known medieval antecedents. Reciting these prayers despite limited access to the Eucharist, Schaupin would have reaffirmed her vocational commitment as a

---

[58]   For a detailed account of this closure, see Amy Leonard, *Nails in the Wall: Catholic Nuns in Reformation Germany*, Women in Culture and Society (Chicago: University of Chicago Press, 2005), 130–45.

[59]   Bodleian Library, uncatalogued manuscript from St. Nicolas in Undis, f 118r–119v. My thanks to Nigel Palmer for arranging for me to spend a few hours with this manuscript before it was catalogued. A brief description of the manuscript and its history was prepared for an exhibition catalogue in 2009. Nigel F. Palmer, "Strasbourg & the History of the Book: Five Centuries of German Printed Books and Manuscripts," ed. Taylor Institution Library and University of Oxford St. Giles' (2009), 36–7.

bride of Christ. Considering the difficulties involved in receiving the Eucharist at St. Nicolas in Undis, the prayers might have also offered comfort and patience against persecution.

For some fifteenth-century Christians, Christ truly was the spouse to every soul. This late medieval belief that marrying Jesus could be achieved by every Christian circulated through, and likely originated in, medieval convents. Nuns and their secular friends turned to exempla and devotional manuals to understand Christ's role as spouse, and sought advice on prayer techniques from both their confessors and sisters at local convents. Late medieval nuns viewed each Christian who passed their convent's walls to be capable of wedding Christ in heaven. In fourteenth- and fifteenth-century towns, this certainty that Christ was a lover for every soul meant that married laywomen and celibate nuns were recognized as brides of Christ—baptism, monastic profession, and the sacrament of marriage did not make these women adulteresses. As celibacy became a fault line of religious difference, early modern Christians came to understand the ritual marriage to Christ in profession ceremonies as differentiating nuns from a community of regular believers. By the end of the sixteenth century, conversations about nuns' identities as brides of Christ had been partially resolved. In Catholic regions, sisters were only permitted to teach when carefully monitored by their male religious superiors, while in Protestant regions, the nun's marriage to Christ had become an act of adultery. As the newly emerging confessions argued over whether celibate women were brides of Christ, the master narrative of Christ's love for elect souls remained useful on both sides of the confessional divide.

Chapter 7
Confessions of "True" Brides of Christ

In 1546, the Catholic Church in the Spanish Netherlands added to the Index of Banned Books an anonymous Dutch pamphlet on the bride of Christ now ascribed to Ysbrandt Schol (c. 1464–1534), an obscure preacher who was executed for heresy, possibly as a Sacramentist—Netherlandish Protestants who challenged traditional doctrines on the sacraments in the 1520s and 30s.[1] If not for a brief notice of the burning of both the author and his book by representatives of the Inquisition in the Spanish Netherlands, Schol's *Devout Contemplation on the Bride of Christ* could not now be categorized as either Protestant or Catholic, medieval or early modern, much less cause for a death sentence. After Schol's execution, Peter Jansz of Leiden reissued a part of his burned book as *Van dye bruyt Christi een devote contemplatie [A Devout Contemplation on the Bride of Christ]* as a small anonymous pamphlet.[2] This had been the concluding chapter of the *Profitable and consoling little book on belief and hope [Een profitelijck en[de] troostelick boecxken vanden gheloove ende hoope]*, where Schol instructed brides of Christ to prepare for the end of the world using language and theology which closely resembles fifteenth-century Dutch treatises on the bride of Christ. Schol, like some medieval authors as well as early Reformers like Martin Luther, presented the bride's union with Christ as a transaction in salvation that initiated creation's destruction. In the mid-1520s, when Schol first preached his ideas, this genuinely medieval aspect of the bride of Christ alarmed secular and religious authorities responding to Luther's demands for reform. By the 1530s, when Schol was executed and his books burned, this same theological understanding would have deeply worried authorities responding to a prophetic Anabaptist commune in Münster in 1534–35. In the 1540s, when Schol's work was reprinted anonymously, the bride of Christ had become part of a violently contested argument about sacramental theology and a symbol representing newly

---

[1]   Jesús Martínez de Bujanda, Léon-Ernest Halkin, and Patrick Pasture, eds., *Index de l'Université de Louvain: 1546, 1550, 1558* (Sherbrooke: Sherbrooke Centre d'études de la Renaissance, 1986), 183–4. Albert F. Mellink, *De Wederdopers in de noordelijke Nederlanden 1531–1544* (Groningen: J.B. Wolters, 1954), 344.

[2]   Ysbrandt Schol (?), *Een profitelijck en[de] troostelick boecxken vanden gheloove ende hoope wat dat oprechte ghelove is. Ende welcke ghenade die mensche doer dat gelove nach vercrigen. Ende hoe scadeliken dat onghelove is. Noch een boecxken va[n] die liefde die God tot ons heeft, ende wat die liefde werct, ende hoe scadelick die liefde des werelts is allen menschen seer troostelic. Met noch een deuote contemplatie aan dye bruyt Christi* (Anvers: Adriaen van Bergen, 1534); Ysbrandt Schol (?), *Van dye bruyt Christi een devote contemplacie* (Leiden: Peter Janszoon, 1540). Unless otherwise specified, all quotations and page references are to Peter Janszoon's edition.

forming Christian denominations. In the early 1520s, theologians began rejecting the doctrine of transubstantiation, questioned the efficacy of clerical celibacy, and seriously reconsidered baptismal practices, three of the most important ways medieval Christians engaged with Christ as a spouse. As the new confessions differentiated themselves from one another and from what had been medieval Christianity, most still recognized their own gathering to be the one true bride of Christ while labeling their opponents adulteresses or brides of the devil. Schol's execution and the reprinting of his banned book offer testimony that aspects of the bride of Christ popular in the late medieval north were not just a passing fad.

In art, music, and theology, Catholics and Protestants often shared theological and social uses of the bride of Christ even as they vehemently disagreed about who might be the "true" bride of Christ. I leave to other historians of early modern Europe the task of documenting the more intricate details of this history and here sample only representative examples which express the situational needs of Christians in regions experiencing religious tumult and testify that *each* aspect of the late medieval bride of Christ survived the Reformation. In the Low Countries during and after the Eighty Years' War, marrying Jesus resonated with Christians of all denominations who advocated religious tolerance. In German-speaking principalities, the bride of Christ, so important to Luther's theology, vanished from view during the political and military negotiations of the mid-sixteenth century, then reappeared in hymnals and prayer books soon after the Peace of Augsburg in 1555. In France, Spain, and Italy, the bride of Christ was central to the reform of women's religious communities, but also central to the writing of persecuted seventeenth-century Quietists. Anabaptist hymns and martyrologies represented death as a return to the bridegroom's embrace using imagery also found in Catholic hagiographies and convent documents. In the eighteenth century, Lutheran, Anabaptist, and Methodist hymnals contained newly authored songs addressed to Christ-as-spouse which sometimes borrowed musical phrasings or shared lyrics with Catholic liturgical music. Across Europe and in New World colonies, Catholics and Protestants retained medieval theological understandings of the bride which exceeded the traditional definitions of bride as Ecclesia, the Virgin Mary, or a consecrated virgin. In opposition, Protestants advocated marriage over chastity; following Luther and his medieval predecessors, many Protestant denominations still consider married parents able to wed Jesus. In contrast, post-Tridentine Catholics knew few brides of Christ who were not chaste women. Thus, while Catholics and Protestants continue to associate marriage to Jesus with sacramental theology, with personal salvation, and with the end of the world, Protestants have more overwhelmingly preserved the late medieval certainty that Jesus was a spouse for every Christian soul, while Catholics alone have retained the bride of Christ as a pious virgin. These and other early modern vignettes demonstrate that the late medieval understanding of Christ as a spouse had been accepted and disseminated among the German- and Dutch-speaking Christians of the fourteenth and fifteenth centuries and remained largely unchanged by the theological revolutions of the Reformation.

Sixteenth- and seventeenth-century Christian disputations show that the bride of Christ remained central to popular religious culture. The bride of Christ was not quickly disassembled by angry theologians seeking doctrinally sound imagery for their new, "true" churches. Instead, as religious disputes dissolved into relatively amicable cohabitation in the seventeenth century, reflections of the medieval bride of Christ continued to influence western Christianity. During and after the Reformation, newly emerging denominations adapted the bride of Christ to suit their own communal needs. These new representations of the bride of Christ continue to influence modern scholars' understanding of how the bride of Christ was understood in medieval Europe. Because individual denominations embraced particular aspects of the medieval bride of Christ and rejected others, sixteenth- and seventeenth-century brides of Christ contain important evidence about what was widely accepted by the Christians of the late fifteenth century. For Catholics, the bride became primarily associated with the sexually pure bodies of nuns, saints, and the Virgin Mary, meanings Protestants eventually rejected. As a result of these new theological norms, manuscripts, music, and art depicting medieval brides of Christ which conformed with early modern values are more likely to survive to the present day.

The Illusion of Confessional Difference

The bride of Christ was central to the first theological disputes of the sixteenth century. Perhaps through the influence of Martin Luther's allusion to marrying Jesus in his seminal 1520 response to Pope Leo X in *On Christian Freedom*, the bride of Christ began marking fault lines between the church of Rome and the new denominations of Protestation. In addition to debates over monastic celibacy in the 1520s and 30s, apocalyptic preachers like Ysbrandt Schol understood the bride's presence in the world to be evidence of coming judgment. And, for Sacramentists, Anabaptists, Lutherans, and other early Protestants, the bride came to mark the "true" church of Jesus and the Apostles from the corrupted church in Rome. Even after rejecting medieval sacramental theology and soteriology, Luther retained some medieval aspects of the bride of Christ. Like Ruusbroec, he criticized professional religious who performed rote prayers. Like David of Augsburg, he insisted that Christ was a spouse for every pure believing soul. When Luther redrew the line dividing the true Church, Christ's bride, from the brides of the devil—Catholics, pagans, Jews—he recycled the medieval division between the realms of saved and damned, making "papists" a subspecies of "heretics." Luther argued that individuals became Christ's brides when they received the word of God in pure belief and explicitly denied the special status conferred to nuns as a bride of Christ. He wrote hymns praising Christ as spouse, and warned that anyone who broke with the Protestant Church's good teachings would find themselves married to the devil. For Luther, betraying Christ and wedding the devil marked heretics, heathens, and false prophets who endangered Christian souls.[3]

---

[3]   Luther, WA, vol. 23, 304–5, 934.

194   *Marrying Jesus in Medieval and Early Modern Northern Europe*

When Martin Luther and other sixteenth-century theologians sat down to write out their own views of the sacraments, creation, or of the relationship between God and humanity, they recognized the bride of Christ to be an image appropriate for their task. Consequently, the bride appeared in polemical works advocating reform as well as those defending Rome. Arguments over who might be the true bride of Christ appeared frequently in short vernacular polemic pamphlets and broadsheets [*Flugschriften, Flugblättern*]. Protestant authors like David Joris, Menno Simons, Martin Luther, and Jakob Boehme used the master narrative of Christ's marriage to the bride in polemic and catechesis. Determining whether a particular aspect of the bride of Christ was becoming "protestant" or "catholic" is not a simple matter. For instance, in the Low Countries and northern Germany, the bride as a harbinger of the apocalypse and a representative of the "true" Church appeared among Anabaptists, Lutherans, and Catholics. Ysbrandt Schol's bride of Christ, which seemed dangerously Lutheran, was little different from the brides of Christ described by leading Anabaptists Menno Simons and David Joris, or from the brides portrayed by Catholic humanist Dirck Coornhert. By the seventeenth century, these modest denominational differences between brides of Christ had largely disappeared, as in the blended alchemical writing of authors like Jakob Boehme and Jan Luyken.

To return to Schol's condemned book on the bride of Christ, in the 1520s and 30s, explaining theological nuances through the marriage between Christ and humanity had been a standard trope for sacramental theologians, but rapidly became a dangerous sign of religious dissent. Schol's reading of 2 Corinthians, Revelation, and the Gospel of John originates in orthodox medieval beliefs about the bride of Christ. Like medieval authors, Schol explained the mechanisms of human salvation through learning to accept God's love. God joined himself to his people, the Christians, by sending Christ, his only created son, to wed them all, thus purifying their sinful souls. He wrote that "Christ was sent as the most beautiful bridegroom of human nature, drawing the sinful soul to him like he was drawn into flesh and sickness in the world.... Christ, this worthy Bridegroom takes his elect bride by the hand and arrays her genially and presents to her all the riches of his father's kingdom."[4] Carefully grounded in scriptural citations, Schol's language would not have been questioned two decades earlier. When Schol's Christ says: "I have found no one I love so well as you, thus I set myself [as payment] for your sins and misdeeds because I have given my flesh and blood for you in bitterest death," his medieval imagery also evokes Luther's new doctrine of

---

[4] "So heeft hi ons Christus zum woert gesonden als een die alder schoonste Bruydegom die de menscelike nature die sondighe siele tot hem soude trecken als hi met haer in dese werlt een vleesch ende crancheit is geworden Op dat hi ons alte samen met hem seluen soude vertroosten als hi hemseluen so liefliken gaft tot ons.... Christus dese waerdige Bruydegom nemende bi der hant zijn wtuercoren Bruyt ende siet haer vriendelijc aen ende presenteert haer alle dier rijcdommen zijns vaders." Schol, *Van dye bruyt Christi een devote contemplacie*, a3r.

salvific love.[5] For Schol, the wedding feast of the lamb is "to be understood as the highest union of God himself in his godly nature, which he has given to us in our sickness, on account of the glorious love he has for humankind, so that we can all know him and feast together with him with such pleasure as if we had been brought to know him ourselves in our souls and so that we can all be together, called to him in glory."[6] In the 1540s, a period of religious warfare, it was perhaps inevitable that the *Devout Contemplation on the Bride of Christ* would be condemned as dangerous. Not only did Schol's loving Christ recall Luther, his Wedding of the Lamb echoed the apocalyptic language of persecuted Anabaptists, for whom the bride of Christ had come to represent a persecuted community of true believers.

Before and after the fall of the commune at Münster, Anabaptists understood the persecution of their community to be an immediate precursor to the Wedding of the Lamb. For instance, Sacramentist martyr Cornelius Hendrickz Hoen (d. 1523/24) identified Christ as a bridegroom who married the collective Anabaptist Church during every Eucharistic meal in his *Epistola Christiana admodum*, an attack on Luther's interpretation of the Eucharist, and the Hutterite chronicler Kaspar Braitmichel (d. 1573) described Anabaptists gathering in the "wilderness of Moravia" as the bride of the Lord.[7] So central was the bride of Christ to Anabaptist identity that when prominent leaders Menno Simons and David Joris fell into dispute in the 1540s, both men published pamphlets insisting their own followers were the only true brides of Christ.

The rhetoric of their disagreement models how late medieval representations of the bride as individual Christian were adjusted to explain revisions to sacramental theology. In 1539, Simons challenged David Joris in print in his influential *Fundamentboeck* [*Foundation Book*], a comprehensive defense of Anabaptist Christianity. Joris issued a formal rebuttal in 1542 the same year he published his own lengthy theological statement in *'t Wonderboeck* [*The Book of Wonders*].[8]

---

[5] "mer ic en hebbe niemant geuonden die u so lief hadde als ick. Soe hebbe ic mi seluen voer u misdaet ende schult geset / als ic mijn vleysch ende bloet voer u / gaf in den bitteren doot." Schol, *Van dye bruyt Christi een devote contemplacie*, Biii, r–v.

[6] "Laten wi ons verblijden ende vrolic zijn ende laet ons hem glorie geuen / want die bruyloften des lams zijn ghecomen / ende zijn huysvrouwe heeft haer bereyt. Ende het is haer ghegeuen dat si haer aendoen soude met schone ende blinckende side / want die syde is die rechtuaerdichmakinghe der heylighen ende heeft mi gheseyt / salich zijn si die tot die bruyloft ende auontmael des lams gheroepen zijn In dese bruyloft is te verstaen die hochwaerdige vereeninghe / als God hem seluen in zijn godlike natuere heeft ghegeuen tot onse crancheit / op dat zijn liefde die hi tot den mensche hadde in suclken gloriosen werc soude werden bekent ende dat wi alle te samen met hem ni suicken feeste mede souden vrolic zijn / als wi inden geest doer da geloue consten bekennen dat wi al te samen tot dese glorie geroepen zijn." Schol, *Van dye bruyt Christi een devote contemplacie*, a vii r.

[7] George Huntston Williams, *The Radical Reformation*, 3rd ed. (Kirksville, MO: Truman State University Press, 2000), 107–8, 1077.

[8] Gary K. Waite, *David Joris and Dutch Anabaptism, 1524–1543* (Waterloo, ON: Wilfrid Laurier University Press, 1990), 164–7; Williams, *The Radical Reformation*, 729.

196   *Marrying Jesus in Medieval and Early Modern Northern Europe*

The pair argued the matter out through a flurry of pamphlets on the sacraments and the apocalypse, including letters in which both Simons and Joris claimed the role of true bride of Christ.[9] In 1556, almost certainly in response to Joris and other "false prophets," Simons reissued part of his *Fundamentboeck* as a notice addressed to the "bride of Christ," his community of followers, elect for their right understanding of the sacraments and their pious living. Joris responded with a pamphlet written from the perspective of the God-bride, using the striking double-subject, "Ick-se" [I-she]. Joris urged his followers to hear the voice of their spouse and prepare for a wedding feast, warning that those who reject his prophecies rejected their bridegroom. Simons chastises the bride who follows false prophets, while Joris praises an elect gathering of "brothers" drawing close to their spouse. Joris describes the landscape of the apocalyptic wedding using the voice of Christ the groom to inspire his bride-brothers to prepare for a glorious (if bloody) wedding. Simons's bride is fenced against the horrors of the world; should the bride leave her garden's borders, she will fall into hell. Simons admonishes a straying community through chilling parallels with the capture, rape, and exile of Israel. Despite their differences, Joris and Simons both focus on the same details (the bridegroom's white clothes and bride's beauty), list the same existential threats, and warn against the distracting allure of Satan and the false prophets.

These same elements also appear in contemporary art and literature produced by Catholics in the Low Countries and should not be thought of as uniquely Anabaptist, but instead as part of a regional visual and theological vocabulary for describing sacraments and human-divine interactions. For instance, the engraving series *Jacob's Ladder*, a visual narrative of personal salvation I first discussed in Chapter 2, was created around 1550 by the Catholic artists Maarten van Heemskerck and Dirck Coornhert. Though some of their other collaborative prints include depictions of virgin saints and the Virgin Mary, none of their surviving images explicitly poses a female virgin receiving a ring or kissing Christ. Like Joris and Simons, and like Ysbrandt Schol, these Catholic artists portrayed the bride as a community of believers saved through love, a concept they represented visually with the male soul's blissful embrace of Christ. Like Heemskerck and Coornhert, David Joris was a trained artist.[10] Simons served as a priest who experienced a religious conversion while officiating the mass. None were from unusually wealthy or educated families, so their representations of the bride of Christ can be considered to preserve what would have been known to men growing up in the Low Countries in the first half of the sixteenth century. Despite confessional

---

[9]   All translations are my own, from the microfilmed originals. I was also fortunate to be able to consult a rare collection of Joris's pamphlets held by the Bodleian Library (Vet. D1 f.389), all published anonymously at Rostock. On Simons's use of the bride of Christ, see Beth Kreitzer, "Menno Simons and the Bride of Christ," *Mennonite Quarterly Review* 70, no. 3 (1996).

[10]   On Joris's background and writing, see Waite, *David Joris and Dutch Anabaptism*, 107n180.

Confessions of "True" Brides of Christ 197

differences, these Dutch-speaking men all agree that the bride of Christ is not a virgin saint but rather a representative of the individual soul, the right-standing community, and a harbinger of the apocalypse.

This shared understanding of the bride of Christ in the mid-sixteenth-century Low Countries disappeared during decades of religious warfare and political resistance to foreign rule. In 1568 seventeen Dutch-speaking majority-Protestant provinces took up arms to win their independence from Spanish rule; what began as a war of resistance developed into a decades-long civil war, during which Catholics and Protestants committed gruesome sectarian violence, and national borders eventually marked the confessional boundary between a Catholic south and a Protestant North. During the violence of the Eighty Years' War and the prosperous Golden Age of the seventeenth century, Catholic and Protestant authors continued to borrow imagery and share language when writing about the bride of Christ. As a single example of this war period, I turn to the later years of the artist and poet Dirck Coornhert, who had executed the engravings for *Jacob's Ladder*. Coornhert arrived at a new understanding of the bride of Christ through his experiences as a Catholic supporter of the resistance. Coornhert had risen from a young, unknown artist to a humanist thinker famed for his learned translations, fine engravings, and advocacy of religious tolerance. In 1568 Coornhert was briefly imprisoned by the authorities of the Spanish for his role in the uprising but escaped to the town of Xanten in German-speaking Westphalia. He would go on to serve at the court of Protestant rebel William of Orange and publish a harsh condemnation of Anabaptist visionary David Joris. In 1582, following the official secession of the Northern states (1581) and the renewal of open warfare, Coornhert published a short comic play, *On the Bride of Christ* [*Tweeling vanden Bruydt Christi en d'Egipsche Vroeivrouwen*], which clothed a biting social critique within a narrative of Christ's wedding to a sinful bride and the misadventures of pagan Egyptian women. The second dedicatory poem includes a discussion of European national stereotypes (e.g. the Spanish are haughty, the Germans are drunkards), and many of the play's lines covertly critique the audience's failed piety. In one exchange, which perhaps parodies Luther, Coornhert's God the Father asks Christ why he wishes to marry: "What now dear son? This will be a strange marriage! You are noble, she is poor, you are beautiful, she is horrifying, you are a King's son, she is that same king's slave, you are virtuous, pure, chaste, and rich to say the least. She is evil, foul, unchaste, and has less than nothing. And now ask yourself why you want such a Bride?" The bride too seems puzzled by Christ's interest in her, asking "What need does he have for such an unfaithful servant [*maert*]? ... what about my poor sinfulness awakes desire in his godhead?"[11] Christ is a tireless advocate

---

[11] Dirck Volckhertsz Coornhert, *Tweeling Vanden Bruydt Christi En D'egipsche Vroeivrouwen Doet Dees Tweeling Twee Comedien Aenschouwen* (t'Aemsterdam: ghedruct by my Harmen ianszoon Muller, 1582). Digital facsimile: http://www.europeana.eu/portal/re cord/04202/2BB7ED09D0D8E17460A6FAC31457D61F138BE215.html. Modern edition, http://www.dbnl.org/tekst/coor001pvan01_01/coor001pvan01_01_0005.php.

198   *Marrying Jesus in Medieval and Early Modern Northern Europe*

for his bride, who is also wooed by the wicked Pharaoh. With the help of a team of personified virtues and biblical prophets, the pair wed at last in a ceremony officiated by Moses—not God the Father. As Coornhert's *Bride of Christ* teaches its fractured audience, the sinful bride herself is not strange. Despite her absurdity, in fact, all the more because of her depravity, Christ cannot help but desire his father's slave, just as Jesus loved the devil's slave in *Jacob's Ladder*.

Coornhert's audience knew the contested identities of the bride of Christ and may have been amused rather than offended by this precursor to modern secular appropriations of the bride of Christ for satire, parody, and critiques of false piety.[12] For making these criticisms more overtly in print and preaching, Coornhert would die in exile, driven from the Protestant territory he had helped liberate in 1585 by Dutch Calvinists who viewed him as dangerously divisive.[13] His 1582 comedy on the bride of Christ addresses the disastrous confessional conflicts which had disrupted Coornhert's own career. They argue compellingly that even if being Catholic had damned Coornhert to exile, the true bride of Christ would damn all false Christians and show how, in a single lifetime, inherited ideas about the bride of Christ were first used to articulate new religious convictions and were then rewritten during the fragmentation of church and empire.

The Bride of Christ During the Dutch Golden Age

With the return of peace and the development of international trade routes in the seventeenth century, the Low Countries and northern Germany entered a so-called Golden Age of prosperity and religious tolerance. Following decades of cross-confessional confrontation and proselytizing, confessional differences blurred as some Christians identified stringently with only one Church while others defied easy categorization. In the seventeenth century, Catholic and Protestant artists and authors shared iconographic traditions, devotional music, and lived as neighbors. Though, as Els Stronks has recently shown, Dutch Catholics began resisting Protestant appropriations of their imagery in the 1640s, seventeenth-century

---

[12]   For a brief discussion of Coornhert's efforts to teach through entertainment and the relationship between the two plays and several of Coornhert's engravings, see Anneke C.G. Fleurkens, "Leren Met Lust. Coornherts Toneelspelen," in *Dirck Volckertszoon Coornhert. Dwars Maar Recht*, ed. Hendrik Bonger (Zutphen: De Walburg Pers, 1989), 92–4.

[13]   For a recent reconsideration of Coornhert's life, influence, and participation in late sixteenth-century religious discourse, see Mirjam van Veen, "Spiritualism in the Netherlands: From David Joris to Dirck Volckertsz Coornhert," *Sixteenth Century Journal* 33, no. 1 (2002): 129–50; Mirjam van Veen, "'No One Born of God Commits Sin': Coornhert's Perfectionism," *Nederlands archief voor kerkgeschiedenis* 84, no. 1 (2004): 338–57; Ilja M. Veldman, *Coornhert En De Prentkunst* (Amsterdam: De Walburg Pers, 1989); Gerrit Voogt, *Constraint on Trial: Dirk Volckertsz Coornhert and Religious Freedom*, Sixteenth Century Essays and Studies (Kirksville, MO: Truman State University Press, 2000).

Confessions of "True" Brides of Christ 199

understandings of the bride of Christ varied little among the new confessions.[14] Catholics and Protestants continued to cite the medieval master narrative of the bride's courtship and marriage, updating only aesthetics and scientific references. Even Catholic religious vocations, which continued a medieval tradition of linking the bride of Christ to celibate women, did not limit this to consecrated nuns. The Lutheran cobbler Jakob Boehme (1575–1624) harmonized late medieval images, Lutheran and Jesuit theology, personal prayers and visions, and the hermetic science of Paracelsus, into a theological system built around the soul's marriage to Jesus/Sophia. His Remonstrant follower Jan Luyken (1679–1712) incorporated Catholic music and illustrations into devotional emblem books relating the marriage of Jesus and the Soul. In the last half of the seventeenth century, the Spiritual Maidens [*Geestelijke Maagden*], a new movement of unregulated Catholic lay women, were recognized as brides of Christ for their public work on behalf of the Catholic Reformation. Boehme's use of images, both visual and textual, reflects careful design.[15] Boehme's *Way to Christ*, a posthumous anthology of his shorter manuscript writings, Luyken's *Jesus and the Soul*, an emblem book organized around the universal availability of Christ's love, and the private correspondence of seventeenth-century Spiritual Maidens share the language and images of the late medieval world, updated with seventeenth-century theology and scientific knowledge.

The first book of Boehme's *Way to Christ* narrates the soul's conversion, courtship, and marriage to the divine. Boehme writes "for the information of the Christian-minded reader, so that if similar things happen to him he knows what to do," indicating that any Christ-seeking reader might replicate the Soul's experiences.[16] Boehme's male bride weds Christ at the moment of conversion. As for medieval monastic authors, this marriage initiated a period of testing, prayer, and preparation for the final wedding. In his rendition of the bride's master narrative, Boehme writes:

> If he desires Her love, She is willing and kisses him with a beam of Her sweet love, by which the heart receives joy. But She does not immediately enter the marriage bed with the soul, that is, She does not immediately awaken the corrupted heavenly image that was lost in Paradise in it [the Soul] … if she is to crown you, you must be first tested … and judged: you must taste the sour beer that you have poured into yourself by your abominations. You must first come

---

[14] Els Stronks, "Never to Coincide: The Identities of Dutch Protestants and Dutch Catholics in Religious Emblematics," *Journal of Historians of Netherlandish Art* 3, no. 2 (2011), http://www.jhna.org/index.php/past-issues/volume-3-issue-2/144-stronks-never-to-coincide; Els Stronks, *Negotiating Differences: Word, Image and Religion in the Dutch Republic* (Leiden: Brill, 2011).

[15] All citations are to Erb's English translation, which closely follows the 1730 Leyden edition. Jakob Boehme, *The Way to Christ*, trans. Peter C. Erb (New York: Paulist Press, 1978).

[16] Ibid., 46.

200   *Marrying Jesus in Medieval and Early Modern Northern Europe*

to the gates of hell and show your victory in and for Her love in the face of the devil's attacks so that She will again look at you ... although true humility is first born in marriage to Her, but the free will of your soul must stand as a knight.... conquer[ing] the devil in all his attacks, and pays no attention to temporal things for the love of the noble Sophia, the precious conqueror's crown will be given to it as a sign of victory. Then the Virgin will come to the soul. She has revealed herself in the precious name JESUS ... she kisses the soul completely inwardly with her sweet love and presses love into its desire as a sign of victory. Here Adam according to his heavenly part is resurrected from the dead in Christ ... this is the marriage of the lamb.[17]

In this passage, Christ in the role of female Sophia/Wisdom weds an Everysoul modeled on a male author's experiences. Elsewhere, Boehme identified the soul as a knight in service to Wisdom. These elements invite comparisons between Boehme and the fourteenth-century Dominican Henry Suso, though his work shares elements with other medieval authors. Mirrors, naked souls, kisses, and wine were central elements of the medieval master narrative of the bride of Christ, while references to sour beer appear in the visions of Bridget of Sweden.

Though he wrote as a seventeenth-century Lutheran, Boehme's understanding of the soul's marriage to Christ was mediated, first by the sixteenth-century Jesuits, and then by the seventeenth-century Lutherans whose sermons inspired his conversion. While many medieval authors understood nakedness as an unmediated experience with the divine, Boehme instructed his followers to pray while undressing.[18] Boehme's androgyne Jesus-Sophia kissing the soul, transmitting the knowledge of his/her true identity to a bodiless being that in that instant is resurrected into the original androgynous body of Adam, similarly surpasses late medieval accounts of the kiss and consummation of the loving soul and Christ. The double-bodied, dual-sexed human soul who reflects the androgynous alchemical man Jesus-Sophia reflects Boehme's alchemically informed understanding that God-Sophia created Adam as an androgynous and fertile bearer of children of light and fire. Similarly, Boehme's soul-knight imitated veterans of religious wars and distilled the writing of Catholic soldier, saint, and founder of the Jesuits, Ignatius Loyola, with the medieval androgynous soul to adapt elements of a medieval narrative for a seventeenth-century world.

The Dutch Protestant poet and engraver Jan Luyken (1649–1712), sometimes identified as the engraver who illustrated Boehme's *Way to Christ*, also devised emblem books about the bride of Christ. Luyken's personal history reflects the complex relationships between Christian subgroups in Golden Age Amsterdam. He was the secularized son of Remonstrants (Dutch Protestants who subscribed to the views of Arminius over Calvin) or Mennonites who joined the Collegiants (a subset of the Remonstrant church which advocated religious tolerance and offered shelter to persecuted Anabaptists). He married a singer and actress, Maria de Oudaens (d. 1682), and published a collection of secular love poems as an emblem

---

[17]   Ibid., 44–5.

[18]   Ibid., 100.

book, the *Duytse Lier* [*Dutch Lyre*] in 1671. Luyken was baptized in Amsterdam in a Mennonite congregation a year later at the age of 23. In 1675, at the age of 26, Luyken received a vision of Jesus in his heart and joined the followers of Jakob Boehme; he published *Jesus en de Ziel* [*Jesus and the Soul*] three years later.[19] This book traces the soul from her first conversion, through temptations and education, to an eternal union with Christ which is partially blocked by the barrier of human imperfection.

Like medieval blockbooks and illustrated manuscripts, emblem books blended poetic verses, narrative images, and explanatory prose. However, emblem books conformed more closely to a standardized format: each opening paired a complex illustration with a poem. Neither image nor poem could be interpreted alone, nor was one an illustration for the other. A viewer might contemplate the opening, considering possible meanings from clues in text and image, then turn the page to find the author's detailed explanation for the composition. Both secular and religious emblem books required readers to produce their own meanings from each opening, and thus to experience a personal transformation. Luyken's *Jesus and the Soul* follows this format closely. Each chapter opens with a poem facing an engraved emblem depicting Jesus as a youth with curling hair and the soul as a demure young woman. The poems voice the soul's desires, while scriptural citations beneath each image give God's reply. Luyken follows each opening with a "goddelyke antwoord" [Godly response] consisting of scriptural citations and explanatory commentary.

Both the 1685 edition and the redrawn sequence Luyken created for a 1714 reprint are comprehensive retellings of the medieval master narrative of the bride of Christ. Where medieval artists emphasized nakedness, violence, and suffering with the crucified Christ, Luyken's etchings are softened by lush gardens, Christ's boyish body, and the subtle treatment of potentially violent scenes. In one chapter, the soul rests her head on Jesus's breast as he protects her from a terrible storm. Though their small rock is menaced by sea monsters and buffeted by crashing waves, the soul sleeps tranquilly in Jesus's embrace as if she were John resting at the Last Supper (Figure 7.1). The facing poem explains that the most beautiful of all things is to lie peacefully on Christ's breast, with your head above his heart.[20] In the next scene (Figure 7.2) the soul seals her heart with the name of Jesus in a gesture reminiscent of the Dominican Henry Suso cutting his chest with the holy monogram. Both the 1685 and 1714 versions depict a fully clothed soul stamping her heart with Jesus. In this bloodless scene, Jesus holds up a heart-shaped vial which the soul has just pressed with "JEZUS." Her verses say that the

---

[19]   I cite from the Utrecht Emblem Book Project's facsimile and transcription of a 1685 copy. Page numbers refer to the original pagination as preserved in that facsimile. Jan Luyken, "Jesus en de ziel," ed. Emblem Project Utrecht (Amsterdam, 1685), http://emblems.let.uu.nl/lu1685.html.

[20]   "wy leggenstil op Jezus herte, Dat is een plaats daar alle kwaad, hoe groot en sterk voor overgaat: een plaats van waare vrede en vreugden, den loon der onvervalste deugden. O DipesteLiefde uit Gods gemoed, Myn Jezus, ach wat zyt gy zoet!" (154–7).

Figure 7.1   *De Ziele rust op de Borst Jesu* [*The Soul rests on Jesus's Chest*], Jan Luyken, *Jesus en de Ziel*. Amsterdam: Pieter Arentsa, 1685, 155, RB 35565. Reproduced by permission of The Huntington Library, San Marino, California.

Figure 7.2 *De Ziele heeft haer herte met Jesus versegelt* [*The Soul seals her heart with Jesus*], Jan Luyken, *Jesus en de Ziel*. Amsterdam: Pieter Arentsa, 1685, 150, RB 35565. Reproduced by permission of The Huntington Library, San Marino, California.

soul has received a second treasure, a ring which seals the heart of even unfaithful servants [*ontrouwe knecht of maagd*]. Though Luyken's illustration is bloodless, the opening explicitly links the soul's stamped heart to Christ's pierced body on the cross with scriptural citations ("zet my als een zegel op uw herte" [Set me as a seal upon your heart], Song VIII, 6; "ikk ben met Christus gekruist" [I am crucified with Christ], Gall II, 20). Where medieval artists would have drawn a bleeding heart or a crucified bride, Luyken has positioned text and image to subtly link suffering with Christ to personal salvation. The Divine Response glosses this opening as a stamp or seal which saves the soul from the devil. "Ons herte moet zyn gelyk een penning des hoogsten Konings, die met zyn beeld is betekent" [Our hearts should be like a coin from the highest King, through which his image is known], Luyken explains, borrowing imagery Aquinas introduced to describe the reflection of God the Father in the Son.[21] For Luyken, who may not have ever encountered Aquinas, each bride walking in the world bears God's image in her heart, and thus is a token of God's sovereignty.

In *Jesus and the Soul*, Luyken addresses a community of Protestants who strive to discover the image of God within themselves, insisting that "Jesus blessed for all eternity, desires us to live in him and he in us."[22] Though he was raised by Remonstrants and Anabaptists, influenced by the Lutheran Boehme, and guided by his own revelations, Luyken's emblem book also borrows design elements from Catholic artists, and writes new lyrics addressed to Jesus for Giulio Caccini's (d. 1618) *Amarille mia Belle*. The original aria expresses a lover's fear of betrayal using a melody which arguably alludes to sexual penetration.[23] Though Luyken's verses delight in Christ's newly acquired love, the erotic gestures of the melody remained. Luyken's emblem book blends Boehme's Lutheran Pietism, Luyken's Catholic exemplars, and the devotional routines of seventeenth-century Mennonite and Remonstrant Amsterdam. As a father, grandfather, husband, and visionary, Luyken embodies how marriage to Jesus had become part of domestic lay Christianity, as relevant to married men as to single women.

Jakob Boehme and Jan Luyken were both Protestants who experienced life-changing visions, but their books do not represent a distinctly Protestant theology. Instead, the blending of medieval narratives, contemporary science, personal revelation, and evangelism characterized both Catholic and Protestant representations of the bride of Christ in the seventeenth century. After the Council of Trent, the institutional Church promoted organization of unregulated brides of Christ in the Low Countries known as the "Geestelijke Maagden" [Spiritual Maidens] or *klopjes*, many of whom recorded their own visions. According to Marit Monteiro's comprehensive study, at least 5,000 women were involved in the movement during the seventeenth century, and at least 34 printed books were

---

[21] Thomas Aquinas, *Summa Theologiae*, I–II, 93, a 1, ad 2.

[22] "Jezus gebenedyd in der eeuwigheid, / lust heeft, om hy ons, en in ons te woonen." A3v.

[23] Susan McClary, *Desire and Pleasure in Seventeenth-century Music* (Berkeley: University of California Press, 2012), 23–5.

composed for their use. Manuscript copies of the women's own journals and correspondence also survive. These unmarried women and widows performed acts of charity without taking vows but were distinct from the beguines, who remained a presence in the early modern Low Countries.[24] This extensive body of literary evidence reveals that the Spiritual Maidens were viewed as, and identified one another as, brides of Christ.

Like medieval nuns and beguines, the Spiritual Maidens comprised a community of Christ's brides—writing for and supporting one another—and an audience for guiding literature from their male confessors. They experienced Christ's burning love during communion and wrote to encourage their sisters. Agnes Heilsbach (1597–1640), a Spiritual Maiden, kept a personal diary recording daily activities, personal correspondence, and spiritual experiences between 1637 and 1639, which characterizes the importance of Jesus as a spouse to women in the movement. The diary consists of faded folded leaves covered on every available space with extraordinarily small letters, suggesting Agnes was attempting to conserve paper. Entries describe being filled with the fire of love when receiving the Eucharist and repeatedly reference Christ as Agnes's bridegroom and spouse to all other Spiritual Maidens, saints, and the Virgin Mary. The letters represent the advice and consolation sent between Agnes Heilsbach and Joanna van Randereth (1610–84), for whom Agnes served as a mentor. Both frequently refer to Jesus by the shorthand of spouse.[25] In a letter sent to Agnes, Joanna describes her throat burning as she is lit like a fire and weeps with love, "ick spoeijden mij mijnen Brudegom te ontfangen" [I desire to speedily receive my bridegroom], in reference to the Eucharist.[26] Joanna always addresses Agnes as mother [*moeder*], but also expresses their sisterhood as brides of Christ, an identity Agnes also presents in her diary.

---

[24] The definitive study remains M.E. Monteiro, *Geestelijke maagden: leven tussen klooster en wereld in Noord-Nederland gedurende de zeventiende eeuw* (Hilversum: Verloren, 1996). Amanda Pipkin's research on rape in literary documents produced by this movement examines the physical threats posed to women participating in an active branch of the Counter-Reformation. See, for instance, Amanda Pipkin, "'They were not humans, but devils in human bodies': Depictions of Sexual Violence and Spanish Tyranny as a Means of Fostering Identity in the Dutch Republic," *Journal of Early Modern History* 13, no. 4 (2009): 229–64. The movement is also discussed in Renée Nip, "To Safeguard a Life's work: The Autobiography of Elisabeth Strouven (1600–1661)," in *Ein Platz für sich selbst. Schreibende Frauen und ihre Lebenswelten (1450–1700) / A Place of their own. Women Writers and their Social Environments (1450–1700)*, ed. Anne Bollmann (Frankfurt am Main: Peter Lang, 2011), 215–42.

[25] Both women would be memorialized in posthumous lives by their Jesuit confessors, and Joanna gained a reputation for near-saintly piety. Both women recorded many of their experiences at the request of their confessors. Agnes van Heilsbach, "Letters and Spiritual Diary," KBR MS 20422.

[26] The letter dates to August 29, on the feast day of Saint John. Joanna describes spending five hours at church that day waiting to receive the sacrament of communion (127v).

206 *Marrying Jesus in Medieval and Early Modern Northern Europe*

These glimpses into the daily life of two Spiritual Maidens defy expectations about gender, experience, and Catholic piety in early modern Europe. Like medieval holy women, they wrote to one another as brides of Christ, and enjoyed the company of their spouse each time they received communion. The Spiritual Maidens were Catholic missionaries, celibate women, and brides of Christ. But they were not members of a formal religious order and did not have to be virgins. Neither nuns nor laywomen, the Spiritual Maidens made outposts in Protestant territories and traveled through Catholic towns as brides of Christ, acting as a rampart against Protestantism and a source of inspiration for an embattled community of Catholics. Though they worked in the southern Low Countries, reestablishing Catholicism in the aftermath of the Dutch Revolt, the Spiritual Maidens had as much in common with Jakob Boehme and Jan Luyken as they did with their sisters enclosed in the convents. They understood Jesus to be a communal spouse, recognized that their labor and prayer could win his love, and like their Protestant neighbors, Agnes Heilsbach and her sisters converted others through preaching and writing, keeping the content of their visions mostly private. Despite the trauma of war and the introduction of new religious communities and modes for pious living, Catholics, Protestants, and Anabaptists generally agreed that Jesus was wed to small communities of the faithful, that his love saved sinners, and that individuals could learn how to become a bride of Christ.

Unholy Households

Though the Spiritual Maidens show that the reforms of Trent did not definitively limit Catholic women's opportunities to become brides of Christ to inmates of enclosed convents, in both Protestant and Catholic communities, women who identified as brides of Christ continued to be evaluated against social standards for female comportment. In the same decades that the exemplary father Jan Luyken designed expensive emblem books about the bride of Christ for urban Protestants in Amsterdam, and the publicly pious Spiritual Maidens sought to win souls back for the Catholic Church in Flanders, two London wives, mothers, and visionaries, Anne Wentworth (1629–93?) and Mary Gadbury (c. 1610–50), left difficult marriages to warn the world of the coming of their bridegroom.[27] Apocalyptic predictions were rampant in mid-seventeenth-century England, and prophets often linked social turmoil to the wedding of the Lamb. When they resigned family obligations to become apocalyptic preachers, Gadbury as a revolutionary, Wentworth a prophetic pamphleteer, their forceful rhetoric attracted eager followers. Mary Gadbury was

---

[27] Neither woman's books are available in a modern edition, though most of their published works have been digitized. For biographies and social context on both women, see Phyllis Mack, "Women as Prophets during the English Civil War," *Feminist Studies* 8, no. 1 (1982): 19–45; Katharine Gillespie, *Domesticity and Dissent in the Seventeenth Century: English Women Writers and the Public Sphere* (Cambridge: Cambridge University Press, 2004); Richard Rambuss, *Closet Devotions*, 84, 92.

Confessions of "True" Brides of Christ 207

abandoned by her husband, James, and pursued him to the Netherlands with their young daughter to discover that he had remarried. After returning to London, she supported herself and her daughter with handiwork until she met William Franklin, a married man she recognized as Jesus, and began living with him as the bride. Anne Wentworth married Christ in visions while still living at home and explains that Jesus instructed her to divorce her physically abusive husband.[28] Their visions and warnings were not outlandish for the period, but some male Protestants, for whom marriage was a perfect Christian life, condemned them for abandoning their families. Their stories show that in the seventeenth century, those who claimed to be brides of Christ were judged primarily by gendered social expectations, not theological orthodoxy.

Anne Wentworth received visions in domestic spaces, often at night when everyone else was sleeping, and possibly copied them into a diary before preparing them for print.[29] Anne regularly urged others to repent and join her among Christ's brides: "Will you sleep unto death, and not see King *Jesus* on his Throne? Will you not awake, and trim your Lamps, to meet the Bridegroom?" she asks.[30] In each of her surviving publications, Anne Wentworth invited those who read her pamphlets to "repair to *Kings-Head-Court* in *Whitestreet* where she hath lived these 12 years," to discuss the revelations further.[31] This address was the site for legal disputes linked to Anne's clouded reputation: her husband threw her out of their home in 1677, she won it back in 1678, but the couple remained separated.[32] Despite her careful use of scriptural citations, the leaders of her former church, a Baptist congregation, sided with her estranged husband and excommunicated her for "Catholicism." In response to her claim that she had left her legal husband

---

[28] Humphrey Ellis, *Pseudochristus: or, A true and faithful relation of the grand impostures, horrid blaspemies, abominable practises, gross deceits; lately spread abroad and acted in the county of Southampton, by William Frankelin and Mary Gadbury ... The one ... professing and asserting himself to be the Christ ... The other as wickedly professing and asserting her self to be the spouse of Christ* (London: Printed by John Macock, for L. Fawn, 1650); Thomas H. Luxon, "'Not I, But Christ': Allegory and the Puritan Self," *English Literary History* 60, no. 4 (1993): 899–937; Thomas H. Luxon, *Literal Figures: Puritan Allegory and the Reformation Crisis in Representation* (Chicago: University of Chicago Press, 1995); Jerome Friedman, "Their Name Was God: Religious Charlatans in the Seventeenth-Century English Popular Press," *The Journal of Popular Culture* 25, no. 1 (1991): 55–66. There is also a manuscript, Trial of Mary Gadbury, Clarke MS 18, held by Worcester College, Oxford, f. 27v–28v.

[29] The visions recorded in her *Revelation of Jesus Christ* are all dated and note where she was when Christ appeared. Several revelations happened in bed or while sitting at home. Anne Wentworth, *The Revelation of Jesus Christ Just as He Spake It in Verses at Several Times, and Sometimes in Prose, Unto His Faithful Servant Anne Wentworth, Who Suffereth for His Name: Containing Mercy and Judgment, Comforts to Zion, but Woes to Babylon* (London?, 1679), 3, 10, 13, 16, 17, 21.

[30] Ibid., 3.

[31] Ibid.

[32] Ibid., 22–3.

208 *Marrying Jesus in Medieval and Early Modern Northern Europe*

because she was wed to Christ, they accused her of being an "impudent Hussey a disobedient Wife to him, one that run away from her Husband and the like." For Anne Wentworth, as for her accusers, her authority as a prophet was directly related to her reputation as a respectable wife. In a published defense, she explained that her abusive husband had insisted that she had not left willingly, but was thrown out of the house for refusing to "deny the Lord."[33] Though she complains that her husband's supporters have claimed that she kept "men company, and [had her] Rogues come to [her], and live[d] a scandalous life in an Alms house," Wentworth insisted that she had maintained marital chastity and been left homeless for obeying God's will over obeying her husband.[34] In 1676, she published a defense of her faithful service to worldly and heavenly husbands:

> I shall not be an unfaithful wife for obeying the voice of my heavenly Husband, in answering his call, and submitting to his will, after I had spent out all my natural strength of body in obedience to satisfy the unreasonable will of my earthly Husband, and laid my body as the ground, and as the street for him to go over for 18 years together, and keep silent, for thou O Lord did'st it, and afflicted me less than I deserved, and now the Lord sees my Husband hath as much need of this as I had of his being so great a scourge and lash to me ... I have so much love for him, that I wish his soul as well as my own, and would rather see him a convert, a new man, if I begg'd my bread with him, than to see him made Lord Mayor of *London* and remain with this spirit; for I had better be a Cobblers wife of a mild meek nature, and have the spirit of God in him, and knows the life of the new man, than to be the greatest mans wife in the world, of such a terrible spirit, and put on a form of Religion for a cloak to hide it from the world.[35]

In one exhalation, Anne Wentworth justified her prophetic career, her broken marriage, and her status as a good wife. By openly discussing these slanderous accusations, she was able to portray her husband and his supporters as godless hypocrites. Both she and her opponents understood that her authority as a prophet was related to her reputation as a respectable woman.

A contemporary case of another London wife, Mary Gadbury, reaffirms that a broken marriage could ruin a female prophet's reputation, destroying her authority as a self-proclaimed bride of Christ. Unlike Wentworth, who was able to publish her own writing with the help of her supporters, Gadbury is known primarily through an indignant and pejorative pamphlet authored by Humphrey Ellis, a *Minister of the Word in the city of Winton*. The pamphlet draws from trial testimony, Assize records, conversations with the accused, and letters sent to Ellis by those involved in the case, but censored "tedious" testimony from Mary Gadbury herself. Although Ellis gives a biased account which silences Gadbury, his pamphlet reveals English society responded to their biblically founded and vision-supported claim of bridal identity with enthusiasm (among the crowds who heard her sermons), and (judicial and ecclesiastical) skepticism and condemnation.

---

[33] Ibid., 21.

[34] Ibid.

[35] Anne Wentworth, *A True Account of Anne Wentworth* (1676), 8.

According to Ellis, while operating a boarding house in London, Mary Gadbury received several body-trembling visions, heard the voice of God, and saw a fast-moving man drop a lamb from the skies. Mary's boarder mentioned that another man in the area, a roper and father of three, had also received visions. Gadbury arranged to meet this second visionary, William Franklin, and they soon realized that Franklin was the Lamb-Christ who had appeared in Gadbury's visions. Her vision then guided them to the land of "Ham," in Southampton (because it was hilly) where they established a household and began publicly proclaiming themselves to be Christ and his bride. Franklin traveled by wagon, preaching in the countryside, leaving Mary in town. As he gathered followers, she delivered a series of sermons during which she writhed on a platform in visible physical pain, until she "brought forth" Christ the infant and other spiritual babies. Several other women in their company experienced spiritual pregnancies. As they drew more followers, the movement attracted considerable concern from the local authorities. Mary Gadbury, William Franklin, and their followers were arrested and put on trial on March 7, 1649. Franklin, perhaps under torture, soon recanted, but Mary Gadbury refused. Ellis's account of the trial emphasizes that both he and the judges were more interested in Gadbury's marital status and possible sexual relationship with Franklin than the content of her visions.

According to Ellis, Mary Gadbury initially refused to acknowledge her legal connection to her first husband and her family: "[S]he had no name according to the flesh, but a new name; to that concerning her husband (there being ground enough to judge that she had an husband) that she now had a husband according to the flesh, but that her maker was her husband, the Lord of Hosts was his name, and he was within her." Though witnesses averred that Franklin and Gadbury shared a bed, "she affirmed, that it was without pollution or defilement, and denied that there had ever been any carnal copulation between them."[36] She would be removed to a bawdhouse, a prison dedicated to reforming prostitutes and other women accused of sexual impropriety. Then, in March of 1650, she was retried at the Western Assize. At the conclusion of this trial she recanted, was released, and sent back to London on a cart. Nothing more is known of her.

Mary Gadbury's and Anne Wentworth's followers believed that Christ and his bride walked among them. Both women's marriages to Christ were informed by and related through contemporary media and reflected the theology of contemporary English Protestantism. Perhaps because of this, their accusers found ecstatic visions, women preachers, and even raising armies less objectionable than broken marriages. For instance, the London Artisan, chronicler, and diarist Nehemiah Wallington (1598–1658) recalls that his pregnant wife Grace comforted him after the death of a daughter, reminding him that "it is your daughter's wedding day and will you grieve to see your daughter go home to her husband Christ Jesus, where she shall never want, but have the fullness of joy forever more?"[37] This Protestant

---

[36]   Ellis, *Pseudochristus*, 41.

[37]   Paul Seaver, *Wallington's World: A Puritan Artisan in Seventeenth-Century London* (Stanford: Stanford University Press, 1985), 87.

210 *Marrying Jesus in Medieval and Early Modern Northern Europe*

understanding that Jesus was espoused to members of pious Christian households would appear again in the New World. In a sermon printed in Boston in 1719, Puritan leader Cotton Mather explained the marriage between Christ and the "children of men" in their souls, and the special relevance of this marriage for worldly marriages.[38] In the late seventeenth and eighteenth centuries, Puritans, Moravians, and Lutherans in Europe and colonial America all sang and preached about the marriage between Christ and the soul.

The medieval understanding that Jesus was a spouse for every pious right-behaving Christian was brought to North America in the seventeenth century by the first European colonists and continues to influence contemporary Christianity. German Pietist Nikolaus von Zinzendorf's *Songs of the Sifting* and sermons were filled with references to Christ as spouse and to the wedding of the Lamb. Under his guidance, the Moravian church taught that the sexual consummation between husband and wife produced grace, rather than sin. This interpretation was perhaps an inevitable consequence of the desanctification of chastity and the late medieval insistence that sex with *God* was salvific. Zinzendorf restated the medieval belief that "Your Creator is your Husband," and often addressed Jesus as bridegroom or husband, portraying religious conversion as a marriage contracted between Christ and the individual believer. Unlike medieval authors, Zinzendorf understood this marriage between Christ and the Christian to foreshadow the worldly marriage between husbands and wives. The husband and wife on earth became representatives reenacting the marriage of God and Soul in heaven, and for Zinzendorf, sex between two Christ-loving Christians produces a form of salvation.[39]

---

[38] This sermon postdates the Salem witch trials and belongs to a period of Mather's most prolific and influential writing. Cotton Mather, *A Glorious espousal: A brief essay, to illustrate and prosecute the marriage, wherein our great Saviour offers to espouse unto himself the children of men. And thereupon to recommend from that grand pattern a good carriage in the married life among them. An essay proper and useful in the hands of those who travel on the noble design of espousing the souls of men unto their Saviour. But more particularly and seasonably to be presented, where a marriage is upon a celebration* (Boston: Printed by S. Kneeland, for B. Gray, and J. Edwards, at their shops on the north and south side of the Town-House in King-Street, 1719). On the image in its context, see Richard Godbeer, "'Love Raptures': Marital, Romantic, and Erotic Images of Jesus Christ in Puritan New England, 1670–1730," *The New England Quarterly* 68, no. 3 (1995): 355–84.

[39] On the Moravians, albeit almost exclusively their influence in Early America, see Paul Peucker, "The Songs of the Sifting: Understanding the Role of Bridal Mysticism in Moravian Piety During the Late 1740s," *Journal of Moravian History*, no. 3 (2007): 51–87; Katherine M. Faull, "Christ's Other Self: Gender, the Body, and Religion in the Eighteenth-Century Moravian Church," *Covenant Quarterly* 62, no. 4 (2004): 28–41; Craig D. Atwood, *Community of the Cross: Moravian Piety in Colonial Bethlehem* (University Park: Pennsylvania State University Press, 2004); Wolfgang Breul, "Ehe und Sexualität im radikalen Pietismus," in *Der Radikale Pietismus: Perspektiven der Forschung*, ed. *Wolfgang Breul, Marcus Meier, Lothar Vogel* (Göttingen: Vandenhoeck and Ruprecht, 2010), 403–18; On Moravian piety and sexuality more generally see Fogleman, *Jesus is Female*; Michele Gillespie and Robert Beachy, eds., *Pious Pursuits: German Moravians in the Atlantic World* (New York: Berghahn Books, 2007).

But Moravians were not the only American Christians to embrace Christ as bridegroom. Moravians, Baptists, and Lutherans sang to Christ as spouse on both sides of the Atlantic.[40] Hand-painted black-letter illustrated manuscripts produced by eighteenth-century German immigrants to North America, known as *Fraktur*, incorporated hymns and scriptural citations addressing Christ as spouse. References to Jesus as spouse, lover, and bridegroom occur in late eighteenth- and early nineteenth-century writing exercises [*Vorschriften*], hymnals, baptismal certificates [*Taufscheine*], bibles, bookplates, and were often exchanged as gifts or presentation pieces by German-speaking immigrants of all denominations. Unlike fifteenth-century woodcuts, which typically conformed to standard iconographies and were reproduced in large quantities, each piece of *Fraktur* was a unique composition. An 1872 leaf produced by Lutheran schoolmaster Johann Adam Eyer (1775–1837) is representative of this New World iconography. Eyer's design incorporates elements of Early American fashion, continental Protestant hymns, and the medieval bride of Christ as individual sinner. His decorations center around a prayer addressed to Christ as spouse voiced by a male devotee (Figure 7.3). Eyer's centerpiece is the hymn, "Du meine Seele Singe," composed by the Lutheran pastor Paul Gerhardt (1607–1676). In alternating black and red *Fraktur*, Eyer has copied out: "Du Meine / Seele Singe, / Wohl auf, Und Singe / schön, dem Welchem alle / dinge, zu Dienst und willen / stehn, ich Will den Herren / droben, hier preisen auf der / Erd, ich will ihn Herzlich lobe, / so lang ich leben werd!" [You my, soul sing, rise up and sing beautifully, to him to whom all things stand willingly to serve, I desire to praise the lord here on the earth and there [in heaven], I desire to heartily praise him so long as I shall live!]. In the upper left corner, trumpeting angels announce, "Halleluja! Gott Und dem LAMM!" [Hallelujah! God and the Lamb!] and "Heilig, Heilig, Heilig ist Gott der Herr Zebaoth" [Holy, holy, holy is God of Sabbath]. In the center register, two men in tricorn hats, red coats with blue linings, and laced black shoes step forward, gesturing through the hymn's border. Beneath their feet, Eyer recorded his own—or the men's?—desire to learn to love, serve, and wed the bridegroom. The lower left box reads: "Ich will Lieben und mich üben, daß ich / Meinen Bräutigam / Nun in allem, Mög / gefallen, welcher an / des Creutzes stamm, hat / sein leben hingege / ben, so geduldig / Wie ein Lamm" [I desire to love and cultivate myself so that I may now please my bridegroom, who gave away his life on the tree of the cross as patiently as a lamb, in all things]. In the lower right corner: "Ich will Lieben, und mich üben, meine ganze Lebens=zeit / mich zu schicken und / zu schmücken, mit / dem weisen Hoch / zeit=kleid, zu Erschei / nen, mit den Rei / nen, auf des Lames / Hoch=Zeit=freud" [I desire to love and cultivate myself, my entire lifetime, to adorn myself with the white Wedding-clothes and send myself to appear with the pure at the Wedding of the Lamb]. As this manuscript and other pieces of American *Fraktur* show,

---

[40] Elizabeth Clarke, "'The glorious lover': Baptist literature of the 1680s and the bride of Christ," *Baptist Quarterly* 43, no. 8 (2010): 452–72.

Figure 7.3   Johann Adam Eyer, "You my soul sing" ["Du meine Seele Singe"], 1782. Courtesy of the Free Library of Philadelphia, FLP 541.

marrying Jesus was limited neither to women, nor to the "fringe" movements of early American Christianity.

Embracing Jesus as spouse remains as central to American Christianity as it had been in fifteenth-century Europe. The hymn "Jesus, Lover of my Soul," written in 1740 by Charles Wesley, cofounder of Methodism, is a representative example of the hymns, sermons, art, and daily devotions which invited American

Christians to embrace Christ as spouse. The lyrics express a desire to rest on Christ's bosom, take shelter in his garden, and be wrapped up in Christ's grace. Wesley's lyrics elaborate on Wisdom 11:26, which addresses God as a "Ruler and Lover of Souls," by citing elements of the medieval master narrative of the bride of Christ. Thus this hymn, like its medieval analogues, required the vocal performer to take on the role of bride and participate in a union with God. The choir or soloist asks Christ to "spring ... up within my heart," to rest on his chest, to be wrapped in his wings. The hymn remains in the Methodist hymn book, has also been professionally recorded by gospel, country, and contemporary Christian musicians, and was cited as among his most influential compositions when Wesley was inducted into the Gospel Music Hall of Fame in 1995.[41] American religious historian Stephen Prothero, who reflexively genders Wesley's vocal soul female despite the gender of the hymnodist and of many of the performers, argues that eighteenth- and nineteenth-century hymns, even those written by men, elicited scenes of domestic piety.[42] But the song has been performed by men and women, children and adults, and has taken on new meaning with each performance, and for each audience.

Much that was central to fifteenth-century Christianity would be abandoned by Catholics and Protestants with corrective embarrassment, yet the bride of Christ survived the sixteenth century and remained important to each new denomination. Before the Wars of Religion subsided, the layered meanings medieval Christians had worked into the image of the bride of Christ had already been apportioned to the new confessions according to communal needs. Catholics retained the bride's saintly and celibate identities to shore up their theological advocacy of celibacy, Protestants the bridegroom as a third partner to earthly marriages in defense of their reconsideration of the sacraments, and most denominations preserved the conviction that baptism espoused Christ to individual souls. Thus marrying Jesus continued to be understood as a sinner's first step to eternal salvation across denominations often unaware of the medieval origins of their theological certainty that each individual had been created as a bride of Christ.

---

[41]   I use the lyrics provided by the United Methodist Church's online historical hymnal. "Jesus, Lover of my Soul," accessed May 18, 2013, http://gbgm-umc.org/umhistory/wesley/hymns/umh479.stm (site discontinued).

[42]   Stephen R. Prothero, *American Jesus: How the Son of God Became a National Icon* (New York: Farrar, Straus and Giroux, 2003), 75–6.

Chapter 8
Brides of Christ, Contemporary Christianity, and American Popular Culture

> What is being said here? What is being asked here? Can Jesus bewilder one so? Our beguines are so misguided that they scandalize Jesus.
> —Ruusbroeck, *The Twelve Beguines*[1]

The medieval transformation of the bride of Christ from a chaste virginal nun into a representation of the individual required the collaboration of generations of Christian teachers, patrons, and artisans. Christianity uses, changes, and is changed by communication technologies. Rather than discarding medieval accretions, early modern, and even contemporary Christians continue to reinterpret medieval iconography such as the bride's adornment, the mirror, and the wedding dress essential to their own narratives, unknowingly elaborating on the invitation of the early medieval plainchant refrain: *Veni, Sponsa Christi* [Come, bride of Christ]. Contemporary American popular understandings of marriage to Jesus as sacramental, salvific, and apocalyptic originate in neither biblical verses nor in the modern American wedding industry, but in late medieval elaborations on and adaptations of the bride of Christ.

In 2011, former Alaska Governor Sarah Palin toured North America in a bus painted like the Declaration of Independence. During a visit to Boston, she shared a historically inaccurate version of the ride of Paul Revere that was widely ridiculed. Satirist and social commentator Stephen Colbert concluded commentary on this event with a close-up of Palin's white suit and ornate southwestern silver and turquoise cross, quipping: "It looks like she robbed the Vatican or is going to marry Jesus in Vegas."[2] Colbert's gender-complicated critique of Sarah Palin as a bride of Christ is a modern analogue to medieval and early modern narratives which used marrying Jesus to simultaneously teach and entertain. As an astute satirist of religion in the contemporary world, Colbert's work focuses on widely recognizable American cultural phenomena. The Vatican retains a treasury of large, ornate crosses, the city of Las Vegas celebrates hasty, gaudy weddings, and contemporary American Christianity still recognizes the bride of Christ as a woman in white, covered in jewels, professing compassion for the crucified Christ. Mocking Palin as a faux-bride of Christ strips away subtle layers of her

---

[1] Jan van Ruusbroec, *Opera Omnia: Vanden XII Beghinen*, ed. M.M. Kors, English translation by H. Rolfson, Latin by L. Surius (1552; Turnhout: Brepols, 2000), vol. 7a, 8–9.

[2] *The Colbert Report*, "Werner Herzog," Season 7, Episode 72, first aired on June 6, 2011.

216   *Marrying Jesus in Medieval and Early Modern Northern Europe*

crafted persona as a Christian wife, mother, and patriot while positioning Colbert's persona as a more genuine form of publicly political Christianity. Colbert's persona uses political satire to model idealized Christian civic engagement, but his performance of a powerful Catholic man criticizing a sexualized Protestant mother's performance of Christianity by labeling her a false bride of Christ also recalls centuries of sectarian polemic.

Colbert and his writers were neither citing the obscure late medieval theologians who popularized marrying Jesus, nor inventing something wholly new. Like Ruusbroec's verse preface to the *Twelve Beguines*, but with more levity, Colbert spotlights the hypocrisy of those who claim to be perfect Christians and yet are scandalously mistaken. And, like Ruusbroec's verse, Colbert's attack on a Christian woman's public piety must be understood as a gendered theologizing performed to resonate with a particular Christian-influenced audience. Colbert's American Christian masculinity defies easy categorization. The actor, Stephen Colbert, a baptized Catholic, considers his church to be the "one true bride of Christ," whom he cannot kiss, while his television character the Reverend Sir Dr. Stephen T. Mos Def Colbert DFA Heavyweight Champion of the World implies that he is far more worthy of wedding Jesus than the Christian woman Sarah Palin.[3] This self-declared "man's man" was also voted 69th sexiest woman in America, and his persona often expresses and then quickly denies same sex attraction.[4] When the Catholic actor Stephen Colbert tears down the Protestant politician Sarah Palin's performance of political Christianity, he performs a public sectarian condemnation of an influential woman's piety. Colbert's commentary on Sarah Palin links back to the discernible network of shared images of the bride of Christ produced in late medieval and early modern Europe. This short clip, written to comment on a now-forgotten gaffe, played briefly on television and then hosted briefly on the internet, is a public adaptation of the bride of Christ meant to amuse even non-Christians while offering a deeper meaning to religious insiders. This fluid discourse across socially constructed community boundaries, whether modern or medieval, best characterizes popular religion.

---

[3]   Stephen Thompson, "Interview: The Daily Show's Stephen Colbert, Rob Corddry, Ed Helms, and Mo Rocca," *The Onion A.V. Club*, January 22, 2003, accessed on May 18, 2013, http://www.avclub.com/articles/the-daily-shows-stephen-colbert-rob-corddry-ed-hel,13795/. According to a report of the recent debate between Stephen Colbert and Cardinal Dolan held at Fordham University in September of 2012, Cardinal Dolan kissed Mr. Colbert's wife, and "when Mr. Colbert feigned offense, the cardinal said, in a remark that brought down the house, 'I can kiss your wife. You can't kiss mine.'" Laurie Goodstein, "A Comedian and a Cardinal Open Up on Spirituality," *New York Times*, September 15, 2012, accessed on May 18, 2013, http://www.nytimes.com/2012/09/16/nyregion/stephen-colbert-and-cardinal-cardinal-timothy-dolan-at-fordham-university.html.

[4]   "2012 Hot 100," *Maxim* (April 17, 2012), accessed on May 19, 2013, http://www.maxim.com/hot-100/2012-hot-100.

Interpenetrating Lineages

As I have documented, devotional media preserve changes and continuities in belief which should inform our historical understanding of both religion and popular culture. Much as early modern theologians adapted medieval understandings of marrying Jesus for their own communities, contemporary brides of Christ emerge from their particular community's needs and express their theology using idiomatic symbols. Some of these modern adaptations begin with medieval and early modern understandings: Catholic nuns still are called brides of Christ and profess in wedding dresses, Moravians continue to sing Zinzendorf's hymns, and some contemporary Protestants and Catholics, like Menno Simons, David Joris, and Martin Luther, consider their own church to be Christ's true bride. Other contemporary understandings of the bride of Christ originate in a distinctly modern scientific understanding of gender, creation, and procreation. For instance, Amy DeRogatis's study of contemporary evangelical sex manuals shows that some American Protestants join Zinzendorf and the Puritans in locating God (and the devil) in semen and instruct married couples to look for God during sexual intercourse to be impregnated with the Holy Spirit. This movement's theology incorporates contemporary scientific concepts such as DNA and the transmission of infectious diseases.[5] The change of clothing which visually marked medieval women as brides of Christ has similarly been adjusted by communities which recognize female ordination, as with Bride of Christ Robes, a Protestant manufacturer of ministerial vestments for women. According to her company's history, seamstress Tina Scott was called by Christ to stop making secular wedding dresses and "dress my Bride."[6] Neither Scott's designs nor her testimony reference the Catholic nun's traditional title as bride of Christ or their continued use of secular wedding clothing during that ritual of profession. Scott's robes are all modified from male clerical vestments, not women's wedding gowns. Most designs are cut in A-Line and Princess seams with fabrics and matching accessories—stiletto heels with rhinestone accents, fringes, and richly colored patterns. These contemporary Americans disagree with one another's understanding of the bride of Christ, and I suspect many would find medieval brides of Christ decidedly peculiar. Through their use of scripture, fashion, and scientific knowledge, contemporary Christians nonetheless reconstruct a bride of Christ and Jesus as lover of souls that closely resembles those originating in late medieval Europe.

---

[5] Amy DeRogatis, "'Born Again Is a Sexual Term': Demons, STDs, and God's Healing Sperm," *Journal of the American Academy of Religion* 77, no. 2 (2009): 275–302.

[6] Bride of Christ Robes: Ministry Robes for Women, "About Bride of Christ Robes," accessed May 18, 2013, http://brideofchristrobes.com/company.htm. Though female ordination is hardly an uncontested issue, it is interesting that some female ministers identify as brides of Christ. This company's use of African-American models also suggests that it may be catering to a specific communal need for personalized and stylish vestments that would not be found in other communities who practice female ordination but have standardized vestments.

Like medieval beguines, nuns, priests, and married couples, modern evangelicals, Catholics, queer nuns, and atheists step into the role of bride of Christ to attain salvation. However, modern brides of Christ relate to Jesus as a fully male adult human. Embracing Jesus as a lover and a spouse has become an experience defined by contemporary scientific models for biological sex, legal definitions of marriage, and cultural constructions of gender. For contemporary Americans, Jesus participates in both queer and heteronormative marriages, but only as a man, a friend, and a brother, never a sister, a bride, or a mother.

Some contemporary Protestant denominations recognize the bride of Christ as one of the central scripturally sourced aspects of Christian womanhood. For these communities, Jesus is an idealized spouse for married women and a boyfriend for abstinent unmarried girls. R. Marie Griffith's ethnography of the Women's Aglow ministry describes women teaching one another to love God as an ideal man or husband, and cites several pamphlets and romance novels which present Jesus as a second husband. One pamphlet asks (as if the author had read Tauler): "How would you like to be married to a husband who is always faithful … and will love you no matter what you do? Surprise! The Bible says we've already got exactly that kind of husband. The God of the Universe is my Husband! What a mind blowing idea."[7] Aglow's gentle spiritual spouse, like the late medieval Christ-as-bridegroom, is a composite figure blending scriptural and secular romance who supports women in difficult marriages.

Aglow's communal reaffirmation that Christ might be a spouse and lover, perfectly masculine yet miraculously gentle, is widespread in contemporary American Christianity. Some American Protestant communities advise teens to view Christ as a lover to encourage abstinence before marriage. The Christian online retailer Virtuous Planet even sells pink and purple "Jesus Christ is my Boyfriend" key fobs, mugs, t-shirts, onesies, and doggie jumpers.[8] A recent Christian response to *Twilight*—itself a Christian romance—redirects readers to chastity by openly sexualizing and romanticizing Christ.[9] The author, Kimberly Powers, is a married mother, youth minister, and self-professed bride of Christ.[10] Enticing Christian teens into romantic relationship with Jesus has been an important part of Evangelical youth culture since the mid-twentieth century.

---

[7] R. Marie Griffith, *God's Daughters: Evangelical Women and the Power of Submission* (Berkeley: University of California Press 1997), 130.

[8] "Jesus Christ is my Boyfriend" t-shirts. Virtuous Planet, "Joy to the World Clothing," accessed on May 18, 2013, http://www.virtuousplanet.com/joy2theworld/s00000000000000065437.

[9] Kimberly Powers, *Escaping the Vampire: Desperate for the Immortal Hero* (Colorado Springs, CO: David C. Cook, 2009). W. Scott Poole discusses *Twilight* and Powers's ministry in *Monsters in America: Our Historical Obsession with the Hideous and the Haunting* (Baylor, TX: Baylor University Press, 2011), 212–16. My thanks to Jennifer L. Welsh for this citation.

[10] This information comes from Powers's own biography and personal webpage. Walk the Talk Youth Ministries, "Kimberly Powers," accessed May 18, 2013, http://www.wttym.org/Walk_the_Talk_Youth_Ministries/Kimberly_Powers.html.

Memoirist Susan Campbell's *Dating Jesus* narrates growing up and leaving a conservative Christian community which, without ever explicitly instructing its members that they were brides of Christ, led a young girl to believe that Jesus was her boyfriend. Queer literary critic Michael Warner identifies Jesus as his first crush in an account of growing up Pentecostal in the south: "Jesus was my first boyfriend. He loved me, personally, and he told me I was his own." Warner recognizes that "Anglo-American Christian culture has developed a rich and kinky iconography of Jesus, the perma-boy who loves us, the demiurge in a dress."[11] Kurt Willems, an Anabaptist pastor and blogger, compares the use of internet-based Christian communities to teenagers explaining their lack of a romantic partner as dating Jesus, a "fling with the King."[12] Pubescents crushing on a boyish savior have interiorized a culture of devotion where Christian parents bring Jesus into the bedroom and pious children sing "Jesus loves me" and believe that love, secular or religious, must eventually lead to marriage.

Unlike the late medieval Christ, whose sexual identity and physical appearance shifted as often as his lovers', the American Jesus is unequivocally male.[13] American Jesus's masculinity reflects a modern medical understanding that chromosomes distinguish male from female, and surgery and hormone therapy are the most common ways to "reassign" sex. Even artistic and theological depictions of Jesus as a woman are biologically limited, superimposing the curving hips and exposed breasts of a woman's body onto the iconography of the crucifixion. While feminist and womanist theologians argue for a womanChrist, and some queer theologians read Christ's ambiguous gender as trans, most depictions of Jesus are designed as theological arguments, not devotional technologies. Thus viewers are challenged to reconsider gender roles and patriarchy, but not drawn into an identification with Christ in the image, nor pushed to slip between male and female, or in and out of the painted body. Nor are there, to my knowledge, cases of contemporary Christians describing a marriage to a female Jesus. Both women and men describe loving Christ as a man—complicated, kinky, feminized, queer, but underneath it all, a physically intact, sexually functioning male.

Modern genetic models of sex and social critiques of gender have made Jesus the bridegroom a bisexual male-bodied figure. Christ's marriages to premodern men have become central to an ongoing theological argument for social inclusion and equal rights. For instance, Gerard Loughlin argues that the wedding at Cana is a marital bond between men, a "queer kind of marriage ... [that] is one of the queerest things about the Christian Church; that it celebrates in its symbols what it denies to its members ... Jesus goes to a wedding at Cana and marries his disciples; John the Baptist marries his friend, the bridegroom Jesus. But this

---

[11]   Michael Warner, "Tongues Untied: Memoirs of a Pentecostal Boyhood," *Curiouser* (2004): 220.

[12]   Kurt Willems, "Jesus is not an Online Boyfriend," May 14, 2012, accessed May 18, 2013, http://www.relevantmagazine.com/god/deeper-walk/blog/29190-jesus-is-not-an-online-boyfriend.

[13]   Prothero, *American Jesus*, 91–4.

is all imaginary, symbolic."[14] Citing fifteenth-century German depictions of John wed to Christ, Loughlin proposes that Jesus is a man whose love for and marriage to other men legitimizes contemporary same-sex relationships.[15] Loughlin's argument hinges on his modern assumptions about Jesus's fixed masculinity and his sexualized interpretation of consummation. In other words, he has transformed these historical men into exemplary sacred bodies who authorize the sacrality of embodied same-sex love.

Contemporary artists and performers also continue the late medieval and early modern anti-clerical and pornographic literature by representing sexualized and sexually violated nuns as the bride of Christ.[16] From nunsploitation films to the mass-produced line drawings of sexy brides of Christ by American artist Chris Cooper, often sold alongside kitschy boxing nuns and Jesus action figures, contemporary media depictions of nuns as sexually frustrated yet available.[17] These sexualized depictions assume the viewer knows and understands that the vow of chastity made when nuns wed Christ sublimates their erotic potential. The nun as bride-of-Christ has also been embraced by the Sisters of Perpetual Indulgence, a self-described "leading-edge order of queer Nuns." The founding Sisters (and most of the current members) are sexually active queer male evangelists, public voices in the world for safe sex in a way that intentionally inverts the implicitly suppressed heterosexual desires of enclosed celibate women. The Sisters canonize their own saints, endow charities, and educate the public. Medieval imagery suffuses the movement, and each Sister is made into a bride of Christ. The Sisters of Perpetual Indulgence have playfully modeled their organization after the hierarchies and rituals of medieval convents: they wear habits based on designs worn by fourteenth-century French and Flemish nuns, and during their profession ceremonies, they take new names, don habits, and become brides of Christ. The movement harmonizes acts of charity with public subversions of gender and religion through their use of drag and high camp and by organizing public events like their annual Hunky Jesus Contest, held in San Francisco each Easter.[18] The Sisters' identification as Christ's brides criticizes contemporary

---

[14]   Loughlin, *Queer Theology*, 2.

[15]   This historically grounded argument for incorporating a full spectrum of human sexuality into contemporary Christianity is partially founded on the work of medievalist John Boswell. Mathew Kuefler, *The Boswell Thesis: Essays on Christianity, Social Tolerance, and Homosexuality* (Chicago: University of Chicago Press, 2006).

[16]   See, for instance, the opening of Rambuss's *Closet Devotions*, which compares the pornographic film *More of a Man* to the animated and kissable Christ in Madonna's "Like a Prayer" video. Rambuss, *Closet Devotions*, 12–14.

[17]   Coopstuff, "Brides of Christ Stickers," accessed May 18, 2013, http://www. coopstuff.com/products/item/brides_of_christ_stickers/ (site discontinued).

[18]   Susan Henking, "Queering Easter: The Sisters of Perpetual Indulgence Redefine Sainthood," *Religion Dispatches*, April 2, 2010, accessed May 18, 2013, http://www. religiondispatches.org/archive/sexandgender/2354/queering_easter__the_sisters_of_ perpetual_indulgence_redefine_sainthood. The Sisters of Perpetual Indulgence, "Sistory," accessed May 18, 2013, http://www.thesisters.org/.

Brides of Christ, Contemporary Christianity, and American Popular Culture   221

Christian—especially Catholic—homophobia and continues a medieval tradition of communal education and exemplary performances.

A Wedding at the End of the World

In the fourteenth and fifteenth centuries, spiritual directors like Otto of Passau explicitly linked the wedding of individual souls to the wedding of the lamb in *Revelation*. This late medieval conflation of the weddings of *Revelation* with the unions of individual souls to Christ became an enduring part of Christian tradition. In the sixteenth and seventeenth centuries, persecuted prophets and spiritual leaders like Menno Simons, David Joris, and the married Englishwomen Mary Gadbury and Anne Wentworth were certain both that Christ had wed himself to those selected for salvation and that those marriages promised an almost-immanent Judgment. Christians continue to expect the world to end, and some anticipating the Apocalypse have either declared themselves brides of Christ or written extensively on the wedding of the Lamb. In twentieth-century America, the male prophets Father Divine, Daddy Grace, and David Koresh declared themselves to be iterations of Christ, and their mortal lovers to be Christ's brides. In Australia, Alan John Miller, a divorced father of two and his girlfriend, Mary Suzanne Luck, publicly identify themselves as Jesus and his bride, Mary Magdalene, and are currently gathering followers of "spirit pairs" to their Divine Church outside Adelaide. Though the movement has been the target for government investigation, it continues to draw converts.[19] As in seventeenth-century Puritan England or fifteenth-century Germany, these movements are sometimes ridiculed and marginalized or, as with David Koresh and the Branch Davidians, violently ended by the secular government. Though they are now studied as New Religious Movements, followers of self-proclaimed brides of Christ and the social institutions which place groups under suspicion retain both the late medieval laity's conviction that individuals may become brides of Christ and late medieval institutional discomfort with self-identified brides of Christ who veer too far from sexual and political norms.

American prophets of the end-times still preach that marrying Jesus signifies communal salvation and acts as a harbinger of the end-times, and some American brides of Christ still struggle with conflicting obligations to worldly and spiritual spouses. At least fifteen Protestant churches and ministries named after the bride of Christ have an internet presence, and at least one, Bride of Christ Ministries, is run by David and Sheila Magiera.[20] Their sermons, videos, books, and website urge Christians to prepare for the Rapture by becoming brides of Christ. Elements of their message closely resemble the late medieval master narrative of the

---

[19]   Alan John Miller, "Divine Truth," accessed May 18, 2013, http://www.divine truth.com/.

[20]   David Magiera, Bride of Christ Ministries, accessed May 18, 2013, http://www. brideofchrist.com/.

soul's marriage to Jesus. Though the Magieras cite only scripture and personal revelation for their descriptions of the bride's transformation, they describe the bride dancing, playing music and receiving gifts of clothing. Like many medieval authors, they insist that "whether you are a man or a woman, you have been created to be the bride of Christ, because there is no distinction of gender in the eyes of our Creator." Their ministry operates several media platforms in addition to the web portal, including a digital newsletter, appearances on television and radio shows, self-published books, and devotional sculptures. They even sell embossed wedding invitations in bulk so that members can "invite everyone to [their] wedding with Jesus!" Each invitation cordially invites the recipient to the wedding of the Lamb and explains that God is "preparing for the wedding of His Son." Rather than the typical RSVP and guest registry information, these wedding invitations instruct guests to surrender and prepare to wed Christ. As a married couple speaking to other brides within Christ's "Bridal Spirit" since 1998, the Magieras have dedicated their marriage to serving their heavenly Groom.

Other American preachers of the end-times shared with late medieval wives the need to leave their worldly spouses before wedding Jesus. African-American folk artist Sister Gertrude Morgan's mission began with conflict between her obligations as a married woman and her call to become a harbinger of the apocalypse and intimate lover of God. Morgan was called by Christ to leave her husband and to pursue a ministry in New Orleans and preached the Apocalypse until her death.[21] There, she painted several visions of herself as Christ's bride to serve as visual aids for her street ministry. A 1957 painting of Morgan in heavenly Jerusalem has been dated to the year she wed and was "crowned out" by Christ (Figure 8.1). Morgan painted herself in a white wedding gown, posed alongside Jesus. Morgan painted on anything available at the moment of inspiration—this scene was painted on the lid of a paint tin—and used her paintings to illustrate sermons and songs. In this portrait, which echoes medieval iconography, Morgan is enthroned, a bouquet of roses in one hand. She portrays Jesus as fair-skinned with wide eyes open to the viewer. He rests one hand on her shoulder, the other positioned near her hair as if he has just placed the white crown on Morgan's head. Morgan painted several versions of her marriage to Jesus: in each scene, Morgan wears a white dress, and Jesus is fair-skinned, typically dressed in a white tuxedo rather than the casual white buttoned shirt, tan slacks, and the bow tie shown here. Heaven's walls are bordered by white-faced, red-haired angels; Jerusalem's shotgun houses contain rocking chairs and televisions. Gertrud Morgan's visions of heavenly Jerusalem often are covered with handwritten passages from scripture; in this painting only three words, "Sister Morgan Gertrude," run along the western wall of Jerusalem.

---

[21] My thanks to Emily S. Clark, who first introduced me to Sister Gertrude Morgan. Emily Clark, "She's the Four-Leaf Clover in the City Katrina Turned Over: The Historical Sister Gertrude Morgan and Her Post-Hurricane Katrina Specters" (MA thesis, University of Missouri-Columbia, 2009); William A. Fagaly et al., eds., *Tools of Her Ministry: The Art of Sister Gertude Morgan* (New York: Rizzoli International Publications, 2004).

Brides of Christ, Contemporary Christianity, and American Popular Culture 223

Figure 8.1   Sister Gertrude Morgan (1900–80), *New Jerusalem*, New Orleans, Louisiana, c. 1957–74. Acrylic and/or tempera on metal lid, 12 in. × 19 in. Collection of the American Folk Art Museum, New York, gift of Bliss Carnochan in honor of Gerard C. Wertkin, American Folk Art Museum director (1991–2004), 2004.7.1. Photo by Gavin Ashworth, New York.

As in medieval depictions of the bridal pair, this smiling couple is dressed in the fashion of their day, their marital status marked through clothing, accessories, and scriptural references. However, unlike medieval depictions which posed the bridal pair gazing into one another's eyes as a visual depiction of the beatific vision, Morgan and Jesus gaze forward to the viewer, as if posed by a modern wedding photographer. Gertrude Morgan's crowning-out cites the iconography the medieval bride of Christ—the embrace, the crown or the garland of roses, and her white wedding clothes. Morgan painted herself and her world by transposing the streets and troubles of contemporary New Orleans onto scenes of heaven

224 *Marrying Jesus in Medieval and Early Modern Northern Europe*

derived from scripture. Her art, songs, and sermons recall the apocalyptic visions of married prophets like Mary Gadbury, Anne Wentworth, Bridget of Sweden, and David Joris. Gertrude Morgan too had married Jesus, and the sinners of the world should repent because the world was about to end.

Then, as Now

This fragmentary survey of contemporary brides of Christ reveals the enduring importance of the bride of Christ to Christian popular piety. As I have argued, brides of Christ in medieval and early modern Europe incorporated elements of contemporary popular culture and reflected new developments in Christian theology and practice. Though it was not until the late thirteenth century that European Christians demonstrably began teaching basic theology to secular audiences with stories of the bride, early Christian authors like Origen and John Chrysostom had also invited the lay men and women to participate in Christ's wedding in sermons and baptismal instructions. By the mid-fourteenth century, the bride of Christ had become a container within which authors and artists could organize and disseminate information about salvation, creation, and the interpenetration of the spiritual and material worlds. In collaboration with nuns, beguines, and lay men and women, medieval clergy thus used the bride's master narrative to popularize techniques of self-transformation appropriate for use by both lay and religious. The laicization of marrying Jesus coincided with the religious renewal in women's houses when female-authored devotional literature created both new lay women saints and clerical suspicion of women's visions, and would be codified during the Reformations, as newly emerging denominations each identified themselves as the true bride of Christ. By offering individual Christians a path to salvation through Christ's salvific love, marrying Jesus has remained a valuable didactic framework for pious living in a devil-filled world. Christ and his bride have also become a means of protest, a source of amusement, and the premise for subversive irony in contemporary western culture. When modern Christians present Christ as bridegroom, whether to urge penitence, to displace sexual desire, reject asexual purity in favor of redemptive love, or to challenge assumptions about gender and sexuality, they revive the medieval innovation that Jesus was a bridegroom for any body, and for every soul.

Each retelling of Christ's wedding with a soul links strands of society and history together, penetrating illusory boundaries between secular and sacred. With the assistance of artists, and the authorizing precedents gleaned from the lives of saints and the wisdom of biblical exegetes, spiritual directors, confessors, devotional authors, and preachers—male *and* female—made Christ's courtship with the loving soul into a template for religious reform. But their depictions of Christ's bride are only a small part of a more complex story of the relationship between media, community, and religious reform in medieval and modern Christianity.

The resemblance between medieval, early modern, and contemporary representations of the bride of Christ testifies that late medieval popular culture continues to influence late modern American Christianity. Then, as now, images of the bride of Christ are mosaics combining idiosyncratic interests with widely accepted interpretations of scripture and doctrine. Then, as now, individuals aspire to marry Jesus in response to media infusing every aspect of their daily lives. This ongoing process of remaking the bride of Christ satisfies the needs and values of an always-immediate now by respectfully—if unknowingly—gesturing to historical precedents. The late modern bride of Christ continues to make mysteries comprehensible, to demarcate the boundaries between saved and damned, and to invite individual believers, no matter their worldly station, to learn to love God. The late medieval laity's identification with the bride of Christ did not fade into oblivion when the material technologies of their devotion became obsolete. The networks of preachers, nuns, artists, scribes, and visionaries who remade the medieval bride of Christ for the laity survived the theological and technological revolutions of the sixteenth century, and their traces still glimmer in this postindustrial age.

Bibliography

Manuscripts

Book of Hours. Oxford BL Rawl Lit f8.

David of Augsburg. *Bruder Davids von Augsburg Geistliche Lehre und Betrachtungen*. BSB CGM 183.

———. *Mystikertexte. Gebete und Betrachtungen, Predigten und Traktate, hauptsächlich von David von Augsburg und Berthold von Regensburg. On the Incarnation of Christ*, early 14th century. BSB CGM 176.

Einsiedeln Stiftsbibliothek Codex 710 (322). *Heinrich Seuse, Writings*. e-codices, http://www.e-codices.unifr.ch/en/list/one/sbe/0710.

Gebet-und Andachtsbuch, including "Von der bruderschaft oder mahelschaft d[er] ewige[n] weißheit vn[d] wie sich halten sullen die Iunger d[er] ewigen weißheit." Karlsruhe Badische Landesbibliothek, MS Lichtenthal 99 (1469). Digital facsimile: http://digital.blb-karlsruhe.de/urn/urn:nbn:de:bsz:31-29469.

Gebet-und Betrachtungsbuch, Karlsruhe Badische Landesbibliothek St. Peter, pap. 9. http://digital.blb-karlsruhe.de/urn/urn:nbn:de:bsz:31-8328.

Getijden-en gebedenboek: Kalender. Gebeden en devote excerpten. 1525, KBR MS II 5573.

Heilsbach, Agnes van. "Letters and Spiritual Diary." KBR MS 20422.

Henry Suso's *Exemplar*. Wolfenbüttel, Herzog August Bibliothek., Cod. 78.5. August 2, Augsburg [1482?].

Honorius Augustudonensis. *Commentary on the Song of Songs*. MS CLM. 30172. BSB (1403).

———. MS CLM. 4550. BSB (12th century).

———. MS CLM. 18125. BSB (c. 1200).

Leben der Heiligen Altväter, containing manuscript additions related to the life of Nikolaus von Flüe. Luzern, Bibliothek des Kapuzinerklosters Wesemlin: Leben der heiligen Altväter, deutsche Inkunabel Kod. 32b (c. 1480).

Life of Gertrud Von Ortenberg. c. 1475. KBR, 8507–9, Codex 368.

Mechthild von Hackeborn. *Liber specialis gratiae*. Oxford, BL: Douce 44.

Miscellany. Basel, Universitätsbibliothek. MS Cod. G2 II 58 (14th century).

Müller, Jerome, scribe. *Miscellany of Mystical Treatises [Sammelhandschrift, z.T. mystiche Texte]* (Augsburg, 1436). Munich: Bavarian State Library/Bayerische StaatsBibliothek. MS CGM 411 48v. Münchener Digitalisierungszentrum. MDZ: http://daten.digitale-sammlungen.de/~db/0006/bsb00064431/images.

Private Devotions. Oxford, BL: MS Dutch f1.

Profession statement of Jacomijne Costers, f 166 in "Dutch Devotional Tracts." Mariendaal, Antwerp. Before 1481. New York: Jewish Theological Seminary of America, Library, MS NH108.

228 *Marrying Jesus in Medieval and Early Modern Northern Europe*

Sammelhandschrift: Elisabeth-Vita des Dietrich von Apolda / Tösser Schwesternbuch. Karlsruhe, Landesbibl., Cod. Donaueschingen 452.

Seuse, Thomas Peuntner. *"Hymnen, dt.* including Von der bruderschaft oder mahelschaft d[er] ewige[n] weißheit vn[d] wie sich halten sullen die Iunger d[er] ewigen weißheit." 1453, Nuremburg (BSB CGM 405), 107r.

Speculum virginum. British Library MS Arundel 44.

————. MS Walters 72.

Spiritual DiceGame, Eckhart and Tauler Sermons. Heidelberg, Universitätsbibl., Cod. Sal. VIII 77.

Spiritual Spouseship [Gemahelschaft Christi mit der gläubigen Seele]. BSB CGM 516, c. 1459. MDZ: http://daten.digitale-sammlungen.de/bsb00035383/image_1.

Suso, Heinrich. Dresden Landesbibliothek MS M 277, 89v–106r (1450). Digital facsimile available at http://digital.slub-dresden.de/ppn279351666.

The 21-Year-Old Wife. BSB CGM 1109 f 337 v. MDZ: http://daten.digitale-sammlungen.de/bsb00035397/image_694.

Tractaten, including Pomerius's *Exercitium Super Pater Noster.* KBR MS 4328–33.

Trial of Mary Gadbury. Clarke MS 18, held by Worcester College, Oxford. f. 27v–28v.

Uncatalogued MS from St. Nicolas in Undis. Bodleian Library.

Von der Gemahlschaft Christi und der gläubigen, andächtigen Seele. BSB CGM 7241, 88r, 1499. MDZ http://daten.digitale-sammlungen.de/~db/0003/bsb00034597/images/.

Printed Items (Before 1750)

Biblia Pauperum. Nuremburg: Hans Sporer, 1477. http://arks.princeton.edu/ark:/88435/ht24wj49c.

Christus und die minnende Seele. Xylographic blockbook formerly in a lost manuscript from Mondsee Abbey. Albertina Inv. DG1930/197/1–5, DG1930/198/6–9.

Coornhert, Dirck Volckhertsz. *Tweeling Vanden Bruydt Christi En D'egipsche Vroeivrouwen Doet Dees Tweeling Twee Comedien Aenschouwen.* t'Aemsterdam: ghedruct by my Harmen ianszoon Muller, 1582. Digital facsimile, http://www.europeana.eu/portal/record/04202/2BB7ED09D0D8E17460A6FAC31457D61F138BE215.html. Modern edition, http://www.dbnl.org/tekst/coor001pvan01_01/coor001pvan01_01_0005.php.

Ellis, Humphrey. *Pseudochristus: or, A true and faithful relation of the grand impostures, horrid blaspemies, abominable practises, gross deceits; lately spread abroad and acted in the county of Southampton, by William Frankelin and Mary Gadbury ... The one ... professing and asserting himself to be the Christ ... The other as wickedly professing and asserting her self to be the spouse of Christ.* London: Printed by John Macock, for L. Fawn, 1650.

Bibliography 229

Gabriel à Sancto Joanne-Baptista. *De bruydt Christi Christina, ghekleedt naer de mode van Parys en paradys, betoonende aen alle maeghden hoe sy hedendaeghs naer siel ende lichaem konnen verciert gaen.* Antwerpen: Augustinus Graet, 1690.

Het Hofken Van Devocien: Inhoudende Hoemen Devotelijc Misse Hooren Sal. Een Devote Oeffeninghe in Die Seven Ghetiden Vanden Daghe. Hoemen God Inwendelijc Aenbidden Sal Een Troostelike Onderwisinge Der Passien Christi Doer Vraghe Ende Antwoerde. Een Minnelicke Tsamensprekinge Des Bruydegoms Der Sielen Ende Zijnre Bruyt. Hoemen Dat Gheloove Inwendich Oeffenen Sal Om Daer Ghestadich in Te Bliven. Antwerpen: Symon Cock, c. 1540.

Hier beghint een sueuerlijck boecxken ghenoemt thoofkijn van deuotien. Antwerpen: Gheraert Leeu, 1487.

Joris, David. Pamphlets printed in Rostock. Bodleian Library. Vet. D1 f.389.

Kempe, Margery. *Here begynneth a shorte trystyse of contemplacyon taught by our lorde Jhesu cryste, or taken out of the boke of Margerie kempe of lynn.* London, Fletestrete: Wynken de Worde, c. 1500.

———. *Here foloweth a veray deuoute treatyse (named Benyamyn) of the myghtes and vertues of mannes soule, of the way to true contemplacyon, compyled by ... Rycharde of saynt Vyctor. (Dyuers doctrynes ... taken out of the lyfe of ... Saynt Katheryn of Seenes, etc.-A shorte treatyse of contemplacyon taught by our lorde Jhesu cryst, or taken out of the boke of Margery kempe ancresse of Lynne.-A deuoute treatyse called the Epystle of prayer.-A deuoute treatyse compyled by mayster Walter Hylton of the songe of aungelles.-A verary necessary Epystle of dyscrecyon in styrynges of the soule.-A deuoute treatyse of dyscernynge of sprytes, etc.).* London: Henry Pepwell, 1521.

Luyken, Jan. "Jesus en de ziel." Edited by Emblem Project Utrecht. Amsterdam, 1685. http://emblems.let.uu.nl/lu1685.html.

Mather, Cotton. *A Glorious espousal: A brief essay, to illustrate and prosecute the marriage, wherein our great Saviour offers to espouse unto himself the children of men. And thereupon to recommend from that grand pattern a good carriage in the married life among them. An essay proper and useful in the hands of those who travel on the noble design of espousing the souls of men unto their Saviour. But more particularly and seasonably to be presented, where a marriage is upon a celebration.* Boston: Printed by S. Kneeland, for B. Gray, and J. Edwards, at their shops on the north and south side of the Town-House in King-Street, 1719.

Passau, Otto von. *Dat Boeck des gulden throens of der XXIV ouden.* Utrecht: [Drukker met het monogram], March 1480.

———. *Diß Buch ist genannt die Vier und czwentzig Alten, oder der güldin Tron, geseczet von bruder Otten von Passowe.* Augsburg: Anton Sorg, 1480.

———. *Die vierundzwanzig Alten, oder Der goldne Thron.* Cologne: Johann Koelhoff the Elder, May 26, 1492.

Pomerius, Henricus. *Exercitium Super Pater Noster.*1447. XYLO 30 BNF.

———. *Exercitium Super Pater Noster [Latin-Flamand].* 1460. XYLO 31 BNF.

230 *Marrying Jesus in Medieval and Early Modern Northern Europe*

Schol, Ysbrandt (?). *Een profitelijck en[de] troostelick boecxken vanden gheloove ende hoope wat dat oprechte ghelove is. Ende welcke ghenade die mensche doer dat gelove nach vercrigen. Ende hoe scadeliken dat onghelove is. Noch een boecxken va[n] die liefde die God tot ons heeft, ende wat die liefde werct, ende hoe scadelick die liefde des werelts is allen menschen seer troostelic. Met noch een deuote contemplatie aan dye bruyt Christi.* Anvers: Adriaen van Bergen, 1534.

————. *Van dye bruyt Christi een devote contemplacie.* Leiden: Peter Janszoon, 1540.

Seüsse, Heinrich, Rulman Merswin, and Henricus de Herph. *Hie seind geschriben die capitel des büchs d[as] do der Seüsse heisset ... Vita; Büchlein der ewigen Weisheit; Büchlein der Wahrheit; Briefbüchlein. - Merswin, Rulman: Neunfelsenbuch. Mit Kap. 60 aus dem Spieghel van Volcomenheit von Henricus Herp.* Augsburg: Anton Sorg, 1482. 103v–104r. MDZ: http://daten.digitale-sammlungen.de/~db/0003/bsb00031701/image_1.

Spitzer, Konrad von (?). *Buch der Kunst, dadurch der weltlich Mensch mag geistlich werden.* Augsburg: Johann Bämler, 1477.

Tauler, Johannes and Rulman Merswin. *Sermon des gross gelarten in gnade erlauchten doctoris Johannis Thauleri predigerr ordens, weisende auff den nehesten waren wegk, yn geiste czu wandern durch uberschwebenden syn, vnour acte von geistes ynnigen vorwandelt i deutsch manchen menschen zu selikeit.* Leipzig: Conrad Kachelofen, 1498.

Vervoort, Frans. *Bruygoms mantelken, vanden inwendighen nauolghen des leues en des cruycen ons liefs Heeren Ihesu Christi.* [Antwerp?]: Godefridi, Petrus Ghelen, Jan van, 1554.

Von der ynnigen selen wy sy gott casteyet vnnd im beheglich mach. Erfurt: Wolfgang Schenck, 1499.

Wentworth, Anne. *A True Account of Anne Wentworths Being Cruelly, Unjustly, and Unchristianly Dealt with by Some of Those People Called Anabaptists, of the Particular Opinion, and All the Cause She Gave, and What She Hath Done Who Would Never Appear in Publick, but Forced to Declare the Tender Mercies of God, and Cruelty of Man; That Will Not Hear Truth If It Were to Save Her Life or Soul, Having Tendred by All Just and Legal Ways, but They Reject and Refuse to Hear Her, When So Weak as a Dying Woman. Also Her Discovering the Two Spirits Which Are in the World, and Her Giving Warning of What E're Long Will Surely and Suddenly Come to Pass.* 1676.

————. *The Revelation of Jesus Christ Just as He Spake It in Verses at Several Times, and Sometimes in Prose, Unto His Faithful Servant Anne Wentworth, Who Suffereth for His Name: Containing Mercy and Judgment, Comforts to Zion, but Woes to Babylon.* [London?], 1679.

New Media

"2012 Hot 100." *Maxim*. April 17, 2012. Accessed May 19, 2013. http://www.maxim.com/hot-100/2012-hot-100.

Bourdain, Anthony. *Anthony Bourdain: No Reservations*. "Food Porn." Episode 67, first aired on February 9, 2009, by the Travel Channel. http://www.travelchannel.com/tv-shows/anthony-bourdain/episodes/food-porn.

———. *Anthony Bourdain: No Reservations*. "Food Porn 2." Episode 93, first aired on April 19, 2010, by the Travel Channel. http://www.travelchannel.com/tv-shows/anthony-bourdain/episodes/food-porn-2-1.

Bride of Christ Robes: Ministry Robes for Women. "About Bride of Christ Robes." Accessed May 18, 2013. http://brideofchristrobes.com/company.htm.

Coopstuff. "Brides of Christ Stickers." Accessed May 18, 2013. http://www.coopstuff.com/products/item/brides_of_christ_stickers/ (site discontinued).

Goodstein, Laurie. "A Comedian and a Cardinal Open Up on Spirituality." *New York Times*. September 15, 2012. Accessed May 18, 2013. http://www.nytimes.com/2012/09/16/nyregion/stephen-colbert-and-cardinal-cardinal-timothy-dolan-at-fordham-university.html.

Magiera, David. Bride of Christ Ministries. Accessed May 18, 2013. http://www.brideofchrist.com/.

Miller, Alan John. "Divine Truth." Accessed May 18, 2013. http://www.divinetruth.com/.

The Sisters of Perpetual Indulgence. "Sistory." Accessed May 18, 2013. http://www.thesisters.org/.

Thompson, Stephen. "Interview: The Daily Show's Stephen Colbert, Rob Corddry, Ed Helms, and Mo Rocca." *The Onion A.V. Club*. January 22, 2003. Accessed May 18, 2013. http://www.avclub.com/articles/the-daily-shows-stephen-colbert-rob-corddry-ed-hel,13795/.

Virtuous Planet. "Joy to the World Clothing." Accessed May 18, 2013. http://www.virtuousplanet.com/joy2theworld/s00000000000000065437.

Walk the Talk Youth Ministries. "Kimberly Powers." Accessed May 18, 2013. http://www.wttym.org/Walk_the_Talk_Youth_Ministries/Kimberly_Powers.html.

Willems, Kurt. "Jesus is not an Online Boyfriend." May 14, 2012. Accessed May 18, 2013. http://www.relevantmagazine.com/god/deeper-walk/blog/29190-jesus-is-not-an-online-boyfriend.

Scholarly Editions and Facsimiles

Augustine of Hippo. *De bono coniugali, De sancta virginitate*. Translated by P.G. Walsh. Oxford: Oxford University Press, 2001.

Backer, Hector Marie Auguste de. *L'Exercitium Super Pater Noster; Contribution À L'histoire Des Xylotypes*. Mons: L. Dequesne, 1924.

Banz, Romuald. *Christus und die Minnende Seele: zwei spätmittelhochdeutsche mystische Gedichte*. Hildesheim: G. Olms, 1977.

Berger, Lothar. *Die Goldene Muskate, Ein Spätmittelalterlicher Passionstraktat*. Marburg, 1969.

Bernard of Clairvaux. *Bernard of Clairvaux: Selected Works*. Edited by G.R. Evans. New York: Paulist Press, 1987.

232 *Marrying Jesus in Medieval and Early Modern Northern Europe*

Bevan, Frances A. *Three Friends of God: Records from the Lives of John Tauler, Nicholas of Basle, Henry Suso*. London: J. Nisbet, 1887.

Boehme, Jakob. *The Way to Christ*. Translated by Peter C. Erb. New York: Paulist Press, 1978.

Boekenoogen, Gerrit J. *Een suverlijc Exempel, hoe dat Jesus een heydensche maghet een soudaens dochter wech leyde, wt haren lande naar den Delftschen druk van Frans Sonderdanck uit het begin der 16de eeuw*. Leiden: Brill, 1904.

Bollmann, Anne and Nikolaus Staubach. *Schwesternbuch Und Statuten Des St. Agnes-Konvents*. Emmerich: Emmericher Geschichtsverein e.V., 1998.

Borries, Ekkehard. *Schwesternspiegel Im 15. Jahrhundert: Gattungskonstitution, Editionen, Untersuchungen*. Berlin: Walter De Gruyter, 2008.

Brinkerink, D.A., ed. *Van den doechden der vuriger ende stichtiger susteren van Diepen Veen: ('Handschrift D')*. Leiden: A.W. Sijthoff, 1904.

Bruning, E. et al. *Het geestelijk lied van Noord-Nederland in de vijftiende eeuw. De Nederlandse liederen van de handschriften Amsterdam (Wenen ÖNB 12875) en Utrecht (Berlijn MG 8o 190)*. Amsterdam: Vereniging voor Nederlandse Muziekgeschiedenis, 1963.

Bujanda, Jesús Martínez de, Léon-Ernest Halkin, and Patrick Pasture, eds. *Index de l'Université de Louvain: 1546, 1550, 1558*. Sherbrooke: Sherbrooke Centre d'études de la Renaissance, 1986.

Burns, Robert Ignatius. *Underworlds: The Dead, the Criminal, and the Marginalized*. Translated by Samuel Parsons Scott. Philadelphia: University of Pennsylvania Press, 2001.

Chrétien de Troyes. *Le chevalier de la charrette*. Éd. Bilingue by Catherine Croizy-Naquet. Paris: H. Champion, 2006.

Chrysostom, John. *Baptismal Instructions*. Translated by Paul W. Harkins. Westminster, MD: Newman Press, 1963.

Cramer, Thomas. *Maeren-Dichtung*. München: W. Fink, 1979.

De Man, Dirk. *Hier Beginnen Sommige Stichtige Punten Van Onsen Oelden Zusteren: Naar Het Te Arnhem Berustende Handschrift Met Inleiding En Aanteekeningen*. The Hague: M. Nijhoff, 1919.

Derkits, Hans. "Die Lebensbeschreibung Der Gertrud Von Ortenberg." PhD dissertation, Universität Wien, 1990.

Eschenbach, Wolfram von. *Parzival*. Edited by Karl Lachmann and Bernd Schirok. Berlin: De Gruyter, 2003.

Fallersleben, Hoffmann von. *Horae Belgicae. Studio Atque Opera Hoffmanni Fallerslebensis*. Hannoverae: C. Ruempler, 1836.

Gertrud of Helfta. *Spiritual Exercises*. Translated by Gertrud Jaron Lewis and Jack Lewis. Cistercian Fathers series, 49. Kalamazoo, MI: Cistercian Publications, 1989.

Hadewijch. *Brieven*. Edited by J. van Mierlo. Antwerp: Standaard-Boekhandel, 1947.

———. *The Complete Works*. Translated by Columba Hart. New York: Paulist Press, 1980.

Haggh, Barbara Helen. *Two Offices for St. Elizabeth of Hungary: Gaudeat Hungaria and Letare Germania.* Ottawa: Institute of Mediaeval Music, 1995.

Herp, Hendrik. *Spieghel der Volcomenheit.* OGE, vols. 1–2. Antwerpen: Uitgever Neerlandia, 1931.

Huber, Werner T. "Visionsbericht Des Caspar Am Büel." *Bruder Klaus.* March 19, 2012. Web. Accessed September 2, 2012. http://www.nvf.ch/que_m.asp?num=bkq068#anf.

"Jan van Ruusbroecs 'Brulocht' in oberdeutscher Überlieferung: Untersuchungen und kritische textausgabe." In *Münchener Texte und Untersuchungen zur deutschen Literatur des Mittelalters, Bd. 22,* edited by Wolfgang Eichler, 83–97. München: Beck, 1969.

Jeitteles, Adalbert. *Altdeutsche Predigten Aus Dem Benedictinerstifte St. Paul in Kärnten.* Innsbruck: Verlag der Wagner'schen Universitaets-Buchhandlung, 1878.

Jostes, Franz. *Meister Eckhart Und Seine Jünger; Ungedruckte Texte Zur Geschichte Der Deutschen Mystik.* Freiburg: Commissionsverlag der Universitaetsbuchhandlung, 1895.

Kempe, Margery. *The Book of Margery Kempe: The Text from the Unique MS. Owned by Colonel W. Butler-Bowdon.* Ed. S.B. Meech and Hope Emily Allen. Early English Text Society 212 (London: Oxford University Press,1940).

Kristeller, Paul. *Exercitium Super Pater Noster, Nach Der Ältesten Ausgabe Der Bibliothèque Nationale Zu Paris, in 8 Lichtdrucktafeln.* Berlin: B. Cassier, 1908.

Landmann, Florenz. "Zwei Andachtsübungen Von Strassburger Klosterfrauen." *Archiv für Elsässische Kirchengeschichte* 6 (1931): 217–28.

Langmann, Adelheid. "Die Offenbarungen Der Adelheid Langmann, Klosterfrau Zu Engelthal." Edited by Philipp Strauch. Strassburg: K.J. Trübner, 1878.

Lebeer, Louis. *Spirituale Pomerium: (Bibliothèque Royale De Belgique, Manuscrit 12070).* Bruxelles: Société des Bibliophiles et Iconophiles de Belgique, 1939.

De Limburgse sermoenen. Edited by J.H. Kern. Leiden: A.W. Sijthoff, 1895. http://www.dbnl.org/tekst/_lim003limb01_01/_lim003limb01_01_0037.php.

Luther, Martin. *D. Martin Luthers Werke; Kritische Gesamtausgabe.* Weimar: H. Böhlau, 1883–1929.

Mande, Hendrik. *Een minnentlike claege.* Edited by Thom Mertens. Erftstadt: Lukassen, 1984.

Marienwerder, Johannes von. *Das leben der seligen frawen Dorothee.* Marienburg: Jacob Karweysse, 1492.

———. *Das Leben der heiligen Dorothea.* Edited by Max Toeppen. In *Scriptores Rerum Prussicarum.* Vol. 2. Leipzig: Hirzel, 1863.

———. *The Life of Dorothea von Montau, a Fourteenth-Century Recluse.* Edited by Ute Stargardt. Lewiston: E. Mellen Press, 1997.

Mauz, Jörg. *Das Büchlein Der Ewigen Weisheit: Nach Der Handschrift Nr. 40 Des Suso-Gymnasiums in Konstanz.* Konstanz: Verlag am Hockgraben, 2003.

Mechthild of Magdeburg. *Das fliessende Licht der Gottheit: Nach der Einsiedler Handschrift in kritischem Vergleich mit gesamten Überlieferung.*

Edited by Hans Neumann and Gisela Vollmann-Profe. München; Zürich: Artemis Verlag, 1990.

———. *Das fliessende Licht der Gottheit*. Edited by Margot Schmidt. Stuttgart-Bad Canstatt: F. Frommann, 1995.

———. *The Flowing Light of the Godhead*. Translated by Frank J. Tobin. New York: Paulist Press, 1998.

Meister Eckhart. *The Complete Works of Meister Eckhart*. Translated by Maurice O'C Walshe. New York: Crossroad, 2009.

Merswin, Rulman. "Das Buch Von Den Neun Felsen: Von Dem Strassburger Bürger Rulman Merswin 1352: Nach Des Verf. Autograph." Edited by Karl Schmidt. Leipzig: Hirzel, 1859.

Meulen, Paulus Van der. *Het Roerspel En De Comedies Van Coornhert: Uitgegeven En Van Commentaar Voorzien, Door Dr P. Van Der Meulen*. Leiden: E.J. Brill, 1955.

Mittermaier, Franz Paul. "Lebensbeschreibung Der Sel. Christina, Gen. Von Retters Aus MS 324, Fol. 211 Sequ. Der Bibliothèque Nationale Et Universitaire De Strasbourg." *Archiv für Mittelrheinische Kirchengeschichte* 17 (1965): 209–52; and 18 (1966): 203–38.

Morris, Richard. *An Old English Miscellany Containing a Bestiary, Kentish Sermons, Proverbs of Alfred, Religious Poems of the Thirteenth Century, from Manuscripts in the British Museum, Bodleian Library, Jesus College Library, etc.* London: N. Trübner, 1872.

Nicolaus von Basel. Bericht von der Bekehrung Taulers. Edited by Charles Guillaume Adolphe Schmidt. Straßburg, 1875.

Nider, Johannes. *Formicarius*. Graz: Akadem. Druck-u. Verlagsanst, 1971.

Ohly, Friedrich and Nicola Kleine. *Das St. Trudperter Hohelied: Eine Lehre Der Liebenden Gotteserkenntnis*. Frankfurt am Main: Deutscher Klassiker Verlag, 1998.

Pfeiffer, Franz. *Deutsche Mystiker Des Vierzehnten Jahrhunderts I. Bd., Hermann Von Fritslar, Nicolaus Von Strassburg, David Von Augsburg*. Göttingen: Vandenhoec und Ruprecht, 1907.

Pseudo-Engelhart von Ebrach. "Das Buch der Vollkommenheit." In *Das Buch der Vollkommenheit*, edited by Karin Schneider. Berlin: Akademie Verlag, 2006.

Rasmussen, Ann Marie and Sarah Westphal-Wihl, eds. *Ladies, Whores, and Holy Women: A Sourcebook in Courtly, Religious, and Urban Cultures of Late Medieval Germany*. Kalamazoo: Medieval Institute Publications, Western Michigan University, 2010.

Richard of St. Victor. *Selected Writings on Contemplation*. Translated by Clare Kirchberger. New York: Harper and Brothers, 1957.

Rieger, Max. *Das Leben Der Heiligen Elisabeth, Vom Verfasser Der Erlösung*. Stuttgart: Litterarischer Verein, 1868.

Roth, F.W.E. "Aufzeichnungen über das mystische Leben der Nonnen von Kirchberg bei Sulz." *Alemannia* 21 (1893): 103–48.

Rupert of Deutz. *Ruperti Tuitiensis Commentaria in Canticum canticorum*. Edited by Hrabanus Haacke. Turnholti: Brepols, 1974.

Ruusbroec, Jan van. *Opera omnia*. Edited by M.M. Kors. English translation by H. Rolfson. Latin by L. Surius (1552), 10 vols. Turnhout: Brepols, 2000.

Sancti Thomae de Aquino. *Summa theologiae*. Edited by Petrus Caramello. Taurini: Marietti, 1952.

Savage, Anne and Nicholas Watson. *Anchoritic Spirituality: Ancrene Wisse and Associated Works*. New York: Paulist Press, 1991.

Schaff, Philip, ed. *The Principal Works of St. Jerome*. Nicene and Post-Nicene Fathers, Second Series. Vol. 6. New York: Christian Literature, 1893.

————. *A Select library of the Nicene and Post-Nicene Fathers of the Christian Church*. 14 vols. Grand Rapids, MI: Eerdmans, 1974.

Scheepsma, Wybren. *Hemels verlangen*. Amsterdam: Querido, 1993.

Schiewer, Hans-Jochen. "Auditionen und Visionen einer Begine: Die 'Selige Schereri', Johannes Mulberg und der Basler Beginenstreit; mit einem Textabdruck." In *Die Vermittlung geistlicher Inhalte im deutschen Mittelalter: internationales Symposium, Roscrea 1994*, edited by Timothy R. Jackson, Nigel F. Palmer, and Almut Suerbaum, 289–318. Tübingen: M. Niemeyer Verlag, 1996.

Schiewer, Regina D. *Die St. Georgener Predigten*. Berlin: Akademie Verl., 2010.

Schönebeck, Brun von. "Das Hohe Lied." In *Bibliothek des Litterarischen Vereins in Stuttgart*, 198, edited by Arwed Fischer. Stuttgart, 1893.

Schülke, Ulrich. *Konrads Büchlein von der geistlichen Gemahelschaft; Untersuchungen und Text*. München: Beck, 1970.

Seyfarth, Jutta, ed. *Speculum Virginum*. Corpus Christianorum Continuatio Mediaevalis. Turnholti: Brepols, 1990.

Solomon, Michael R. *The Mirror of Coitus: A Translation and Edition of the Fifteenth-Century Speculum al Foderi*. Madison, WI: Hispanic Seminary of Medieval Studies, 1990.

Spaapen, B. "Middeleeuwse Passiemystiek, III: De Autobiografie van Alijt Bake (Vervolg); IV: De Brief Uit De Ballingschap." *Ons Geestelijk Erf* 40, no. 1 (1967): 5–64.

St. Birgitta of Sweden. *The Revelations of St. Birgitta of Sweden*. Edited by Bridget Morris. Translated by Denis Michael Searby. Oxford: Oxford University Press, 2006.

Stannat, Werner. *Das Leben Der Heiligen Elisabeth in Drei Mittelniederdeutschen Handschriften Aus Wolfenbüttel Und Hannover*. Neumünster: K. Wachholtz, 1959.

Suso, Henry. *Heinrich Seuse: Deutsche Schriften*. Edited by Karl Bihlmeyer. Stuttgart, 1907.

————. *Henry Suso: The Exemplar, with Two German Sermons*. Edited and translated by Frank J. Tobin. New York: Paulist Press, 1989.

————. *Wisdom's Watch Upon the Hours*. Translated by Edmund Colledge. Washington, DC: Catholic University of America Press, 1994.

Tauler, Johannes. *Die Predigten Taulers aus der Engelberger Handschrift Sowie aus Schmidts Abschriften der Ehemaligen Strassburger Handschriften*. Edited by Ferdinand Vetter. Dublin: Weidmann, 1968.

236 *Marrying Jesus in Medieval and Early Modern Northern Europe*

Tucher, Katharina. *Die "Offenbarungen" Der Katharina Tucher*. Edited by Ulla Williams and Werner Williams-Krapp. Tübingen: M. Niemeyer Verlag, 1998.

Vastovius, Johannes. *Vitis aqvilonia*. In *S:ta Elin av Skövde - kulten, källorna, kvinnan*, edited by Sven-Erik Pernler, Anders Piltz, Jan Brunius, and Johnny Hagberg, 237–42. Skara: Skara stiftshistoriska sällskap, 2007.

Visser, Gerard. "Een Mynlike vuerighe begerte der ynniger zielen tot horen ghemynden here." *Nederlands archief voor kerkgeschiedenis*, Band 1 Heft 3 (1902).

Wackernagel, Wilhelm. *Altdeutsche Predigten und Gebete aus Handschriften*. Hildesheim: G. Olms, 1964.

Waterworth, James. *The canons and decrees of the sacred and ecumenical Council of Trent, celebrated under the sovereign pontiffs, Paul III, Julius III and Pius IV*. London: C. Dolman, 1848.

Wiesner, Merry E., trans. and ed. *Convents Confront the Reformation: Catholic and Protestant Nuns in Germany*. Women of the Reformation. Vol. 1. Milwaukee: Marquette University Press, 1996.

Williams, Ulla and Werner Williams-Krapp. "Eine Warnung an Alle, Dy Sych Etwaz Duncken. Der 'Sendbrief Vom Betrug Teuflischer Erscheinungen' (Mit Einer Edition)." In *Forschungen Zur Deutschen Literatur Des Spätmittelalters. Festschrift Für Johannes Janota*, edited by Horst Brunner and Werner Williams-Krapp. Tübingen: Max Niemeyer Verlag, Imprint von de Gruyter, 2003.

Catalogues

Deschamps en H. Mulder. *Inventaris van de Middelnederlandse handschriften van de Koninklijke Bibliotheek van België*. Vol. 10. Brussels, 1998–. http://belgica.kbr.be/nl/coll/ouvRef/ouvRefCatal_nl.html.

Die Deutsche Literatur Des Mittelalters: Verfasserlexikon (VL). Edited by Wolfgang Stammler, Karl Langosch, and Kurt Ruh. 14 vols. Berlin: De Gruyter, 1978–2008.

Frings, Jutta and Jan Gerchow, eds. "Krone Und Schleier: Kunst Aus Mittelalterlichen Frauenklöstern: Ruhrlandmuseum, Die Frühen Klöster Und Stifte 500–1200: Kunst-Und Ausstellungshalle Der Bundesrepublik Deutschland, Die Zeit Der Orden 1200–1500." München: Hirmer, 2005.

Frühmorgen-Voss, Hella and Norbert H. Ott. "Katalog der Deutschsprachigen Illustrierten Handschriften des Mittelalters." München: In Kommission bei der C.H. Beck'schen Verlagsbuchhandlung, 1986.

Hoffmann, Werner J. *Die deutschsprachigen mittelalterlichen Handschriften der Sächsischen Landesbibliothek - Staats- und Universitätsbibliothek (SLUB) Dresden*. Vol. 132, 462.

Palmer, Nigel F. and Andrew Honey. "Cantica Canticorum." In *A Catalogue of Books Printed in the Fifteenth Century now in the Bodleian Library, Oxford*, edited by Alan Coates. Oxford: Oxford University Press, 2005.

Bibliography
237

Schneider, Karin. *Die deutschen Handschriften der Bayerischen Staatsbibliothek München. CGM 201–350.* Catalogus codicum manu scriptorum Bibliothecae Monacensis V, 2. Wiesbaden, 1970.

Wüstefeld, Helen C. and Anne S. Korteweg. *Sleutel tot licht: getijdenboeken in de Bibliotheca Philosophica Hermetica.* Amsterdam: In de Pelikaan, 2009.

Scholarly Studies

Allen, Peter L. *The Art of Love: Amatory Fiction from Ovid to the Romance of the Rose.* Philadelphia: University of Pennsylvania Press, 1992.

Antier, Jean Jacques. *Le Mysticisme Féminin: Épouses Du Christ.* Paris: Librairie académique Perrin, 2001.

Areford, David S. *The Viewer and the Printed Image in Late Medieval Europe.* Burlington, VT: Ashgate, 2010.

Astell, Ann W. *The Song of Songs in the Middle Ages.* Ithaca: Cornell University Press, 1990.

Atwood, Craig D. *Community of the Cross: Moravian Piety in Colonial Bethlehem.* University Park: Pennsylvania State University Press, 2004.

Badel, P.-Y. "Pierre d'Ailly, auteur du 'Jardin amoureux.'" *Romania* 97 (1976): 369–81.

Baumann, Gerlinde. *Love and Violence: Marriage as Metaphor for the Relationship between Yhwh and Israel in the Prophetic Books.* Collegeville, MN: Liturgical Press, 2003.

Berger, Kurt. *Die Ausdrücke der Unio mystica im Mittelhochdeutschen. Berlin, 1935.* Nendeln: Kraus Reprint, 1967.

Berlinerblau, Jacques. "Max Weber's Useful Ambiguities and the Problem of Defining 'Popular Religion.'" *Journal of the American Academy of Religion* 69, no. 3 (2001): 605–26.

Bernards, Matthäus. *Speculum Virginum: Geistigkeit Und Seelenleben Der Frau Im Hochmittelalter.* 2.unveränderte Aufl. ed. Beihefte Zum Archiv Für Kulturgeschichte, Heft 16. Köln: Böhlau Verlag, 1955.

Bilinkoff, Jodi. *The Avila of Saint Teresa: Religious Reform in a Sixteenth-Century City.* Ithaca: Cornell University Press, 1989.

Blick, Sarah and Rita Tekippe. *Art and Architecture of Late Medieval Pilgrimage in Northern Europe and the British Isles.* Leiden: Brill, 2005.

Bollmann, Anne. "'Being a woman on my own': Alijt Bake (1415–1455) as Reformer of the Inner Self." In *Seeing and Knowing: Women and Learning in Medieval Europe 1200–1550*, edited by Anneke B. Mulder-Bakker, 67–96. Turnhout: Brepols, 2004.

——. *Frauenleben und Frauenliteratur in der Devotio moderna: Volkssprachige Schwesternbücher in literarhistorischer Perspektive.* Groningen: Rijksuniversiteit Groningen, 2004.

Bornstein, Daniel Ethan. *Medieval Christianity.* Minneapolis, MN: Fortress Press, 2009.

Brand, Margit. *Studien zu Johannes Niders deutschen Schriften*. Institutum Historicum Fratrum Praedicatorum Romae. Dissertationes Historicae 23. Rome, 1998.

Brandenbarg, Ton. "Heilig familieleven: Verspreiding en waardering van de historie van Sint-Anna in de stedelijke cultuur in de Nederlanden en het Rijnland aan het begin van de moderne tijd (15de/16de eeuw)." PhD dissertation, University of Amsterdam/Universiteit van Amsterdam, 1990.

Breul, Wolfgang. "Ehe und Sexualität im radikalen Pietismus." In *Radikale Pietismus: Perspektiven der Forschung*, edited by Wolfgang Breul, Marcus Meier, and Lothar Vogel, 403–18. Göttingen: Vandenhoeck and Ruprecht, 2010.

Brundage, James A. *Law, Sex, and Christian Society in Medieval Europe*. Chicago: University of Chicago Press, 1987.

Bugge, John. *Virginitas: An Essay in the History of a Medieval Ideal*. The Hague: Martinus Nijhoff, 1975.

Burns, E. Jane. *Courtly Love Undressed: Reading Through Clothes in Medieval French Culture*. Philadelphia: University of Pennsylvania Press, 2002.

Burrus, Virginia. *The Sex Lives of Saints: An Erotics of Ancient Hagiography*. Philadelphia: University of Pennsylvania Press, 2004.

———. *Saving Shame: Martyrs, Saints, and Other Abject Subjects*. Philadelphia: University of Pennsylvania Press, 2008.

Bynum, Caroline Walker. *Jesus as Mother: Studies in the Spirituality of the High Middle Ages*. Berkeley: University of California Press, 1982.

———. *Holy Feast and Holy Fast: The Religious Significance of Food to Medieval Women*. New Historicism. Berkeley: University of California Press, 1987.

———. "Wonder." *American Historical Review* 102, no. 1 (1997): 1–17.

———. *Wonderful Blood: Theology and Practice in Late Medieval Northern Germany and Beyond*. Philadelphia: University of Pennsylvania Press, 2007.

———. "Patterns of Female Piety in the Later Middle Ages." In *Crown and Veil: Female Monasticism from the Fifth to the Fifteenth Centuries*, edited by Jeffrey F. Hamburger and Susan Marti, 172–90. New York: Columbia University Press, 2008.

Camille, Michael. "The Image and the Self: Unwriting Late Medieval Bodies." In *Framing Medieval Bodies*, edited by Sarah Kay and Miri Rubin, 62–99. Manchester: Manchester University Press, 1994.

———. *The Medieval Art of Love: Objects and Subjects of Desire*. New York: Abrams, 1998.

Carlson, David R. "Structural Similarities between the Literatures of Mysticism and *Fin'amors*." PhD dissertation, University of Toronto, 1984.

Carqué, Bernd and Hedwig Röckelein, eds. *Das Hochaltarretabel der St. Jacobi-Kirche in Göttingen*. Göttingen: Vandenhoeck and Ruprecht, 2008.

Certeau, Michel de. *The Mystic Fable*. Religion and Postmodernism. Chicago: University of Chicago Press, 1992.

———. *The Possession at Loudun*. Translated by Michael B. Smith. Chicago: University of Chicago Press, 2000.

Chidester, David. *Authentic Fakes: Religion and American Popular Culture*. Berkeley: University of California Press, 2005.

Clark, Elizabeth A. "The Celibate Bridegroom and His Virginal Brides: Metaphor and the Marriage of Jesus in Early Christian Ascetic Exegesis." *Church History* 77, no. 1 (2008): 1–25.

Clark, Emily. "She's the Four-Leaf Clover in the City Katrina Turned Over: The Historical Sister Gertrude Morgan and Her Post-Hurricane Katrina Specters." MA thesis, University of Missouri-Columbia, 2009.

Clarke, Elizabeth. "'The Glorious Lover': Baptist Literature of the 1680s and the Bride of Christ." *Baptist Quarterly* 43, no. 8 (2010): 452–72.

Classen, Albrecht, ed. *Discourses on Love, Marriage, and Transgression in Medieval and Early Modern Literature*. Tempe: Arizona Center for Medieval and Renaissance Studies, 2004.

Coakley, John Wayland. *Women, Men, and Spiritual Power: Female Saints and Their Male Collaborators*. New York: Columbia University Press, 2006.

Cohen, Jeremy. "Synagoga Conversa: Honorius Augustodunensis, the Song of Songs, and Christianity's 'Eschatological Jew.'" *Speculum* 79, no. 2 (2004): 309.

Constable, Giles. "The Ceremonies and Symbolism of Entering Religious Life and Taking the Monastic Habit from the Fourth to the Twelfth Century." In *Segni e riti nella chiesa altomedioevale occidentale* (Spoleto: Presso la sede del Centro, 1987): 771–834.

Cooper, Kate. *The Virgin and the Bride: Idealized Womanhood in Late Antiquity*. Cambridge, MA: Harvard University Press, 1996.

Curschmann, Michael. "Imagined Exegesis: Text and Picture in the Exegetical Works of Rupert of Deutz, Honorius Augustodunensis, and Gerhoch of Reichersberg." *Traditio: Studies in Ancient and Medieval History, Thought, and Religion* (1988): 145–69.

Cyrus, Cynthia J. *The Scribes for Women's Convents in Late Medieval Germany*. Toronto: University of Toronto Press, 2009.

Déchanet, William and Jean Déchanet. *Exposition on the Song of Songs*. Spencer, MA: Cistercian Publications, 1970.

Decker, John. *The Technology of Salvation and the Art of Geertgen tot Sint Jans*. Burlington, VT: Ashgate, 2009.

DeRogatis, Amy. "'Born Again Is a Sexual Term': Demons, STDs, and God's Healing Sperm." *Journal of the American Academy of Religion* 77, no. 2 (2009): 275–302.

Dinzelbacher, Peter. *Heilige Oder Hexen? Shicksale Auffalliger Frauen in Mittelalter Und Fruhneuzeit*. Zurich: Artemis and Winkler, 1995.

DuBois, Thomas A. *Sanctity in the North: Saints, Lives, and Cults in Medieval Scandinavia*. Toronto; Buffalo, NY: University of Toronto Press, 2008.

Duby, Georges. *Medieval Marriage: Two Models from Twelfth-Century France*. Translated by Elborg Forster. Baltimore: Johns Hopkins University Press, 1978.

Duffy, Eamon. *The Stripping of the Altars: Traditional Religion in England, c. 1400–c. 1580*. New Haven, CT: Yale University Press, 1992.

240 *Marrying Jesus in Medieval and Early Modern Northern Europe*

Durkheim, Émile. *The Elementary Forms of Religious Life*. Translated by Karen E. Fields. New York: The Free Press, 1995.

Dusar, L. "Het Huwelijk in De Vlaamse Schilderkunst." *Vlaanderen: Tweemaandelijks tijdschrift voor kunst en letteren* 24, no. 145 (1975).

Ehrenschwendtner, Marie-Luise. *Die Bildung Der Dominikanerinnen in Süddeutschland Vom 13. Bis 15. Jahrhundert*. Stuttgart: Steiner, 2004.

Eichler, Wolfgang. *Van den blinckenden Steen in oberdeutscher Texttradition by Jan Van Ruusbroec*. München: W. Fink, 1968.

Eisenstein, Elizabeth L. *The Printing Press as an Agent of Change: Communications and Cultural Transformations in Early Modern Europe*. Cambridge: Cambridge University Press, 1979.

Eliade, Mircea. *The Sacred and the Profane: The Nature of Religion*. Translated by Willard R. Trask. Orlando: Harcourt, 1987.

Elliott, Dyan. *Spiritual Marriage: Sexual Abstinence in Medieval Wedlock*. Princeton, NJ: Princeton University Press, 1993.

————. *Proving Woman: Female Spirituality and Inquisitional Culture in the Later Middle Ages*. Princeton, NJ: Princeton University Press, 2004.

————. *The Bride of Christ Goes to Hell: Metaphor and Embodiment in the Lives of Pious Women, 200–1500*. Philadelphia: University of Pennsylvania Press, 2012.

Evangelisti, Silvia. "Wives, Widows, and Brides of Christ: Marriage and the Convent in the Historiography of Early Modern Italy." *The Historical Journal* 43, no. 1 (2000): 233–47.

Fagaly, William A. et al., eds. *Tools of Her Ministry: The Art of Sister Gertude Morgan*. New York: Rizzoli International Publications, 2004.

Falkenburg, Reindert Leonard. *The Fruit of Devotion: Mysticism and the Imagery of Love in Flemish Paintings of the Virgin and Child, 1450–1550*. Philadelphia: John Benjamins, 1994.

Faull, Katherine M. "Christ's Other Self: Gender, the Body, and Religion in the Eighteenth-Century Moravian Church." *Covenant Quarterly* 62, no. 4 (2004): 28–41.

Fenten, Sandra. *Mystik Und Körperlichkeit: Eine Komplementär-Vergleichende Lektüre Von Heinrich Seuses Geistlichen Schriften*. Würzburg: Königshausen and Neumann, 2007.

Fleurkens, Anneke C.G. "Leren Met Lust. Coornherts Toneelspelen." In *Dirck Volckertszoon Coornhert. Dwars Maar Recht*, edited by Hendrik Bonger, 80–97. Zutphen: De Walburg Pers, 1989.

Fogleman, Aaron Spencer. *Jesus is Female: Moravians and the Challenge of Radical Religion in Early America*. Philadelphia: University of Pennsylvania Press, 2007.

Friedman, Jerome. "Their Name Was God: Religious Charlatans in the Seventeenth-Century English Popular Press." *The Journal of Popular Culture* 25, no. 1 (1991): 55–66.

Friesen, Ilse E. *The Female Crucifix: Images of St. Wilgefortis since the Middle Ages*. Waterloo, ON: Wilfrid Laurier University Press, 2001.

Bibliography

Garber, Rebecca L.R. *Feminine Figurae: Representations of Gender in Religious Texts by Medieval German Women Writers 1100–1375*. London: Routledge, 2003.

Gebauer, Amy. *"Christus Und Die Minnende Seele": An Analysis of Circulation, Text, and Iconography*. Wiesbaden: Reichert Verlag, 2010.

Gillespie, Katharine. *Domesticity and Dissent in the Seventeenth Century: English Women Writers and the Public Sphere*. Cambridge: Cambridge University Press, 2004.

Gillespie, Michele and Robert Beachy, eds. *Pious Pursuits: German Moravians in the Atlantic World*. New York: Berghahn Books, 2007.

Ginzburg, Carlo. *The Cheese and the Worms: The Cosmos of a Sixteenth-Century Miller*. Baltimore: Johns Hopkins University Press, 1980.

Godbeer, Richard. "'Love Raptures': Marital, Romantic, and Erotic Images of Jesus Christ in Puritan New England, 1670–1730." *The New England Quarterly* 68, no. 3 (1995): 355–84.

Grabes, Herbert. *The Mutable Glass: Mirror Imagery in Titles and Texts of the Middle Ages and Engilsh Renaissance*. Cambridge: Cambridge University Press, 1982.

Graziano, Frank. *Wounds of Love: The Mystical Marriage of Saint Rose of Lima*. Oxford: Oxford University Press, 2004.

Green, D.H. *Medieval Listening and Reading: The Primary Reception of German Literature, 800–1300*. Cambridge; New York: Cambridge University Press, 1994.

Green, John D. *A Strange Tongue: Tradition, Language, and the Appropriation of Mystical Experience in Late Fourteenth-Century England and Sixteenth-Century Spain*. Leuven: Peeters, 2002.

Greenhill, Eleanor Simmons. *Die geistigen Voraussetzungen der Bilderreihe des Speculum virginum; Versuch einer Deutung*. Münster: Aschendorff, 1962.

Greenspan, Karen. "Erklaerung des Vaterunsers: A Critical Edition of a Fifteenth-century Mystical Treatise by Magdalena Beutler of Freiburg." PhD dissertation, University of Massachusetts-Amherst, 1984.

Gregory, Rabia. "Thinking of their Sisters: Authority and Authorship in Late Medieval Women's Religious Communities." *Journal of Medieval Religious Cultures* 40, no. 1 (2014): 75–100.

Griese, Sabine. *Text-Bilder und ihre Kontexte: Medialität und Materialität von Einblatt-Holz-und-Metallschnitten des 15. Jahrhunderts*. Zürich: Chronos, 2011.

Griffith, R. Marie. *God's Daughters: Evangelical Women and the Power of Submission*. Berkeley: University of California Press 1997.

Griffiths, Fiona J. *The Garden of Delights: Reform and Renaissance for Women in the Twelfth Century*. Middle Ages Series. Philadelphia: University of Pennsylvania Press, 2007.

Grundmann, Herbert. *Religious movements in the Middle Ages: The historical links between heresy, the Mendicant Orders, and the women's religious movement in*

242 *Marrying Jesus in Medieval and Early Modern Northern Europe*

the twelfth and thirteenth century, with the historical foundations of German mysticism. Translated by Steven Rowan. Notre Dame, IN: University of Notre Dame Press, 1995.

Gurevich, Aron. *Medieval Popular Culture: Problems of Belief and Perception.* Translated by János M. Bak and Paul A. Hollingsworth. Cambridge: Cambridge University Press, 1988.

Hamburger, Jeffrey F. "The Use of Images in the Pastoral Care of Nuns: The Case of Heinrich Suso and the Dominicans." *The Art Bulletin* 71, no. 1 (1989): 20–46.

———. *The Rothschild Canticles: Art and Mysticism in Flanders and the Rhineland Circa 1300.* Yale Publications in the History of Art. New Haven, CT: Yale University Press, 1990.

———. *Nuns as Artists: The Visual Culture of a Medieval Convent.* Berkeley: University of California Press, 1997.

———. *The Visual and the Visionary: Art and Female Spirituality in Late Medieval Germany.* New York: Zone Books; MIT Press, 1998.

———. *St. John the Divine: The Deified Evangelist in Medieval Art and Theology.* Berkeley: University of California Press, 2002.

———, ed. *Frauen - Kloster - Kunst: Neue Forschungen Zur Kulturgeschichte Des Mittelalters: Beiträge Zum Internationalen Kolloquium Vom 13. Bis 16. Mai 2005 Anlässlich Der Ausstellung "Krone Und Schleier".* Turnhout: Brepols, 2007.

———. "Overkill, or History That Hurts." *Common Knowledge* 13, no. 2–3 (2007): 404–28.

Hamburger, Jeffrey F. and Anne-Marie Bouché. *The Mind's Eye: Art and Theological Argument in the Middle Ages.* Princeton, NJ: Princeton University Press, 2006.

Hamburger, Jeffrey F. and Susan Marti. *Crown and Veil: Female Monasticism from the Fifth to the Fifteenth Centuries.* New York: Columbia University Press, 2008.

Hamm, Berndt. *The Reformation of Faith in the Context of Late Medieval Theology and Piety: Essays by Berndt Hamm.* Leiden: Brill, 2004.

Harrington, Joel F. *Reordering Marriage and Society in Reformation Germany.* Cambridge: Cambridge University Press, 1995.

Hart, Columba, OSB. "*Consecratio Virginum*: Thirteenth-Century Witnesses." *The American Benedictine Review* 23, no. 2 (1972): 258–74.

Hasebrink, Burkhard. "Ein Einic Ein. Zur Darstellbarkeit Der Liebeseinheit in Mittelhochdeutscher Literatur." *Beiträge zur Geschichte der deutschen Sprache und Literatur* 124, no. 3 (2002): 442–65.

Heiland-Justi, Werner. *Elisabeth: Königstochter von Ungarn, Landgräfin von Thüringen und Heilige: "diese fröwe ist gewesen törlich wise und wiszklich torecht."* Lindenberg: Fink, 2007.

Henking, Susan, "Queering Easter: The Sisters of Perpetual Indulgence Redefine Sainthood." *Religion Dispatches.* April 2, 2010. Accessed May 18, 2013. http://www.religiondispatches.org/archive/sexandgender/2354/queering_easter__the_sisters_of_perpetual_indulgence_redefine_sainthood.

Bibliography 243

Heslop, T.A. "The English Origins of the Coronation of the Virgin." *The Burlington Magazine* 147, no. 1233, Sculpture (Dec. 2005): 790–97.

Hess, Cordelia. *Heilige Machen Im Spätmittelalterlichen Ostseeraum: Die Kanonisationsprozesse Von Birgitta Von Schweden, Nikolaus Von Linköping Und Dorothea Von Montau.* Berlin: Akademie Verlag, 2008.

Hindsley, Leonard Patrick. *The Mystics of Engelthal: Writings from a Medieval Monastery.* New York: St. Martin's Press, 1998.

Holloway, Julia Bolton. *Saint Bride and Her Book: Birgitta of Sweden's Revelations.* Newburyport, MA: Focus Texts, 1992.

Hollywood, Amy M. *The Soul as Virgin Wife: Mechthild of Magdeburg, Marguerite Porete, and Meister Eckhart.* Notre Dame, IN: University of Notre Dame, 1995.

———. *Sensible Ecstasy: Mysticism, Sexual Difference, and the Demands of History.* Religion and Postmodernism. Chicago: University of Chicago Press, 2002.

———. "Queering the Beguines: Mechthild of Magdeburg, Hadewijch of Anvers, Marguerite Porete." In *Queer Theology: Rethinking the Western Body*, edited by Gerard Loughlin, 163–75. Malden, MA; Oxford: Basil Blackwell, 2007.

Hoover, Stewart M. *Religion in the Media Age.* London; New York: Routledge, 2006.

Hummel, Regine. *Mystische Modelle im 12. Jahrhundert: St. Trudperter Hoheslied, Bernard von Clairvaux, Wilhelm von St. Thierry.* Göppingen: Kümmerle, 1989.

Irigaray, Luce. *Speculum of the Other Woman.* Ithaca: Cornell University Press, 1985.

James, William. *The Varieties of Religious Experience.* Cambridge, MA: Harvard University Press, 1985.

Jantzen, Grace M. "Mysticism and Experience." *Religious Studies* 25, no. 3 (1989): 295–315.

Jaye, Barbara H. *The Pilgrimage of Prayer: The Texts and Iconography of the Exercitium Super Pater Noster.* Salzburg: Institut für Anglistik und Amerikanistik Universität Salzburg, 1990.

Jenkins, Henry. *Convergence Culture: Where Old and New Media Collide.* New York: New York University Press, 2006.

Johnston, Warren. "Prophecy, Patriarchy, and Violence in the Early Modern Household: The Revelations of Anne Wentworth." *Journal of Family History* 34, no. 4 (2009): 344–68.

Jundt, Auguste. *Histoire du panthéisme populaire au Moyen Age et au seizième siècle (suivie de pièces inédites concernant les Frères du libre esprit, maître Eckhart, les libertins spirituels, etc.) Paris 1875.* Frankfurt am Main: Minerva, 1964.

Kieckhefer, Richard. *Unquiet Souls: Fourteenth-Century Saints and Their Religious Milieu.* Chicago: University of Chicago Press, 1984.

Keller, Hildegard Elisabeth. *Wort und Fleisch: Körperallegorien, mystische Spiritualität und Dichtung des St. Trudperter Hoheliedes im Horizont der Inkarnation.* Frankfurt am Main; New York: P. Lang, 1993.

244 *Marrying Jesus in Medieval and Early Modern Northern Europe*

————. "Die minnende Seele in des Teufels Netz. Geschlechterpolemik kontrafaziert." In *Text im Kontext: Anleitung zur Lektüre deutscher Texte der frühen Neuzeit*, edited by Alexander Schwarz and Laure Ablanalp, 109–26. Bern: Lang, 1997.

————. *My Secret Is Mine: Studies on Religion and Eros in the German Middle Ages*. Studies in Spirituality, Supplement, 4. Leuven: Peeters, 2000.

Kessler, Michael and Christian Sheppard. *Mystics: Presence and Aporia*. Chicago: University of Chicago Press, 2003.

King, J. Christopher. *Origen on the Song of Songs as the Spirit of Scripture: The Bridegroom's Perfect Marriage-Song*. Oxford: Oxford University Press, 2005.

King, Richard. *Orientalism and Religion: Postcolonial Theory, India and 'The Mystic East.'* London: Routledge, 1999.

Kingma, Eloe. *De mooiste onder de vrouwen: een onderzoek naar religieuze idealen in twaalfde-eeuwse commentaren op het Hooglied*. Hilversum: Verloren, 1993.

Klaniczay, Gábor. *Holy Rulers and Blessed Princesses: Dynastic Cults in Medieval Central Europe*. Cambridge: Cambridge University Press, 2002.

Kleinberg, Aviad M. *Prophets in Their Own Country: Living Saints and the Making of Sainthood in the Later Middle Ages*. Chicago: University of Chicago Press, 1992.

Klug, Martina B. *Armut und Arbeit in der Devotio moderna: Studien zum Leben der Schwestern in niederrheinischen Gemeinschaften*. Münster: Waxmann, 2005.

Kreitzer, Beth. "Menno Simons and the Bride of Christ." *Mennonite Quarterly Review* 70, no. 3 (1996): 299–318.

Kuefler, Mathew. *The Boswell Thesis: Essays on Christianity, Social Tolerance, and Homosexuality*. Chicago: University of Chicago Press, 2006.

Küsters, Urban. *Der Verschlossene Garten: Volkssprachliche Hohelied-Auslegung Und Monastische Lebensform Im 12. Jahrhundert*. Studia Humaniora, Bd. 2. Düsseldorf: Droste, 1985.

Ladurie, Emmanuel Le Roy. *Montaillou: Cathars and Catholics in a French village, 1294–1324*. London: Scolar Press, 1978.

Lahaye-Geusen, Maria. *Das Opfer der Kinder: Dienst und Leben der pueri oblati im hohen Mittelalter. Ein Beitrag zur Liturgie und zur Sozialgeschichte des Mönchtums*. Münsteraner theologische Abhandlungen, no. 13. Althenberge: Oros, 1991.

Latour, Bruno. *Reassembling the Social: An Introduction to Actor-Network-Theory*. Oxford: Oxford University Press, 2005.

Lavin, Marilyn Aronberg and Irving Lavin. *The Liturgy of Love: Images from the Song of Songs in the Art of Cimabue, Michelangelo, and Rembrandt*. Lawrence: Spencer Museum of Art, University of Kansas, 2001.

Lavrín, Asunción. *Brides of Christ: Conventual Life in Colonial Mexico*. Stanford: Stanford University Press, 2008.

Lee, Becky R. "The Treatment of Women in the Historiography of Late Medieval Popular Religion." *Method & Theory in the Study of Religion* 8, no. 4 (1996): 345–60.

Bibliography 245

Lehfeldt, Elizabeth A. *Religious Women in Golden Age Spain: The Permeable Cloister*. Burlington, VT: Ashgate, 2005.

Leonard, Amy. *Nails in the Wall: Catholic Nuns in Reformation Germany*. Women in Culture and Society. Chicago: University of Chicago Press, 2005.

Lerner, Robert E. *The Heresy of the Free Spirit in the Later Middle Ages*. Berkeley: University of California Press, 1972.

Lewis, Gertrud Jaron. *By Women, for Women, About Women: The Sister-Books of Fourteenth-Century Germany*. Toronto: Pontifical Institute of Mediaeval Studies, 1996.

Lewis, Katherin J. "Model Girls? Virgin-Martyrs and the Training of Young Women in Late Medieval England." In *Young Medieval Women*, edited by Katherin J. Lewis, Nöel James Menuge, and Kim M. Phillips, 25–46. New York: St. Martin's Press, 1999.

Lie, Orlanda S.H. "Middelnederlandse Literatuur Vanuit Genderperspectief: Een Verkenning." *Tijdschrift voor Nederlandse taal- en letterkunde* 117, no. 3 (2001): 246–67.

Lindgren, Erika Lauren. *Sensual Encounters: Monastic Women and Spirituality in Medieval Germany*. New York: Columbia University Press, 2009.

Lipton, Emma. *Affections of the Mind: The Politics of Sacramental Marriage in Late Medieval English Literature*. Notre Dame, IN: University of Notre Dame Press, 2007.

Lochrie, Karma. *Margery Kempe and Translations of the Flesh*. Philadelphia: University of Pennsylvania Press, 1991.

Lochrie, Karma, Peggy McCracken, and James Schultz, eds. *Constructing Medieval Sexuality*. Minneapolis: University of Minnesota Press, 1997.

Long, Charles H. "Popular Religion." In *Encyclopedia of Religion*, edited by Lindsay Jones. 2nd ed. Vol. 11, 7324–33. Detroit: Macmillan Reference USA. *Gale Virtual Reference Library*. Web. Accessed October 3, 2012.

Loughlin, Gerard, ed. *Queer Theology: Rethinking the Western Body*. Malden, MA; Oxford: Blackwell, 2007.

Lowe, Kate. "Secular Brides and Convent Brides: Wedding Ceremonies in Italy During the Renaissance and Counter-Reformation." In *Marriage in Italy, 1300–1650*, edited by Trevor Dean and Kate Lowe. Cambridge: Cambridge University Press, 1999.

Lücker, Maria Alberta. *Meister Eckhart Und Die Devotio Moderna*. Studien Und Texte Zur Geistesgeschichte Des Mittelalters; Bd. 1. Leiden: E.J. Brill, 1950.

Luxon, Thomas H. "'Not I, But Christ': Allegory and the Puritan Self." *English Literary History* 60, no. 4 (1993): 899–937.

———. *Literal Figures: Puritan Allegory and the Reformation Crisis in Representation*. Chicago: University of Chicago Press, 1995.

Mack, Phyllis. "Women as Prophets during the English Civil War." *Feminist Studies* 8, no. 1 (1982): 19–45.

Mahmood, Saba. *Politics of Piety: The Islamic Revival and the Feminist Subject*. Princeton, NJ: Princeton University Press, 2005.

246 *Marrying Jesus in Medieval and Early Modern Northern Europe*

Marsh, Christopher W. *Popular Religion in Sixteenth-Century England: Holding Their Peace*. New York: St. Martin's Press, 1998.

Matter, Anne E. *The Voice of My Beloved: The Song of Songs in Western Medieval Christianity*. Philadelphia: University of Pennsylvania Press, 1990.

————. "Mystical Marriage." In *Women and Faith: Catholic Religious Life in Italy from Late Antiquity to the Present*, edited by Lucetta Scaraffia and Gabriella Zarri, 30–41. Cambridge, MA: Harvard University Press, 1999.

McAvoy, Liz Herbert. *Authority and the Female Body in the Writings of Julian of Norwich and Margery Kempe*. Woodbridge, Suffolk; Rochester, NY: D.S. Brewer, 2004.

McClary, Susan. *Desire and Pleasure in Seventeenth-century Music*. Berkeley: University of California Press, 2012.

McGinn, Bernard. *Meister Eckhart and the Beguine Mystics: Hadewijch of Brabant, Mechthild of Magdeburg, and Marguerite Porete*. New York: Continuum, 1994.

————. *The Flowering of Mysticism: Men and Women in the New Mysticism (1200–1350)*. Vol. 3. New York: Crossroad Herder, 1999.

————. "The Problem of Mystical Union in Eckhart, Seuse, and Tauler." In *Meister Eckhart in Erfurt*, edited by A. Speer and L. Wegener, Miscellanea Mediaevallia 32, 538–53. Berlin: De Gruyter, 2005.

————. "Theologians as Trinitarian Iconographers." In *The Mind's Eye: Art and Theological Argument in the Middle Ages*, edited by Jeffrey F. Hamburger and Anne-Marie Bouché. Princeton, NJ: Princeton University Press, 2006.

————. "Mystical Consciousness: A Modest Proposal." *Spiritus* 8 (2008): 44–63.

McNamara, Jo Ann. *Sisters in Arms: Catholic Nuns through Two Millennia*. Cambridge, MA: Harvard University Press, 1996.

McNamer, Sarah. *The Two Middle English Translations of the Revelations of St. Elizabeth of Hungary: ed. from Cambridge University Library MS Hh.i.11 and Wynkyn de Worke's printed text of ?1493*. Heidelberg: Universitätsverlag C. Winter, 1996.

Meiss, Millard. *Painting in Florence and Siena after the Black Death*. Princeton, NJ: Princeton University Press, 1951.

Meister, Peter. "Suso's (?) Minnebüchlein." *Mystics Quarterly* 15, no. 3 (1989): 125–32.

Mellink, Albert F. *De Wederdopers in de noordelijke Nederlanden 1531–1544*. Groningen: J.B. Wolters, 1954.

Mertens, Thomas. "Mystieke Cultuur En Literatuur in De Late Middeleeuwen." In *Grote Lijnen: Syntheses over Middelnederlandse Letterkunde*, edited by F.P. van Oostrom and W. van Anrooij, 11, 117–35. Amsterdam: Prometheus, 1995.

————. "*Die Gheestelicke Melody*: A Program for the Spiritual Life in a Middle Dutch Song Cycle." In *Women and Experience in Later Medieval Writing: Reading the Book of Life*, edited by Anneke B. Mulder-Bakker and Liz Herbert McAvoy, 123–48. New York: Palgrave Macmillan, 2009.

Metz, René. *La consécration des vierges dans l'église Romaine: Étude d'histoire de la liturgie*. Paris: Presses Universitaires de France, 1945.

Miles, Margaret R. *A Complex Delight: The Secularization of the Breast, 1350–1750*. Berkeley: University of California Press, 2008.

Monteiro, M.E. *Geestelijke maagden: leven tussen klooster en wereld in Noord-Nederland gedurende de zeventiende eeuw*. Hilversum: Verloren, 1996.

Moore, Cornelia Niekus. *The Maiden's Mirror: Reading Material for German Girls in the Sixteenth and Seventeenth Centuries*. Vol. Band 36. Wiesbaden: Otto Harrassowitz, 1987.

Morgan, David, ed. *Keywords in Religion, Media, and Culture*. New York: Routledge, 2008.

Morton, Vera. *Guidance for Women in Twelfth-Century Convents*. Rochester, NY: Boydell and Brewer, 2004.

Muir, Carolyn Diskant. "Art and Religion in Seventeenth-Century Antwerp: Van Dyck's 'Mystic Marriage of the Blessed Hermann-Joseph.'" *Simiolus: Netherlands Quarterly for the History of Art* 28, no. 1/2 (2000): 51–69.

———. "Bride or Bridegroom? Masculine Identity in Mystic Marriages." In *Holiness and Masculinity in the Middle Ages*, edited by P.H. Cullum, 58–78. Cardiff: University of Wales, 2004.

———. *Saintly Brides and Bridegrooms: The Mystic Marriage in Northern Renaissance Art*. London: Harvey Miller, 2012.

Mujica, Barbara Louise. *Sister Teresa: The Woman who Became Saint Teresa of Avila*. Woodstock, NY: Overlook Press, 2007.

———. *Teresa de Avila, Lettered Woman*. Nashville: Vanderbilt University Press, 2009.

Nemes, Balázs J. "*Dis buch ist iohannes schedelin*. Die Handschriften eines Colmarer Bürgers aus der Mitte des 15. Jahrhunderts und ihre Verflechtungen mit dem Literaturangebot der Dominikanerobservanz." In *Kulturtopographie des deutschsprachigen Südwestens im späteren Mittelalter. Studien und Texte*, ed. Barbara Fleith and René Wetzel, 157–214. Berlin: De Gruyter, 2009.

Nevitt, H. Rodney. *Art and the Culture of Love in Seventeenth-Century Holland*. Cambridge Studies in Netherlandish Visual Culture. Cambridge; New York: Cambridge University Press, 2003.

Newman, Barbara. *From Virile Woman to WomanChrist: Studies in Medieval Religion and Literature*. Philadelphia: University of Pennsylvania Press, 1995.

———. *God and the Goddesses: Vision, Poetry, and Belief in the Middle Ages*. Philadelphia: University of Pennsylvania Press, 2003.

Nip, Renée. "To Safeguard a Life's work: The Autobiography of Elisabeth Strouven (1600–1661)." In *Ein Platz für sich selbst. Schreibende Frauen und ihre Lebenswelten (1450–1700) / A Place of their own. Women Writers and their Social Environments (1450–1700)*, edited by Anne Bollmann, 215–42. Frankfurt am Main: Peter Lang, 2011.

Noll, Thomas. "Zur Ikonographie des Hochaltarretabels der St. Jacobi-Kirche in Göttingen." In *Das Hochaltarretabel der St. Jacobi-Kirche in Göttingen*, edited by Bernd Carqué and Hedwig Röckelein, 207–47. Göttingen: Vandenhoeck and Ruprecht, 2008.

Ohly, Friedrich. *Hohelied-Studien: Grundzüge einer Geschichte der Hoheliedauslegung des Abendlandes bis um 1200.* Wiesbaden: F. Steiner, 1958.

Oppenheim, Philipp. *Die Consecratio virginum als geistesgeschichtliches Problem, Eine Studie zu ihrem aufbau, ihrem Wert und ehrer Geschichte.* Rome, 1943.

Otto, Rudolph. *The Idea of the Holy: An Inquiry into the Non-Rational Factor in the Idea of the Divine and Its Relation to the Rational.* Translated by John W. Harvey. London: Oxford University Press, 1958.

Palmer, Nigel F. "Das Buch als Bedeutungsträger bei Mechthild von Magdeburg." In *Bildhafte Rede in Mittelalter und früher Neuzeit: Probleme ihrer Legitimation und Funktion,* edited by Wolfgang Harms and Klaus Speckenbach, 142–57. Tübingen: Niemeyer, 1992.

———. "Strasbourg & the History of the Book: Five Centuries of German Printed Books and Manuscripts." Edited by Taylor Institution Library and University of Oxford St Giles', 2009.

———. "Woodcuts for Reading: The Codicology of Fifteenth-Century Blockbooks and Woodcut Cycles." *Studies in the History of Art* 75 (2009): 91–118.

Panofsky, Erwin. "'Imago Pietatis,' Ein Beitrag zur Typengeschichte des 'Schmertzensmannes' und der 'Maria Mediatrix.'" In *Festschrift für Max J. Friedländer zum 60, Geburtstage,* edited by Max J. Friedländer, 261–308. Leipzig: Verlag von E.A. Seemann, 1927.

Parshall, Peter W. *The Woodcut in Fifteenth-Century Europe.* New Haven, CT: National Gallery of Art, Distributed by Yale University Press, 2009.

Parshall, Peter W. and Rainer Schoch. *Origins of European Printmaking: Fifteenth-Century Woodcuts and Their Public.* Washington: National Gallery of Art, in association with Yale University Press, New Haven, CT, 2005.

Partner, Nancy F. "Did Mystics Have Sex?" In *Desire and Discipline: Sex and Sexuality in the Premodern West,* edited by Jacqueline Murray and Konrad Eisenbichler, 296–311. Toronto: University of Toronto Press, 1996.

Pernler, Sven-Erik, Anders Piltz, Jan Brunius, and Johnny Hagberg. *S:ta Elin av Skövde - kulten, källorna, kvinnan.* Skara: Skara stiftshistoriska sällskap, 2007.

Petev, Todor T. "Spiritual Structures in the Netherlandish Blockbook *Canticum canticorum,* ca. 1465." *E-magazine LiterNet* 15, no. 3 (2008). http://liternet. bg/publish17/t_t_petev/spiritual_en.htm.

Petroff, Elizabeth. *Medieval Women's Visionary Literature.* New York: Oxford University Press, 1986.

Peucker, Paul. "The Songs of the Sifting: Understanding the Role of Bridal Mysticism in Moravian Piety During the Late 1740s." *Journal of Moravian History,* no. 3 (2007): 51–87.

Philipowski, Katharina-Silke and Anne Prior. *Anima und Sêle: Darstellungen und Systematisierungen Von Seele Im Mittelalter.* Philologische Studien und Quellen. Berlin: E. Schmidt, 2006.

Pickford, Cedric Edward. *The Song of Songs: A Twelfth-Century French Version.* London: Oxford University Press, 1974.

Bibliography 249

Pipkin, Amanda. "'They were not humans, but devils in human bodies': Depictions of Sexual Violence and Spanish Tyranny as a Means of Fostering Identity in the Dutch Republic." *Journal of Early Modern History* 13, no. 4 (2009): 229–64.

Poole, W. Scott. *Monsters in America: Our Historical Obsession with the Hideous and the Haunting.* Baylor, TX: Baylor University Press, 2011.

Poor, Sara S. "Mechthild von Magdeburg, Gender, and the 'Unlearned Tongue.'" *Journal of Medieval and Early Modern Studies* 31, no. 2 (2001): 213–50.

———. *Mechthild of Magdeburg and Her Book: Gender and the Making of Textual Authority.* Philadelphia: University of Pennsylvania Press, 2004.

Powell, Morgan. "The *Speculum Virginum* and the Audio-Visual Poetics of Women's Religious Instruction." In *Listen, Daughter: The Speculum Virginum and the Formation of Religious Women in the Middle Ages,* edited by Constant J. Mews, The New Middle Ages, 111–35. New York: Palgrave, 2001.

Powers, Kimberly. *Escaping the Vampire: Desperate for the Immortal Hero.* Colorado Springs, CO: David C. Cook, 2009.

Prothero, Stephen R. *American Jesus: How the Son of God Became a National Icon.* New York: Farrar, Straus and Giroux, 2003.

Rambuss, Richard. *Closet Devotions.* Durham, NC: Duke University Press, 1998.

Rath, Wilhelm. *Der Gottesfreund vom Oberland; sein Leben, geschildert auf Grundlage der Urkundenbücher des Johanniterhauses "Zum grünen Wörth" in Strassburg.* Stuttgart: Verlag Freies Geistesleben, 1955.

Reinhard, Wolfgang. "Reformation, Counter-Reformation, and the Early Modern State: A Reassessment." *The Catholic Historical Review* 75, no. 3 (1989): 383–404.

Rémy, Pierre. "Le mariage, signe de l'union du Christ et de l'église: Les ambiguïtés d'une référence symbolique." *Revue des sciences philosophiques et théologiques* 66, no. 3 (1982): 397–415.

Reynolds, Blair and Patricia Heinicke. *The Naked Being of God: Making Sense of Love Mysticism.* Lanham, MD: University Press of America, 2000.

Riccoboni, Bartolomea and Daniel Ethan Bornstein. *Life and Death in a Venetian Convent: The Chronicle and Necrology of Corpus Domini, 1395–1436.* Chicago: University of Chicago Press, 2000.

Ringler, Siegfried. *Viten- Und Offenbarungsliteratur in Frauenklöstern Des Mittelalters: Quellen Und Studien.* Münchener Texte Und Untersuchungen Zur Deutschen Literatur Des Mittelalters, Bd. 72. München: Artemis Verlag, 1980.

Roest, Bert. *Franciscan Literature of Religious Instruction before the Council of Trent.* Leiden: Brill, 2004.

Roper, Lyndal. *The Holy Household: Women and Morals in Reformation Augsburg.* Oxford: Oxford University Press, 1989.

Rose-Lefmann, Deborah A. "Hendrik Herps 'Spiegel der Volkommenheit' in deutscher Sprache: eine überlieferungsgeschichtkiche Edition." Princeton, NJ: Princeton University Press, 1998.

———. "Lady Love, King, Minstrel: Courtly Depiction of Jesus or God in Late-Medieval Vernacular Mystical Literature." In *Arthurian Literature and*

250 *Marrying Jesus in Medieval and Early Modern Northern Europe*

Christianity: Notes from the Twentieth Century, edited by Peter Meister, 141–61. New York: Garland, 1999.

Rubin, Miri. *Medieval Christianity in Practice*. Princeton, NJ: Princeton University Press, 2009.

Rudy, Gordon. *Mystical Language of Sensation in the Later Middle Ages*. Studies in Medieval History and Culture, vol. 14. New York: Routledge, 2002.

Rudy, Kathryn M. "An Illustrated Mid-Fifteenth-Century Primer for a Flemish Girl, British Library, Harley Ms. 3828." *Journal of the Warburg and Courtauld Institutes* 69 (2006): 51–94.

———. "How to Prepare the Bedroom for the Bridegroom." In *Frauen - Kloster - Kunst: Neue Forschungen Zur Kulturgeschichte Des Mittelalters: Beiträge Zum Internationalen Kolloquium Vom 13. Bis 16. Mai 2005 Anlässlich Der Ausstellung "Krone Und Schleier,"* edited by Jeffrey F. Hamburger, 369–78, 505–6. Turnhout: Brepols, 2007.

Salih, Sarah. *Versions of Virginity in Late Medieval England*. Rochester, NY: D.S. Brewer, 2001.

Scheepsma, Wybren. "De Helletocht van Jacomijne Costers (d. 1503)." *Ons Geestelijk Erf* 70 (1996): 157–85.

———. *Deemoed en devotie: de koorvrouwen van Windesheim en hun geschriften*. Amsterdam: Prometheus, 1997.

———. *Medieval Religious Women in the Low Countries: The 'Modern Devotion,' the Canonesses of Windesheim, and Their Writings*. Translated by David F. Johnson. Woodbridge: Boydell Press, 2004.

———. *The Limburg Sermons: Preaching in the Medieval Low Countries at the Turn of the Fourteenth Century*. Edited and translated by David F. Johnson. Leiden: Brill, 2008.

Schepers, Kees. "A Very Old Fly in *Exercitium Super Pater Noster II* in the Bibliothèque national de France." *Quarendo* 29, no. 2 (1999): 79–95.

———. *Bedudinghe op Cantica Canticorum*. 2 vols. Leuven: Peeters, 2006.

Schilling, Heinz. *Konfessionskonflikt und Staatsbildung: eine Fallstudie über das Verhältnis von religiösem und sozialem Wandel in der Frühneuzeit am Beispiel der Grafschaft Lippe*. Gütersloh: Gütersloher Verlagshaus Mohn, 1981.

———. *Religion, Political Culture, and the Emergence of Early Modern Society: Essays in German and Dutch History*. Leiden; New York: E.J. Brill, 1992.

———. *Early Modern European Civilization and its Political and Cultural Dynamics*. Hanover, NH: University Press of New England, 2008.

Schleif, Corine and Volker Schier. *Katerina's Windows: Donation and Devotion, Art and Music, as Heard and Seen through the Writings of a Birgittine Nun*. University Park: Pennsylvania State University Press, 2008.

Schlotheuber, Eva. "Best Clothes and Everyday Attire of Late Medieval Nuns." In *Fashion and Clothing in Late Medieval Europe / Mode und Kleidung im Europa des späten Mittelalters*, edited by Regula Schorta and Rainer Christoph Schwinges, 139–54. Basel: Joint publication of the Abegg-Stiftung, Riggisberg, and Schwabe Verlag, 2010.

Bibliography 251

Schmidt, Wieland. "Die Vierundzwanzig Alten Ottos Von Passau." *Palaestra*, no. 212 (1938): 1–423.

Schmidtke, Dietrich. *Studien Zur Dingallegorischen Erbauungsliteratur Des Spätmittelalters: Am Beispiel Der Gartenallegorie.* Tübingen: Niemeyer, 1982.

Schwab, Francis Mary. *David of Augsburg's 'Paternoster' and the Authenticity of his German Works.* München: C.H. Beck, 1971.

Scribner, Robert W. *For the Sake of Simple Folk: Popular Propaganda for the German Reformation.* Cambridge: Cambridge University Press, 1981.

Seaver, Paul. *Wallington's World: A Puritan Artisan in Seventeenth-Century London.* Stanford: Stanford University Press, 1985.

Sells, Michael Anthony. *Mystical Languages of Unsaying.* Chicago: University of Chicago Press, 1994.

Sepp, Florian, Bettina Wagner, and Stephan Kellner. "Handschriften und Inkunabeln aus süddeutschen Frauenklöstern in der Bayerischen Staatsbibliothek München." In *Nonnen, Kanonissen und Mystikerinnen: Religiöse Frauengemeinschaften in Süddeutschland,* edited by Eva Schlotheuber, Helmut Flachenecker, and Ingrid Gardill, 317–72. Göttingen: Vandenhoeck and Ruprecht, 2008.

Shinners, John Raymond. *Medieval Popular Religion, 1000–1500: A Reader.* Peterborough: Broadview Press, 1997.

Simons, Walter. *Cities of Ladies: Beguine Communities in the Medieval Low Countries, 1200–1565.* Philadelphia: University of Pennsylvania Press, 2001.

Sluhovsky, Moshe. *Believe Not Every Spirit: Possession, Mysticism, & Discernment in Early Modern Catholicism.* Chicago: University of Chicago Press, 2007.

Smith, Susan L. "The Bride Stripped Bare: A Rare Type of the Disrobing of Christ." *Gesta* 34, no. 2 (1995): 126–46.

Spitz, Hans-Jörg. "Spiegel der Bräute Gottes. Das Modell der Vita Activa und Vita Contemplativa als Strukturierendes Prinzip im St. Trudperter Hohen Lied." In *Abendländische Mystik Im Mittelalter. Symposion Kloster Engelberg 1984,* edited by Kurt Ruh (Germanistische Symposien Berichtsbände, 7). Stuttgart: J.B. Metzlersche Verlagsbuchhandlung, 1986.

Steinberg, Leo. *The Sexuality of Christ in Renaissance Art and in Modern Oblivion,* 2nd ed. Chicago: University of Chicago Press, 1997.

Strasser, Ulrike. *State of Virginity: Gender, Religion, and Politics in an Early Modern Catholic State.* Ann Arbor: University of Michigan Press, 2004.

Stronks, Els. *Negotiating Differences: Word, Image and Religion in the Dutch Republic.* Leiden: Brill, 2011.

———. "Never to Coincide: The Identities of Dutch Protestants and Dutch Catholics in Religious Emblematics." *Journal of Historians of Netherlandish Art* 3, no. 2 (2011). http://www.jhna.org/index.php/past-issues/volume-3-issue-2/144-stronks-never-to-coincide.

Tinsley, David Fletcher. *The Scourge and the Cross: Ascetic Mentalities of the Later Middle Ages.* Paris: Peeters, 2010.

252 *Marrying Jesus in Medieval and Early Modern Northern Europe*

Turner, Denys. *Eros and Allegory: Medieval Exegesis of the Song of Songs*, Cistercian Studies 156. Kalamazoo, MI: Cistercian Publications, 1995.

Van Engen, John H. *Sisters and Brothers of the Common Life: The Devotio Moderna and the World of the Later Middle Ages*. Middle Ages Series. Philadelphia: University of Pennsylvania Press, 2008.

Vandenabeele, Bart. "Strelend wonden helen: over Hadewijch, erotiek en esthetiek." *Uil van Minerva (De): Tijdschrift voor Geschiedenis en Wijsbegeerte* 13, no. 2 (1996–97): 89–95.

Veen, Mirjam van. "Spiritualism in the Netherlands: From David Joris to Dirck Volckertsz Coornhert." *Sixteenth Century Journal* 33, no. 1 (2002): 129–50.

———. "'No One Born of God Commits Sin': Coornhert's Perfectionism." *Nederlands archief voor kerkgeschiedenis* 84, no. 1 (2004): 338–57.

Velden, Hugo van der. "Petrus Christus's Our Lady of the Dry Tree." *Journal of the Warburg and Courtauld Institutes* 60 (1997): 89–110.

Veldman, Ilja M. *Maarten Van Heemskerck and Dutch Humanism in the Sixteenth Century*. Maarssen: G. Schwartz, 1977.

———. *Coornhert en de Prentkunst*. Amsterdam: De Walburg Pers, 1989.

Verdier, Philippe. *Le couronnement de la Vierge: les origines et les premier développements d'un thème iconographique*. Montréal: J. Vrin, 1980.

Vermeulen, Yves G. *Tot profijt en genoegen: motiveringen voor de produktie van Nederlandstalige gedrukte teksten, 1477–1540*. Groeningen: Wolters-Noordhoff/Forsten, 1986.

Volfing, Annete. "Middle High German Appropriations of the Song of Songs: Allegorical Interpretation and Narrative Extrapolation." In *Perspectives on the Song of Songs. Beiheft zur Zeitschrift für die alttestamentliche Wissenschaft*, edited by Anselm Hagedorn, 294–316. Berlin: De Gruyter, 2005.

Voogt, Gerrit. *Constraint on Trial: Dirk Volckertsz Coornhert and Religious Freedom*. Sixteenth Century Essays Studies. Kirksville, MO: Truman State University Press, 2000.

Waite, Gary K. *David Joris and Dutch Anabaptism, 1524–1543*. Waterloo, ON: Wilfrid Laurier University Press, 1990.

Warnar, Geert. *Ruusbroec: Literature and Mysticism in the Fourteenth Century*. Translated by Diane Webb. Leiden: Brill, 2007.

Warner, Michael. "Tongues Untied: Memoirs of a Pentecostal Boyhood." *Curiouser* (2004): 215–24.

Watson, Arthur. *The Early Iconography of the Tree of Jesse*. 1st ed. London: Oxford University Press, 1934.

Weinstein, Donald and Rudolph M. Bell. *Saints and Society: The Two Worlds of Western Christendom, 1000–1700*. Chicago: University of Chicago Press, 1982.

Welsh, Jennifer L. "Mother, Matron, Matriarch: Sanctity and Social Change in the Cult of St. Anne, 1450–1750." PhD dissertation, Duke University, 2009.

Wiethaus, Ulrike. *Ecstatic Transformation: Transpersonal Psychology in the Work of Mechthild of Magdeburg*. Syracuse: Syracuse University Press, 1996.

—————. "Naming and Un-naming Violence Against Women: German Historiography and the Cult of St. Elisabeth of Thuringia (1207–1231)." In *Medievalism and the Academy*, edited by Leslie Workman, Kathleen Verduin, and David D. Metzger, 187–209. Cambridge: D.S. Brewer, 1997.

Williams, George Huntston. *The Radical Reformation*. Kirksville, MO: Truman State University Press, 2000.

Williams-Krapp, Werner. "Bilderbogen-Mystik: Zu Christus Und Die Minnende Seele. Mit Edition Der Mainzer Überlieferung." In *Überlieferungsgeschichtliche Editionen Und Studien Zur Deutschen Literatur Des Mittelalters. Kurt Ruh Zum 75. Geburtstag*, edited by Konrad Kunze, Johannes G. Mayer, and Bernhard Schnell, 31, 350–64. Tübingen: Niemeyer, 1989.

—————. "The Erosion of a Monopoly: German Religious Literature in the Fifteenth Century." In *The Vernacular Spirit: Essays on Medieval Religious Literature*, edited by Renate Blumenfeld-Kosinski, Nancy Bradley Warren, and Duncan Robertson, 239–62. New York: Palgrave, 2002.

Wilson, Adrian and Joyce Lancaster Wilson. *A Medieval Mirror: Speculum Humanae Salvationis, 1324–1500*. Berkeley: University of California Press, 1984.

Winston-Allen, Anne. *Convent Chronicles: Women Writing about Women and Reform in the Late Middle Ages*. University Park: Pennsylvania State University Press, 2004.

Wolf, Kenneth Baxter. *The Life and Afterlife of St. Elizabeth of Hungary: Testimony from Her Canonization Hearings*. Oxford: Oxford University Press, 2010.

Wünsche, Gregor. "Hadewijch am Oberrhein: Niederländische Mystike in den Händen der sogennante Gottesfreunde." In *Kulturtopographie des deutschsprachigen Südwestens im späteren Mittelalter: Studien und Texte*, edited by Barbara Fleith and René Wetzel, 83–98. Berlin: De Gruyter, 2009.

Yardley, Anne Bangall. "The Marriage of Heaven and Earth: A Late Medieval Source of the Consecratio Virginum." *Current Musicology* (1990): 305–24.

Index

Note: Page numbers in **bold** indicate illustrations.

21-Year-Old Wife, The (*Das Frauchen von 22 (21) Jahren*) 165–6
24 Elders (*Die vierundzwanzig alten oder der guldin Tron der minnenden seelen, Boeck des gulden throens of der XXIV ouden*) 20, 69, 71, 113–14

Adalbert, husband of Dorothea of Montau 146–7, 156–7, 164
adornment. *See* jewelry
altar, altarpiece 4, 12, 48, 62, 93–4, 101–10, 156–8, 170; **82, 102–3, 111, 158**
Amsterdam 28, 200–201, 206
Anabaptism 19, 28, 191–7, 200, 204, 206, 219
angels 44, 67, 81–5, 92n44, 106–7, 110, 133, 136, 148, 158–60, 164, 177, 187, 211–12, 222–3; **43, 80, 84, 111, 134, 159, 212, 223**
St. Anne 149, 167, 185
Antwerp 21, 57, 73, 177
Apocalypse 20, 77–8, 83, 98, 196–7, 221–4
bride of the Apocalypse 19, 68, 136, 194
Aquinas, Thomas 71–2, 222
Ardent Desire (*Een Mynlike vuerighe begerte der ynniger zielen tot horen Ghemynden Here*) 90–91
Art of Spiritual Living (*Buch der Kunst, dadurch der weltlich Mensch mag geistlich werden, Büchlein von der geistlichen Gemahelschaft, De Gheestelycke Brvyloft ...*) 71, 74, 81–2, 89, 93; **80, 82, 90**
Augsburg 5–6, 33, 53, 71, 133, 158
Augustine of Hippo 63n66, 71, 165
Avignon papacy 1, 27

Bake, Alijt 20, 120, 142, 188
baptism xi, xvii, 2, 14, 19–20, 23–4, 26, 28–9, 34, 68, 106n57, 122, 128, 163, 188, 190, 192, 213, 224
Baptists 207, 211
Basel 4, 33, 67, 146
beds 60–62, 85–6, 108, 162–5, 169, 176, 207n29, 209, 219
in art 56–7; **58, 86**
cradle 204
deathbed 171, 180–81
marital bed 55, 145–8, 199–200
beguines 1–3, 13, 57, 117–18, 127, 138, 146, 150, 153–6, 205, 215–16
Benedictines 36, 51, 71, 76, 87, 96, 133, 173, 174
Bernard of Clairvaux 15, 22–3, 72, 124, 181
Biblia Pauperum (*Bible for the Poor*) 96–9; **97, 99**
blood 37, 43–4, 94, 101, 110, 114, 123, 127, 129, 133–67, 160, 166, 187, 194; **38–40, 43, 102, 111, 134, 159**
Boehme, Jakob (Jakob Böhme) 15, 27–8, 194, 199–201, 204, 206
Bollandists (Société des Bollandistes) 20
Book of Perfection (*Das Buch der Vollkommenheit*) 1, 52–3, 72
Bourdain, Anthony 60n55
Bride of Christ Ministries 221–2
Bride of Christ Robes 217
Bridget of Sweden (Bride, Birgitta, Birgitta of Vadstena) 55, 100, 148, 150, 153–61, 163–4, 187, 200; **158, 159**
Bridgettines 21, 158
Brotherhood of Eternal Wisdom 21, 31–3, 51, 113, 132
Brun von Schönebeck 29, 36n13, 63–4

catechesis 25, 70, 117, 194
catechumens 3, 23–4, 121
Catherine of Alexandria 26

256   *Marrying Jesus in Medieval and Early Modern Northern Europe*

Catherine of Siena 155–6
Catherine of Sweden 155–8; **158**
celibacy xi, 14–15, 18–23, 25, 32, 117–18,
    145, 149, 157, 165, 184–5, 188,
    190, 192–3, 213
    celibate marriage (*Josephsehe*) 145
chalices 87, 107, 110–12; **111**
Chidester, David 11–12
childcare 145–50, 153, 166, 175
choirs 76–8, 181–2, 213
    stalls 179
Christ and the Loving Soul (*Christus und
    die minnende Seele*) 15, 51–2, 57,
    70, 72, 85, 87–9, 92, 98–100, 113;
    58, 86, 88
Christus, Petrus 83n22, 151–3; **152**
Church (Ecclesia) as bride of Christ 48, 68,
    93, 192
church councils
    Council of Constance 33, 105, 118
    Council of Trent xv, 21, 27, 204
    Lateran Councils 25, 75
cloisters 7, 54, 64, 71, 112–13, 118
clothing 24–5, 63, 67–8, 77–8, 85–90,
    92, 96, 101, 110, 112, 114, 118,
    128–33, 136, 146n5, 148, 150–52,
    161–2, 169–70, 179, 217, 222–4
Colbert, Stephen 215–16
communion. *See* Eucharist
confession 21n45, 114, 141, 145, 165n70,
    189
confessionalization 18–20, 192–3
Consecratio Virginum 175
Coornhert, Dirck Volckertsz (Dirck
    Volckhertsz Coornhert, Dirck
    Volckertszoon Coornhert) 44–8,
    194–8
    Jacob's Ladder (*Jakobs ladder of
    de allegorie van de weg naar
    eeuwige zaligheid*), after designs
    by Maarten van Heemskerck 44–8,
    196; **46, 47**
    On the Bride of Christ (*Tweeling
    vanden Bruydt Christi en
    d'Egipsche Vroeivrouwen*) 197–8
Costers, Jacomijne (Jacoba Custodis) 21,
    177–8
creator 1–3, 23, 41, 55, 63–4, 79–81,
    121–6, 194, 200, 210

crosses 12, 44–5, 83, 89, 100, 106–7, 112,
    160, 215; **43, 103, 108, 159**
crowns 23, 25, 36–48, 48n24, 57, 63,
    67–8, 77–9, 85–6, 92, 94–100,
    107, 110–12, 129, 133, 136–9, 151,
    160–62, 170, 176, 178–9, 181,
    199–200, 222–3; **38–40, 58, 80, 90,
    95, 97, 99, 111, 134, 152, 159, 223**
crucifixions 18, 27, 41, 68, 74, 77–8, 87–9,
    91, 94, 96, 98, 101, 105, 107, 114,
    131, 133–40, 219; **88, 102, 111, 134**

d'Ailly, Pierre 72, 105
Danzig (Gdańsk) xv, 157
Daughter of Zion 114
David of Augsburg 118–23, 127–8, 193
Dietrich of Apolda 145, 150, 151
devils 5–6, 27, 41, 44–5, 78–9, 132, 177, 196,
    198, 200, 204, 217, 224; **43, 46, 203**
    brides of the devil 93, 171, 188–9, 192–3
    demonic possessions 186–8
Devotio Moderna 32, 169, 186
Dominicans 119, 132, 140–42, 155–6, 166,
    173–4, 183, 186, 189
Dorothea of Montau (Dorothea von
    Montau) 146–8, 154–7, 160–64
Durkheim, Émile 11

Eckhart, Meister 52, 60, 122n12, 127
Eckhartian legends 141–3, 165–6
Eliade, Mircea 11
Elizabeth of Hungary (Elizabeth of Thuringia)
    146–8, 151, 153, 155–61; **152**
enclosure 21–2, 27, 185
Eucharist xi, 12, 14, 27, 34, 48, 57, 60,
    68–9, 87, 107, 110, 121–3, 142,
    145, 147, 155, 171, 182–5, 189–90,
    195, 205–6; **111**
Eyer, Johann Adam 211–12; **212**

Fraktur 211; **212**
Franciscans 20, 63, 71, 101, 118, 120, 124,
    150–51, 155, 186
Franklin, William 207, 209

Gadbury, Mary 28, 206, 208–9, 221
Garden of Devotion (*Le Jardin amoureux,
    Thoofkijn van devotien*) 72, 81,
    105–13

Index 257

gardens 37–40, 68, 78, 83, 91–2, 94, 98, 104–13, 178, 196, 201, 213; **38–40, 84, 95, 103, 108–9, 203**

garlands. *See* wreaths

gender 56, 112–13, 126–7, 130–32, 139, 142, 184

of the bride and bridegroom xii–xiv, 14–18, 23–4, 32–3, 35–48, 54, 218–20

and piety 8, 17–18, 187–8, 207

pronouns and translations xvii, 6, 55, 117–18, 213

Gertrud of Helfta 11, 155, 172, 174–6

Gertrud of Ortenberg (Gertrud Rickeldegen) 1–3, 12–13, 23, 148, 153–5, 160, 162–4

Godhead 1, 93, 121–2, 125–9, 133, 139–40, 160, 197

Great Wedding at Diepenveen 179–81

Alijt Comhaers 179

Griete Koetgens 180

Griete ten Kolke 180

Griete Tasten 180

Griete des Vryen 180

Grote, Geert (Geert Groote, Gerhard Groet, Gerrit Groet, Gerardus Magnus) 32, 141, 142

Hours of Eternal Wisdom 32, 141

habit. *See* clothing

Hadewijch of Brabant 57–60, 119–20

hearts 31, 43–4, 54, 57–60, 63, 78n15, 79, 83, 91, 104–5, 107, 118, 124, 132–3, 135, 138–9, 153–4, 166, 179, 189, 201–4, 213; **43, 105, 108, 203**

heaven 2, 25, 37, 41, 53, 67–8, 77–8, 81, 92–3, 107, 110, 112, 117, 121, 125, 132–3, 136–8, 148, 160, 164, 171, 176–84; **80, 137, 223**

Heemskerck, Maarten van (Maerten van Heemskerk, Martin van Heemskerk, Marten Jacobszoon Heemskerk van Veen) 44–8

Jacob's Ladder (*Jakobs ladder of de allegorie van de weg naar eeuwige zaligheid*), designs engraved by Dirck Coornhert 44–8, 196; **46–7**

Heilsbach, Agnes 205–6

Helena of Skövde 148–50, 153, 155–7; **158**

hell 63, 81, 92–3, 109–10, 170, 196, 200

heresy 26–7, 127, 170, 191–2

Herp, Hendrik (Henricus de Herph, Hendrik van Herp, Herpius, Harphius) 20, 73, 119–20, 124, 178

Honorius Augustodunensis (Honorius of Autun) 15, 36–40, 48, 51, 63, 74

Hoppen, Geertruijt 181

image (*Bild*, *figura*) xi, xii, xiv, 3, 5, 9–12, 25–6, 34–5, 55–6, 68, 113–14, 119, 121–7, 130, 142, 174, 184, 194, 199, 216, 225

Irigaray, Luce 56, 60–61, 127

Islam 17, 34, 60

Jenkins, Henry xiii, 9–10

Jesus. *See also* wisdom

as boyfriend xii, 218

as child 15, 83, 91, 122, 129, 131, 154, 160, 163, 183–5; **84, 159**

gender of 6, 36, 127, 218–21

as Man of Sorrows 35, 45, 89, 110, 136, 158–60; **82, 159**

jewelry 11, 65, 68, 78–9, 85, 100, 104, 160–61, 170, 178–9, 215

rings 4, 20, 26, 67–8, 92, 101–4, 113, 136, 155, 169–70, 175, 204; **105, 137**

Joanna van Randereth 205–6

John Chrysostom 23–4, 62–3, 165, 224

Joris, David 194–7, 221

Katherina van Mispelteren 177

Kempe, John 147, 149

Kempe, Margery 147–9, 153–7, 160, 164–5

kisses 12, 56, 60, 63, 68, 77, 91, 94, 96, 113, 127–9, 135, 143, 170, 184, 199–200, 216

kitchens 87, 148

Langmann, Adelheid 173–4, 178–9, 185

Latour, Bruno 9

Limburg Sermons 93, 123–5

London 206–9

Love Bears a Cross (*Kreutztragende Minne, Jesus und die Braut, Nonnenlehre, Die Innige Seele*) 51, 73, 74, 89–90, 98, 101–2; **103**

258 *Marrying Jesus in Medieval and Early Modern Northern Europe*

A Loving Complaint (*Een mynlike clage der mynnender zielen tot horen gemynden, Een minnentlike claege*) 55, 90–91

Ludwig IV, Landgrave of Thuringia (Louis IV) 150–51

Luther, Martin 4–5, 13–15, 22–3, 28, 188, 191–4, 217

Luyken, Jan (Johannes Luiken) 194, 199–204, 206; **202–3**

Magdalena of Freiburg (Magdalena Beutlerin) 176–7, 188

mahelschatz 4–5, 79

marriage rituals 169–79

Mary (mother of Jesus) 22, 63, 92–3, 96, 98, 101, 104, 107, 113–14, 145, 149, 161–2, 177, 183–4, 205; **105, 159**

as bride of Christ 18–19, 25, 68, 78, 80, 192–3

marriage to Eberhart Schutz of Hohenstein 185

Mary Magdalene 96, 98, 157, 221

Mather, Cotton 210

Mechthild of Magdeburg 52, 72, 89, 118–20, 127–42

Merswin, Rulman 4, 15, 64, 118–20, 126, 141, 148

Mirror for Maidens (*Speculum Virginum*) 37–41, 73, 75–8, 80–81, 87, 93, 114, 155, 165

mirrors 1, 45, 77, 81, 107, 121–6, 151, 200

Morgan, Sister Gertrude 222–4; **223**

Müller, Jerome 5–7, 11–13

mysticism 34, 49–54, 56–7, 118, 126–8, 188

nakedness 43–5, 48, 55–7, 60, 63, 68, 85–7, 92, 101, 107, 110, 126–36, 138–40, 160–64, 189, 200–201; **43, 46–7, 82, 86, 88, 102, 134**

Nicholas of Basel (Nicolaus von Basel) 4, 64n73

Nider, Johannes 21, 27, 186

Nikolaus von Flüe (Bruder Klaus) 146, 148

orgasms 57, 60–61

Origen 23–4, 224

Otto, Rudolph 10–11

Otto von Passau 20–21, 69, 85–71, 113–14, 221

Paris 105, 114, 141

Periculoso. See enclosure

periodization xiv–xv, 13

polemic 5, 194, 216

Pomerius, Henry (Henricus Pomerius, Hendrik vanden Boemgaert) 70, 72, 92–3, 106–12

Exercises on the Pater Noster (*Exercitium Super Pater Noster*) 72, 92–3, 104–13; **111**

popular religion xi, 3, 7–14, 49, 216

pornography 55, 59–62, 120, 135, 184, 220

prayer confraternities 32

purgatory 110, 139, 184

Retters, Christina 174, 176, 182

rosaries 107, 157; **158**

rose crowns, rose garlands. *See* wreaths

Rosetum exercitiorum spiritualium et sacrarum meditationum 94–6; **95**

Rupert of Deutz 25

Ruusbroec, Jan van (John of Ruusbroec, Jan van Ruysbroek) 19, 26, 118–20, 125, 127, 130–31, 136, 142, 173, 215–16

Schaupin, Sybilla 189–90

Schol, Ysbrandt 191, 194–6

Schürstab, Ursula 52

Schwesternspiegel 187

Sendbrief vom Betrug teuflischer Erscheinungen 186–7

sermons 1–2, 4, 7, 10–11, 13, 22–4, 63–5, 94, 81–2, 93, 117–18, 121–3, 139, 142, 200, 208–10, 221–2

sexual intercourse 26, 56–62, 147, 204, 210, 217

consummating marriage to Jesus 6, 10, 69, 78, 122–5, 129–30, 176, 184, 200

sexuality 6, 15–18, 34, 41–8, 55–7, 75, 87, 127, 219–20

Silvoorts, Elizabeth 21, 178

Simons, Menno 194–7, 217, 221

Sisters of Perpetual Indulgence 220

Song of Songs 12, 44, 112, 128
  in art **38–40**, **95**, **97**, **99**
  commentaries and sermons on 15,
    22–5, 36–41, 48, 63, 67–8, 74–81,
    85, 93–9
Sophia (Wisdom, Eternal Wisdom) 15,
  18n40, 24, 31–5, 52, 54, 72, 107,
  121–3, 132–6, 119, 200, 213
Sorg, Anton 33, 53, 113, 117–18
soteriology 2–5, 10, 25, 27, 37, 44, 50,
  57, 59–60, 69, 75–8, 122, 135–6,
  139–42, 165–6, 193–5, 215, 224
Souke van Dorsten 177
Spiritual Loveletter (*Den gheesteliken*
  minnenbrief die Jesus Christus
  sendet tot synre bruyt) 73, 82–4; **84**
Spiritual Maidens (*Geestelijke Maagden*)
  28, 119, 204–6
Spiritual Melody (*Geestelijke lied, Die*
  Gheestelicke Melodie) 74, 91, 181
Spiritual Spouseship of Christ
  (*Gemahelschaft Christi mit der*
  gläubigen Seele) 53, 65, 70, 74,
  85–6, 165
suffering 41, 53, 65, 75, 79, 85–90, 101–4,
  132–40, 153, 166, 170–71, 179,
  184, 201, 204
Sunder, Freidrich 15, 174, 183–5
Suso, Henry (Heinrich Seuse, Heinrich von
  Suso, Heinrich von Berg, Henricus
  Suso) 15, 19–21, 31–3, 51–4, 89,
  113, 118–20, 130–42, 167, 183,
  185, 189, 200–201; **134, 137**
Synagogue (Synagoga as personification)
  36

Tauler, Johannes (John Tauler, Johann
  Tauler) 4, 15, 19, 64, 117–20, 136,
  139, 141–3
tears 2, 79, 91, 98, 132, 139, 148–9, 157,
  166, 205
Throne of Mercy (*Gnadenstuhl*) 94, 104;
  105
Tijtes, Gese 180–81
tonsures 23, 35, 44, 92–6, 106, 110–14,
  113, 140, 159; **42, 43, 95, 111, 134,
  137, 159**
transmedia storytelling xii, 10, 67–70,
  75–81, 113–15
St. Trudpert Song of Songs (*Trudperter*
  Hohes Lied) 74, 75–81, 85, 93
Tucher, Katharina 100, 138, 148, 155–6,
  160, 162–3, 186

Ursula of Münsterberg 188–9

veils 37–41, 106, 151, 157, 169–70, 175;
  38–40, 108, 158
virginity 18–20, 23, 62, 75–6, 81, 93,
  141–2, 147, 149, 164–7, 178, 206

wedding dresses. *See* clothing
Wentworth, Anne 28, 206–9, 221, 224
Wesley, Charles 212–13
widows 23, 63, 145, 150, 165, 187, 205
wreaths 77, 101, 104, 107, 132, 136, 223;
  105, 108, 134

Xylographic Cantica Canticorum 93–6

von Zinzendorf, Nikolaus 15, 28, 210, 217